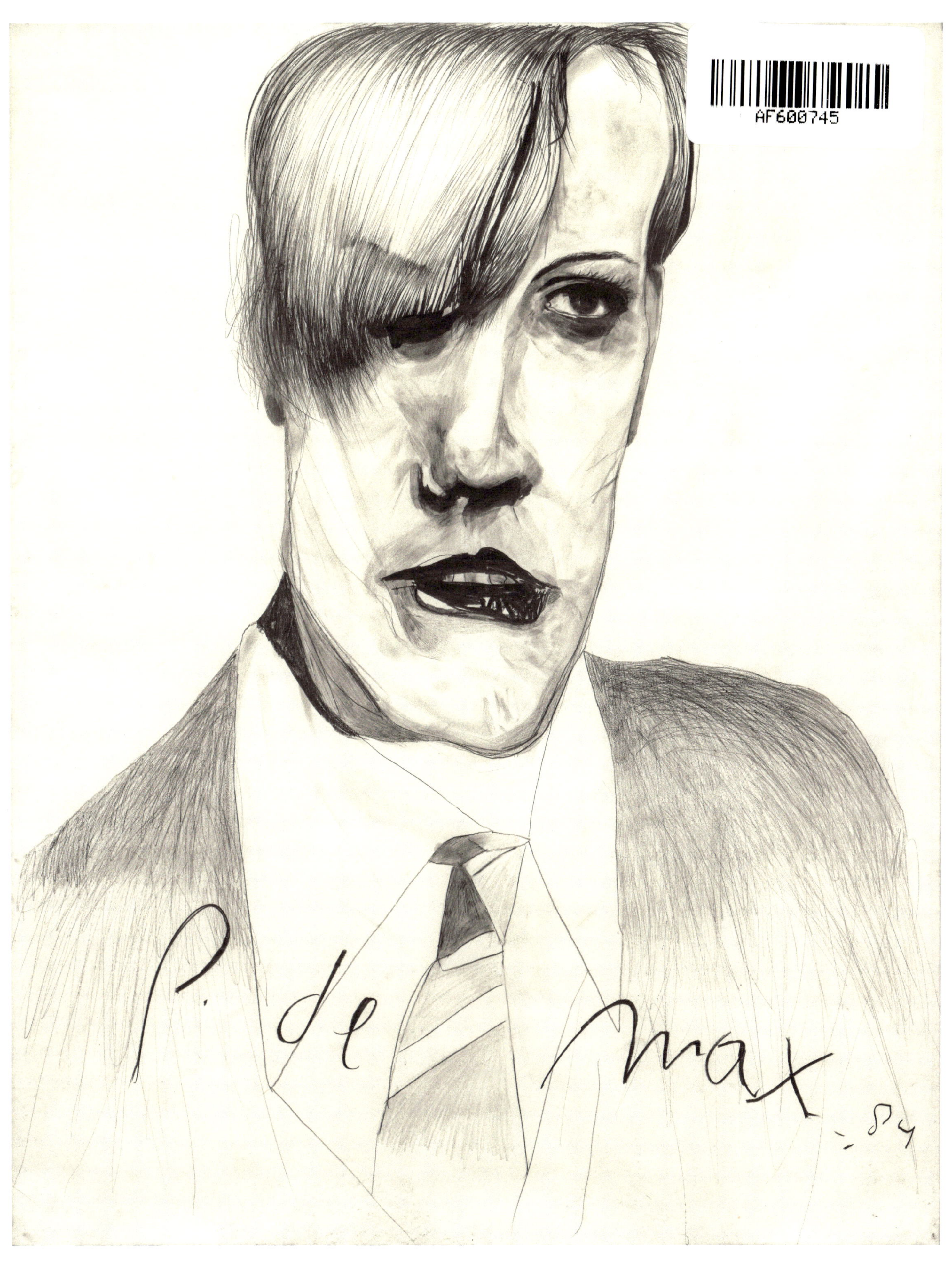

AF600745

*Portrait de Max*, 1984

Dear Stéphane,

It's your birthday. You'd be 61 born in 61. I'm thinking of you as the stars fan out in the sky tonight as I walk my dog. It strikes me that the extreme head racket that occupies so much of your work is stellar: "Oy Suzy" there goes one, yet my feeling about the text written alongside one image or the flowers popped in around the jabber is that it is never very much about "one" speaking at all. The words just constellate, burst into symbols whether pictograph men with guns or a multiple territory of women with their names and each with a little sac attached like aphids then a quick sketch of a nightclub recurs, a dirty mouth, a piggy truck, an old banana, a smile a piece of fruit and often it feels like a contagious memory map of one long strewn night. A life. I look up in the sky again. I know you had difficulty learning to read and what remains is a highly broken process. Which winds up feeling very present. Mandelbaum means almond tree. The faces are broken, your language is frantic and strewn. If you got old, you'd be padding around. Did you know that naming and the mapping of constellations flourished right before the dawn of printing. They were mapping the sky but more so they were reading and writing on it. The sky was an immense easel. I feel your guts as it pours onto the page, like a later improvisation on etching—because you don't so much get it right ever you keep getting it different—and these patches of math make me think how *this* might be read one way at one time and we marked it, so once there was a constellation named Mist and another purported to be an artist's studio and then there was the bee and the hand dragging in the water on the side of a boat and all those renditions fizzled when the stars moved, the astronomer lost his job, and you moving guns into 3D got killed. Crime being an atmosphere that fills the page but ultimately creates a studio unto itself. Pure vivid lack. Whereas *this* (by which I mean the barking and the doodling, the agitation, the pre-crime) is not so much the insides of your head but a deep centralizing of the margins, a magnificent devotion to the uncomfortable, and therefore we are not going to look at your notebooks and we're not going to look at your studio or write bios of your model, instead it simply becomes your time, this beautiful recording, this active endless expansion of something that if we pinpoint we only become dull and look querulously—your father's original first name "Leon" a Brinks truck do you mean the incorrect is correct it's only the expansion that matters in galaxies what is on the edges a little broken mouth with a cigar between its teeth now feels like a crappy truth that never ends, so start there or there make a million dollars tonight or count how many Jews died in Vilnius or one bloody rabbi or one boy hooked to the wall with his bloody junk or how not to get in a tiny boat with a cache of guns the population is speckled the population is standing up because they weren't ever entirely alive, because they were or are *pieces* and there's a Nazi sign, will the swastika ever go away all the damage it has done or is it forever young and fresh its wrongness like an explosive cock or a cunt being fingered by its own owner and her long dazzling nails in exactly the wrong place like the star on a horse's head where all the hairs meet, make the incantations sweet and language again and art again is a message to the next guy in line which is all of us. Medieval monks simply kept copying the bible again and again illuminating the edges dirty illumination this is just that—the Pasolini Bible the Nassar Bible my Jew father the artist again. The piles of tiny icons in some of these drawings, like icons in pools, strike me as what one might find in an archeological dig, in a tell—where you find a lot of them, and the anthropologist admits she does not know the purpose of these there were or are so many. Are they money or gods. Some spatializations of the page feel like war games. Tiny soldiers clustered in forts. If it's called fort in America the Indians are coming Stéphane I most of all am one who listened loyally to both films made about you after your death was treated to twenty-two minutes of French in one case in another twenty-six and there's a biography also in French. Je ne comprends pas. During the films I guessed which thoughtful person was your brother. I could guess this one was your artist friend, once cute now old, like your father the Jew, it seems like you made your father a super Jew since his paternity technically didn't make you a Jew at all. He couldn't be an artist because of you. He was just a Jew. I didn't see him talking in your film. I liked the voice-over which was clearly a voice on the phone. Stuck to a location by a voice and a pan of the contents of a table and desk as one was getting information the coordinates of the wonderful crime. Isn't it criminal enough to be an artist. Nobody wants this shit till you're dead. Addresses dates more guns like fish floating in a vat echoey and dangling in another hapless boat. When you're flying over a place and you see plenty of pools you just think steal. I'm trying to say you learned writing too late or just later so writing is drawing and drawing is a big silly brag. Fanciful it's a little like Rose Wylie. You're so young and dead, and she's so old. Each hero face like a coin do you think art is a mint, Stéphane. A post office. Are these letters to them, these saints. A communing. The face of Pasolini, Stéphane. The face of Pierre Goldman more of an actor than you it seems, the face of George Dyer, the big killjoy, a part of face, a lower part of a face with a texty mask. Let's face it, a partial face means war—"gueule cassée"—the face is barking. Your work is flooded with war. Faces in general are horrible blurred nose, fat lips, full fleshy face shocked eyes. I heard you were beautiful. You looked like a boy ordering a sandwich. Pasolini gets shot by his own films, in here, his portrait bears no resemblance to him, your Pasolini does not look like Pasolini, it looks like Gregg Bordowitz. I did the math. You are the other Gregg. You could have battled AIDS! Resemblance is even less important here than it is to Gertrude Stein, you really don't *do* women here, Stéphane, they are mostly utilitarian to suck a cock at the entrance to Auschwitz to bump it up, an old woman her dugs hang jerking off. There's no woman of note here, no coinage, which in effect makes them simply not the enemy it seems, no target, here, nothing in the future, the clatter of coins falling on the floor, just the present (louder—louder) it seems. Like Claudia, all of Africa the occasional palm tree and its opposite an asshole a pursed mouth with a stick or is it a palm tree sticking out, leaves gone its broken face. Your Bic pen embossed, really dug deep in the page. All sexual relations are class relations. The artist jumps class, but only Simone Weil actually worked in a factory. Rimbaud ran guns *after poetry* and in your etching he looks happy. I watched footage of four Black women (including your wife?) dumping liquor and dancing at your grave. It seems a man must be torn apart, a part of a face, and behind him a fat little Nazi on wheels, surrounded by the scrawl of your bountiful ambition. What else is a sky but a giant clock. Tick tock tick tock Stéphane. What I love about the garish beauty of your work, each phone call portrait to these man's gods, each schmeared day and afternoon has this one breathing constancy of something that could not stop, and even your death is an artful joke that you pursued like a tree standing under that suburban bridge in December.

And yet it kills me. There's something corpsy about being alive if we look at the present through such a past. And I want to bless you Stéphane, pain in the ass that I am. In yoga she read this line attributed to Patanjali. He lived I don't know when. In fact he himself is probably apocryphal. All art is inside he said. He was a holy man so how could *he know*. Why should we search, he asked, running after museums and gardens when every museum and garden [after all] is inside.

Truly,
Eileen

# Stéphane Mandelbaum

With texts by Diedrich Diederichsen, Ralf Marsault, Eileen Myles, Susanne Pfeffer, and Tal Sterngast

Edited by Susanne Pfeffer

MUSEUM MMK FÜR MODERNE KUNST, Frankfurt
Verlag der Buchhandlung Walther und Franz König, Köln

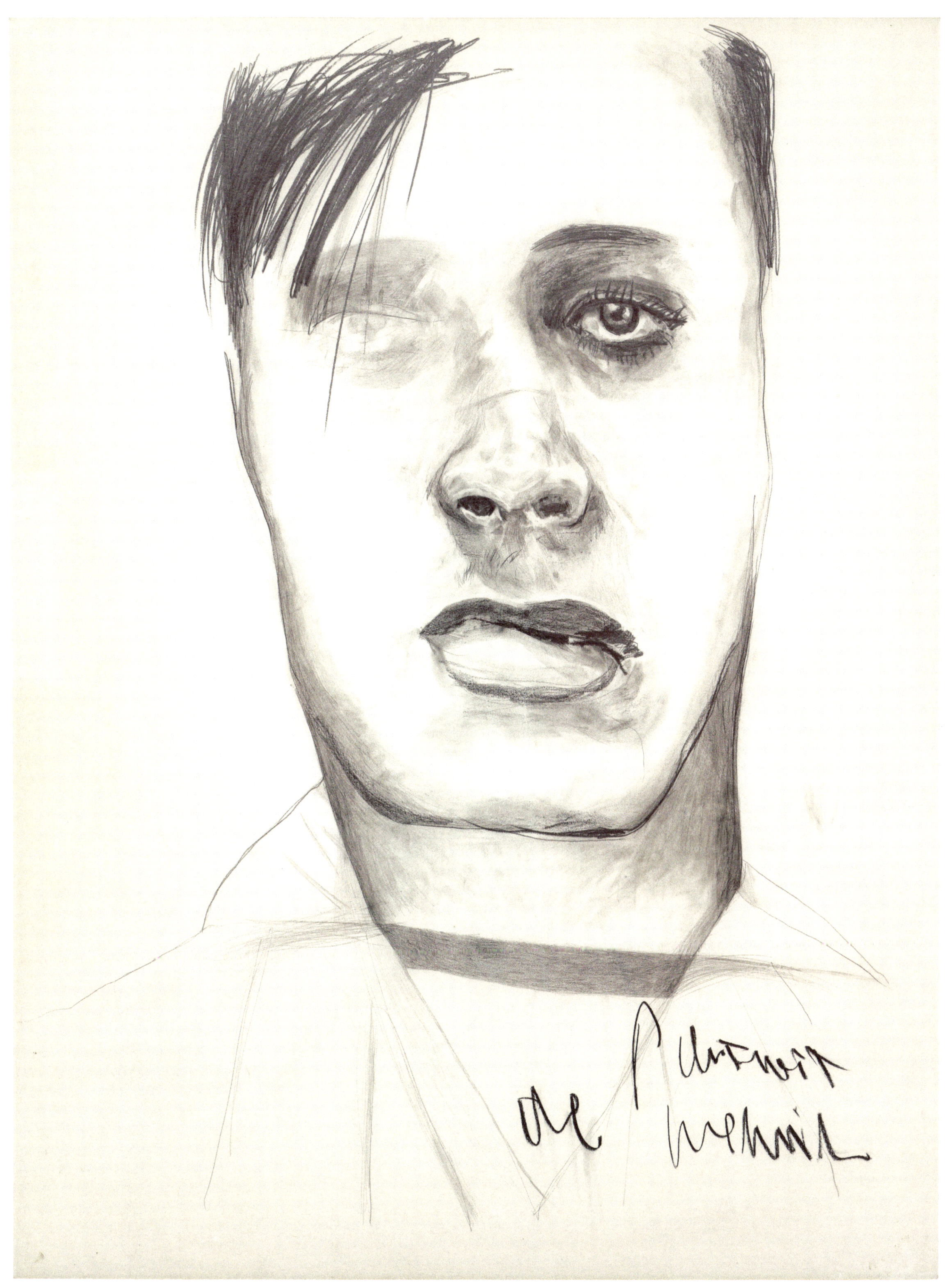

*Portrait de Meknil*, 1985

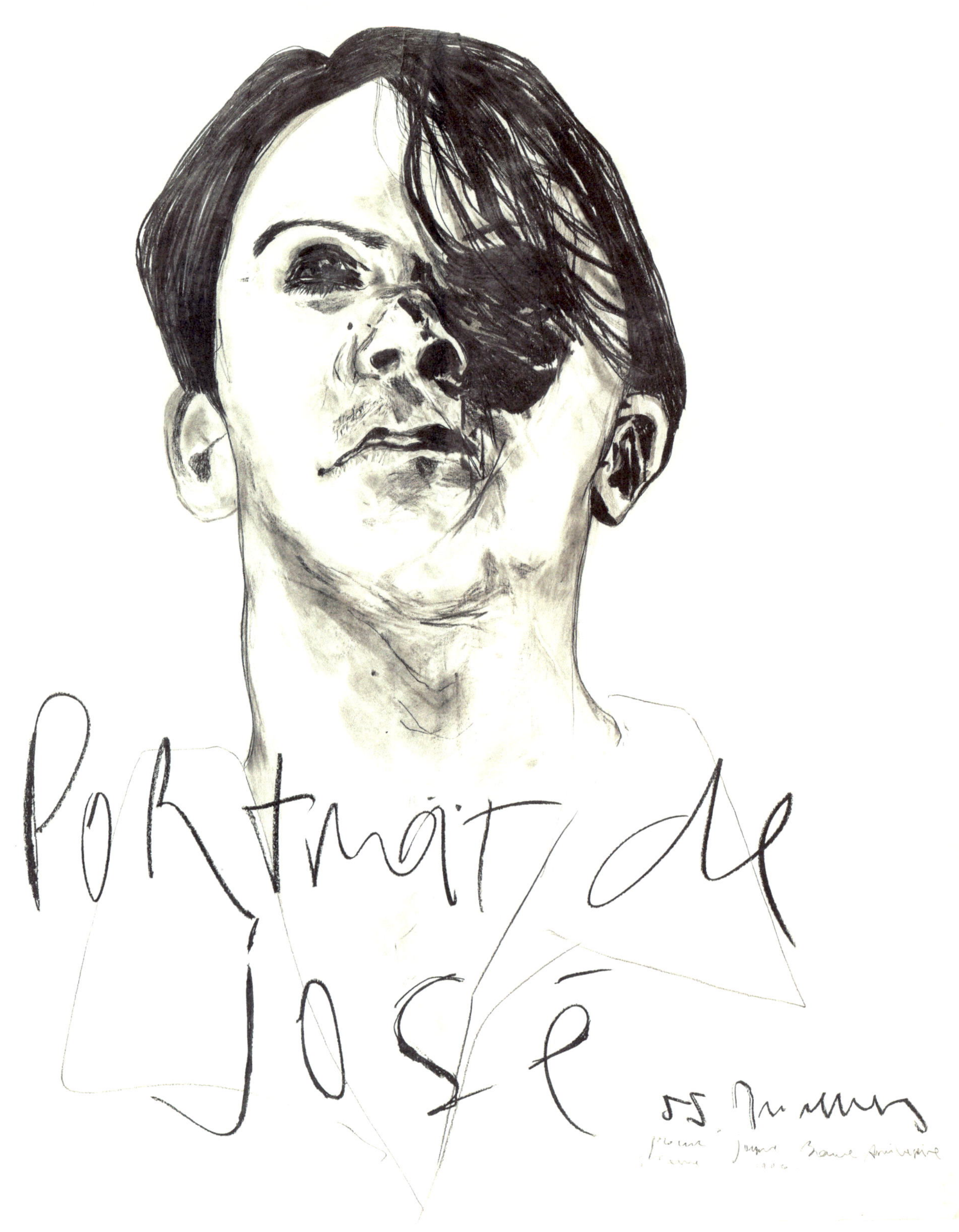


*Portrait de José*, 1985

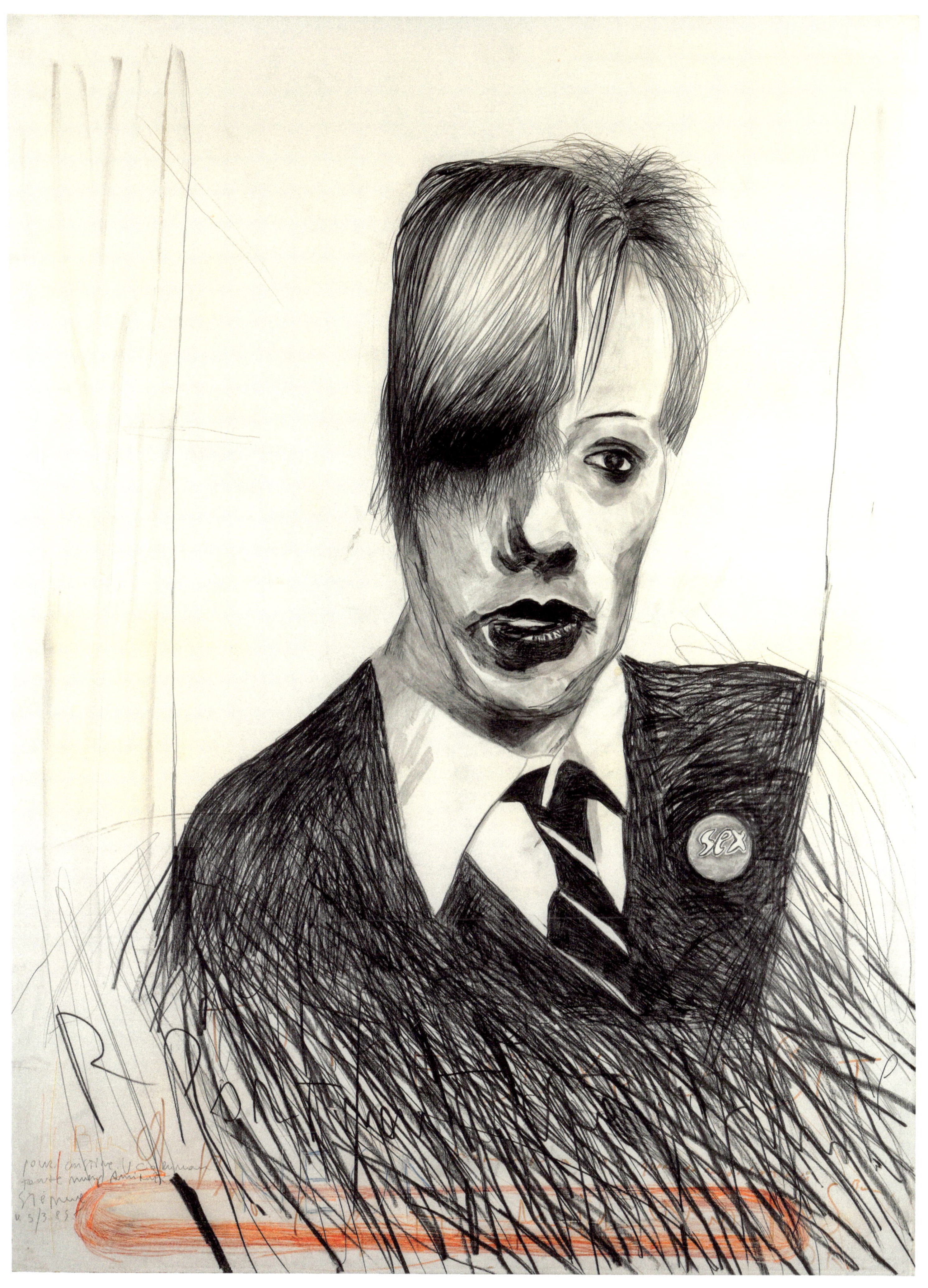


*Portrait de Max*, 1985

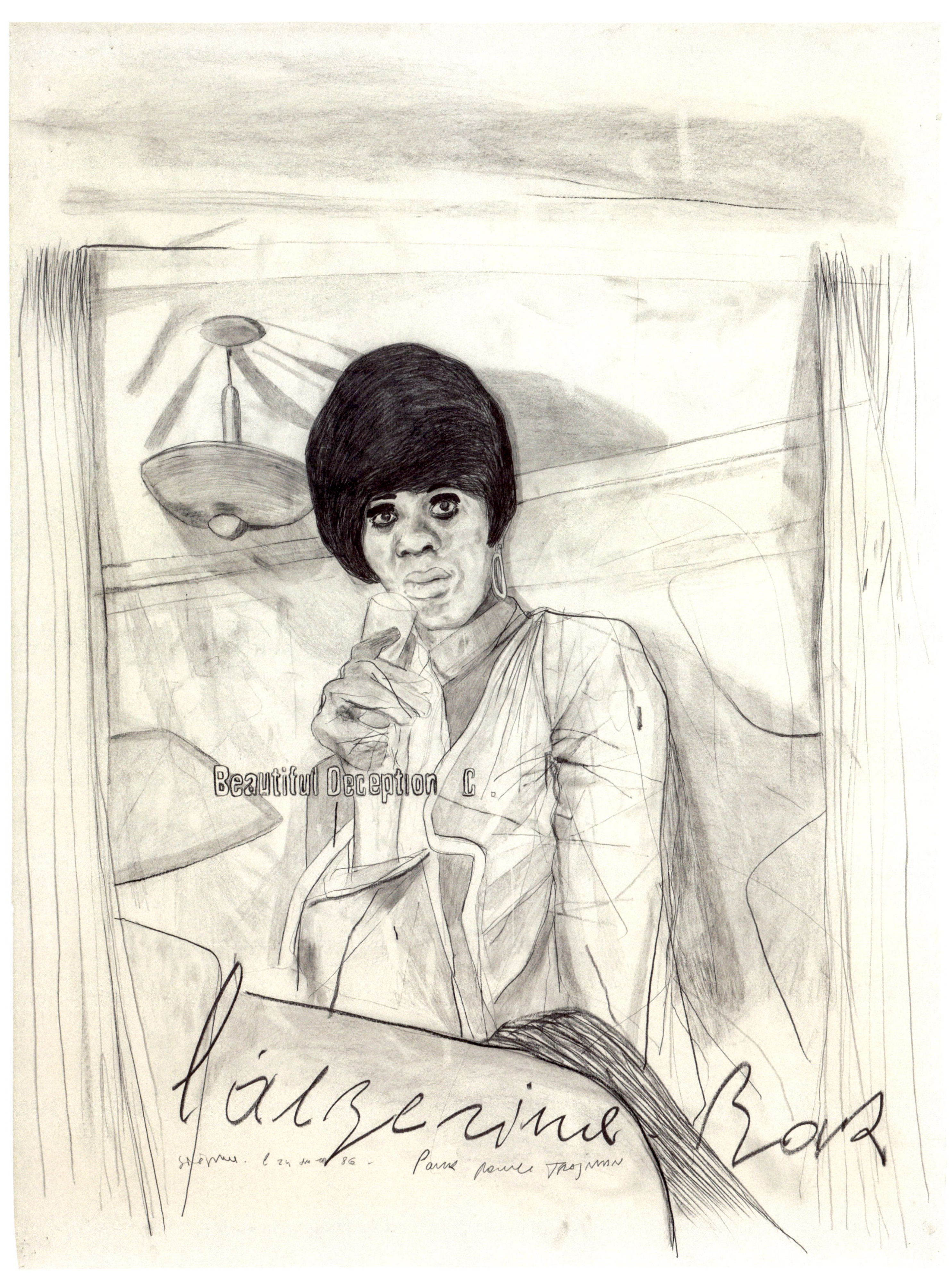


*L’Albertine Bar (Beautiful Deception C.)*, 1986

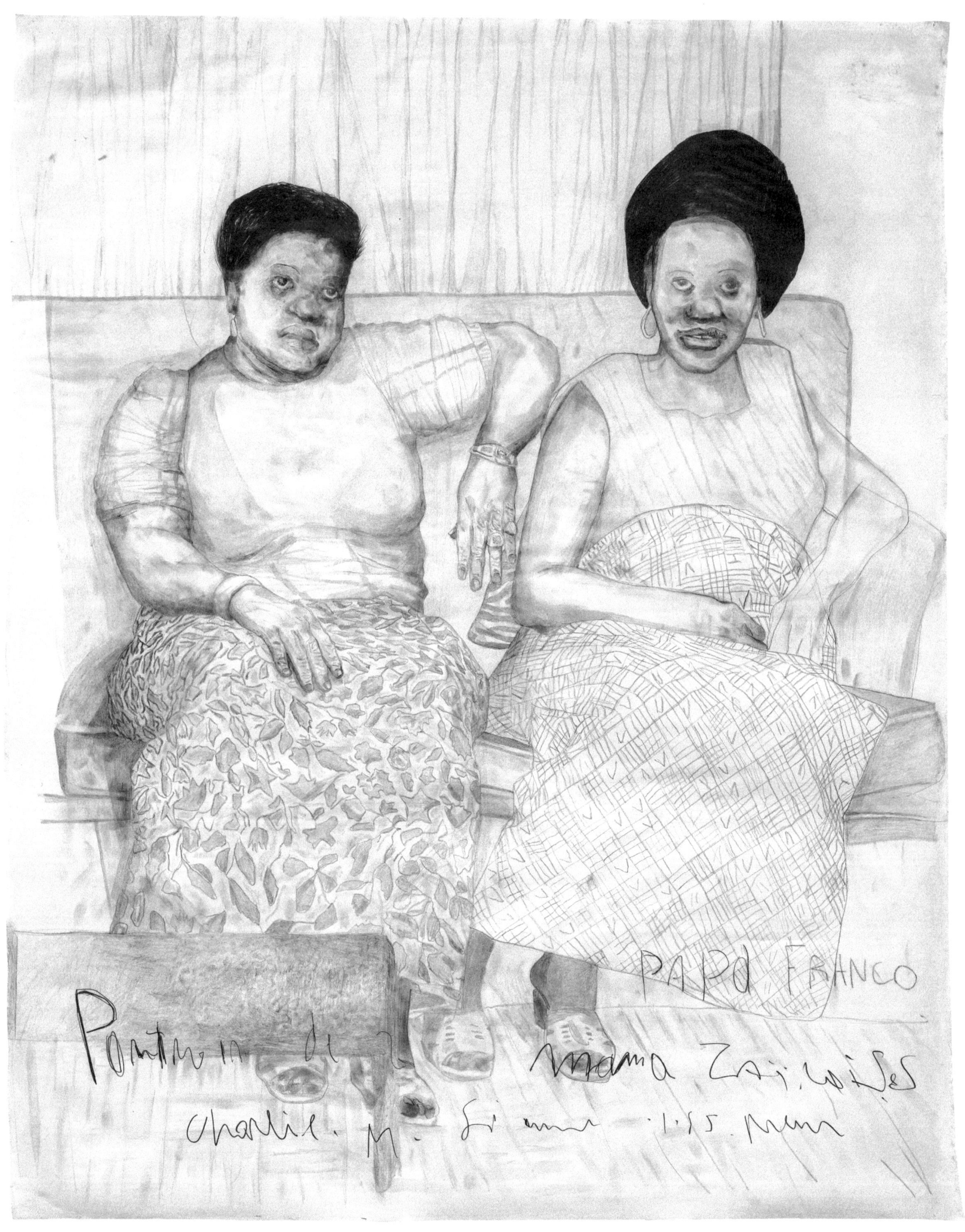


*Papa Franco «Mama zaïroises»*, 1985

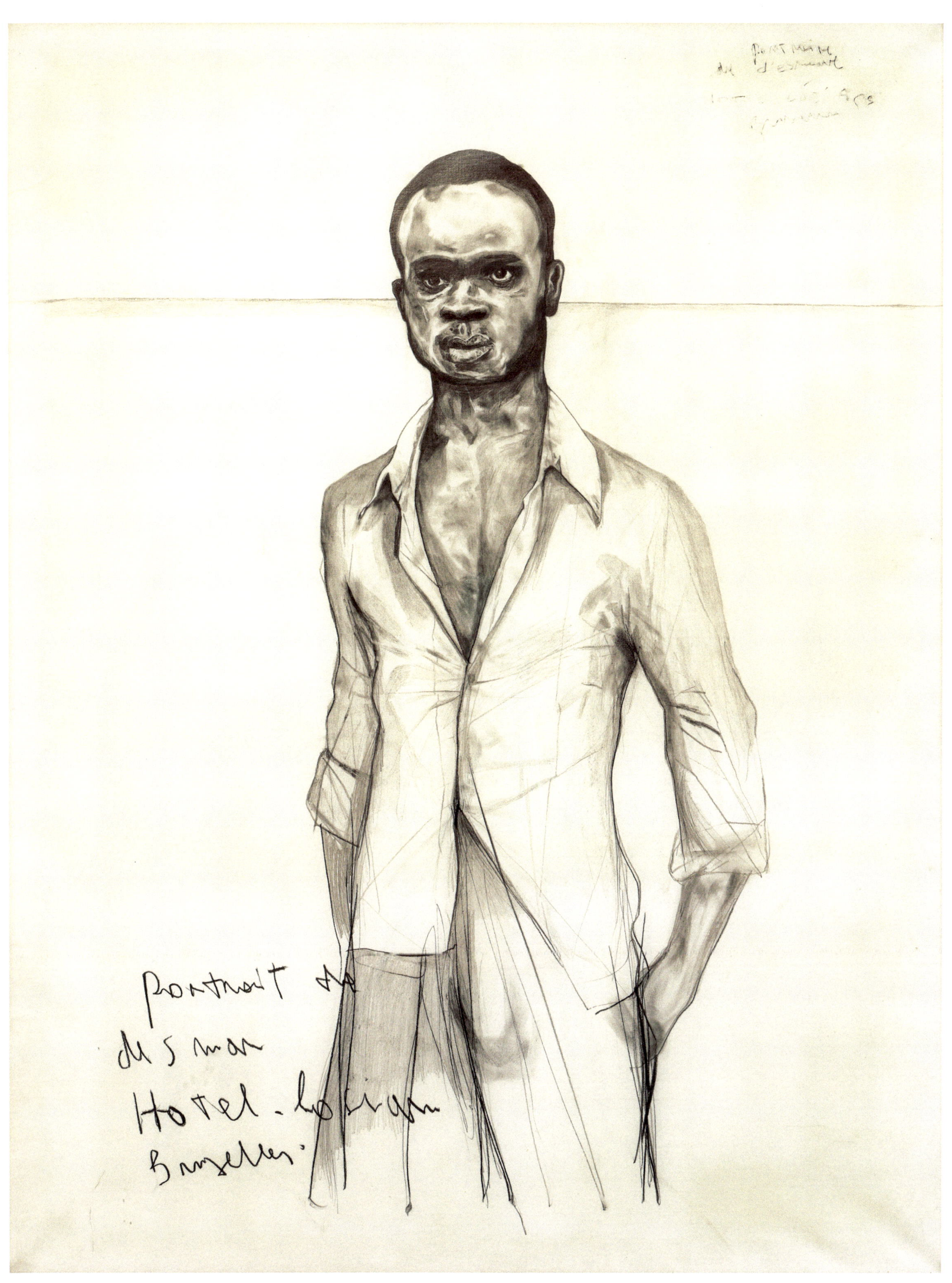

*Portrait de Ousman*, 1985

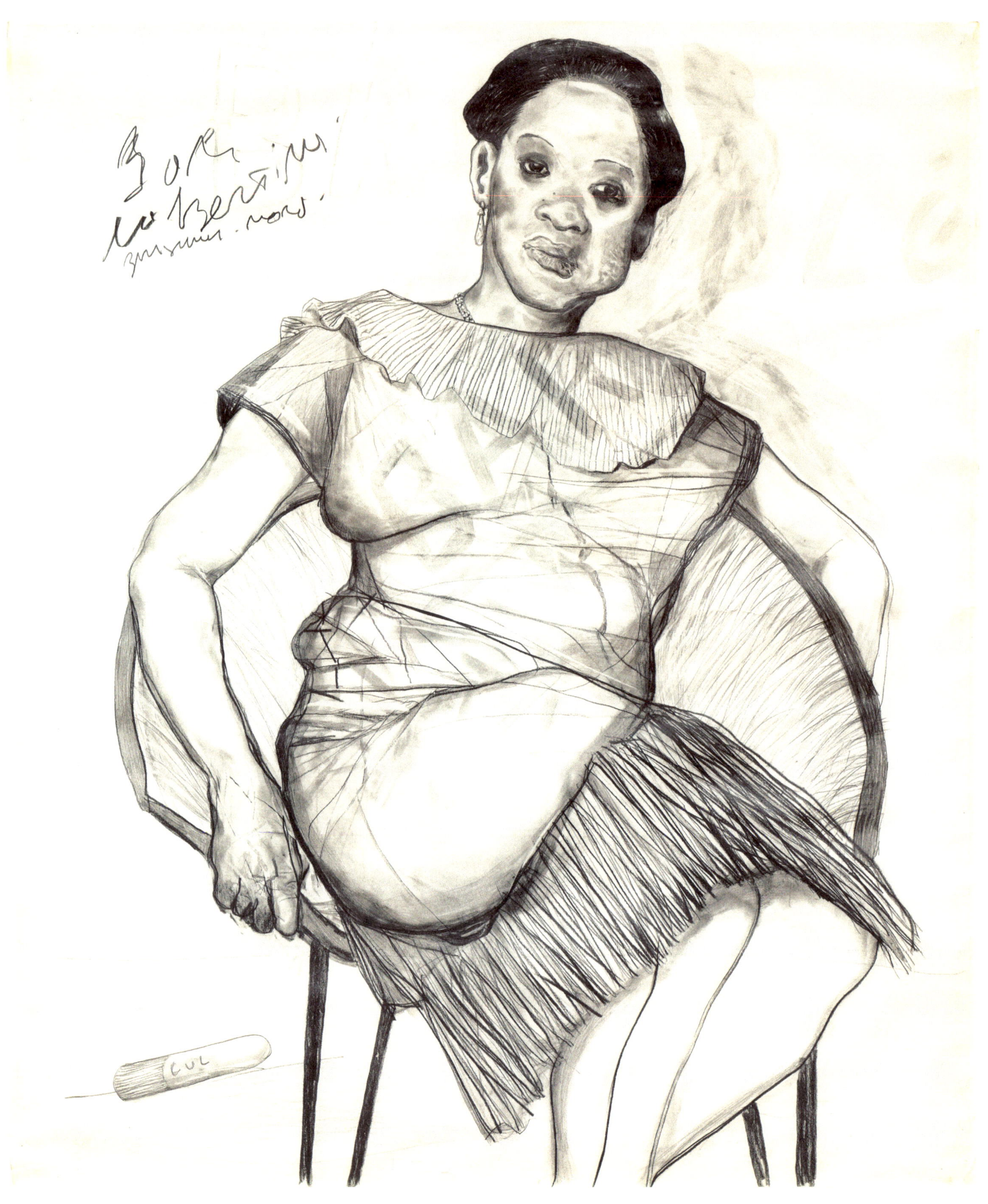

*Bar Albertine Bruxelles Nord*, 1985

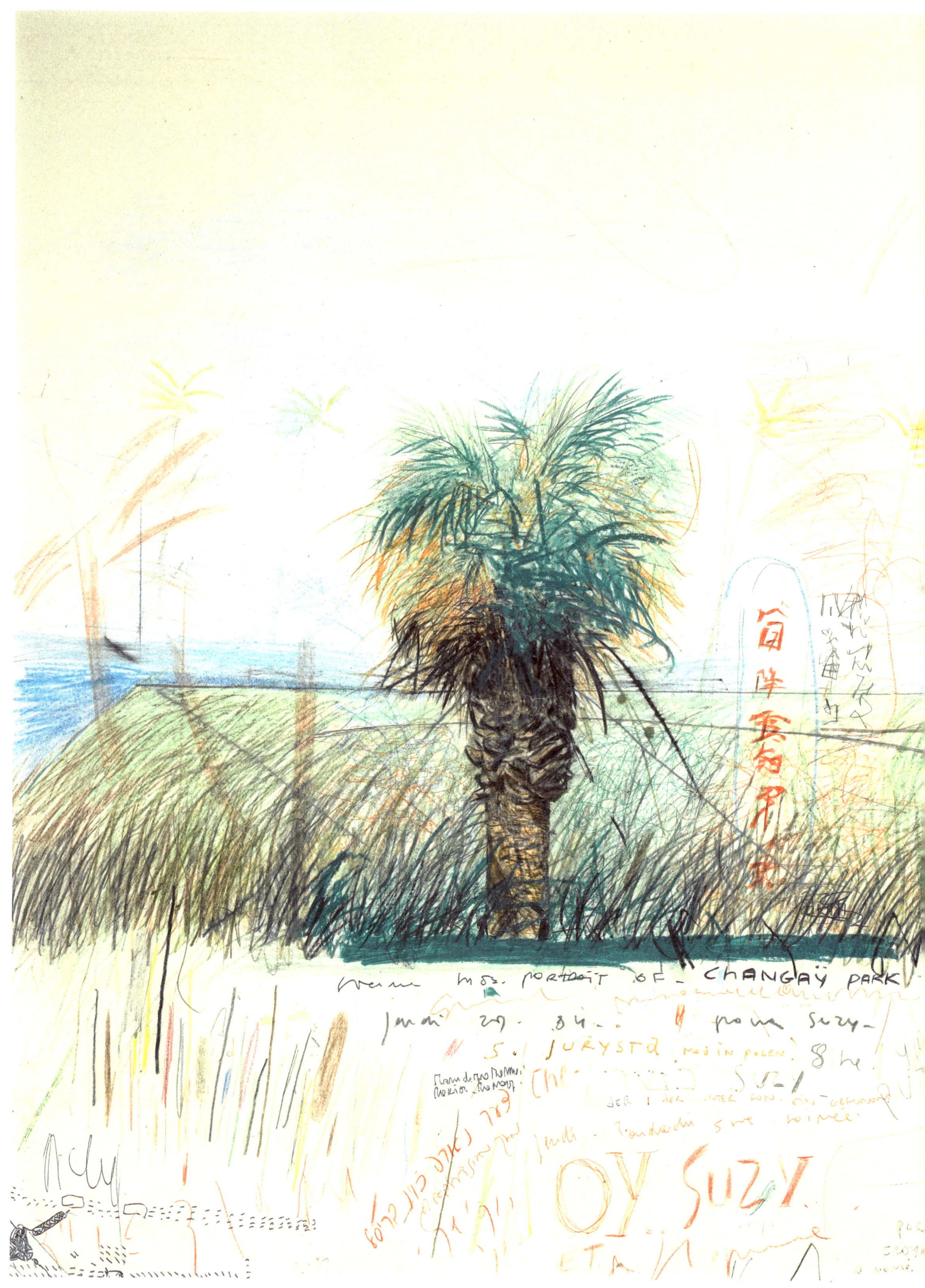


*Porträit of Changaÿ Park*, 1984

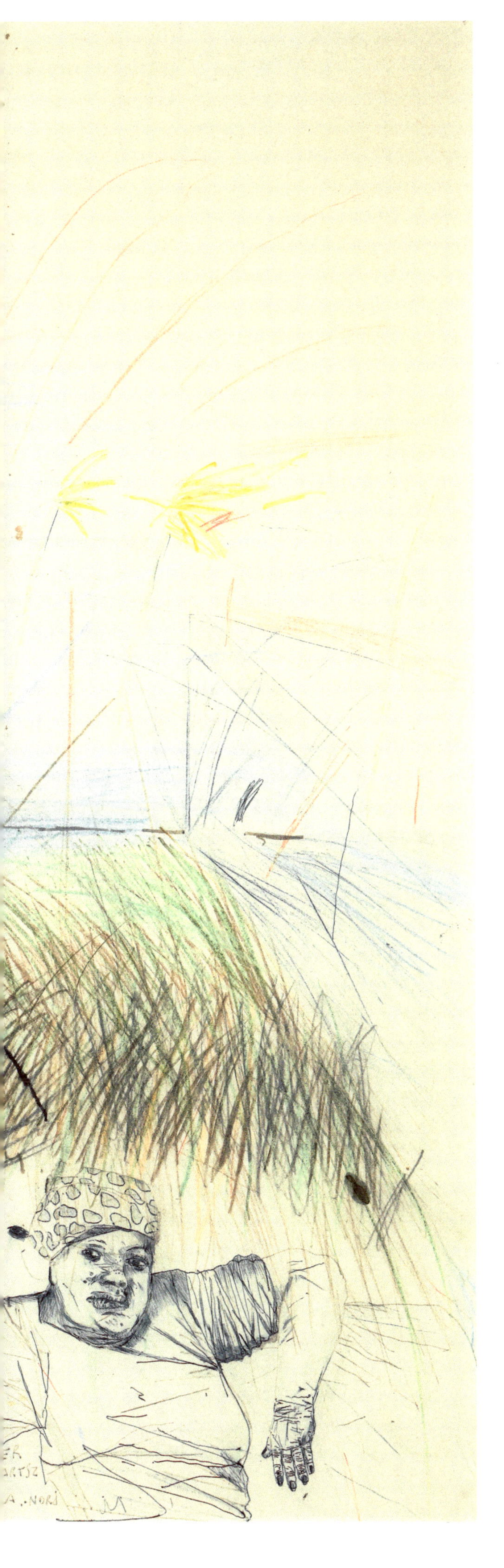

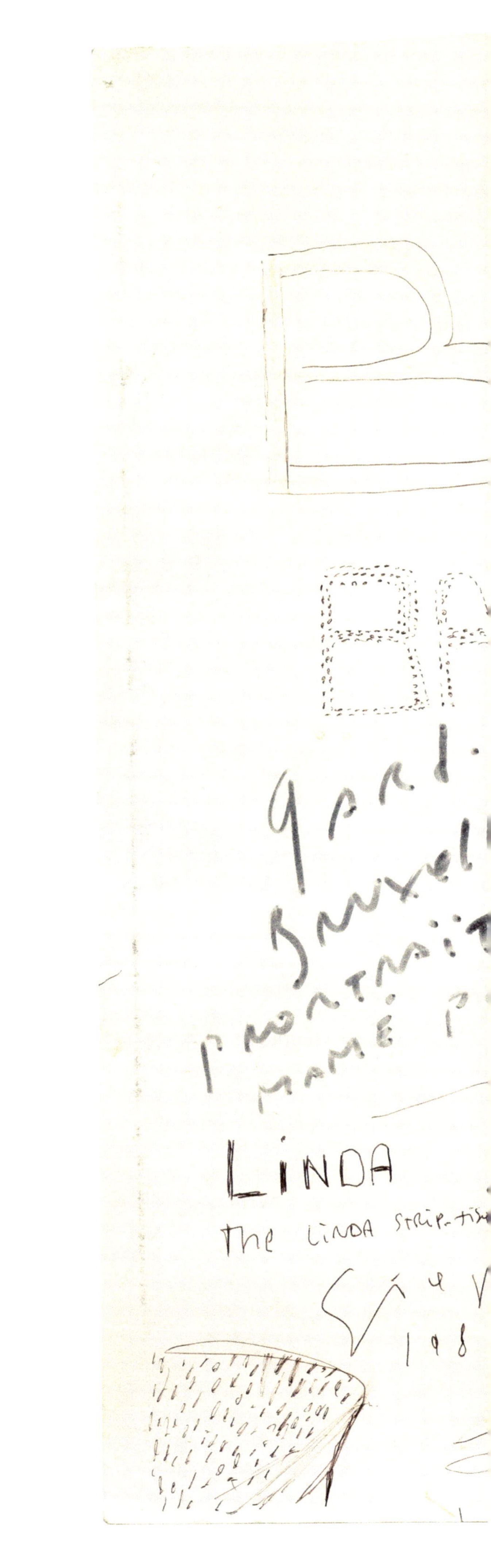
LINDA

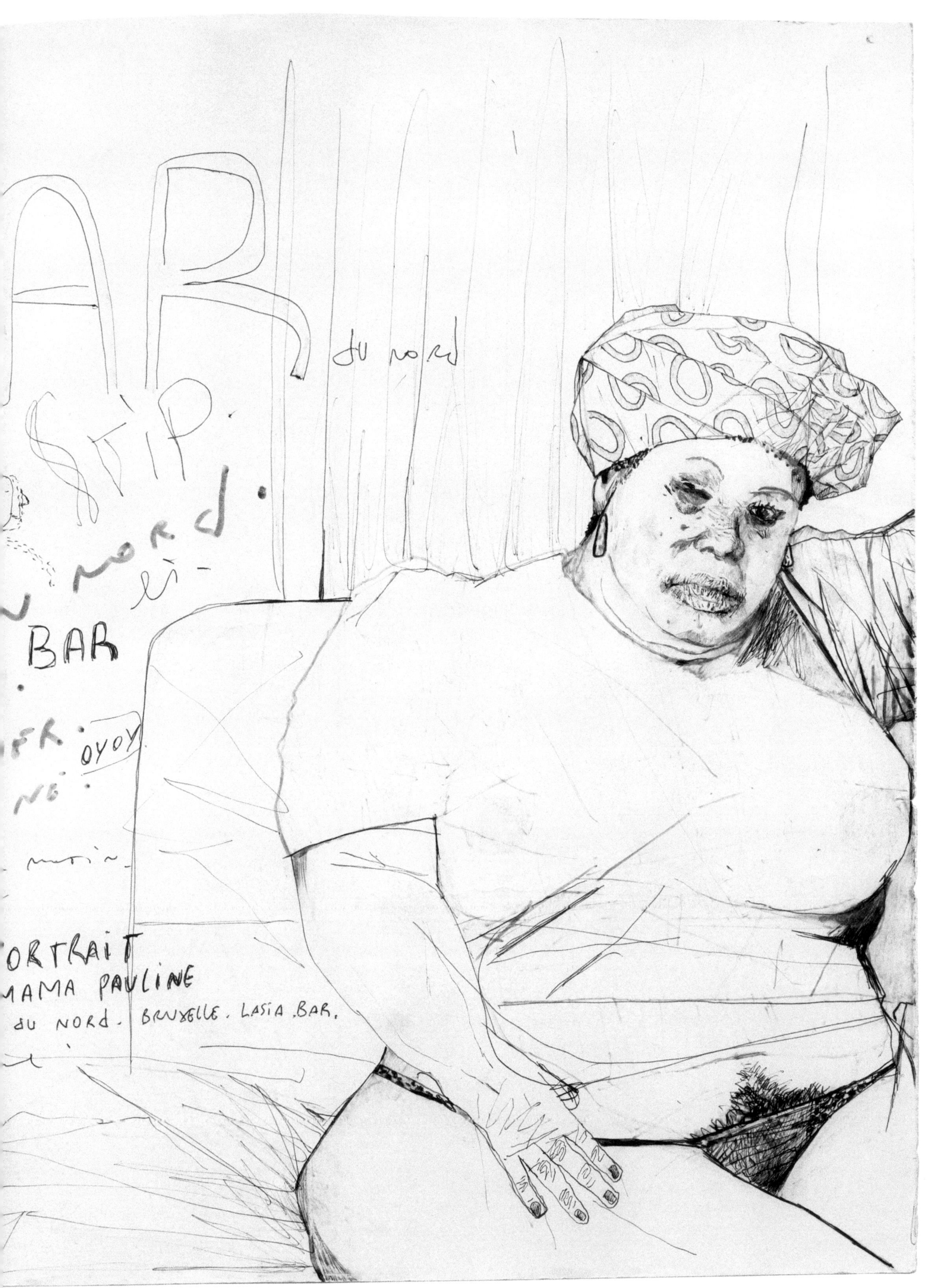


*Portrait de Mama Pauline*, 1984

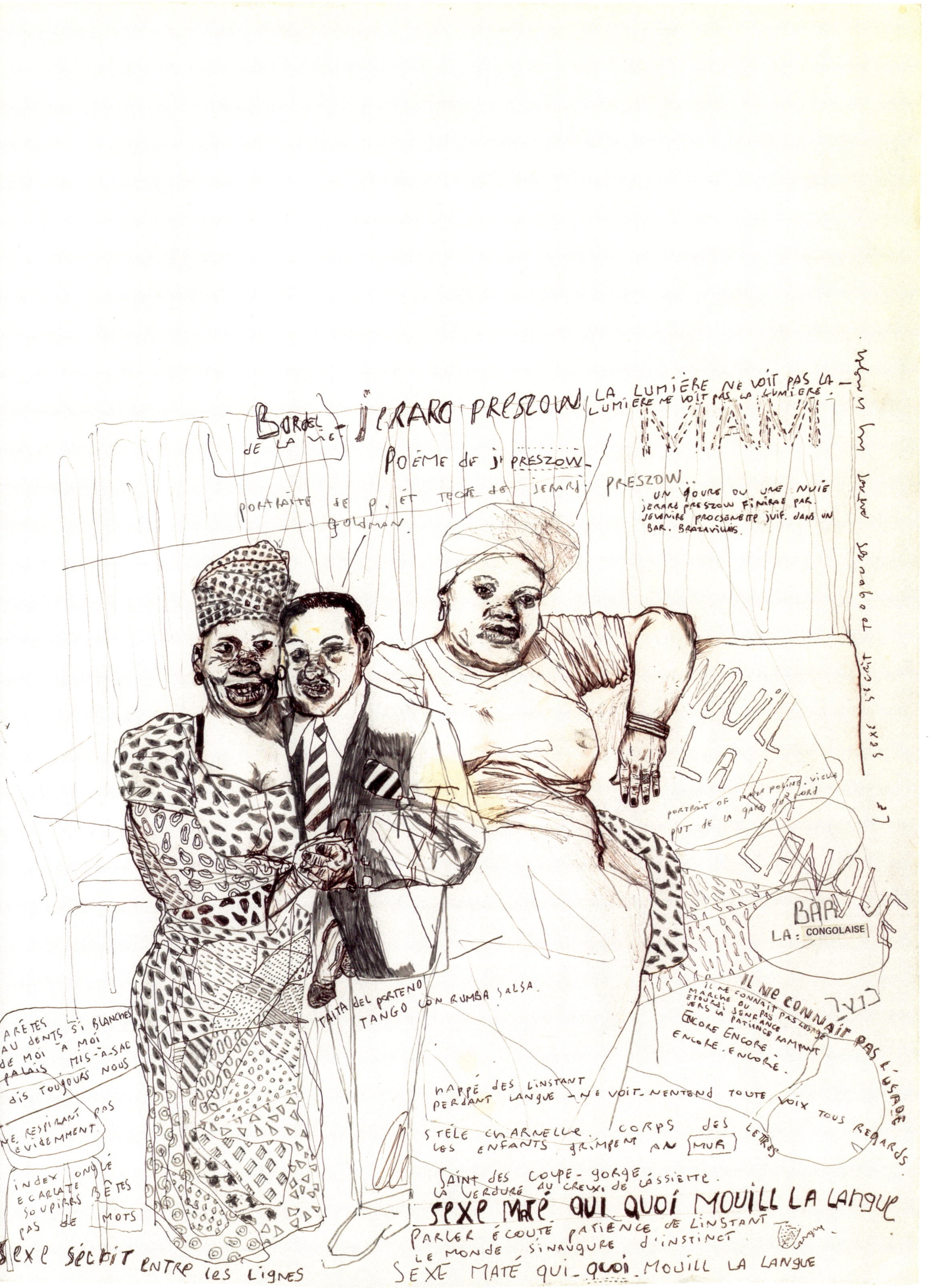


*Bordel de la vie (Jerard Preszow)*, 1986

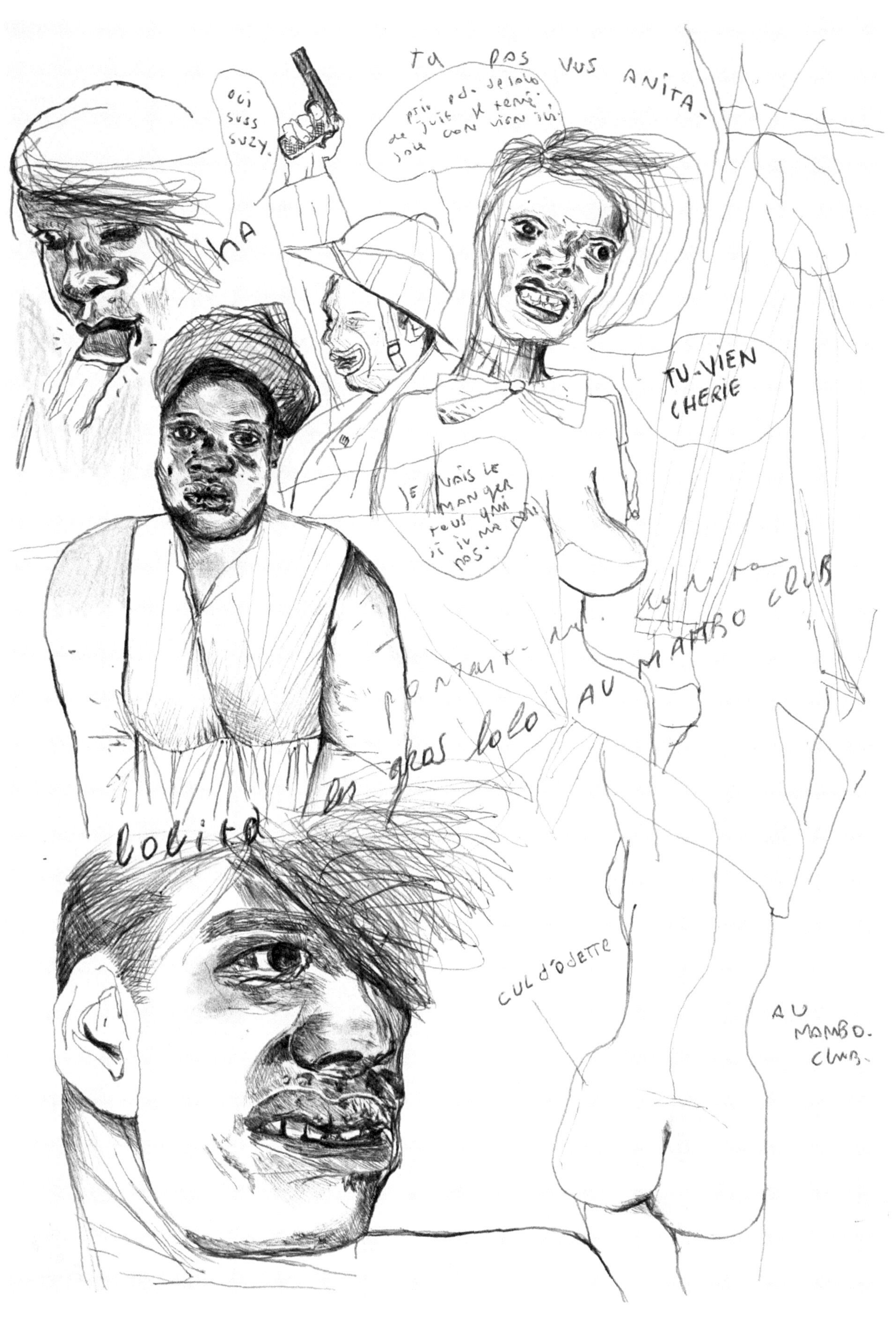


*Lolita les gros lolo au Mambo Club*, 1985

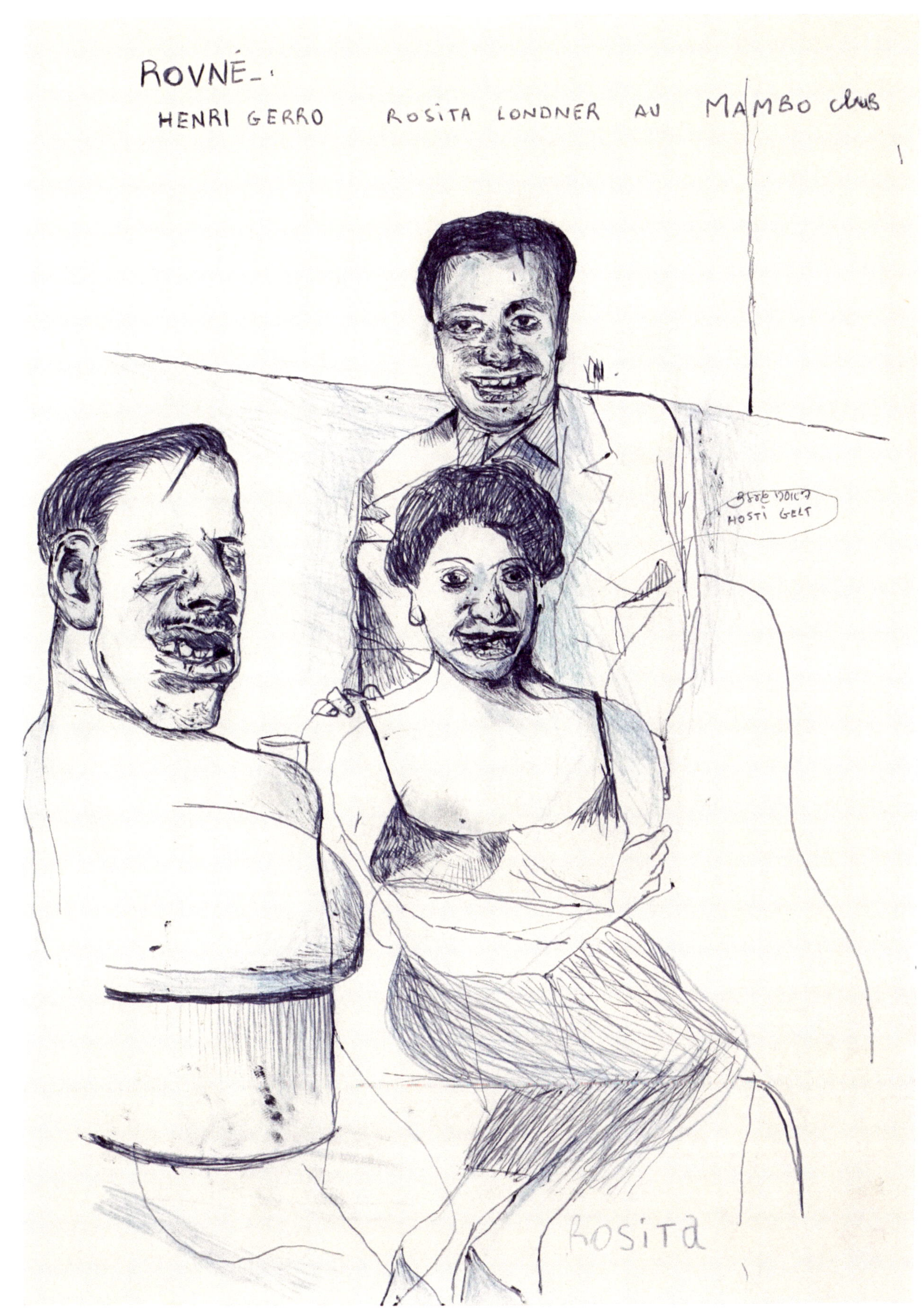


*Rovné (Henri Gerro Rosita Londner au Mambo Club)*, 1985

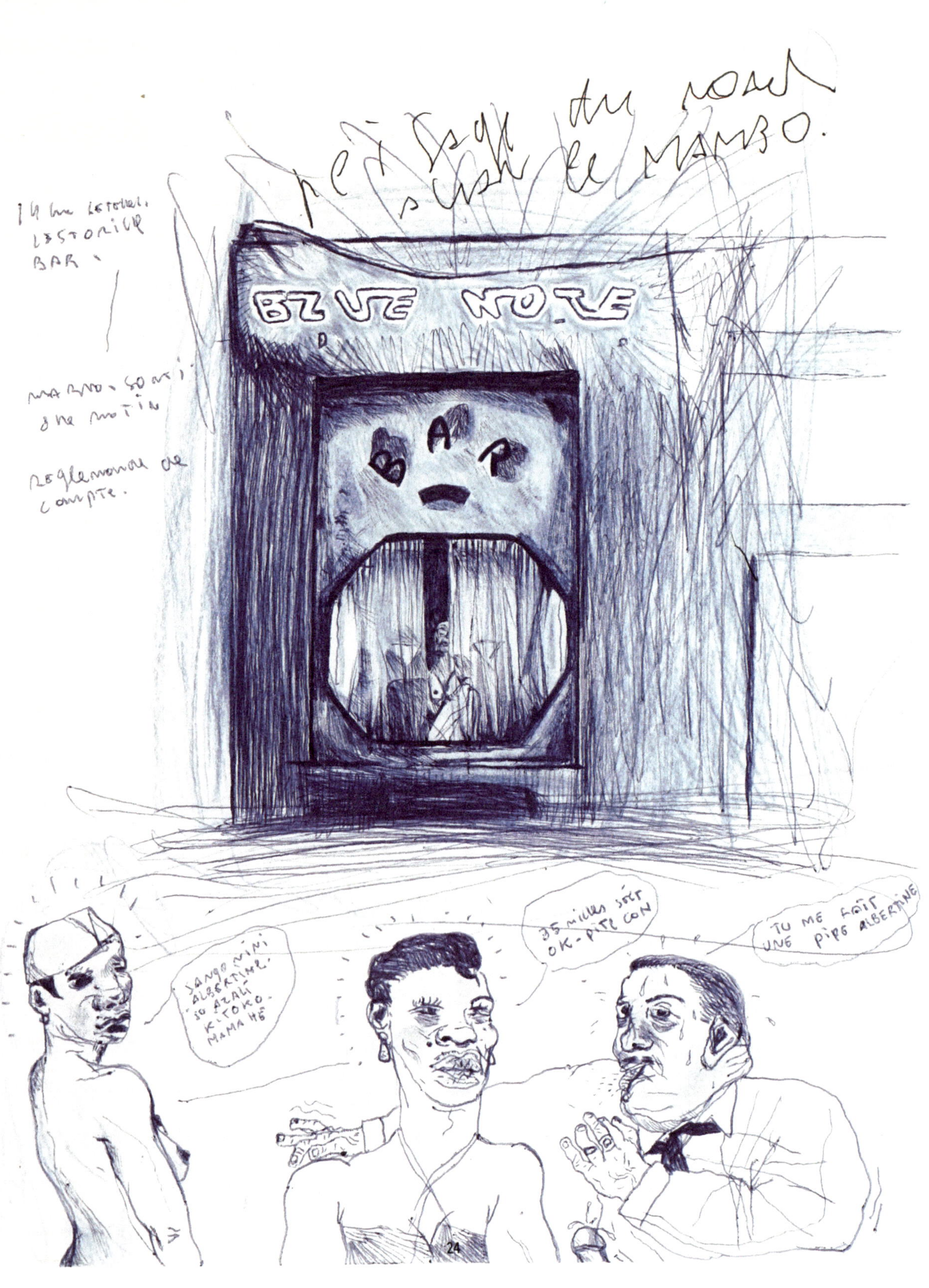


*Blue Note*, 1985

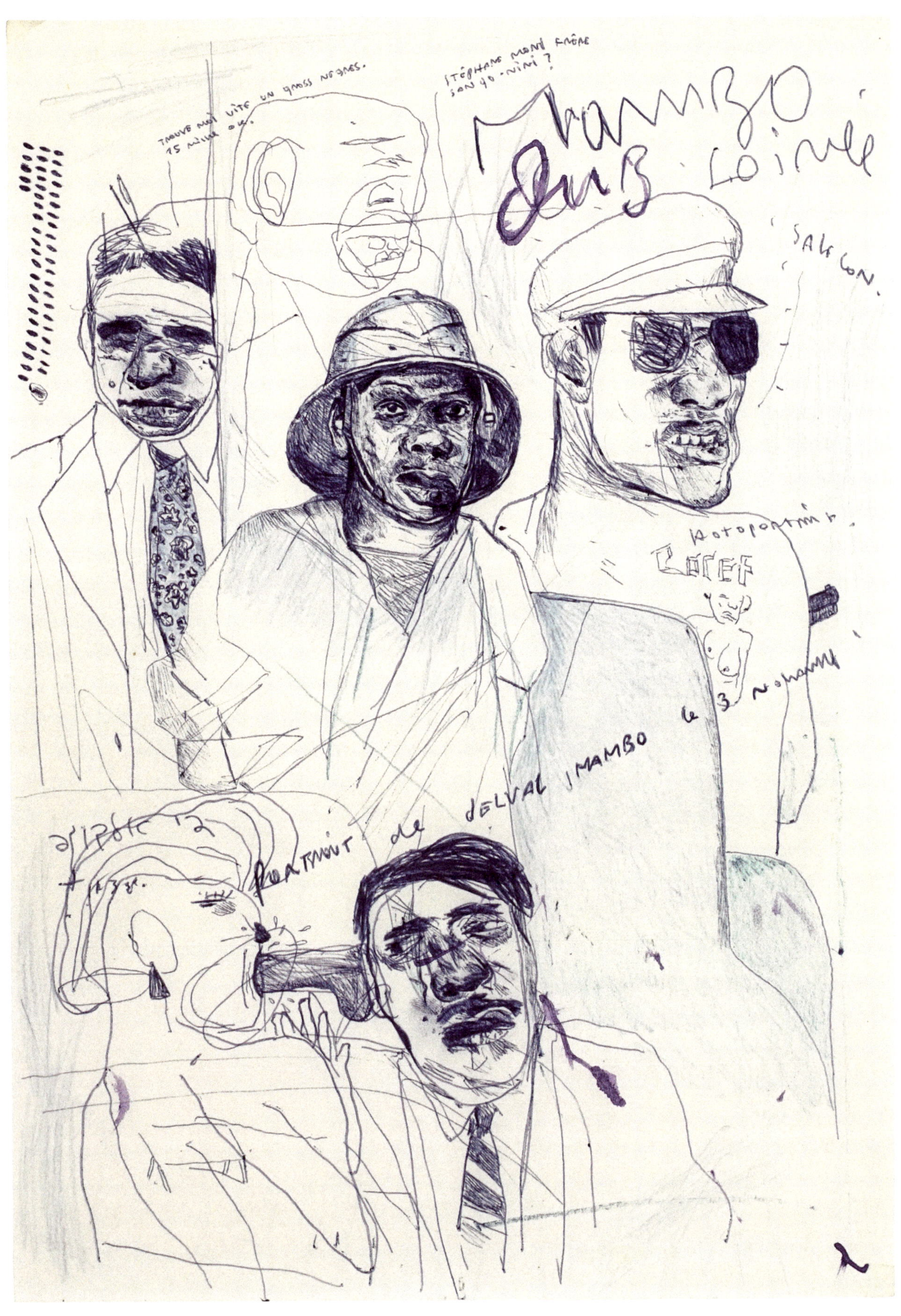


*Mambo Club soirée (Portrait de Delval Mambo)*, 1985

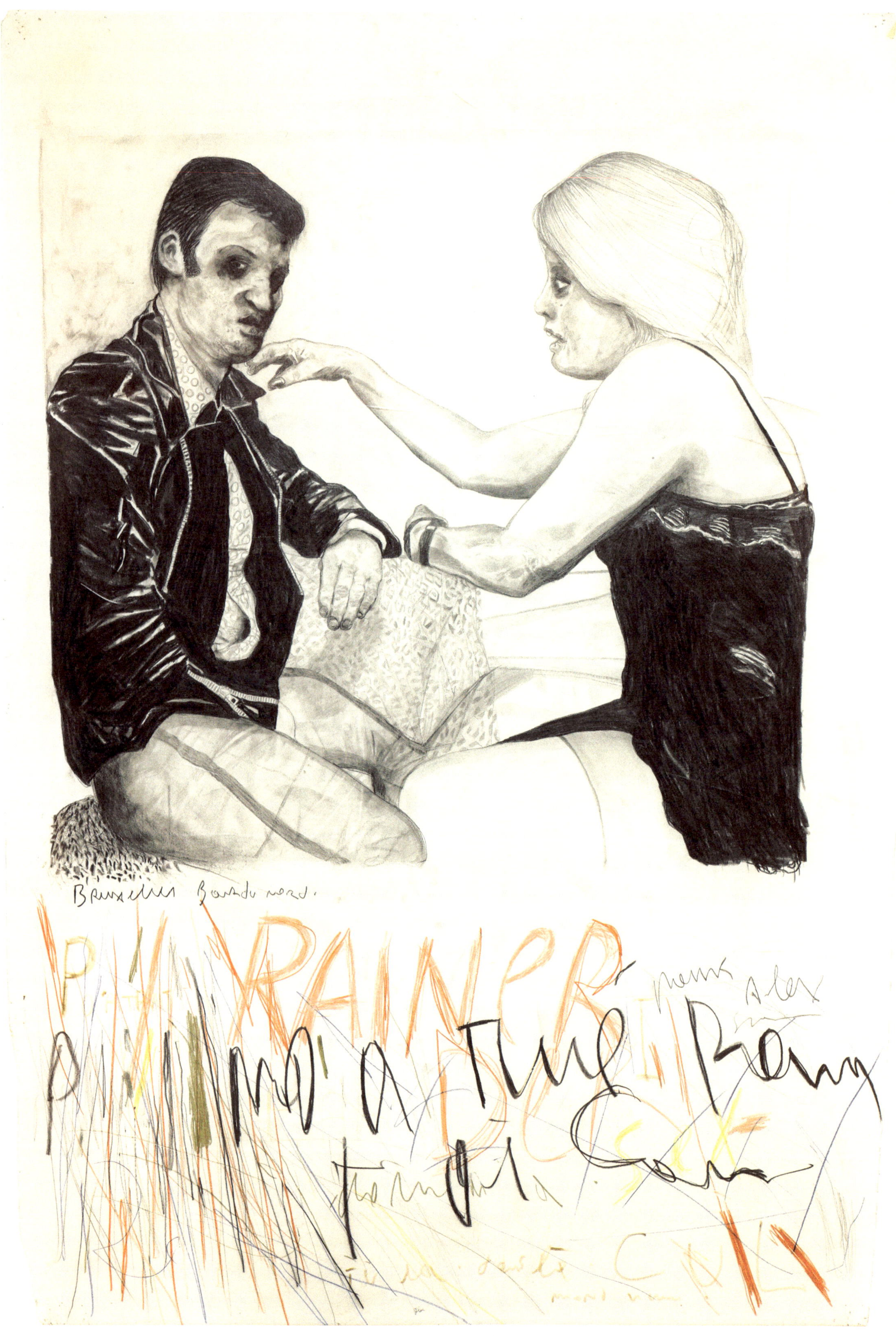


*Rainer (Portrait de Rainer Werner Fassbinder)*, c. 1984

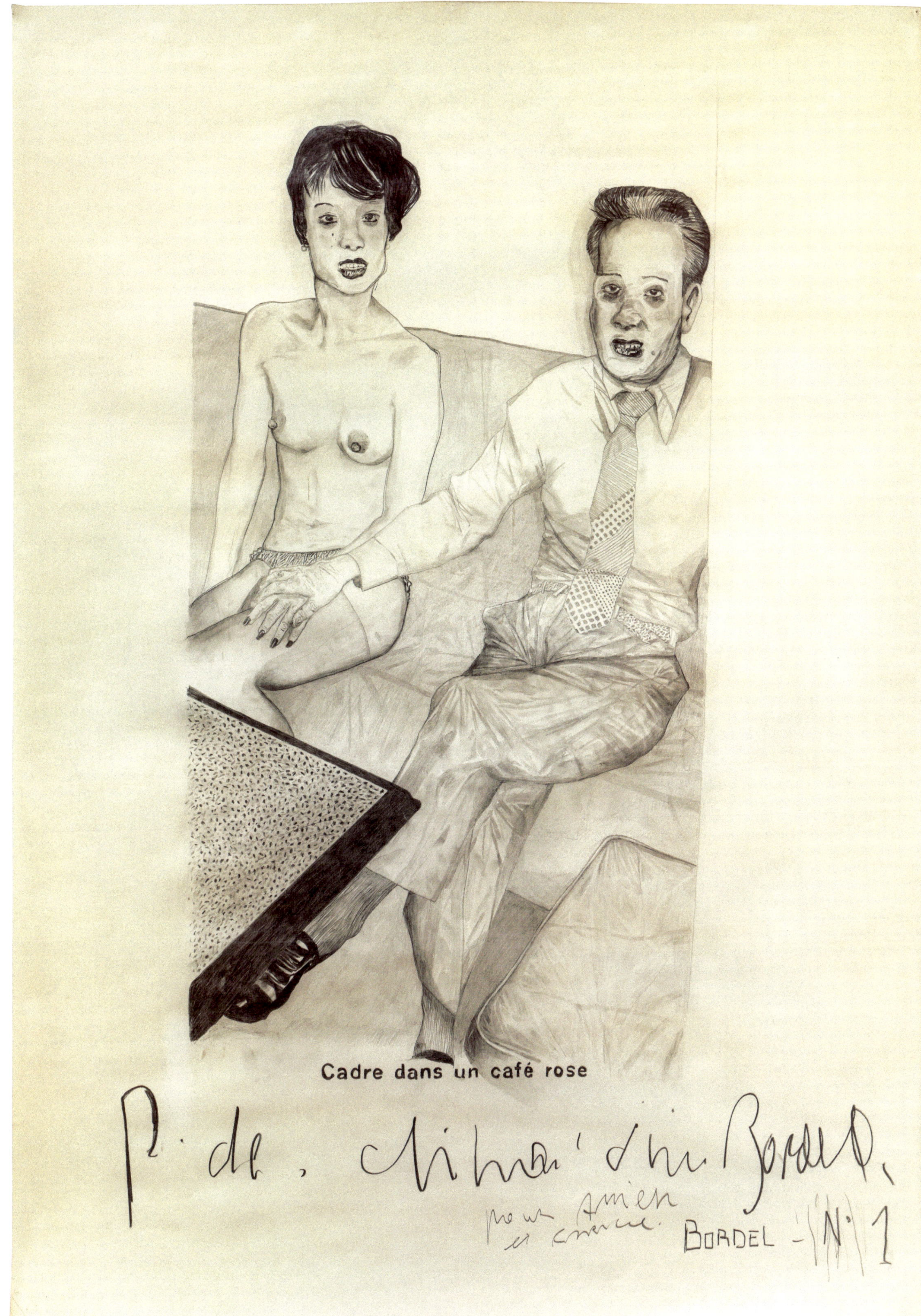


*Cadre dans un café rose*, 1984

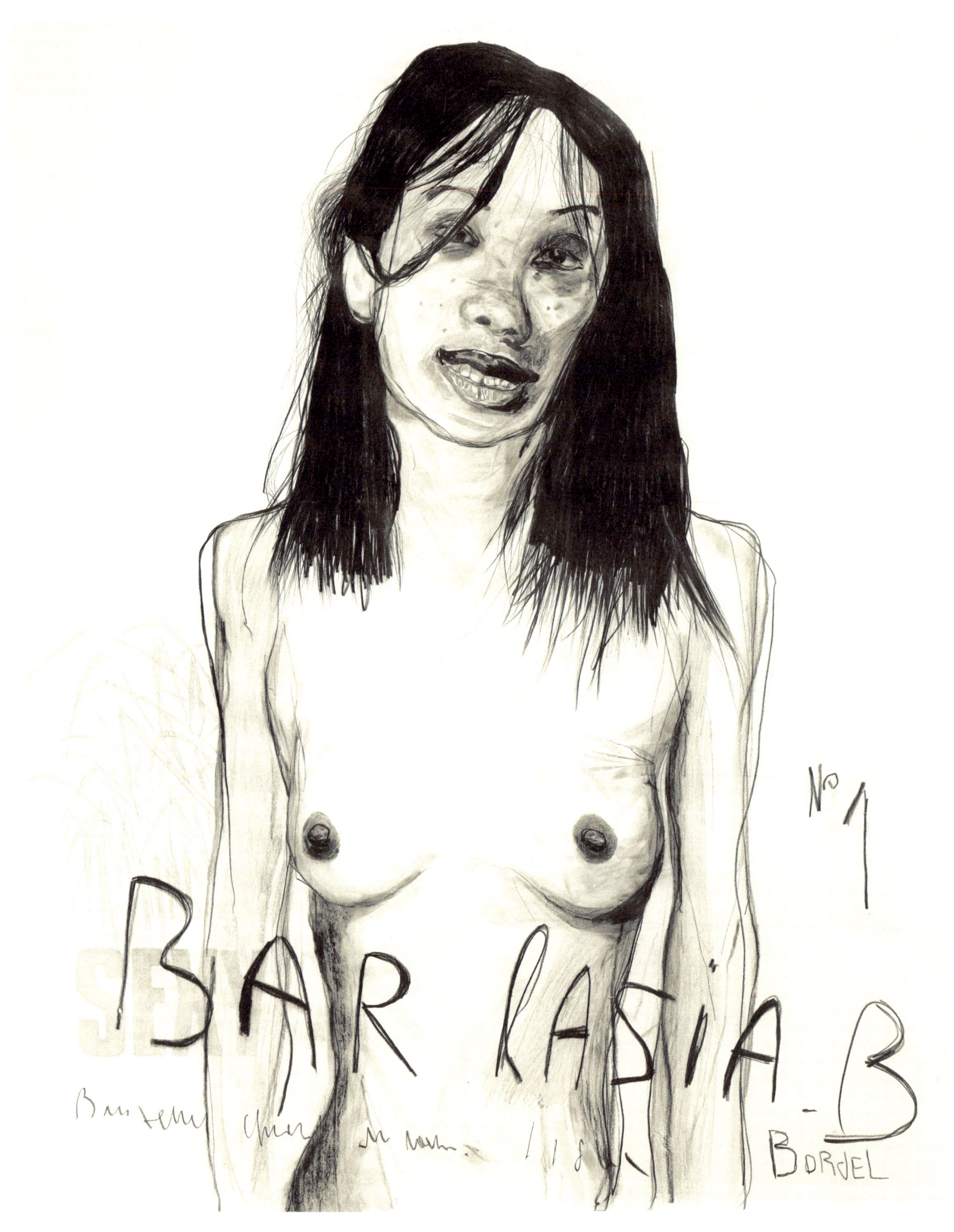


*Bar l'Asia B Nº 1*, 1984

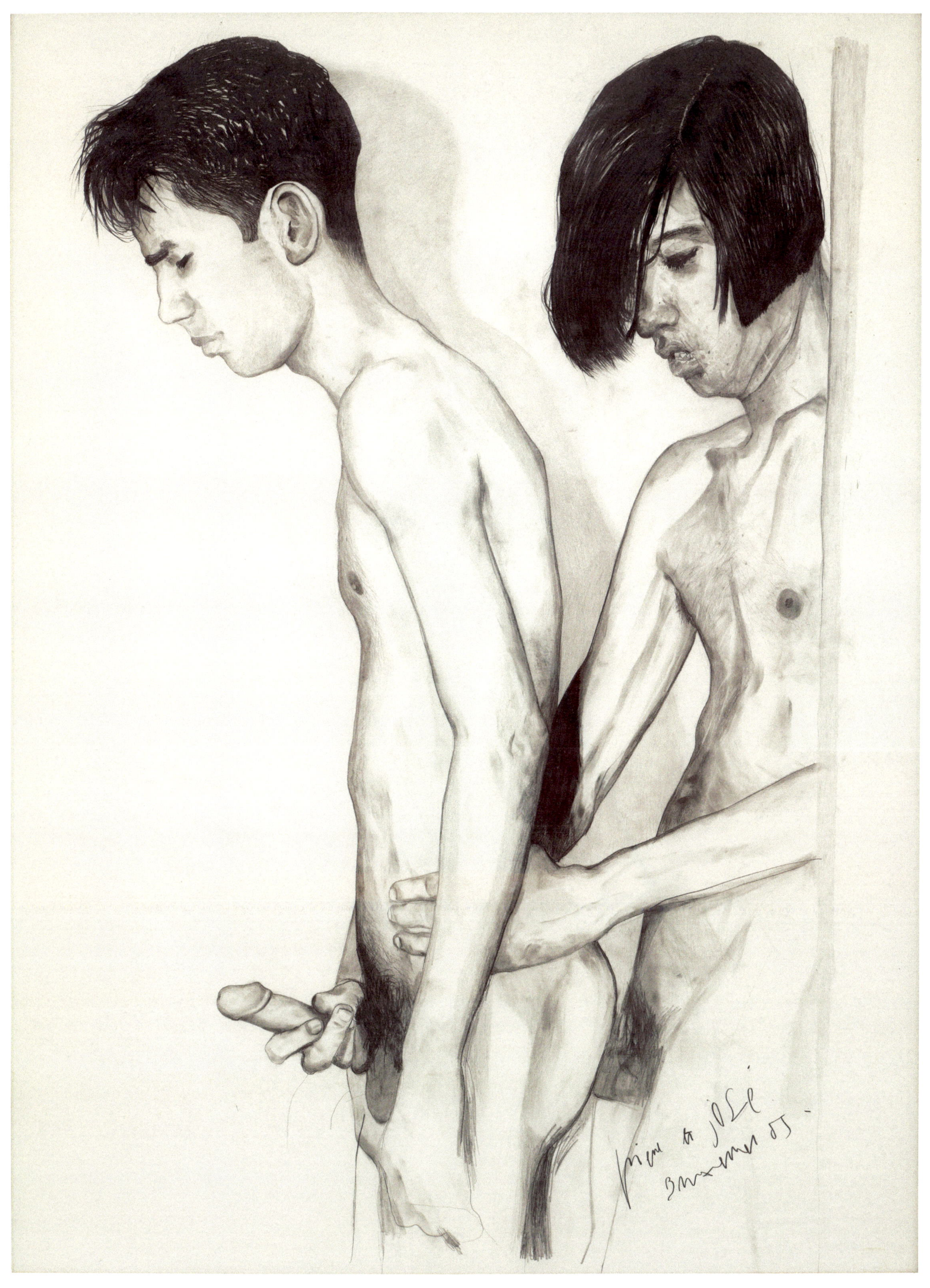

*Pierre et José*, 1985

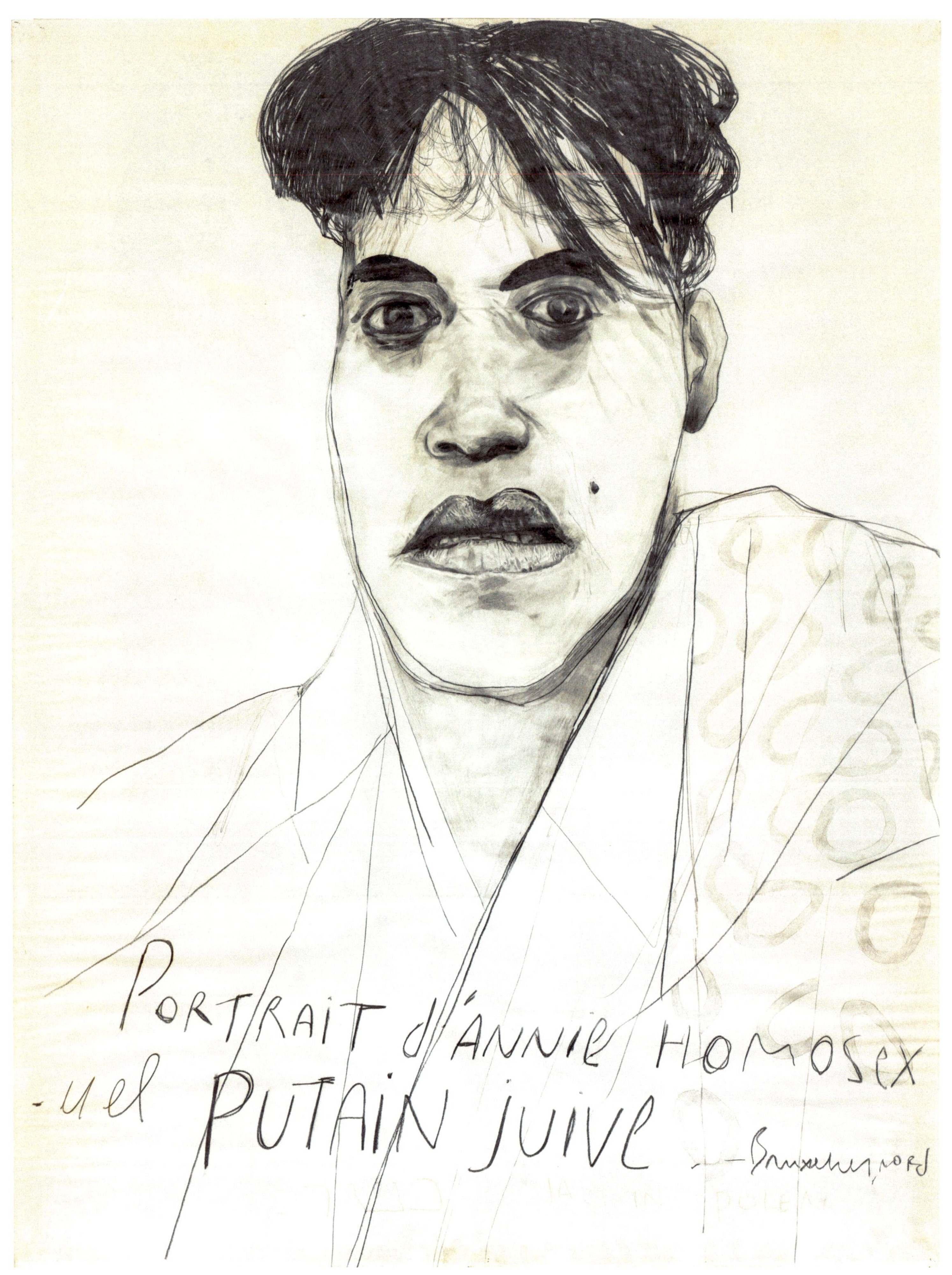


*Portrait d'Annie, Homosexuel, Putain juive*, 1985

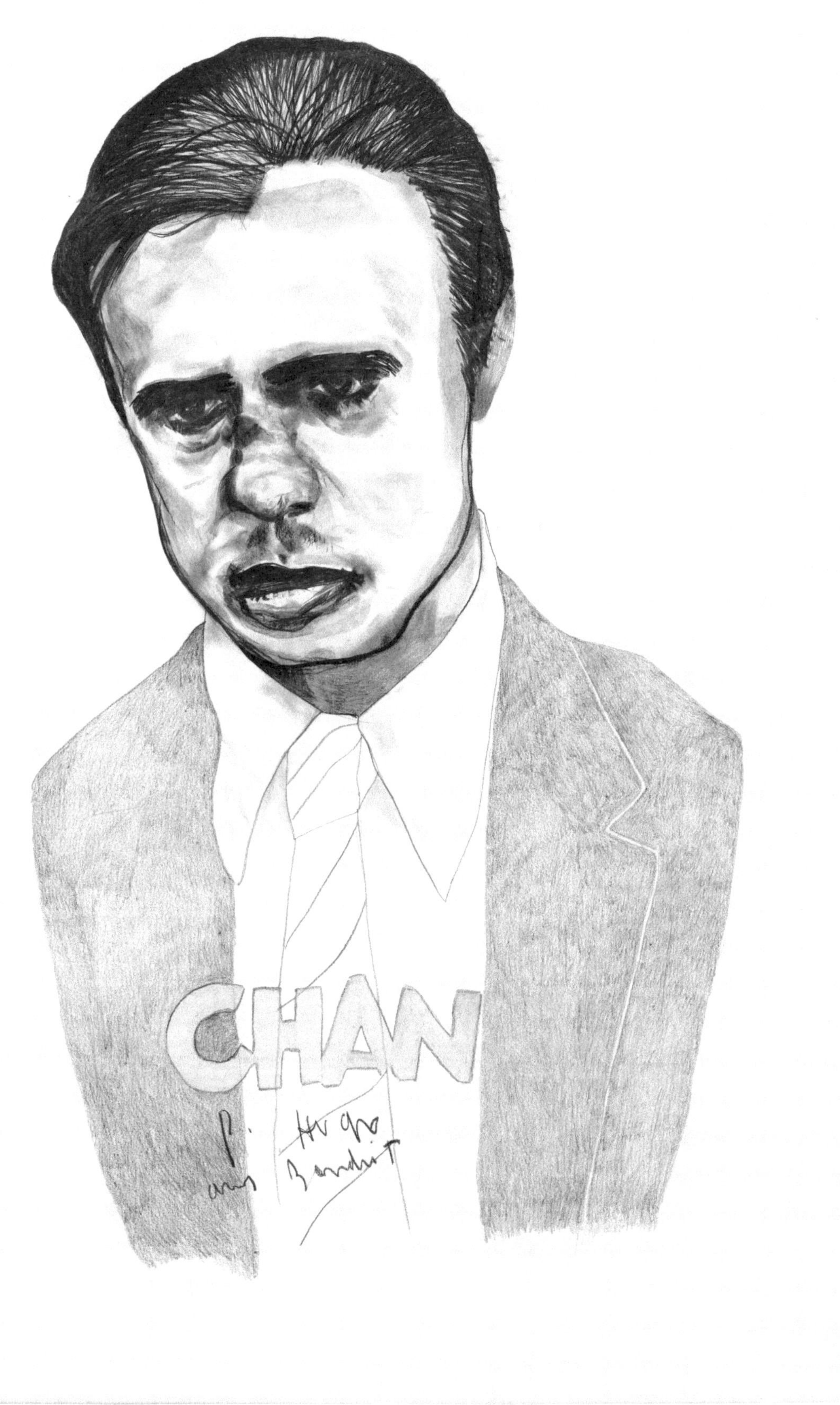


*Portrait de Chan*, 1985

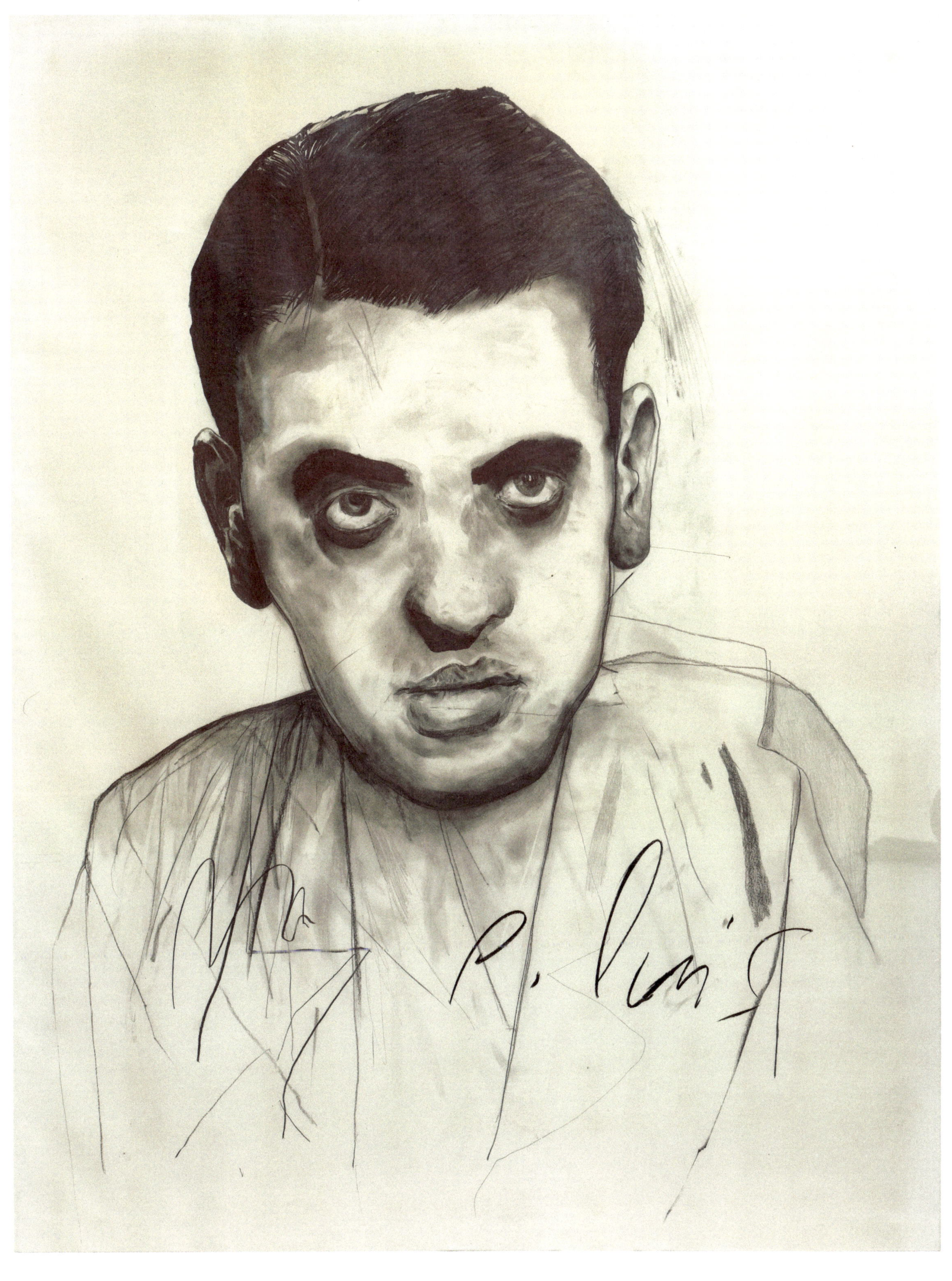

*Buñuel*, c. 1985

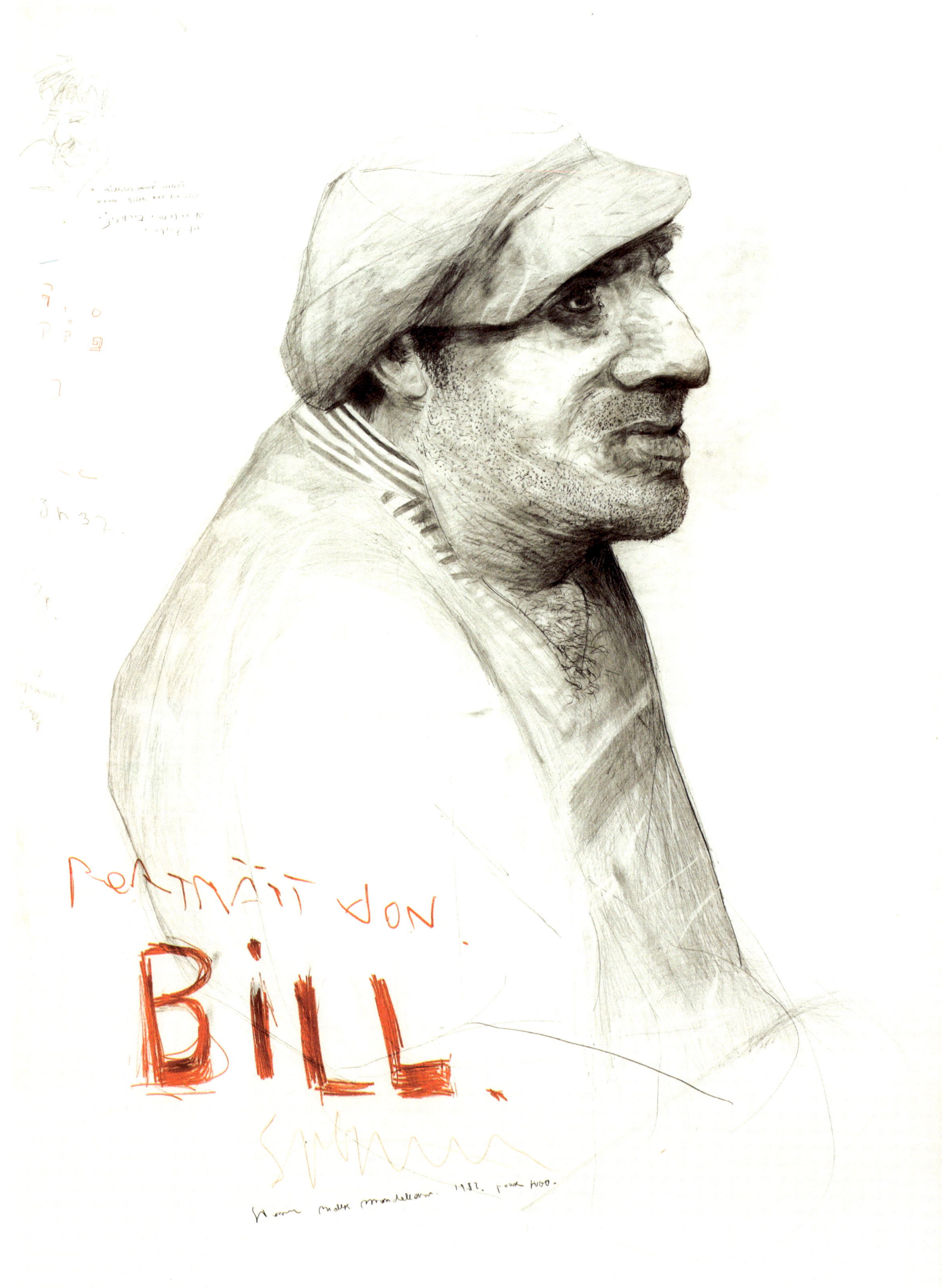


*Portraït von Bill*, 1982

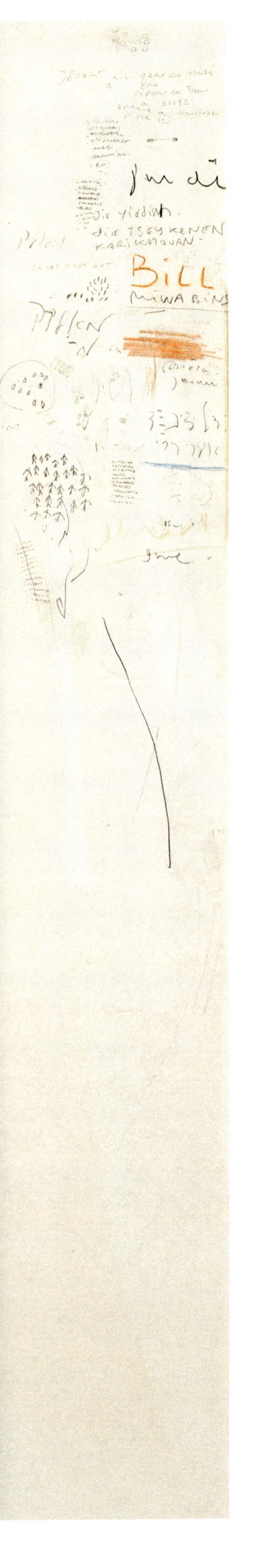

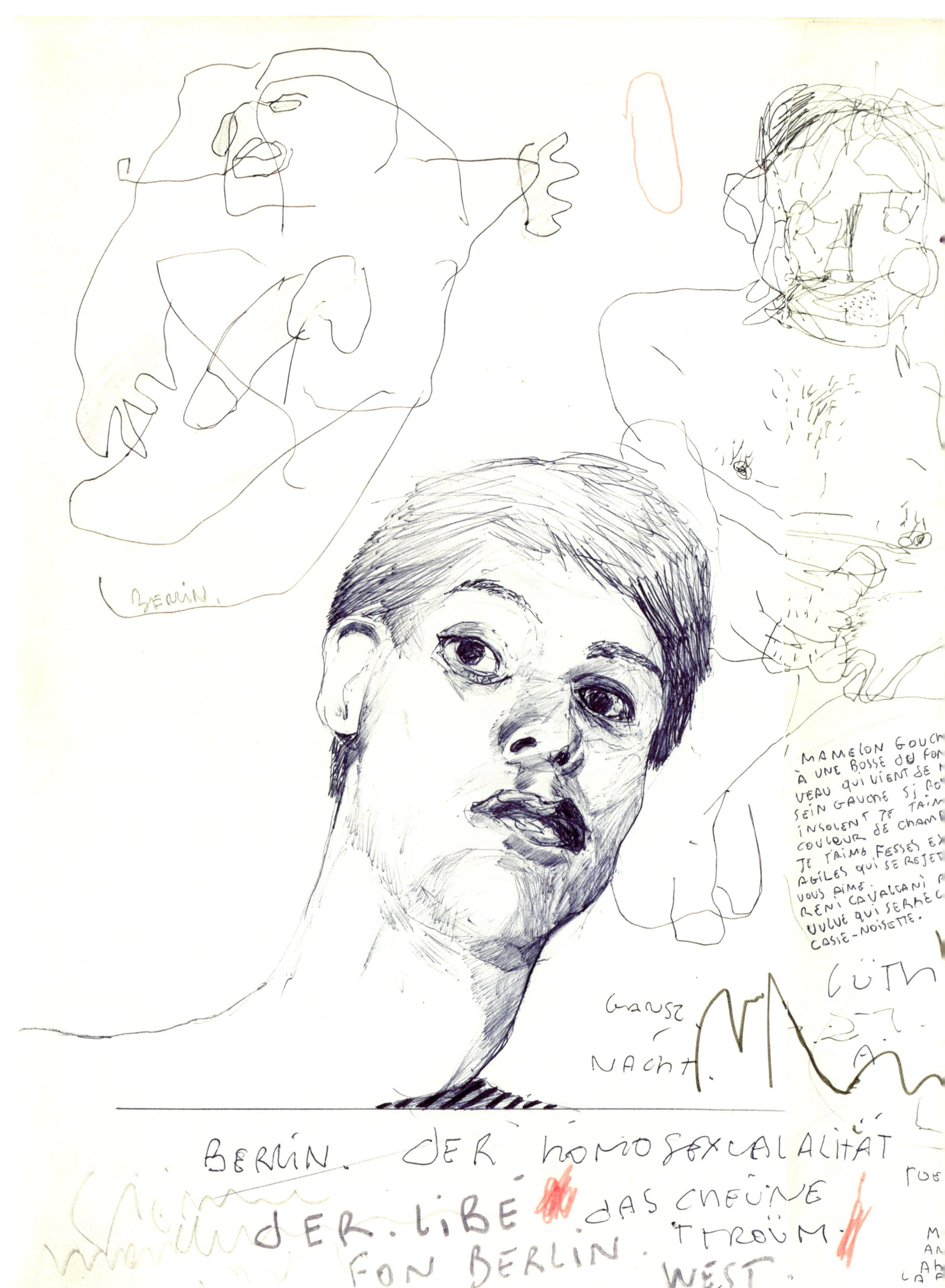


*Composition (Der libé fon Berlin West)*, 1984

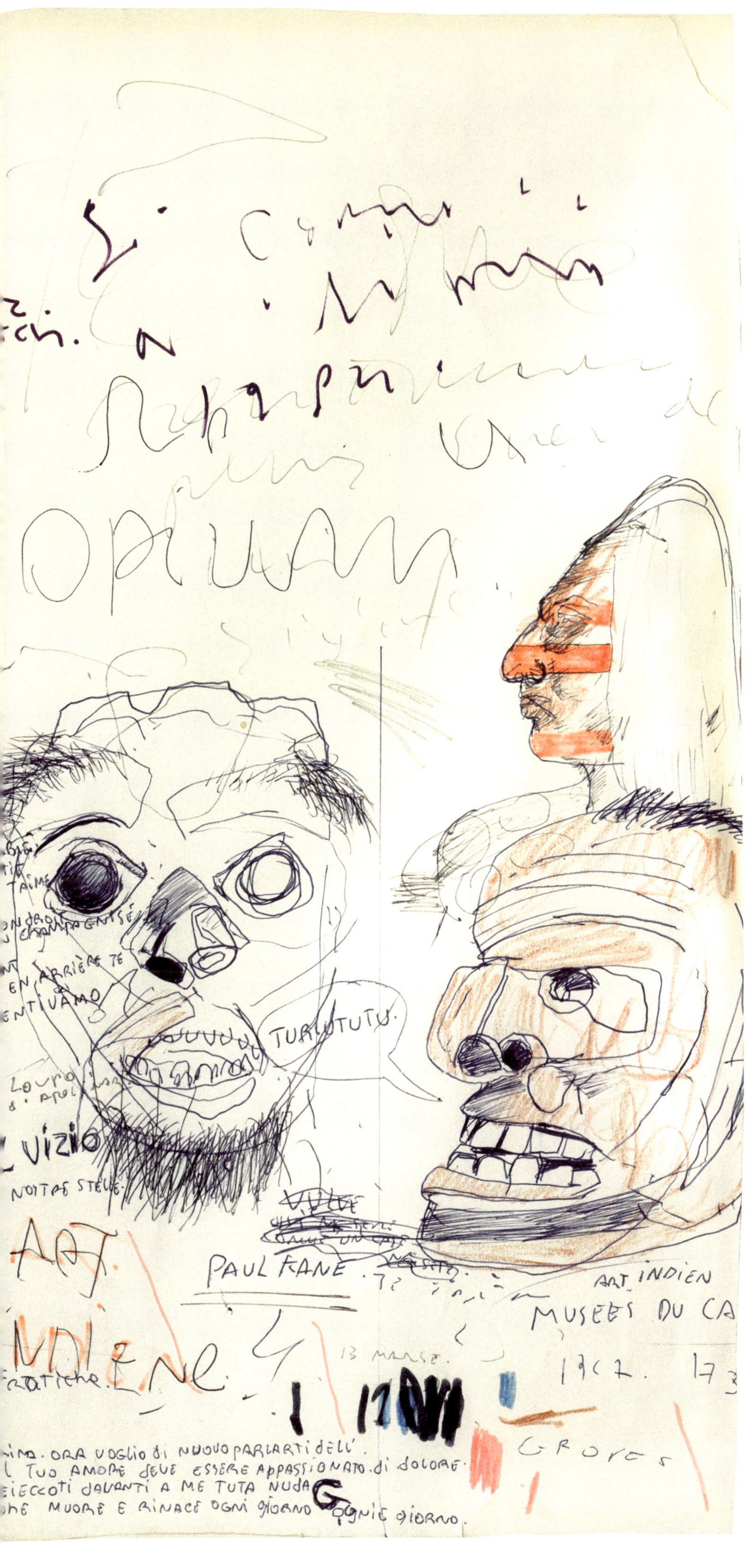

TURLUTUTU
VIZIO
ART
PAUL KANE
ART INDIEN
MUSEES DU CA
ratiche.
13 MARSE.
ima. ORA VOGLIO DI NUOVO PARLARTI DELL'
l TUO AMORE DEVE ESSERE APPASSIONATO. DI DOLORE.
EIECCOTI DAVANTI A ME TUTA NUDA
HE MUORE E RINACE OGNI GIORNO OGNI GIORNO.

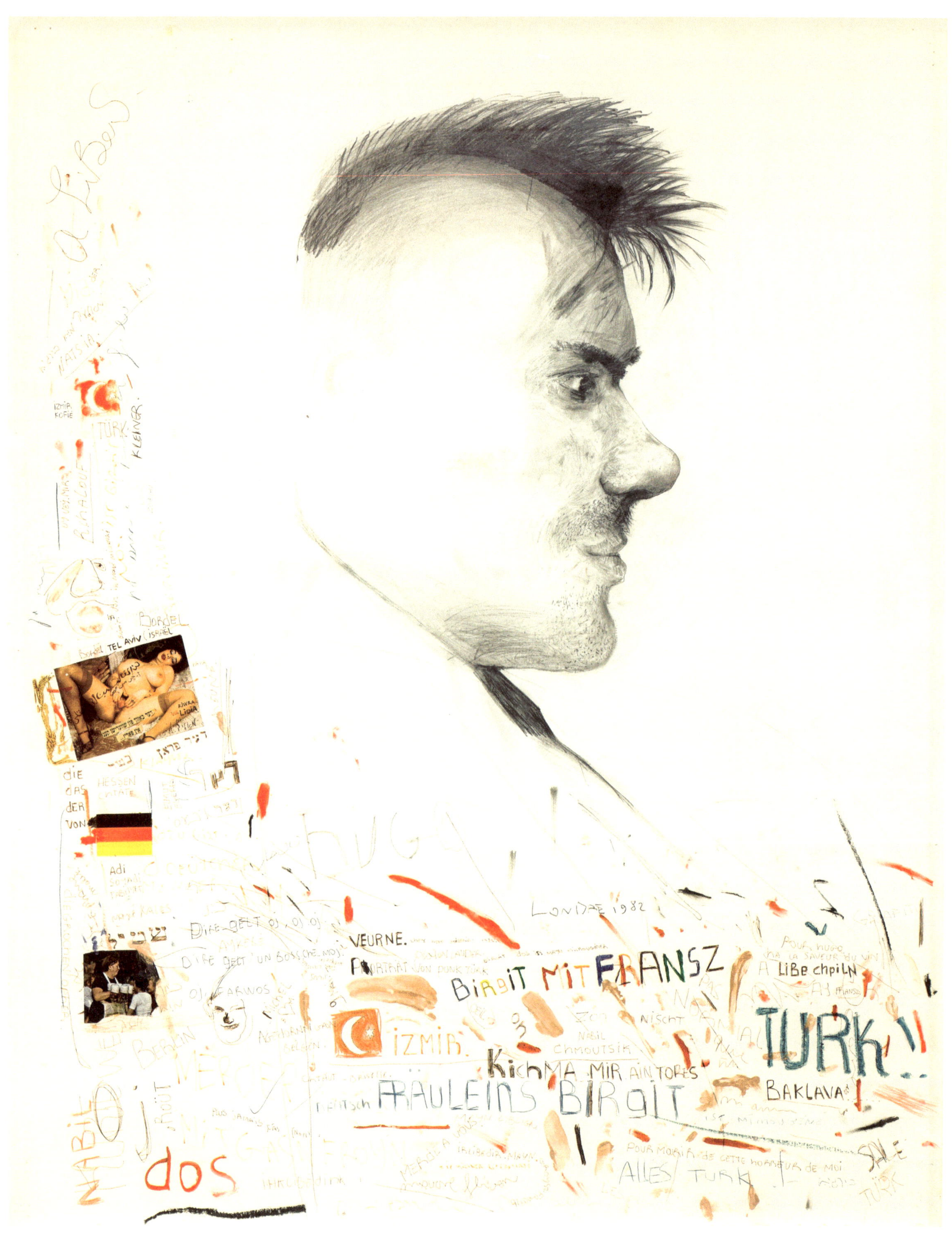

*Portrait von punk türk (Hugo)*, 1984

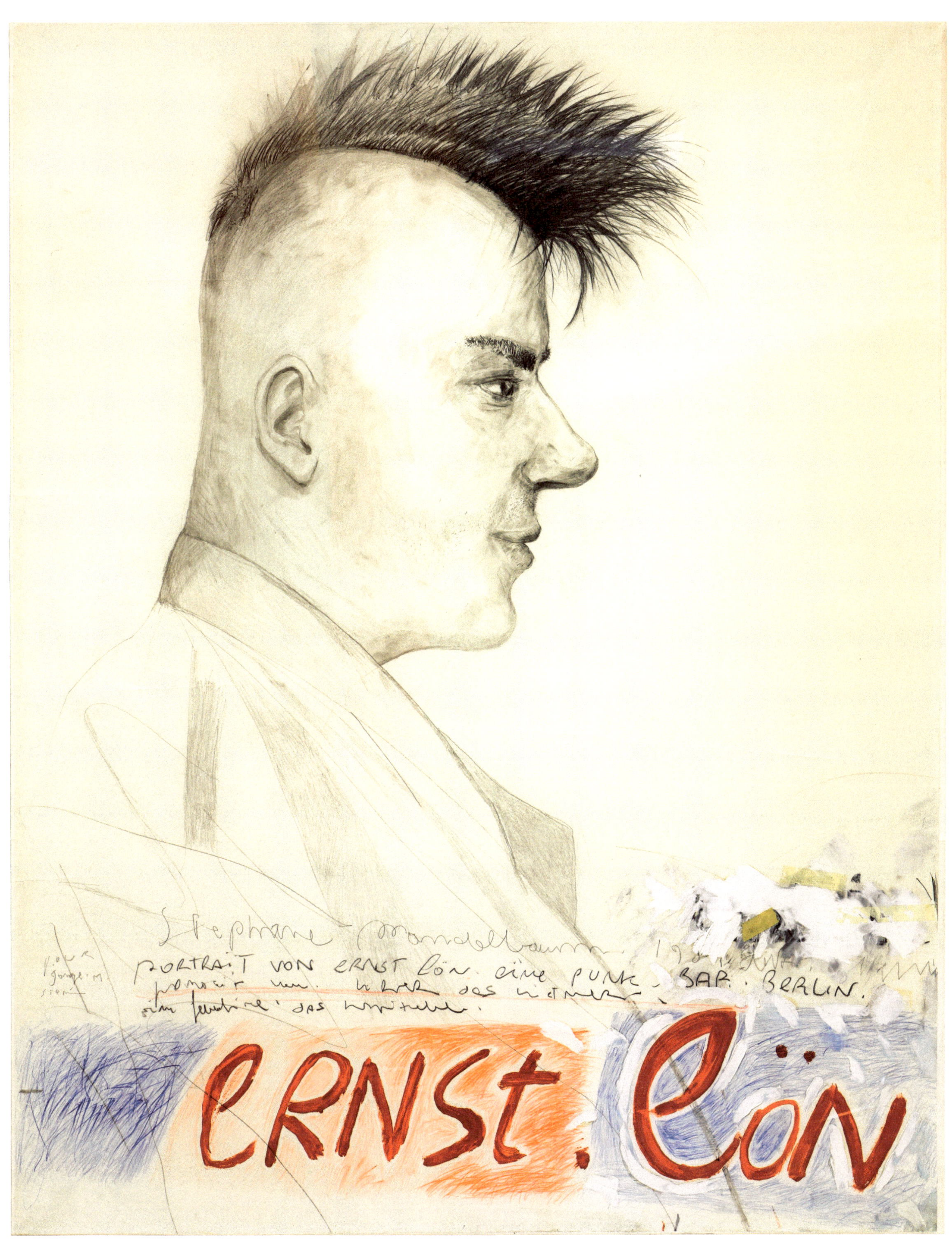


*Ernst Cön (portrait von Ernst Cön, eine Punk)*, 1984

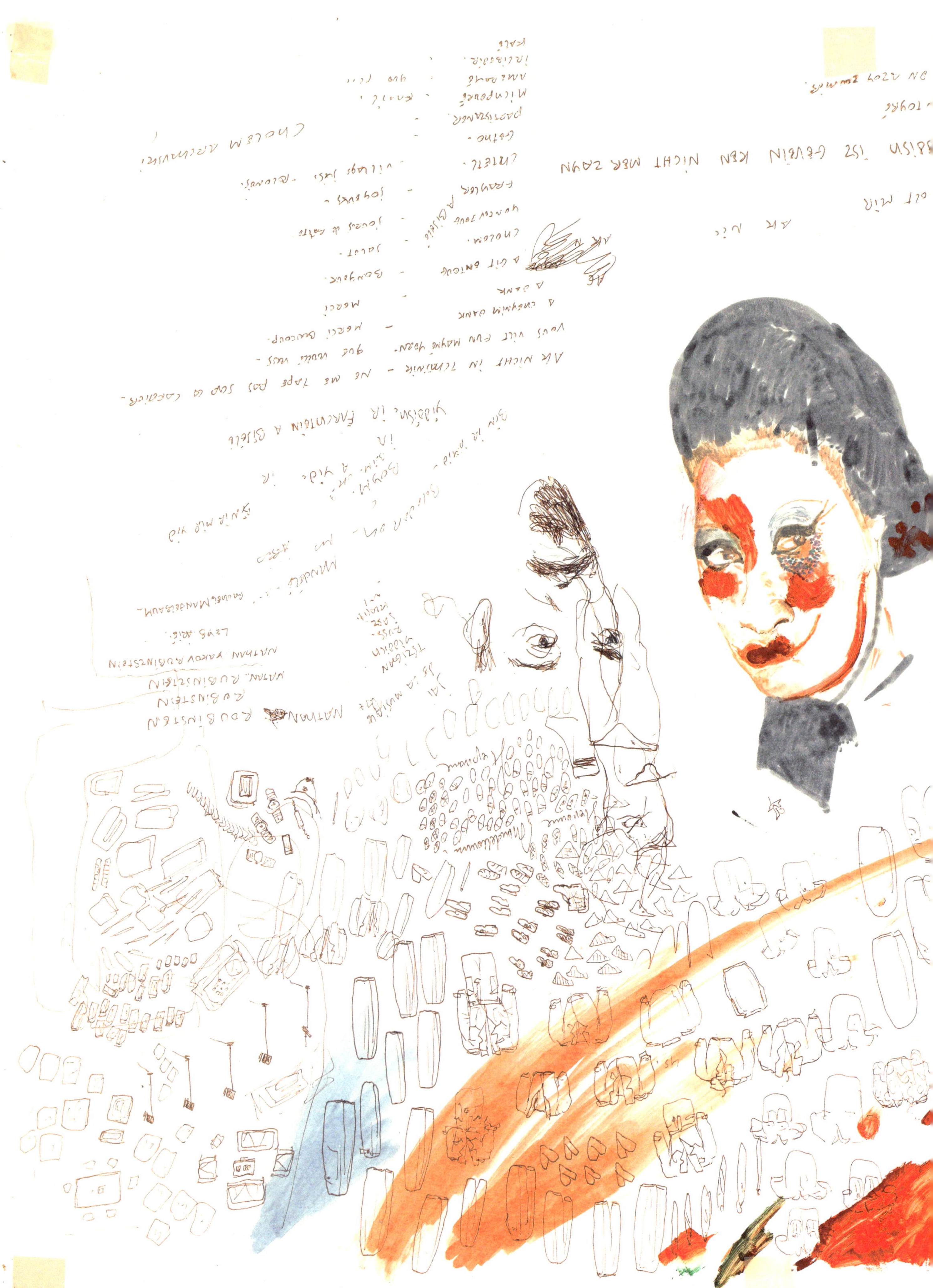


*Composition à la figure rouge*, c. 1984

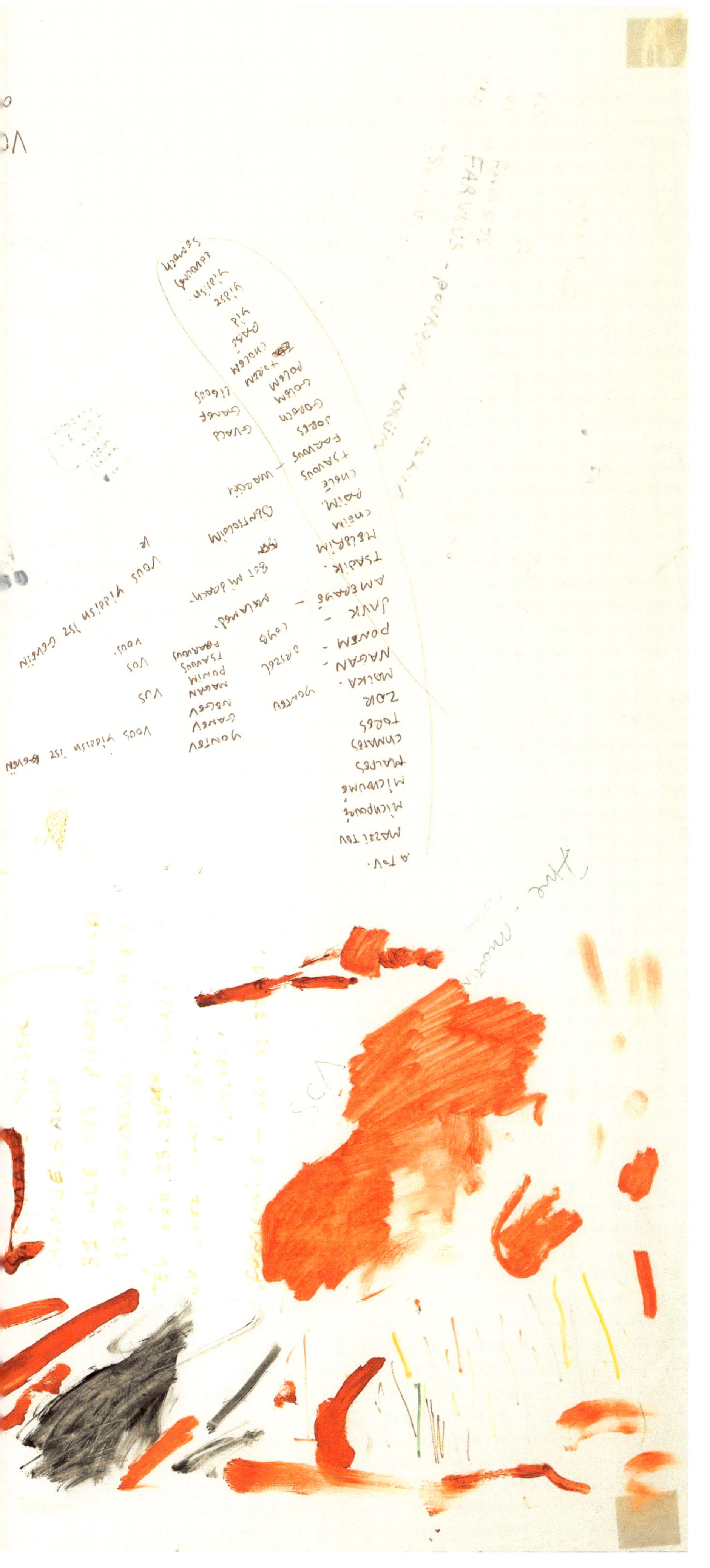

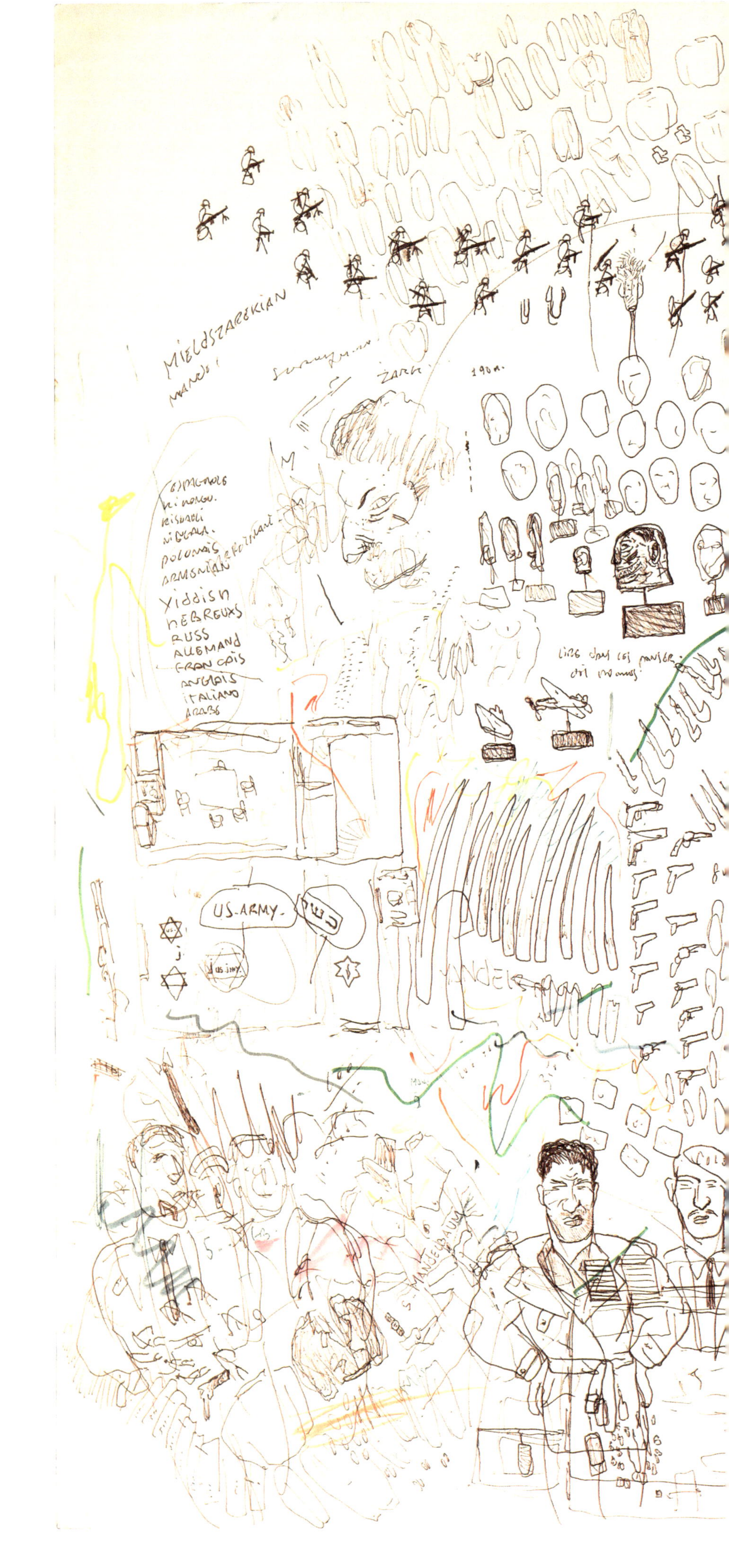
POLONAIS
Yiddish
HEBREUXS
RUSS
ALLEMAND
FRANCAIS
ANGLAIS
ITALIANO
US-ARMY

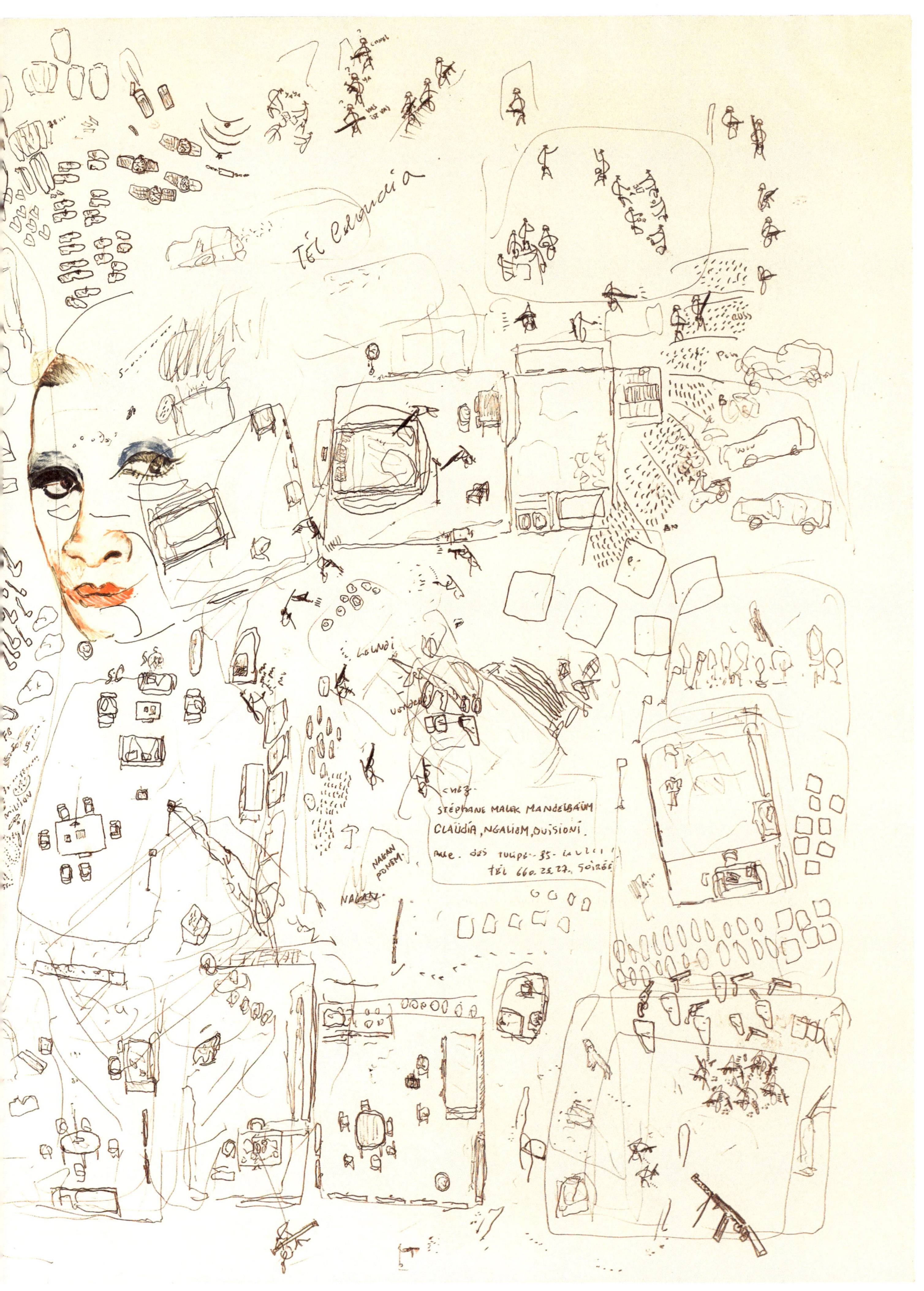


*Composition à la figure rouge*, c. 1984

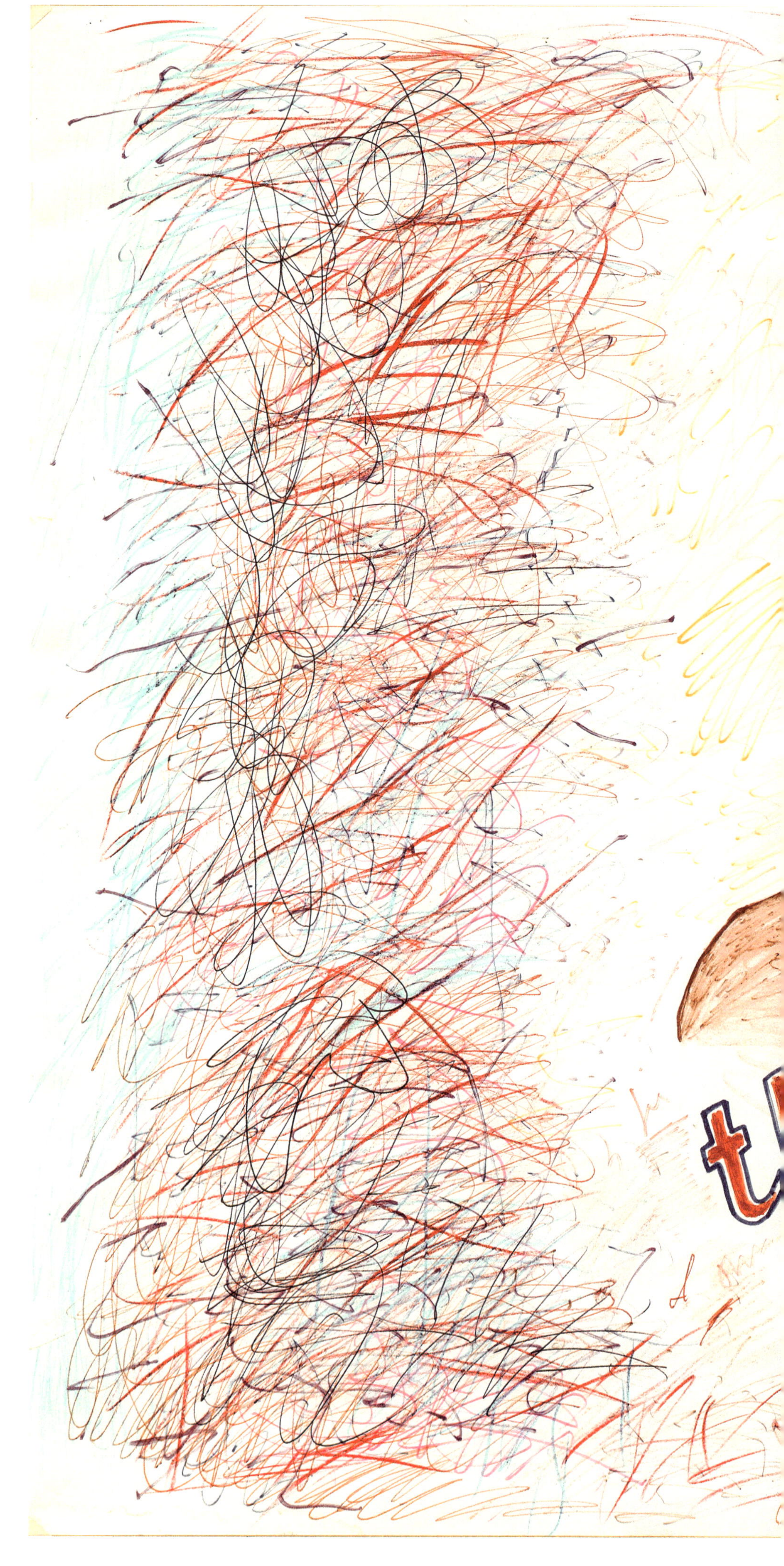

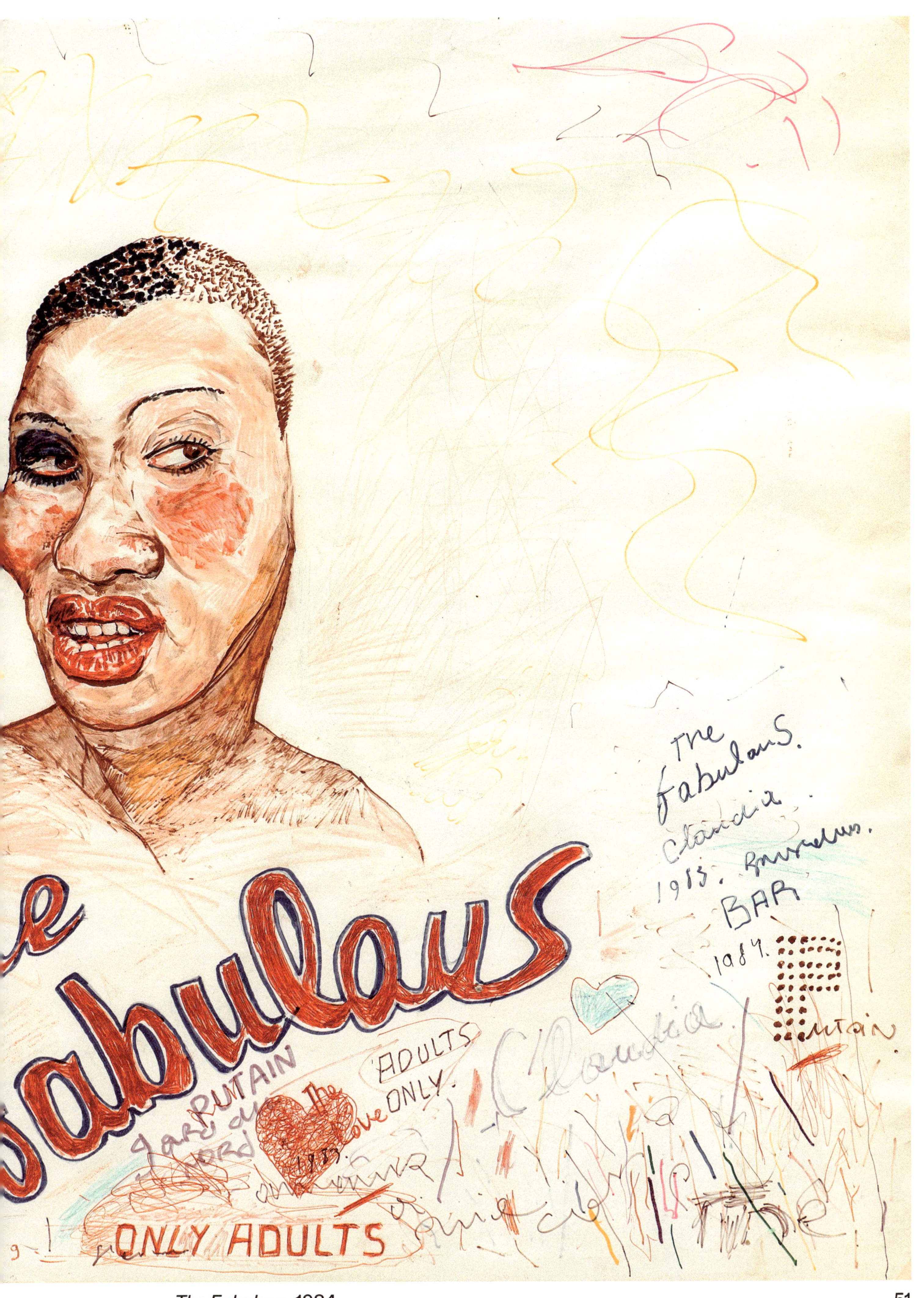


*The Fabulous*, 1984

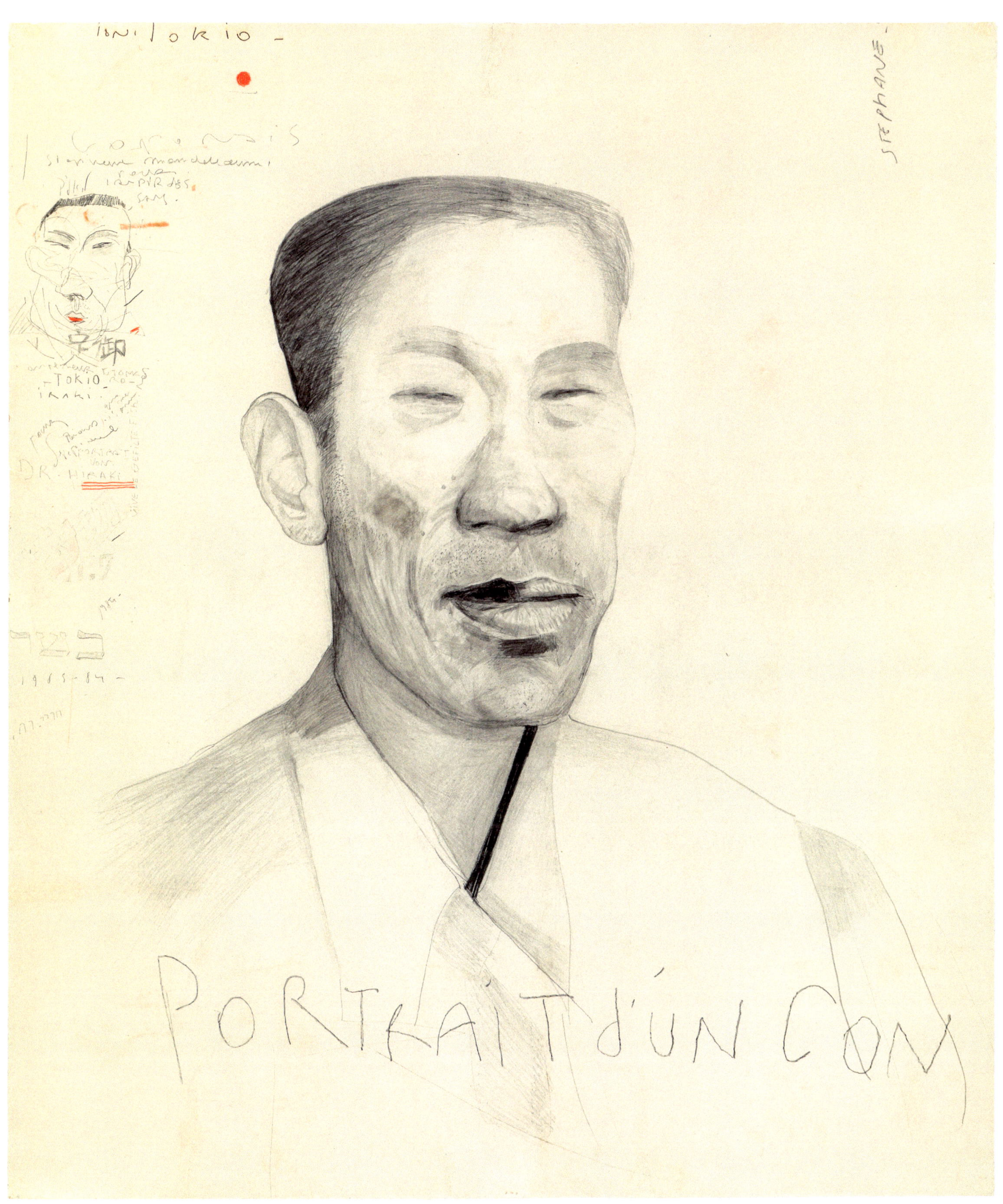


*Portrait d'un con*, 1984

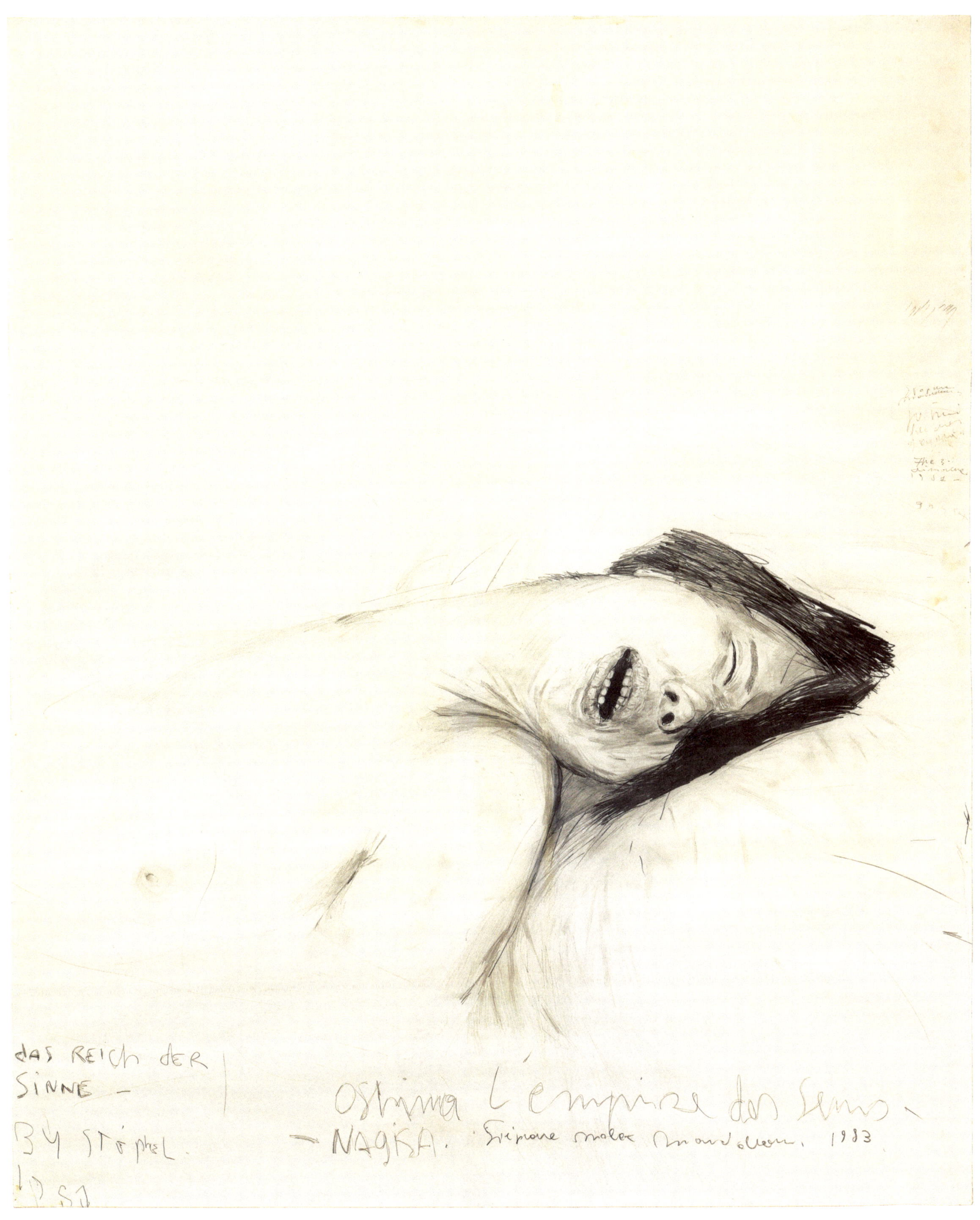


*L'Empire des sens*, 1983

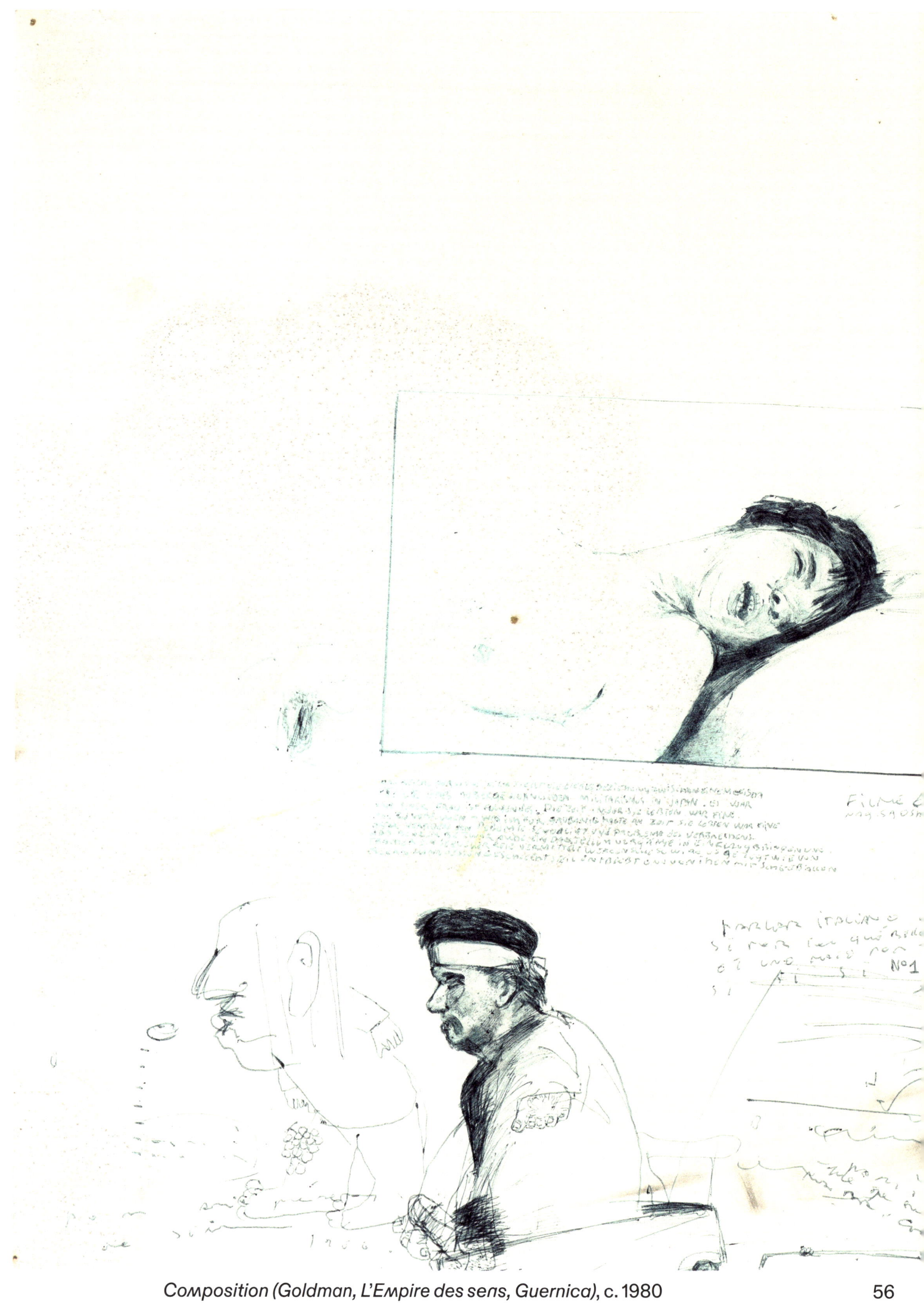

*Composition (Goldman, L'Empire des sens, Guernica)*, c. 1980

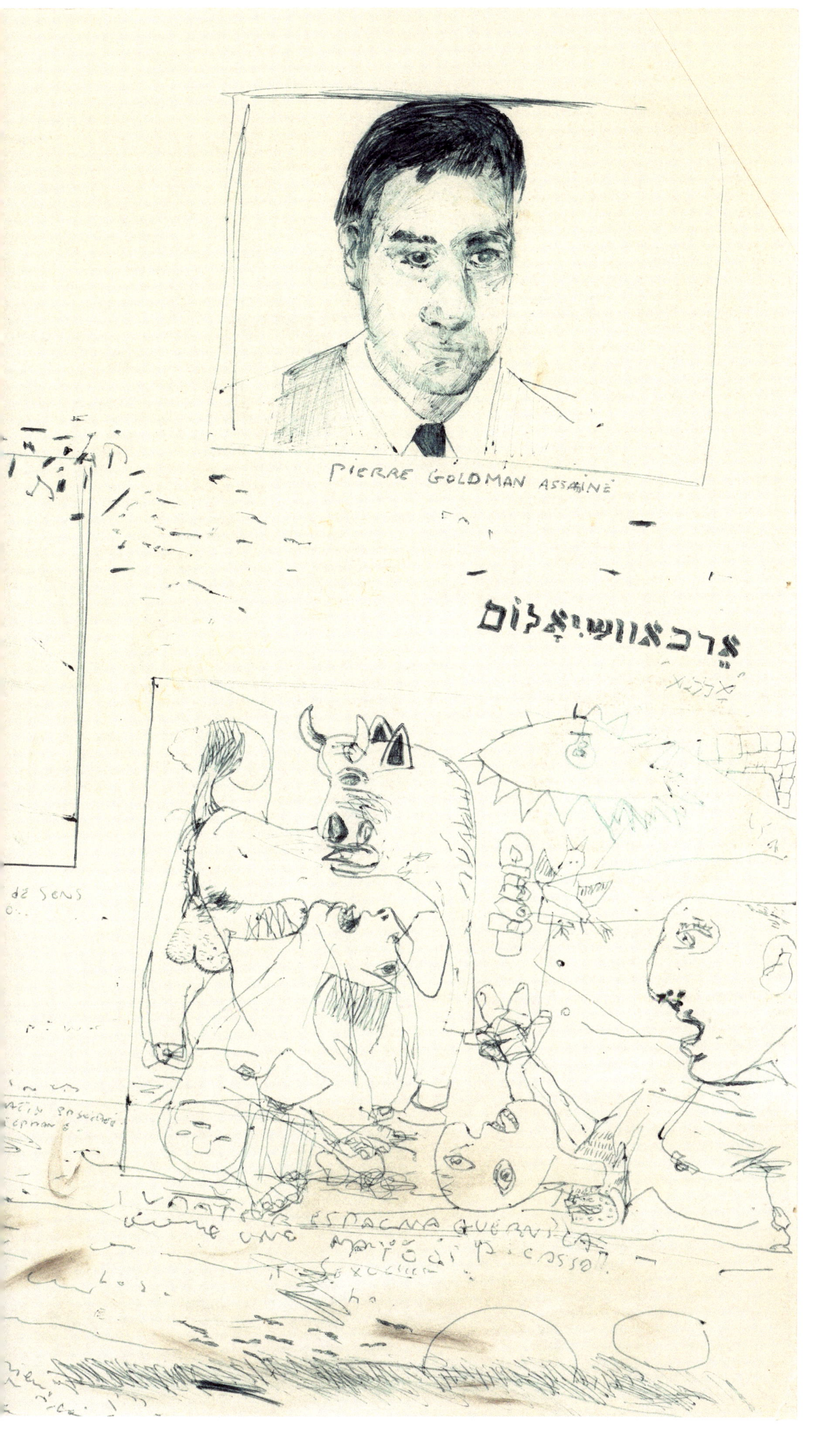
PIERRE GOLDMAN ASSASSINÉ

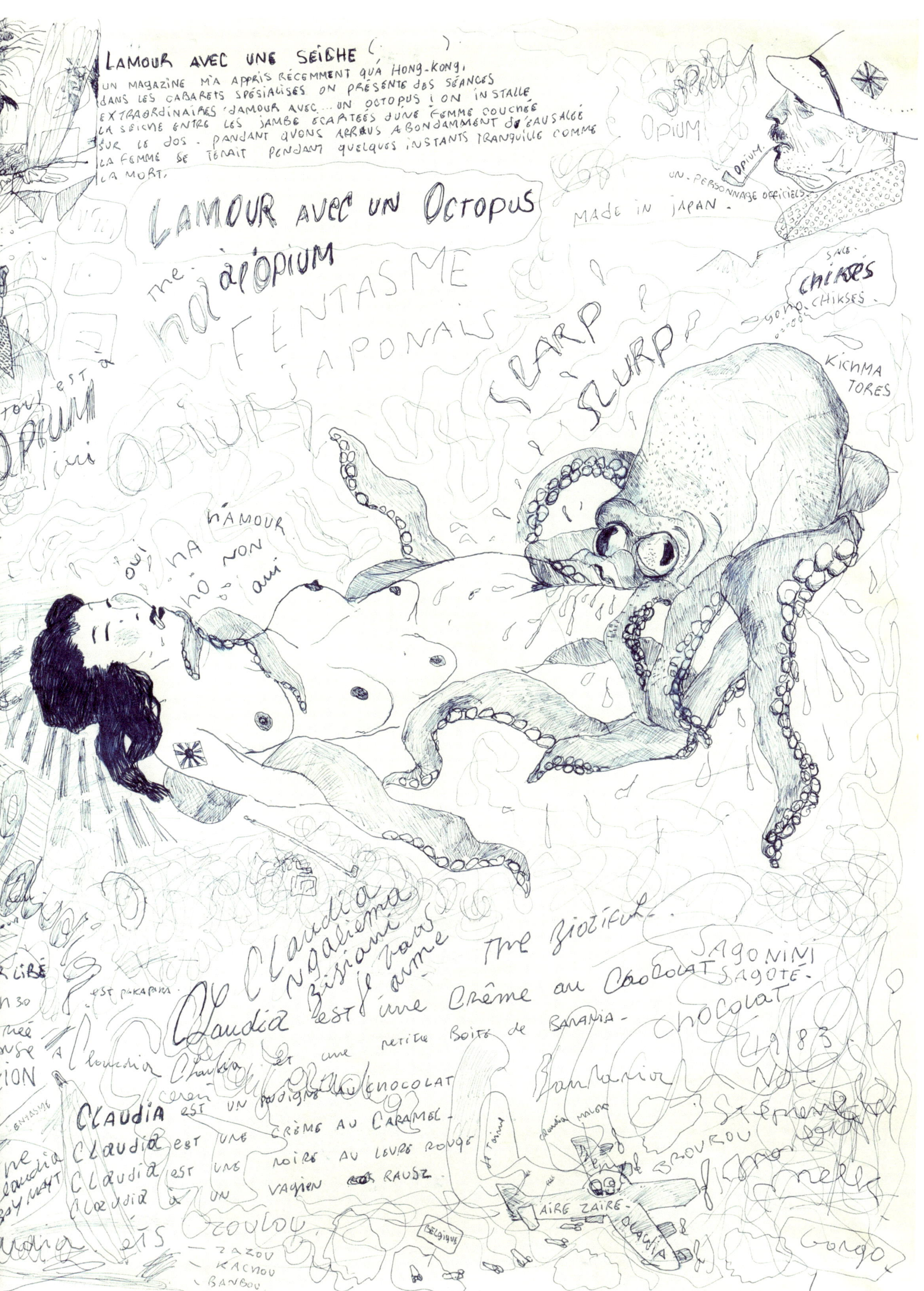


*Composition (Hokusaï, Le Rêve de la femme du pêcheur, 1814)*, 1983

CUANDO ARA
QUE TE HAY

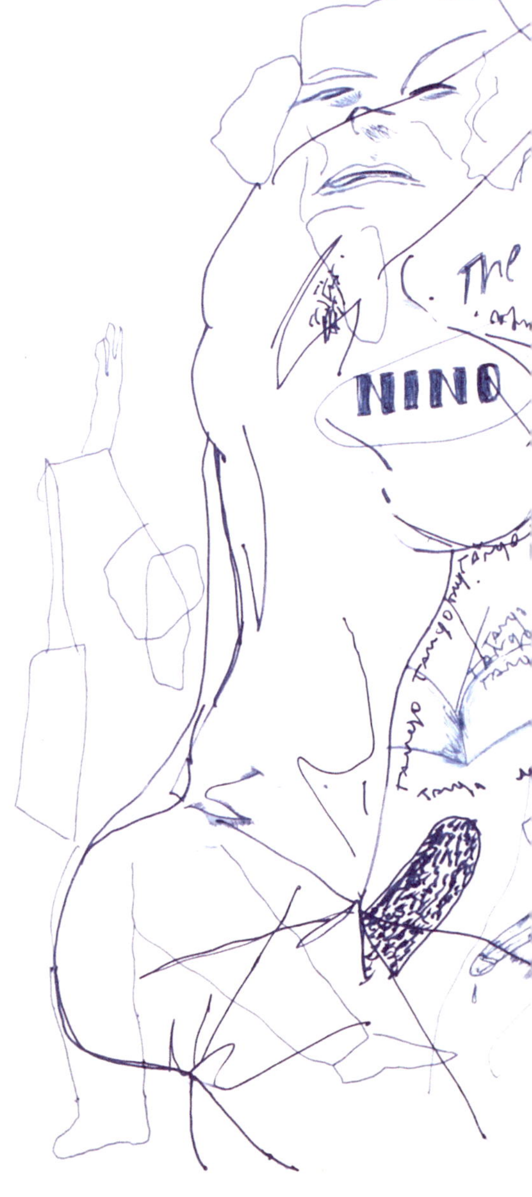

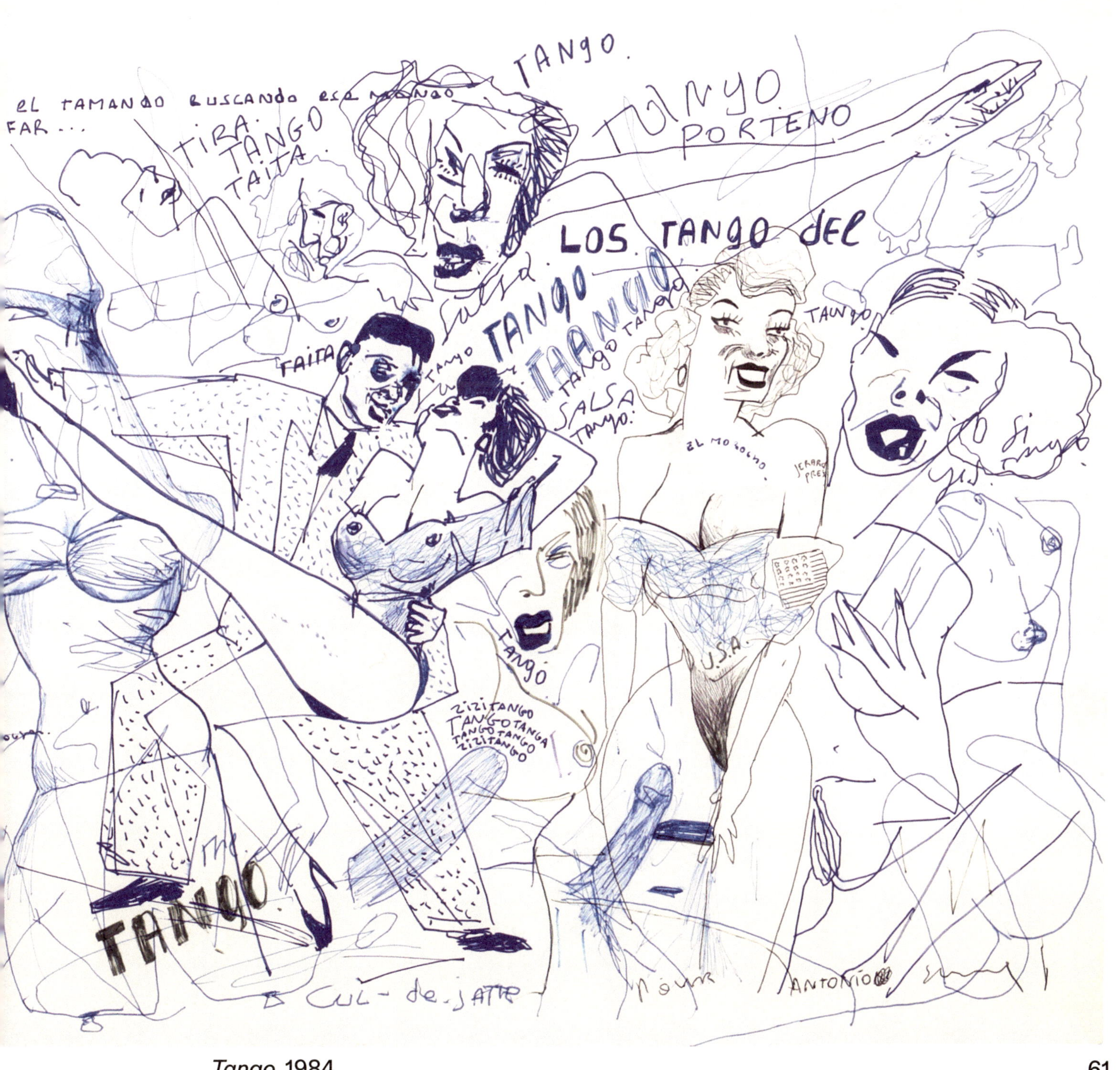


*Tango*, 1984

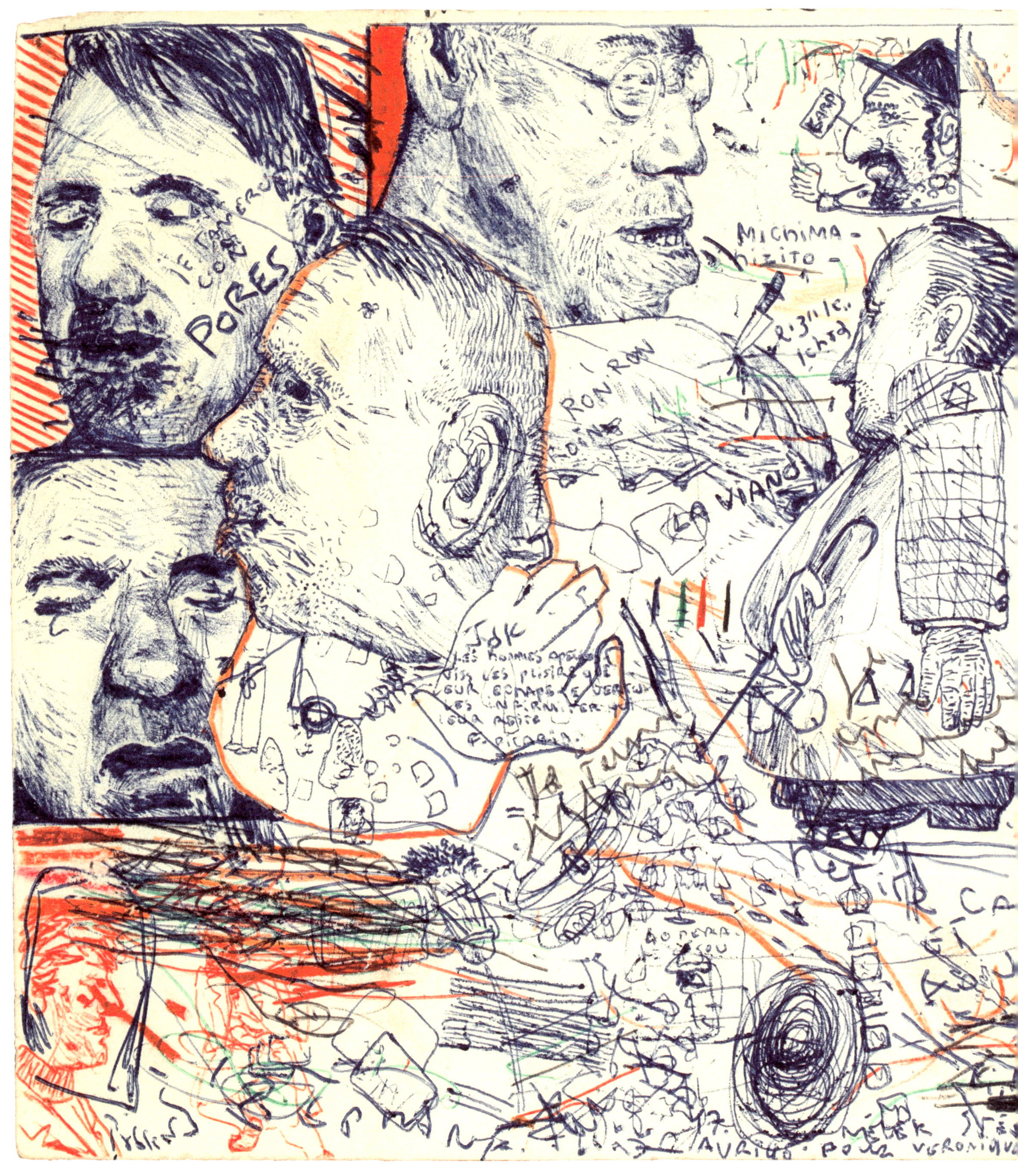


*Composition (Mishima, Bacon...)*, 1980

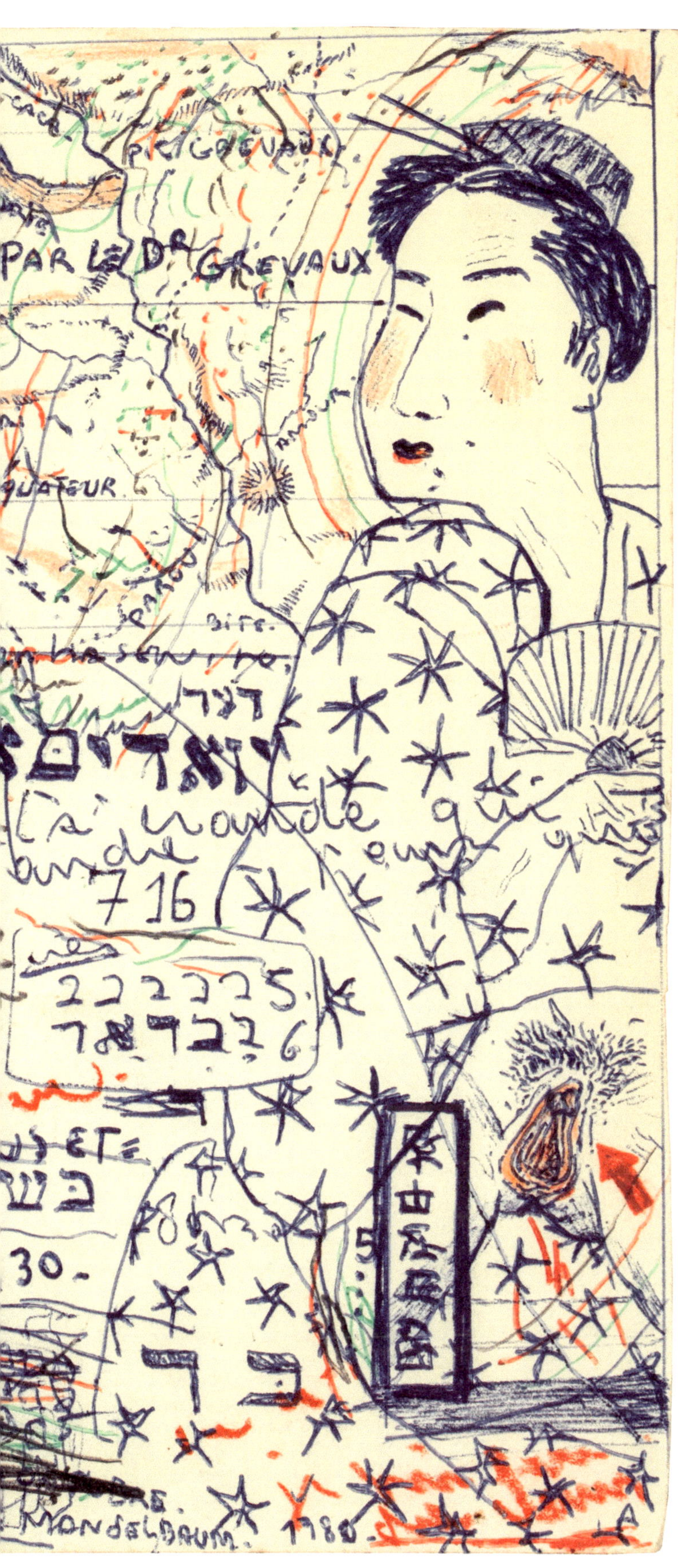

PAR LE Dr CREVAUX
QUATEUR
דער
716
30.
MANDELBAUM 1980

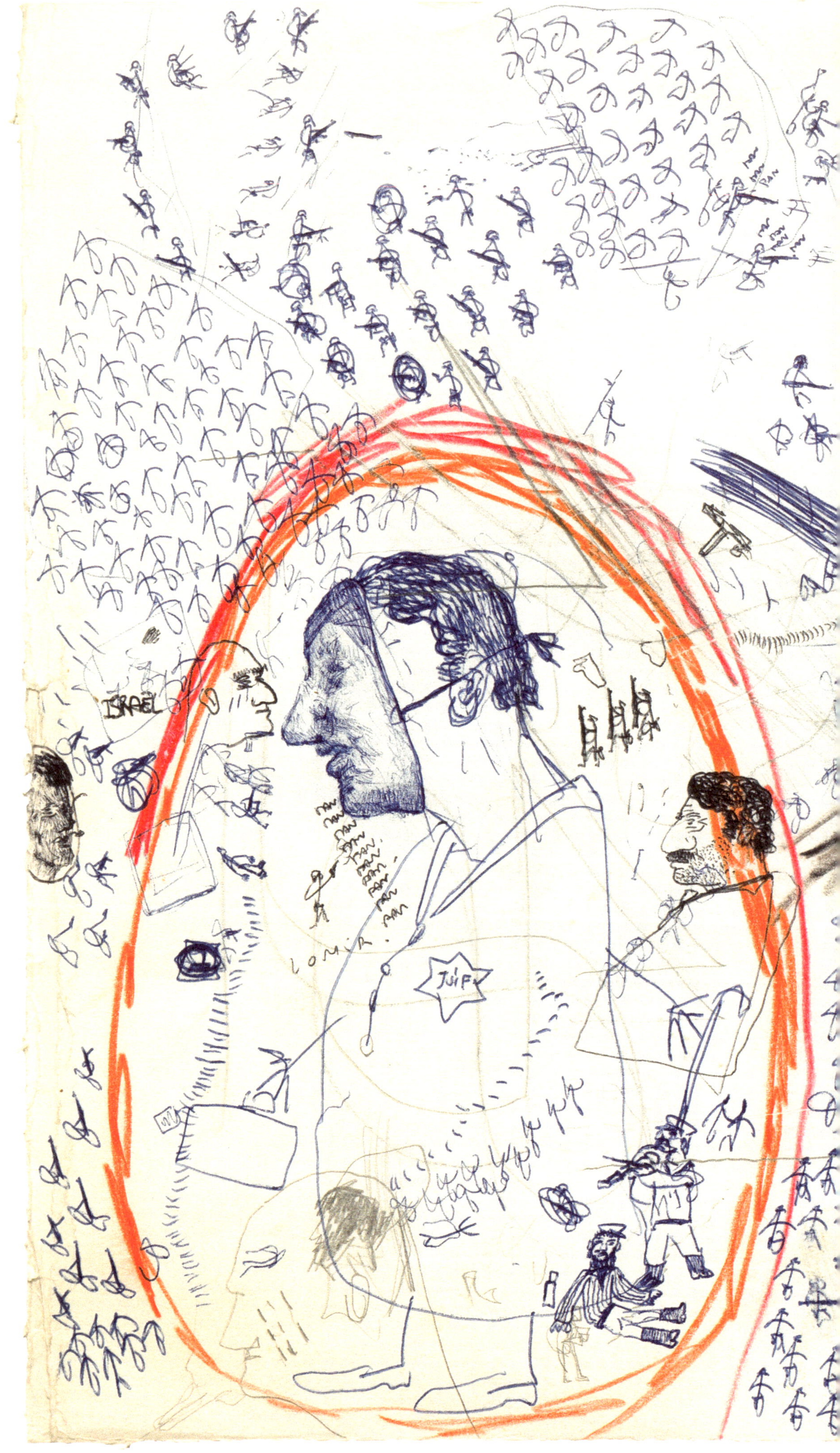
ISRAEL
JUIF

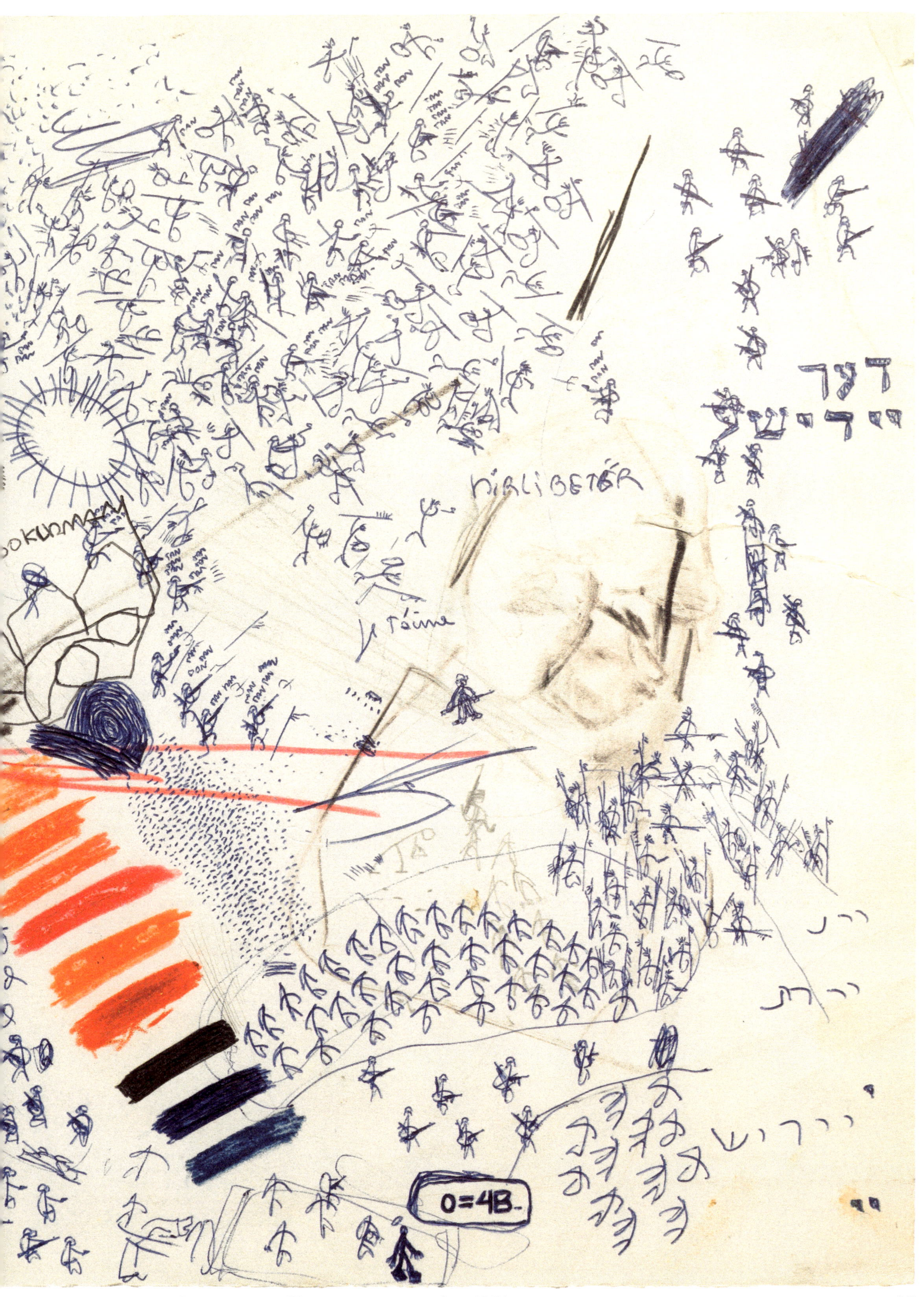

Composition (Figure au masque), c. 1981

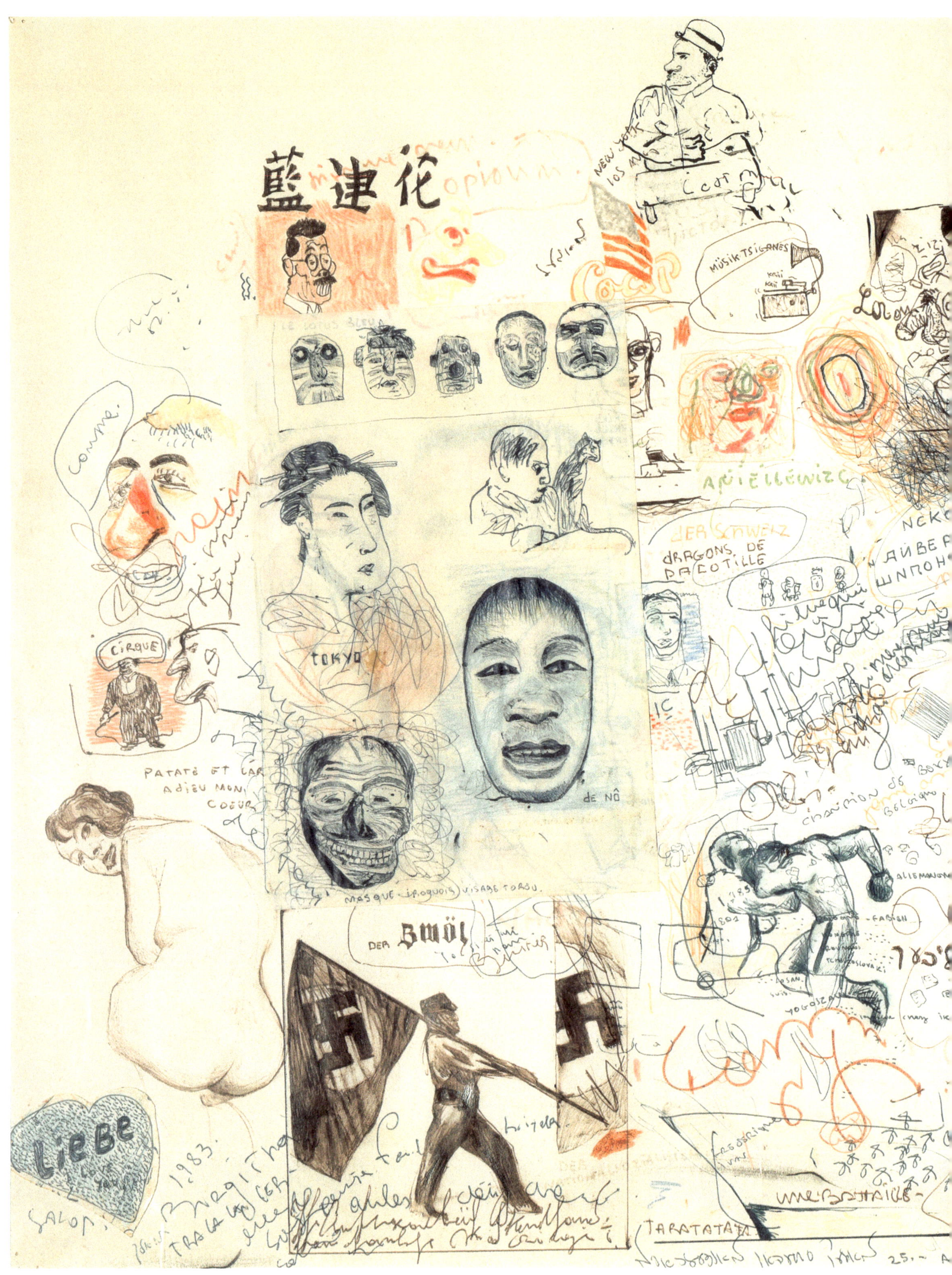


*Composition (Masques Nô)*, 1983

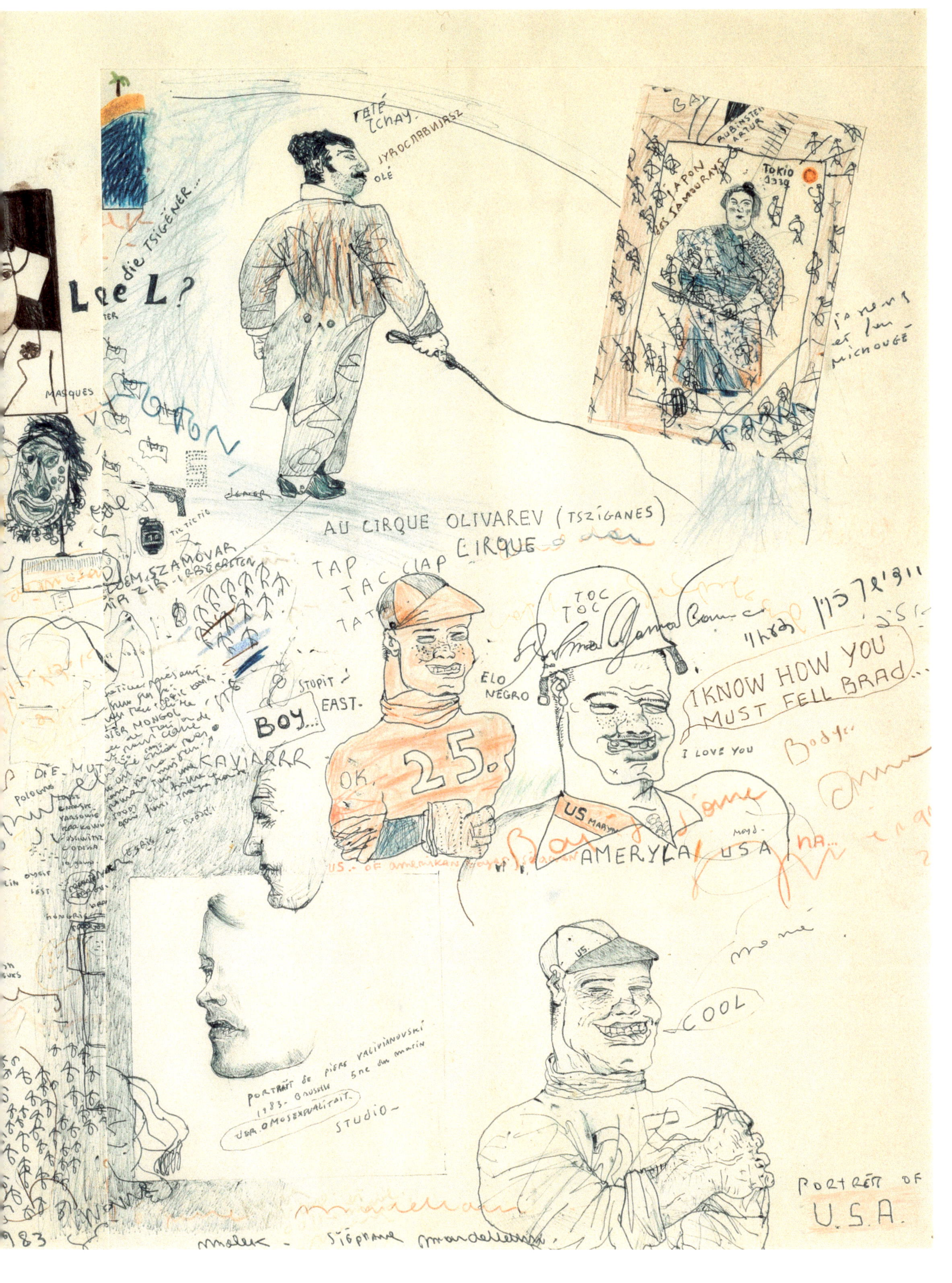
die TSIGÈNER...
OLÉ
JAPON DES SAMOURAYS
TOKIO 1939
MASQUES
AU CIRQUE OLIVAREV (TSZIGANES)
CIRQUE
TAP
TAC CLAP
TATA
TOC
TOC
ELO NEGRO
STUPIT
EAST.
BOY...
KAVIARRR
OK.
25.
I KNOW HOW YOU MUST FELL BRAD...
I LOVE YOU
US
AMERYKA
USA
COOL
STUDIO
PORTRET OF
U.S.A.

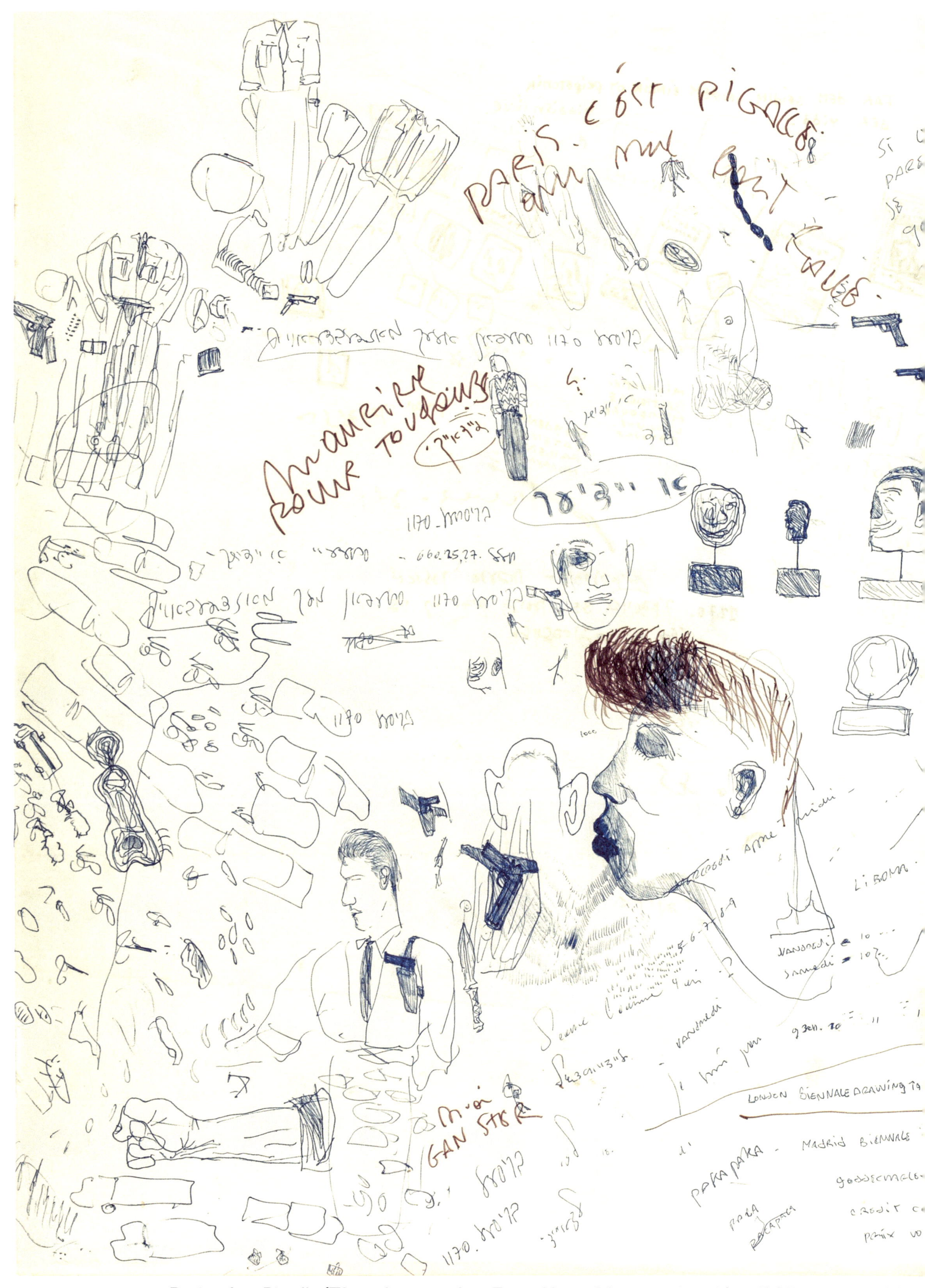


*Paris, c'est Pigalle (Têtes de caractère, Franz Xaver Messerschmidt)*, c. 1985

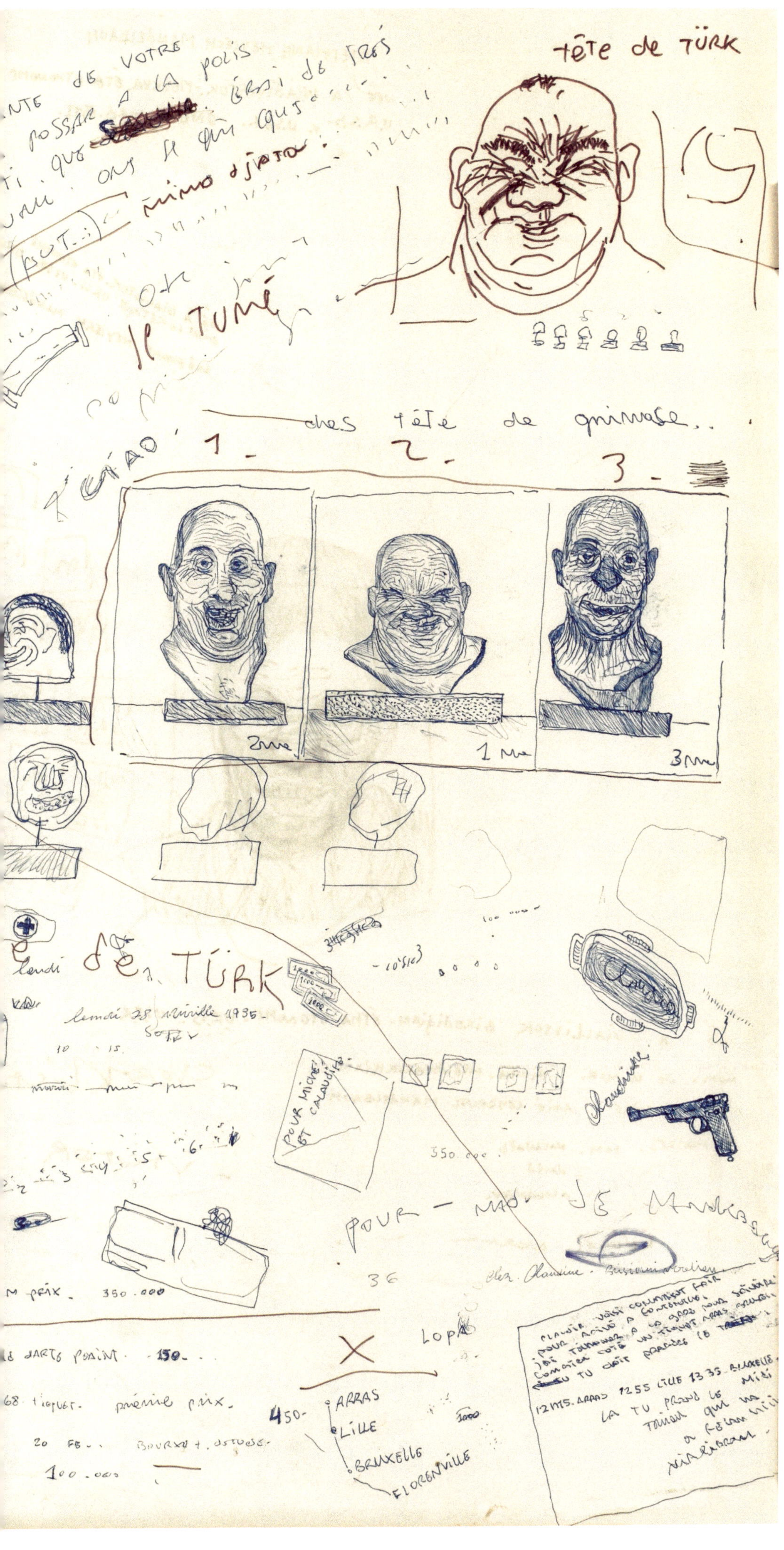
Tête de TÜRK
des tête de grimase..
1 -
2 -
3 -
2me
1 Me
3me
TÜRK
POUR - MAD - JE
36
X
LOPA
ARRAS
LILLE
BRUXELLE
FLORENVILLE
PRIX 350.000
100.000
450-

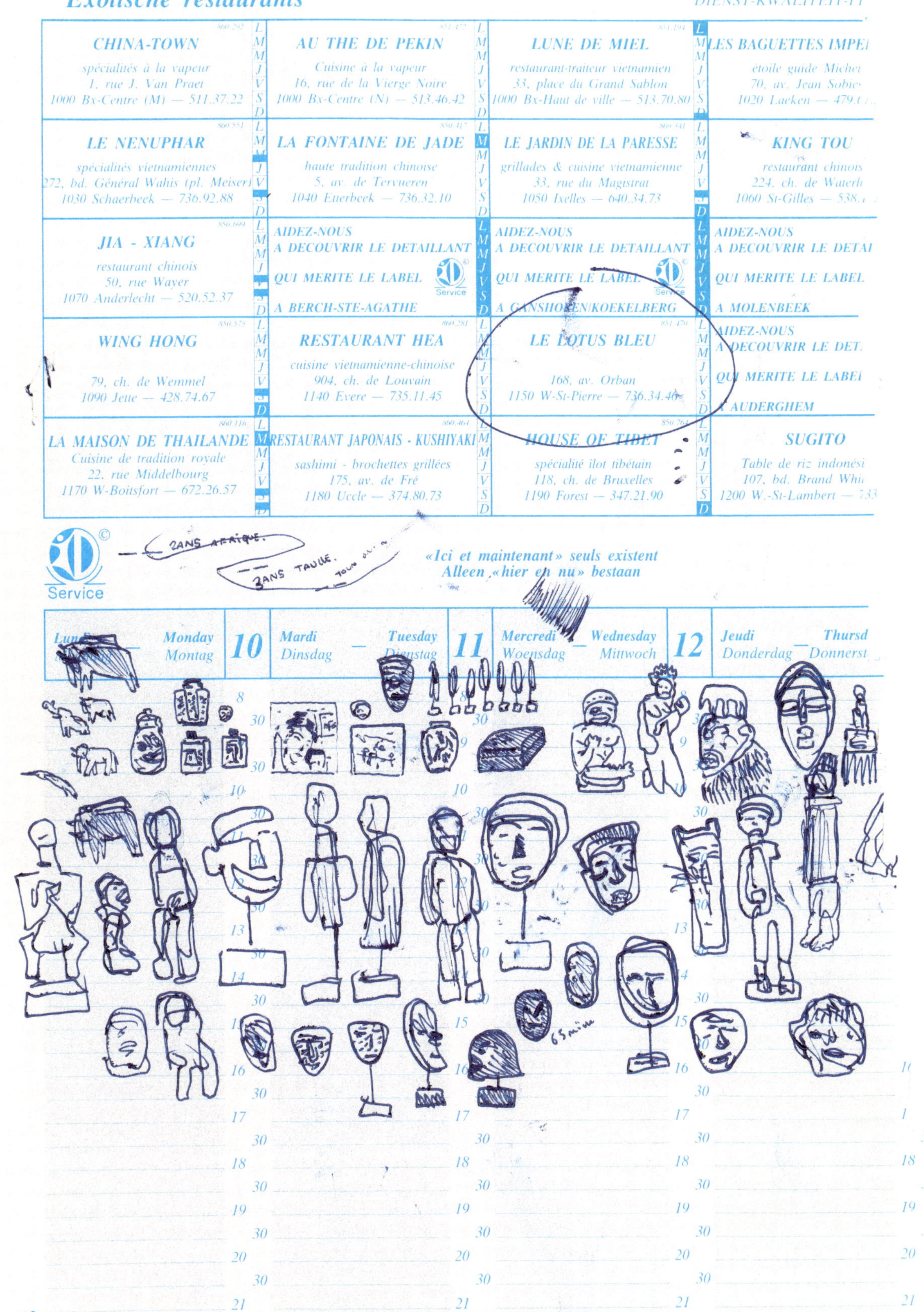
Restaurants exotiques
Exotische restaurants
CHINA-TOWN
spécialités à la vapeur
1, rue J. Van Praet
1000 Bx-Centre (M) — 511.37.22
AU THE DE PEKIN
Cuisine à la vapeur
16, rue de la Vierge Noire
1000 Bx-Centre (N) — 513.46.42
LUNE DE MIEL
restaurant-traiteur vietnamien
33, place du Grand Sablon
1000 Bx-Haut de ville — 513.70.80
LE NENUPHAR
spécialités vietnamiennes
272, bd. Général Wahis (pl. Meiser)
1030 Schaerbeek — 736.92.88
LA FONTAINE DE JADE
haute tradition chinoise
5, av. de Tervueren
1040 Etterbeek — 736.32.10
LE JARDIN DE LA PARESSE
grillades & cuisine vietnamienne
33, rue du Magistrat
1050 Ixelles — 640.34.73
JIA - XIANG
restaurant chinois
50, rue Wayer
1070 Anderlecht — 520.52.37
AIDEZ-NOUS A DECOUVRIR LE DETAILLANT QUI MERITE LE LABEL A BERCH-STE-AGATHE
AIDEZ-NOUS A DECOUVRIR LE DETAILLANT QUI MERITE LE LABEL A GANSHOREN/KOEKELBERG
WING HONG
79, ch. de Wemmel
1090 Jette — 428.74.67
RESTAURANT HEA
cuisine vietnamienne-chinoise
904, ch. de Louvain
1140 Evere — 735.11.45
LE LOTUS BLEU
168, av. Orban
1150 W-St-Pierre — 736.34.46
LA MAISON DE THAILANDE
Cuisine de tradition royale
22, rue Middelbourg
1170 W-Boitsfort — 672.26.57
RESTAURANT JAPONAIS - KUSHIYAKI
sashimi - brochettes grillées
175, av. de Fré
1180 Uccle — 374.80.73
HOUSE OF TIBET
spécialité ilot tibétain
118, ch. de Bruxelles
1190 Forest — 347.21.90
SUGITO
Service
2ANS AFRIQUE
2ANS TAULE
«Ici et maintenant» seuls existent
Alleen «hier en nu» bestaan
Monday
Montag
10
Mardi
Dinsdag
Tuesday
11
Mercredi
Woensdag
Wednesday
Mittwoch
12
Jeudi
Donderdag
118

*Masque japonais* [*Masques Nô*], 1985–86

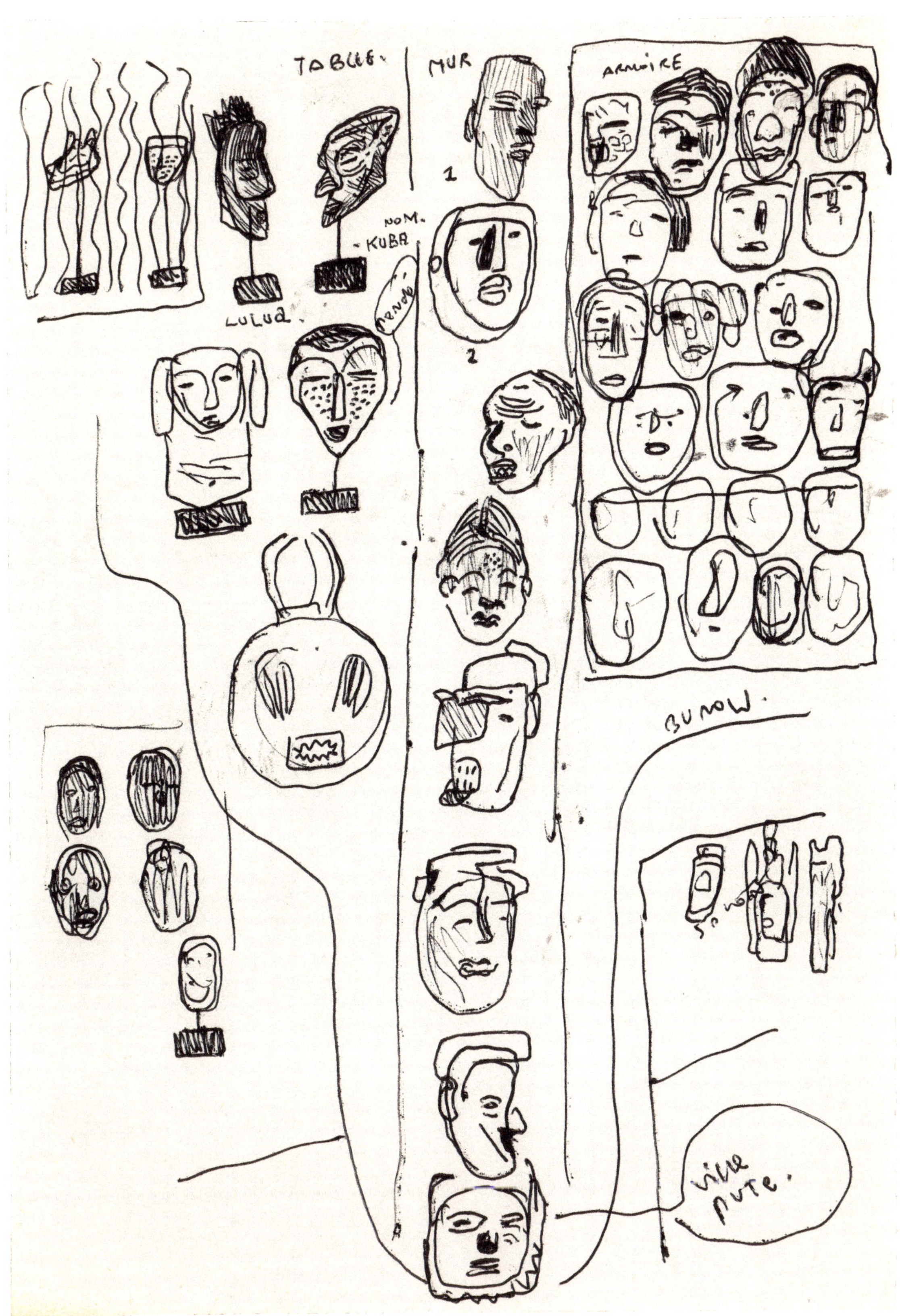


Untitled, 1985–86

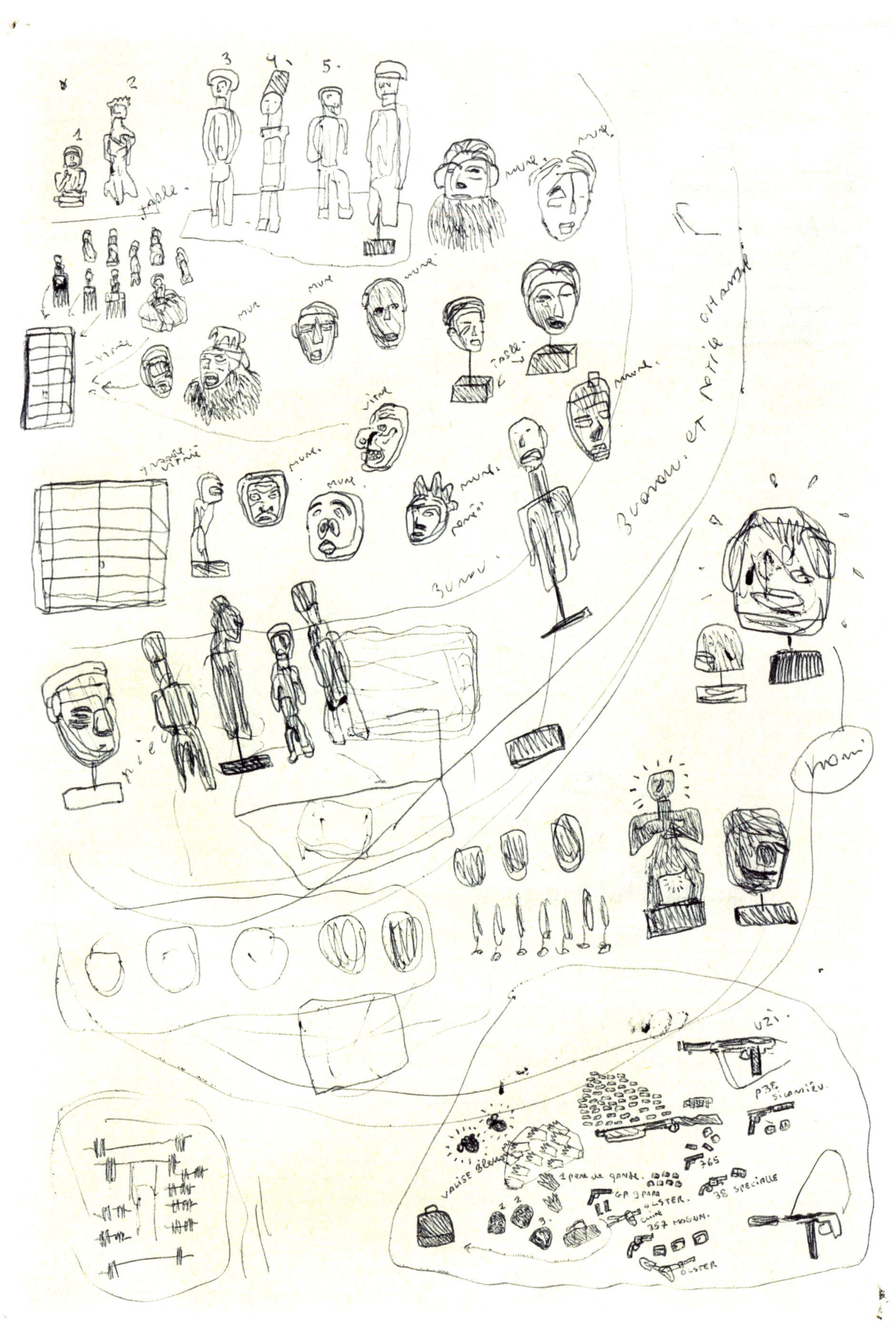


Untitled, 1985–86

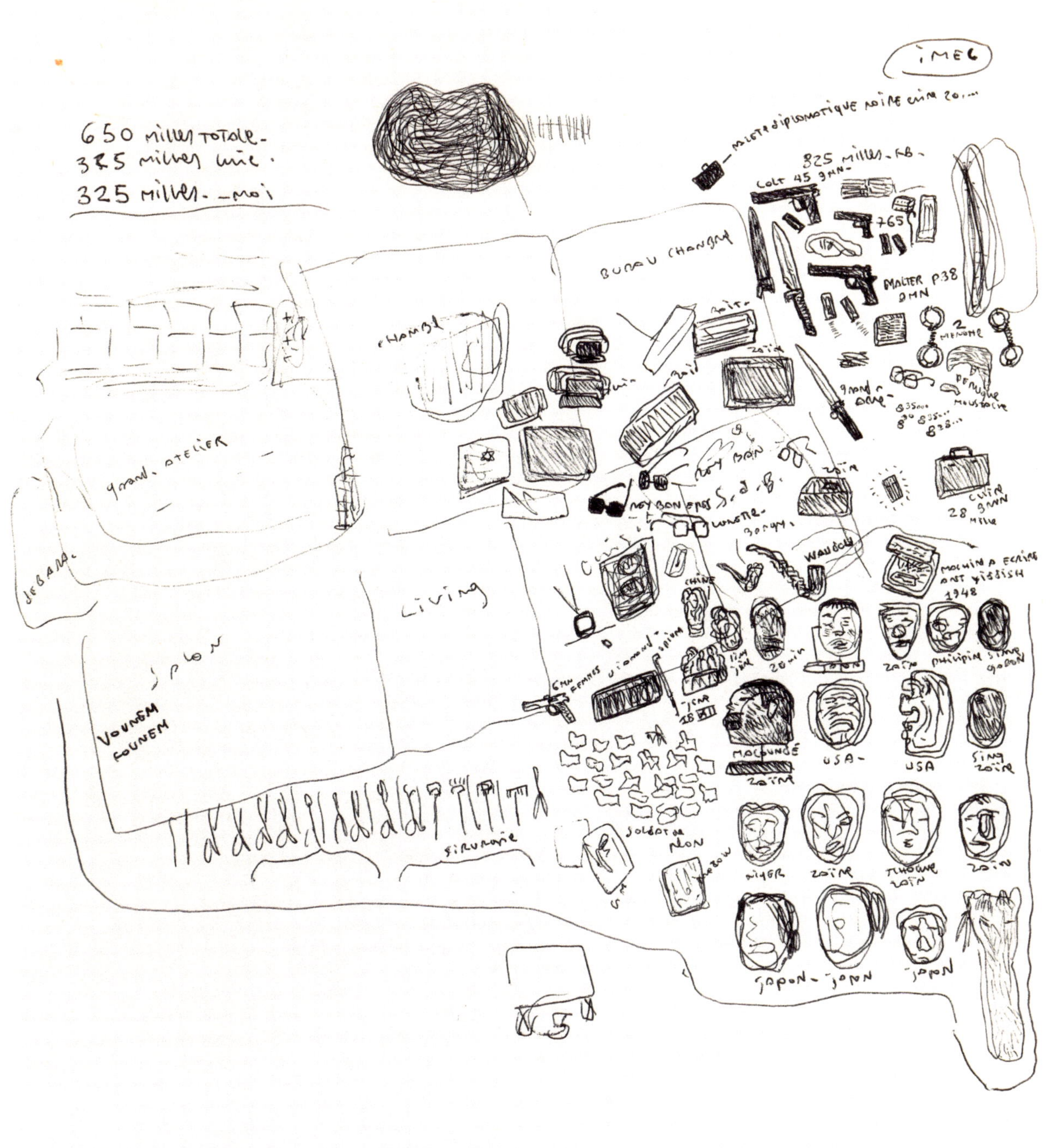


Untitled, 1985–86

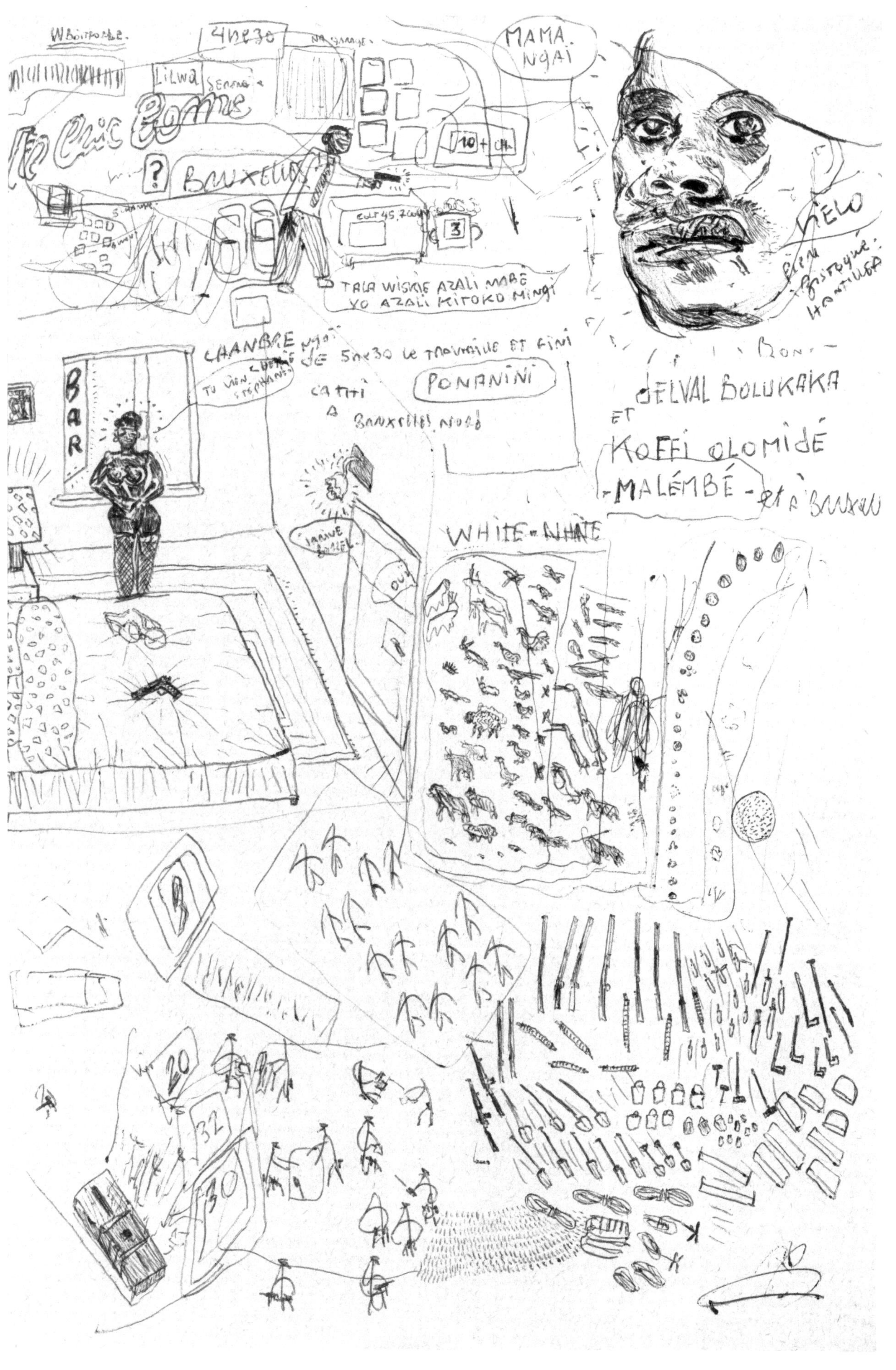


Untitled [*Mama Ngaï*], 1985–86

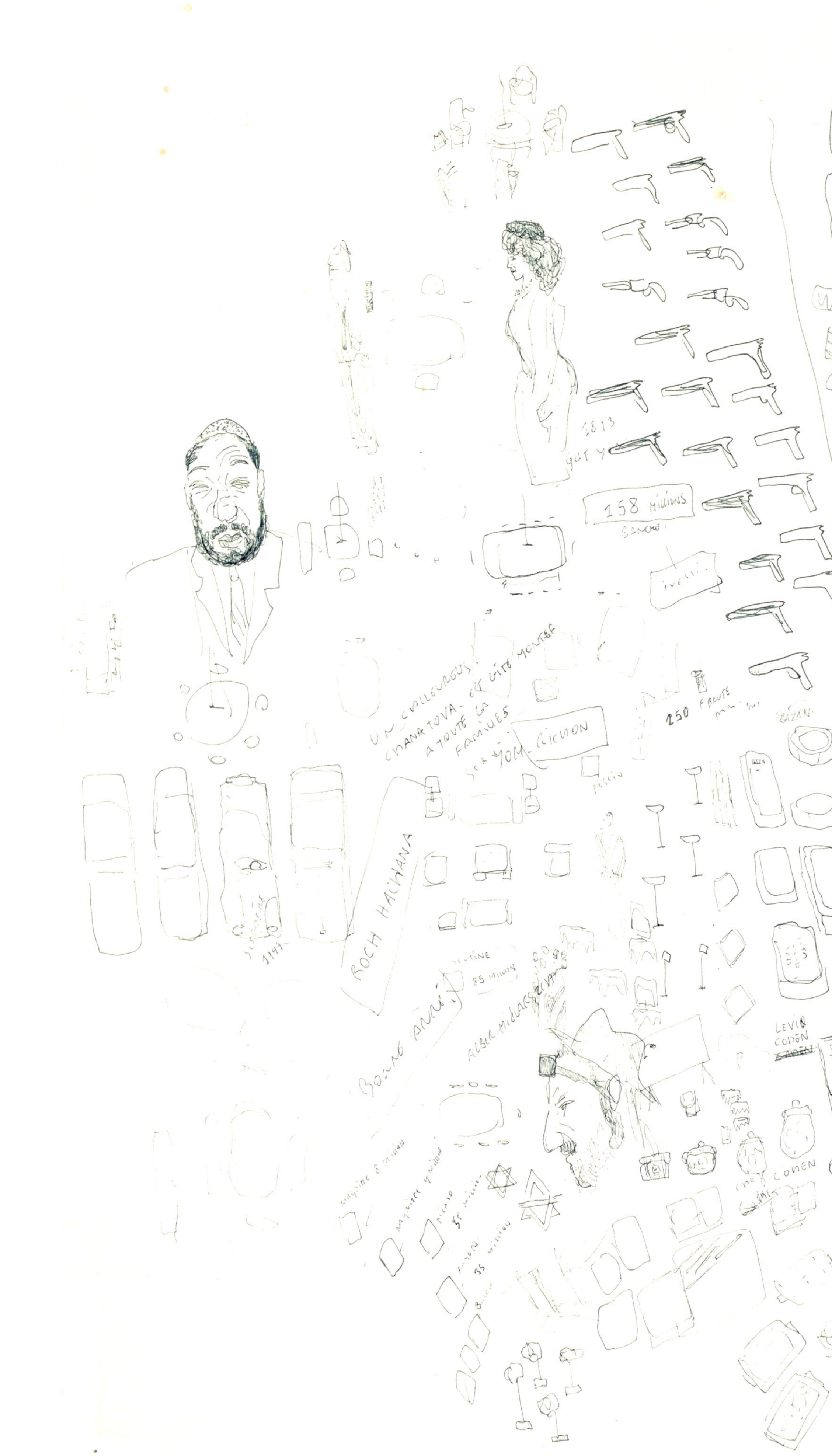

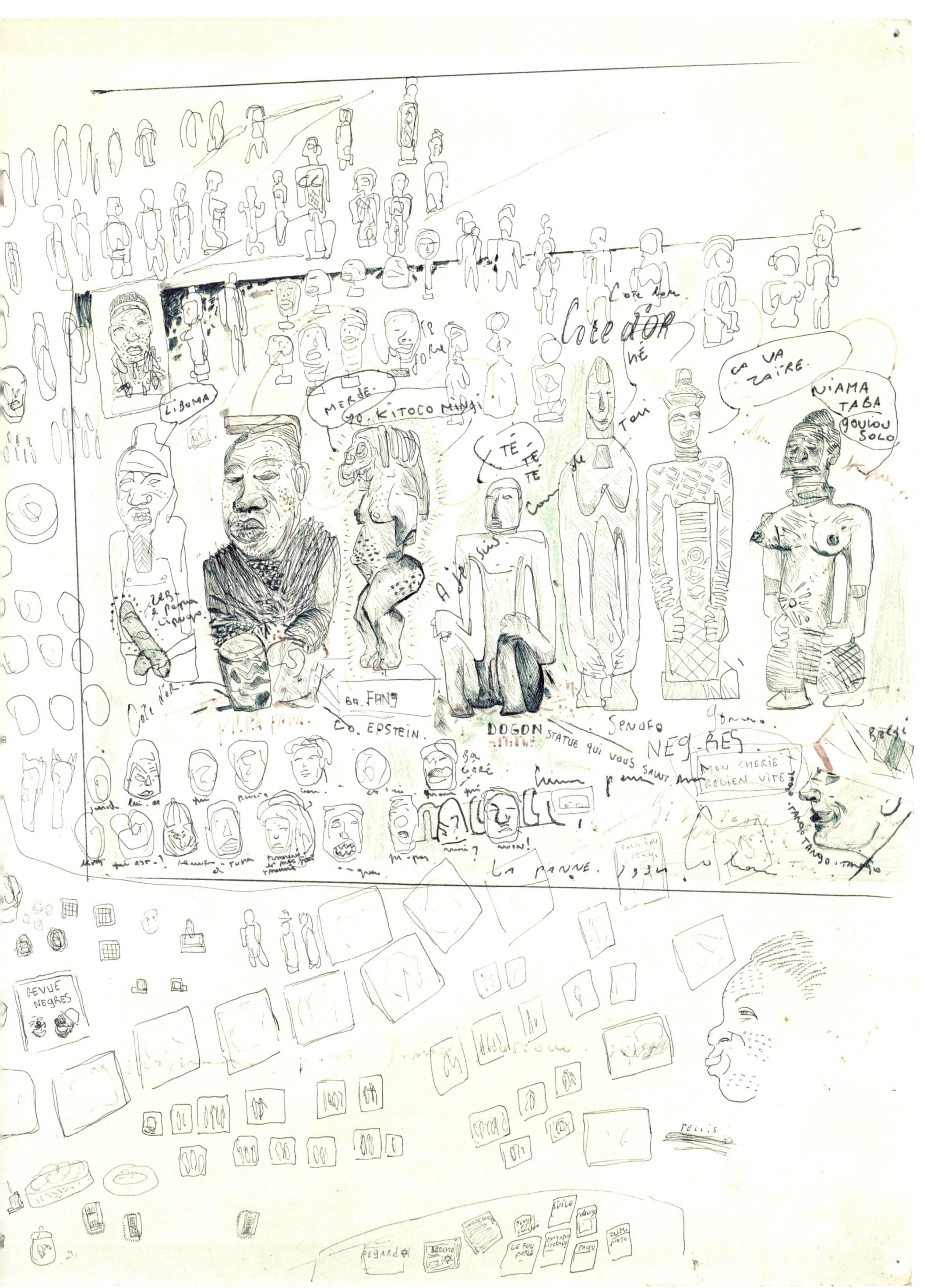


*Fétiches africains*, 1984

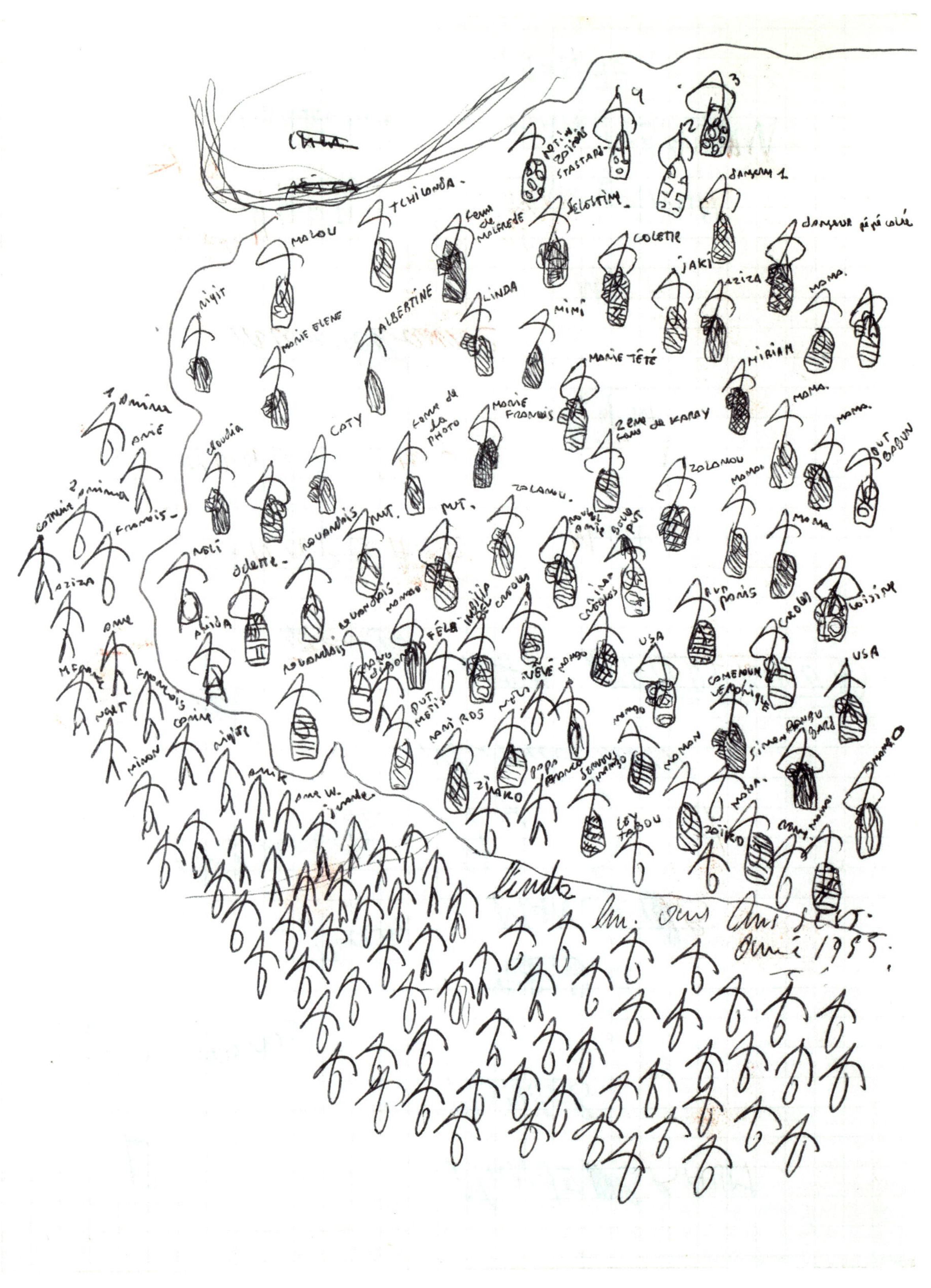

Untitled, 1985–86

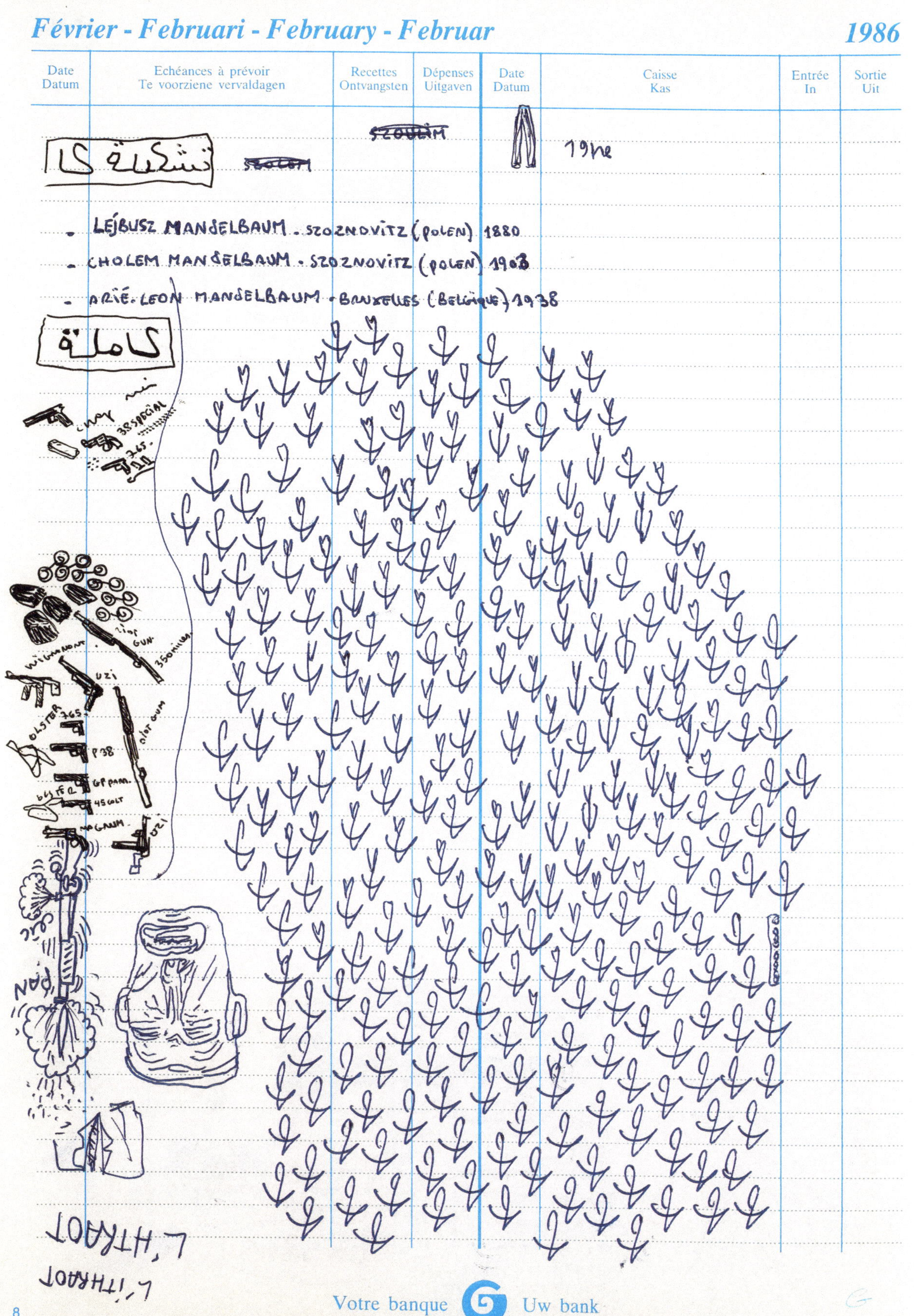


Untitled, 1985–86

UN MAQUEREAU ROUX ET ROSE
CÉTAIT UN JUIF IL SENTAIT L'AIL
IL Y A SURTOUT DES JUIF LEURS FEMMES PORTENT PERRUQUE
ELLES RESTENT ASSISES EXSANGUES AU FOND DES BOUTIQUE.
LES AIGUILLES DE L'ORLOGE DU QUARTIER JUIF DE PRAGUE
TOURNE A REBOURS.
IL FAUT SE SOIR QUE J'ASSASSINE
CE RICHE JUIF AU BORD DU RHIN

FAR DOU. POUR TOI ?
A TICH FAR TSUAJ - UN TABLE POUR DEUX
VIFIL A TOG - COMBIEN PAR JOURS
HOSTOU - TU AS
HOSTOU GELD - TU AS DE L'ARGENT?
BISTOU - TU EST
BISTOU ARIÉ - TU EST ARIÉ
AZOY BIN IR - VOILLA JE SUIS
YIÈTS - RIEN
KEIN NICHT_ IL N'I A PAS
KEIN NICHT BESER - ÇES PAS BON
BISTOU CHAYAL TU ES BELLE.
KIM MIT MIR VIEN AVEC MOI
ÎR - ICI.
JO - OUI
NEIN - NON
A MATOUNÉ FAR DOU UN CADEAUX POUR TOI
DOUS IS MAJN KALÉ. SÉT MA FIANSÉ.
DOUS IS MAJN MIHOUGÉ JÉST MA FOLIE.
REDN YIDDIN - VOUS PARLE YIDDIN
IR REDN YIDDIN. JE PARLE YIDDIN
A BISELE UN PEU
[illegible] FARSHTEIN. JE COMPRE
BESÉDER - D'ACOR
FARSHTEIN NISHT - PAS COMPRIS
HOT AZOY - EN AVANT
TANTÉ AZOY - VOILÀ.
ONKL. ZOYDA - BON [illegible]
MAMÉ - [illegible]
TOTÉ -

HOSTI-GELD-
HOSTI. BISTI
BI
HOST BIS DOU -
BIS DOU ~~[illegible]~~ TU AIS

SO AMERAYÉ QUEL [illegible]
A UAYN PONEM.
TOV
DOU UNGENIK
IN. AZOY. ESN.

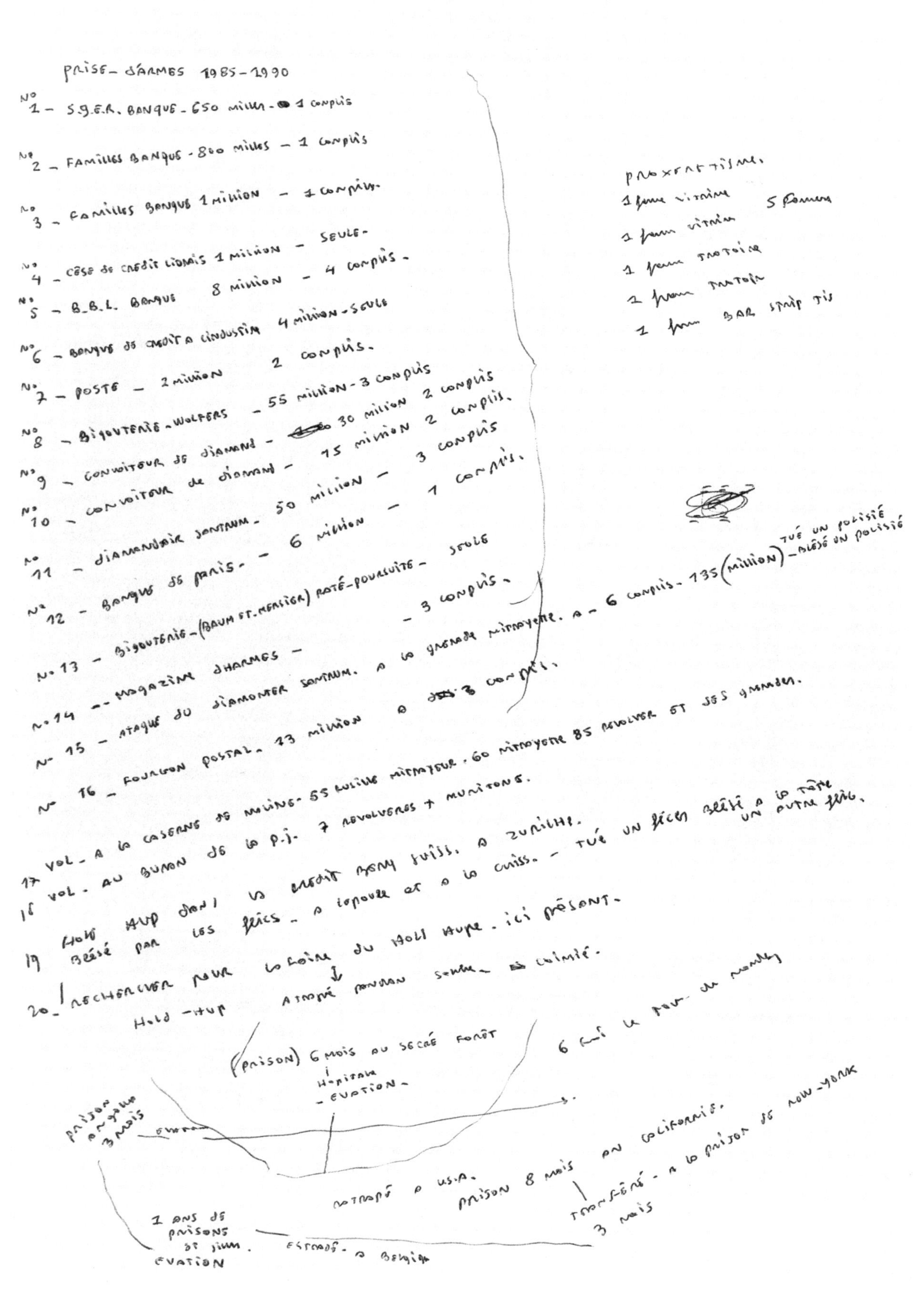


Untitled, 1985–86

police judisier.

dosiei projustitia.

1 VOL. ET INFRACTION DE PROPRIÉTÉ. AN PAR. LUX. POUR AVOIR VOLÉ ET EGORGÉ
— AVEC UN COMPLIS. UN MOUTON. DOSIE. 3 JOURNES DE GARDE A VUS.

2 — ~~pour avoir~~ VOL ET INFRACTION EYAN ÉTÉ SURPRI PAR LA POLIS.
DONS UN VILLA. DE [illegible] BOITFORDE. EYAN
[illegible]. [illegible] BIJOU [illegible]. [illegible]
[illegible] DETANTION 2 JOURNES DE
GUARDE A VUS. ET 8 JOURNE DE PRISON
A ST JILLE.

3 — AVOIRE DONNÉ LE DESPORTE. VOLONTERMENT.
CAFÉ BAR [illegible]. AVOIR CASÉ LES TABLE CHÉSE. VERE. COUTOIRE. POUR UN SOM DANS UN LIEU PUBLIC
DE 155 MILLE FB. ET AVOIR CASÉ LA MACHINE. A [illegible] ET NÉE
[illegible] MINES. — SÉTA ENFUI EN DELIT DE FUITE.

4. POUR AVOIR [illegible]. ACCUSÉ SOUVIRE A LA GENDARMERIE.
qui [illegible] ET AVOIRE. [illegible] UN [illegible].
[illegible] ET SÉTA LIVRÉ A. UNE [illegible]. DONS
[illegible] COUPS. [illegible]
— 3 MOIS DE PRISON (FORÉTE.)

5. DONS LA PERQUISITION LA POLICE [illegible] ET LA P.J.
ON TROUVÉ UNE VOITUR VOLÉ. LA VOITURE SONT [illegible]
[illegible]

6 AVOIR VOLÉ ET AN [illegible] PESAN UN COMPLÉ [illegible]
[illegible] MAGASIN. JONI VERSOGÉ. [illegible]. 1 MOIS DE
ET A. [illegible] DE [illegible] DETANTION
[illegible] A 85 MILLE. [illegible] A MARCHE-
[illegible]

7 AVOIRE ÉTÉ ARRÊTÉ [illegible] DE B.C.R. AU CARTIER [illegible]
BAR [illegible]. S.M. AVOI DONNÉ UN COUPS DE COUTAU. ET [illegible]
JOSÉ. [illegible]. ET APRÉ AVOIRE EGORGÉ [illegible] UN [illegible].
JUSQU [illegible] ET SELON TEMOIN. S.M.
[illegible] UN INFORMÉ [illegible] OU PLUSS
[illegible] DONS [illegible]
[illegible]
[illegible] UN [illegible]
COMPTE. [illegible]
AVOIRE TROUVÉ DES PISTOLÉ ET ARMES DE [illegible]
[illegible]

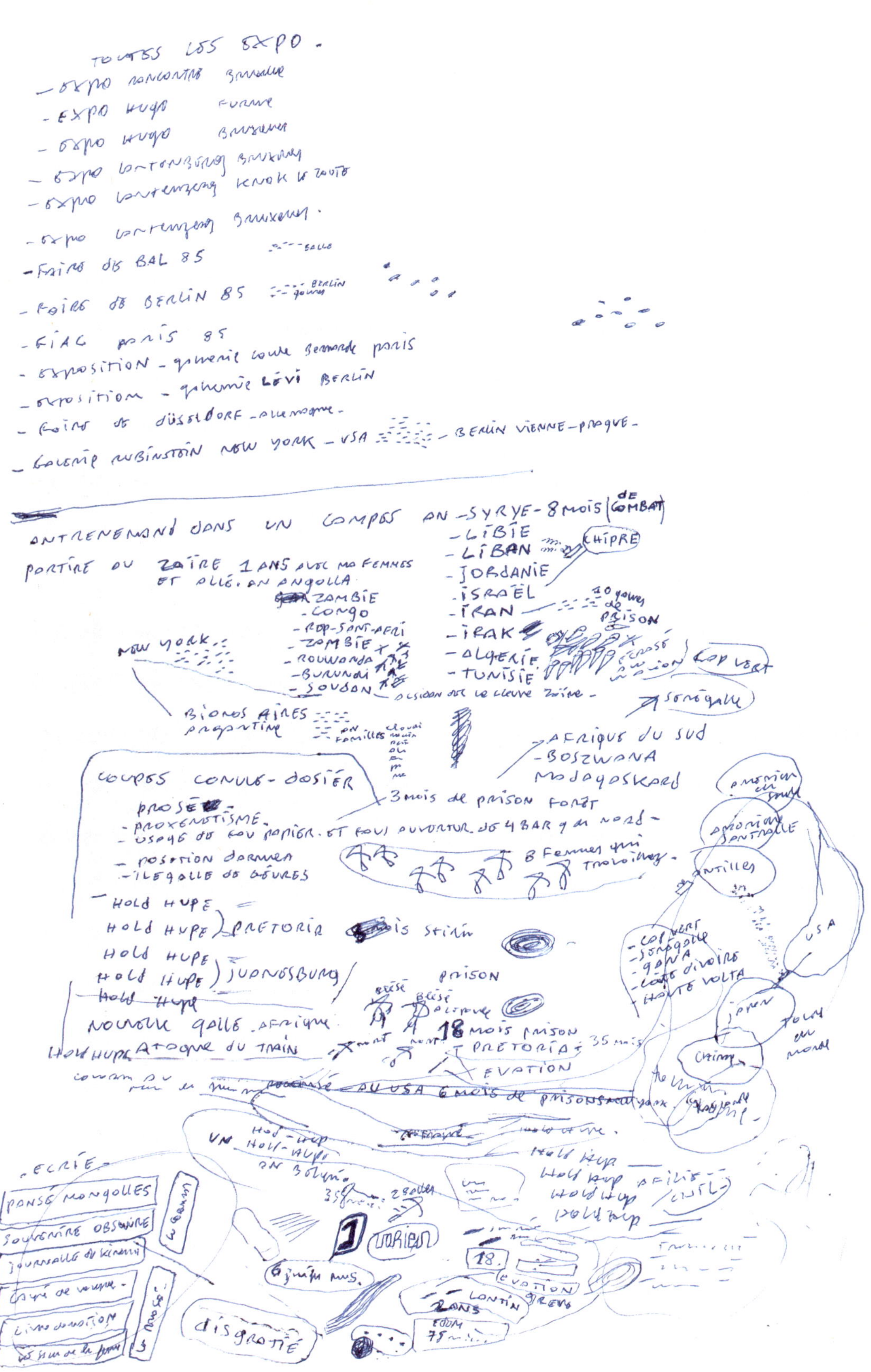

TOUTES LES EXPO.
- FOIRE DE BAL 85
- FOIRE DE BERLIN 85
- FIAC PARIS 85
- EXPOSITION - galerie LÉVI BERLIN
- FOIRE DE DÜSSELDORF - allemagne -
- GALERIE RUBINSTEIN NEW YORK - USA
- BERLIN VIENNE - PRAGUE -
SYRYE - 8 MOIS DE COMBAT
- LIBIE
- LIBAN
CHIPRE
- JORDANIE
- ISRAËL
- IRAN
- IRAK
- ALGERIE
- TUNISIE
CAP VERT
SÉNÉGALLE
PORTIRE DU ZAÏRE 1 ANS AVEC MA FEMMES
ET ALLÉ EN ANGOLLA
ZAMBIE
- CONGO
- ZOMBIE
- ROUWANDA
- BURUNDI
- SOUDON
NEW YORK
BIONOS AIRES
- AFRIQUE DU SUD
- BOSZWANA
MADAGOSKARD
3 mois de prison
HOLD HUPE
PRETORIA
HOLD HUPE
JUONESBURG
PRISON
18 MOIS PRISON
PRETORIA
35 mois
EVATION
DU USA 6 MOIS de PRISON
USA
JAPAN
ANTILLES
- ECRIE -
PONSÉ MONGOLLES
SOUVENIRE OBSEURE
18.
disgRATié

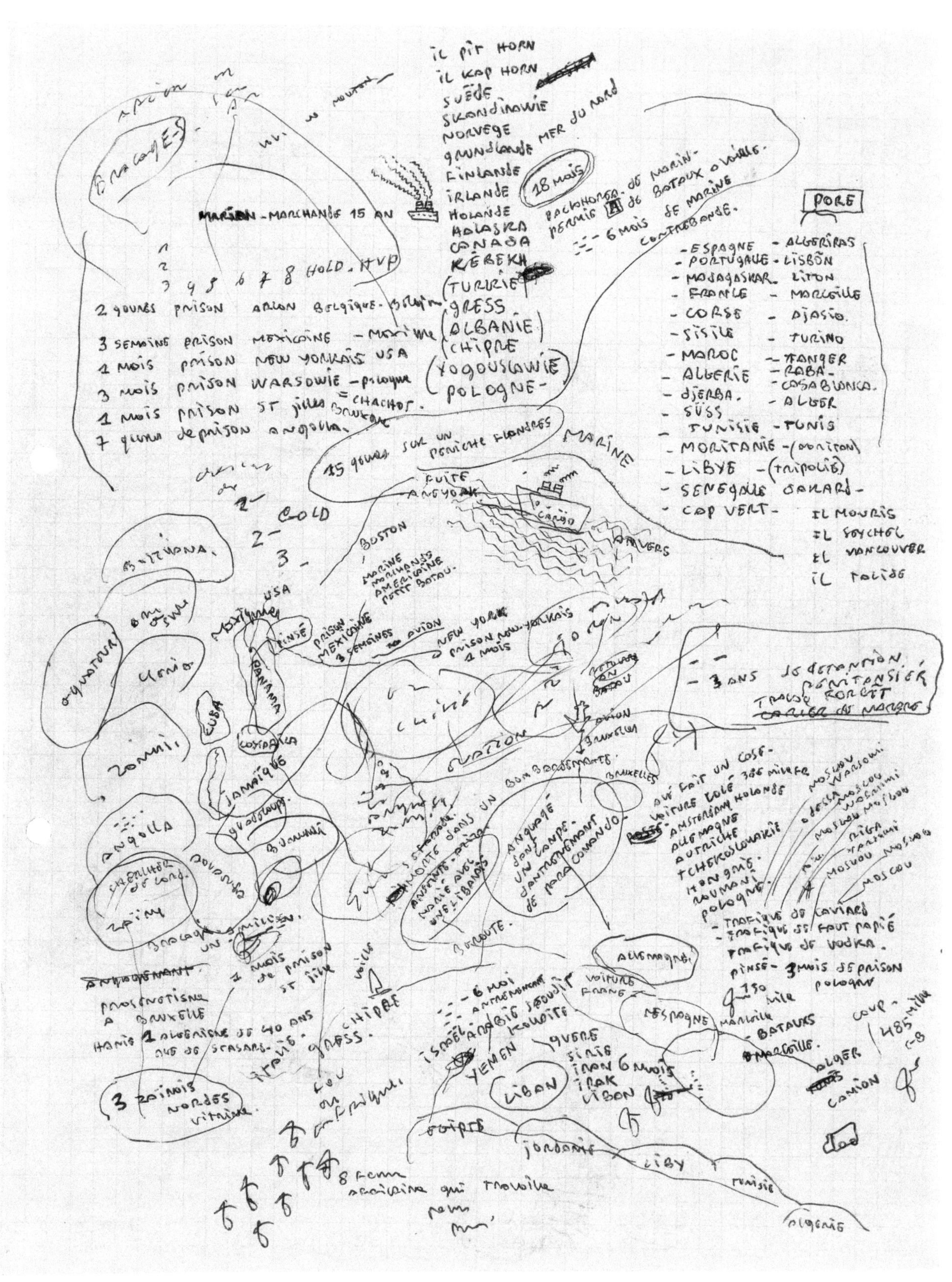


Untitled, 1985–86

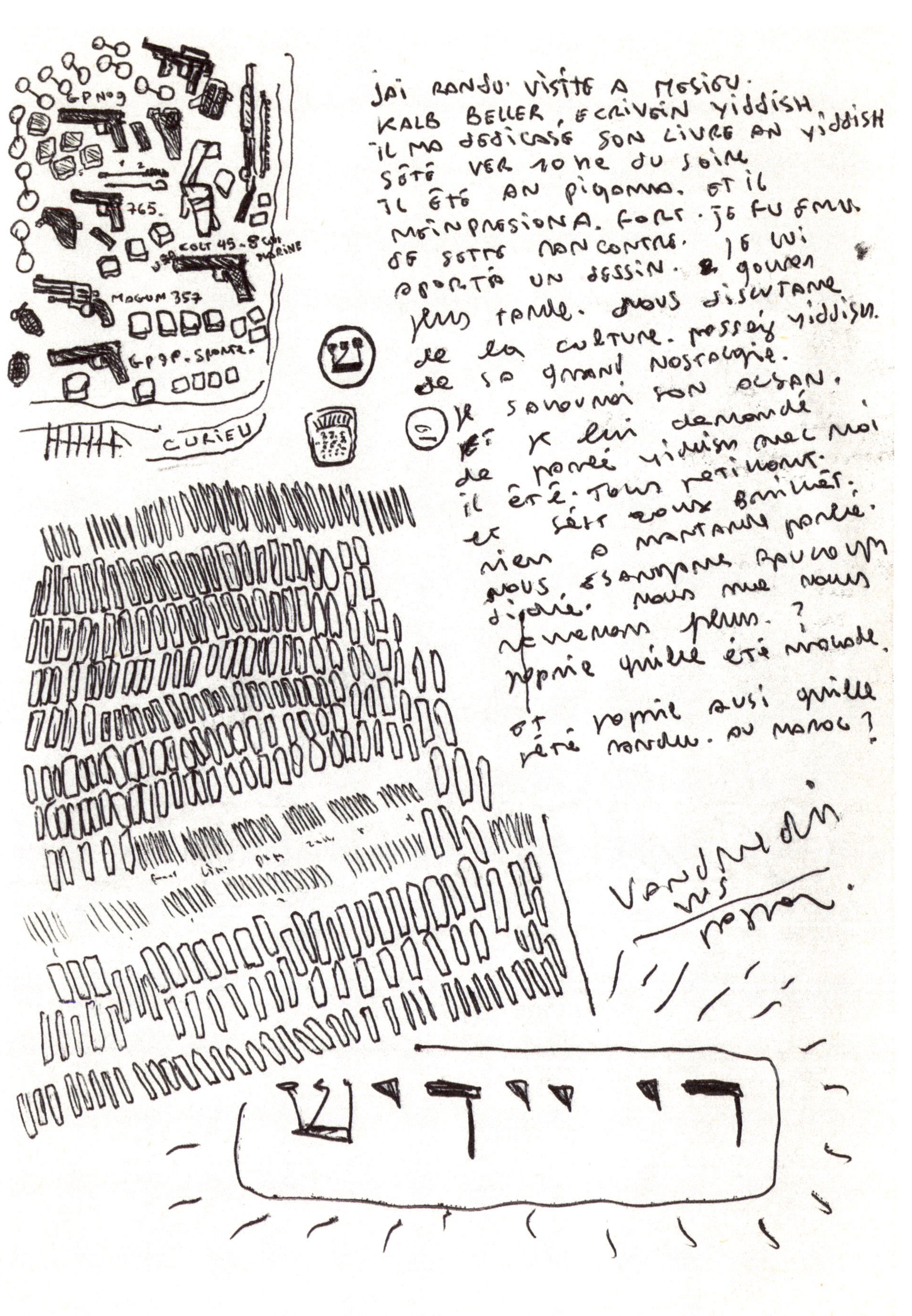


Untitled, 1985–86

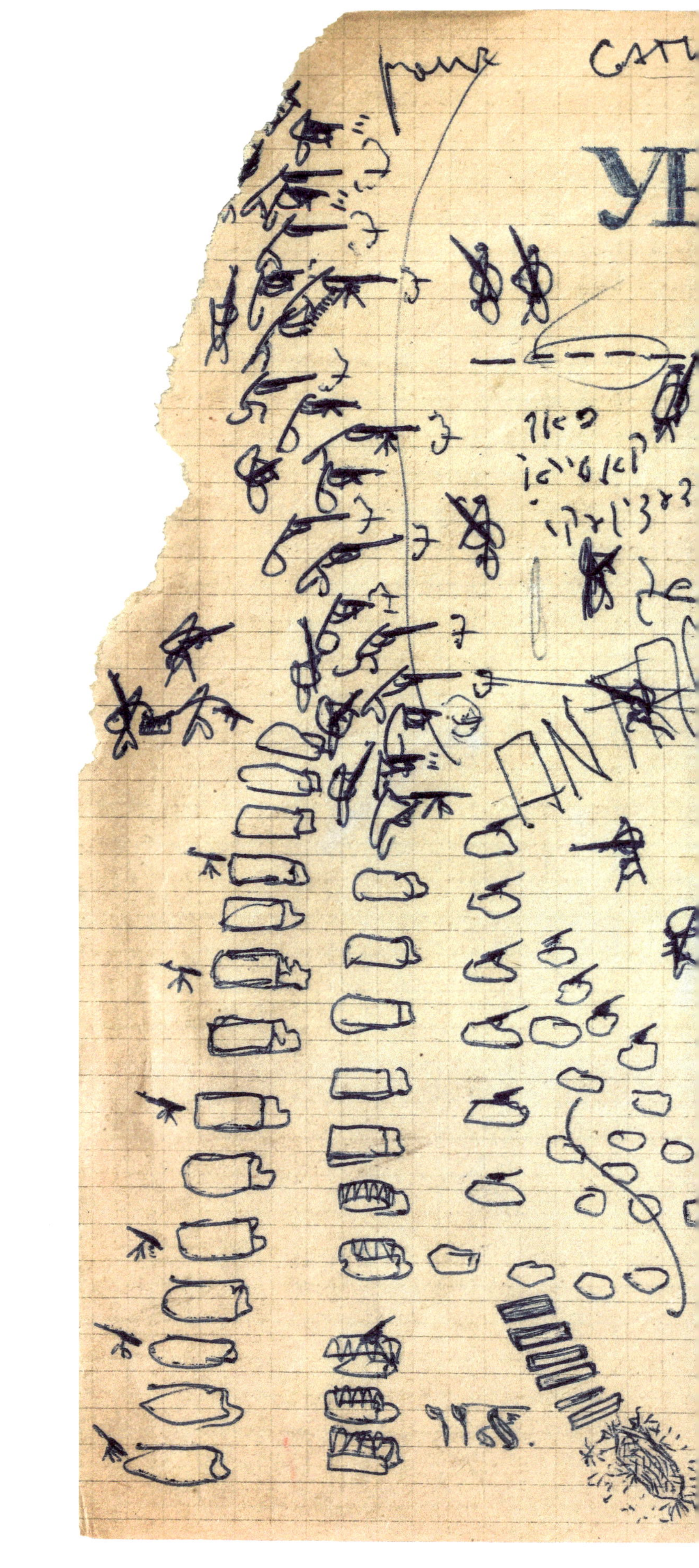

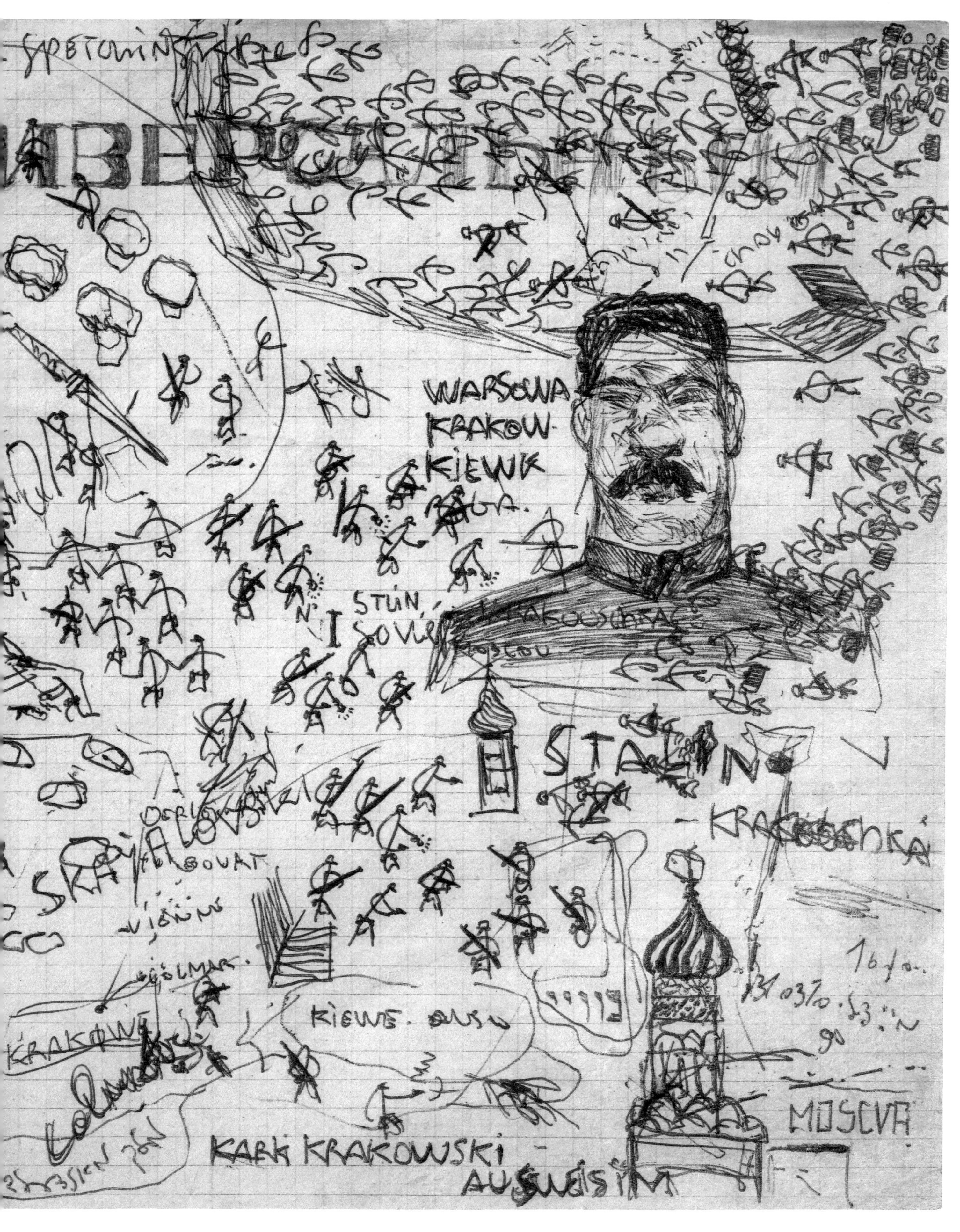


*Stalin*, c. 1985

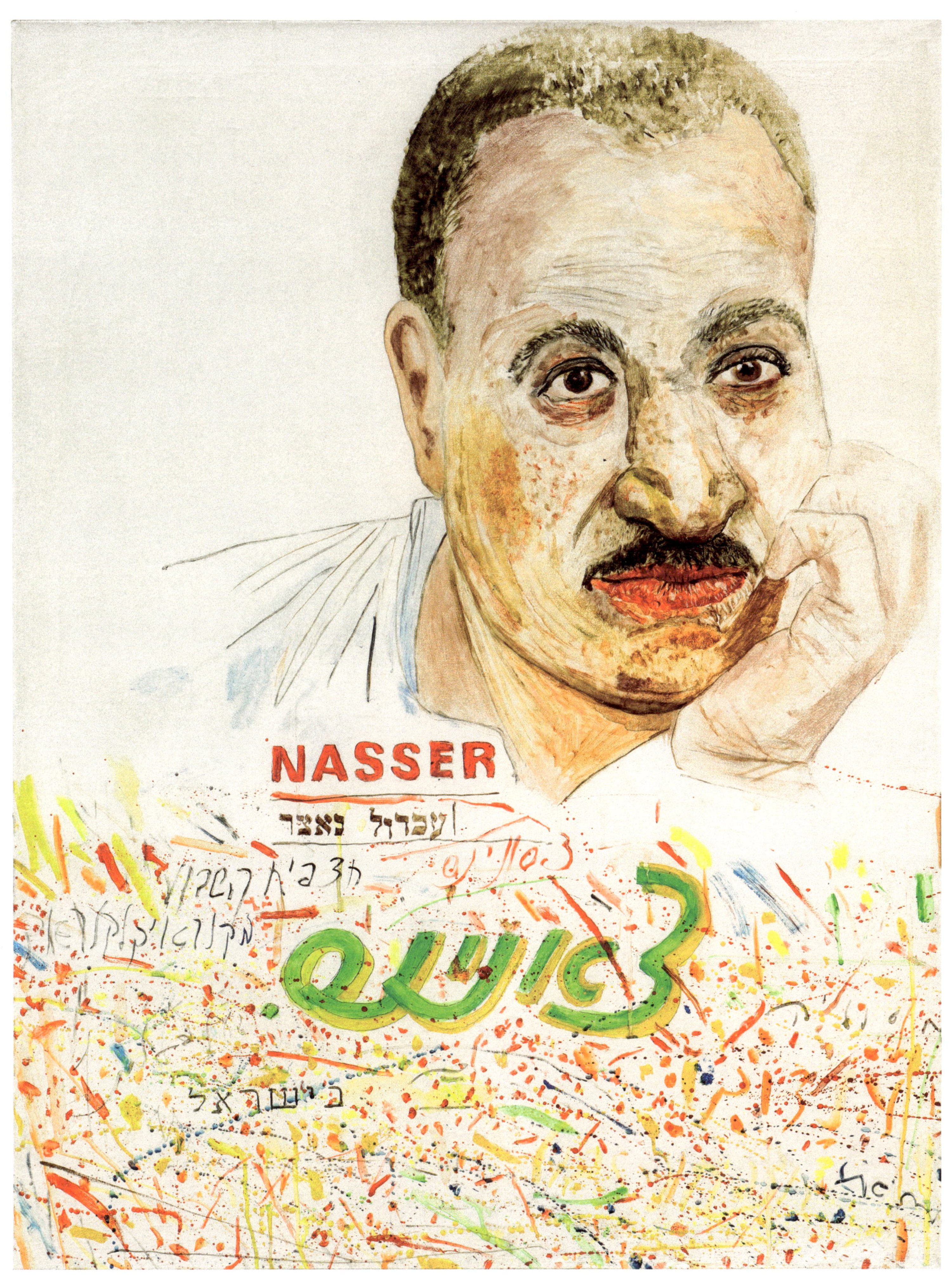


*Gamal Abdel Nasser*, 1983

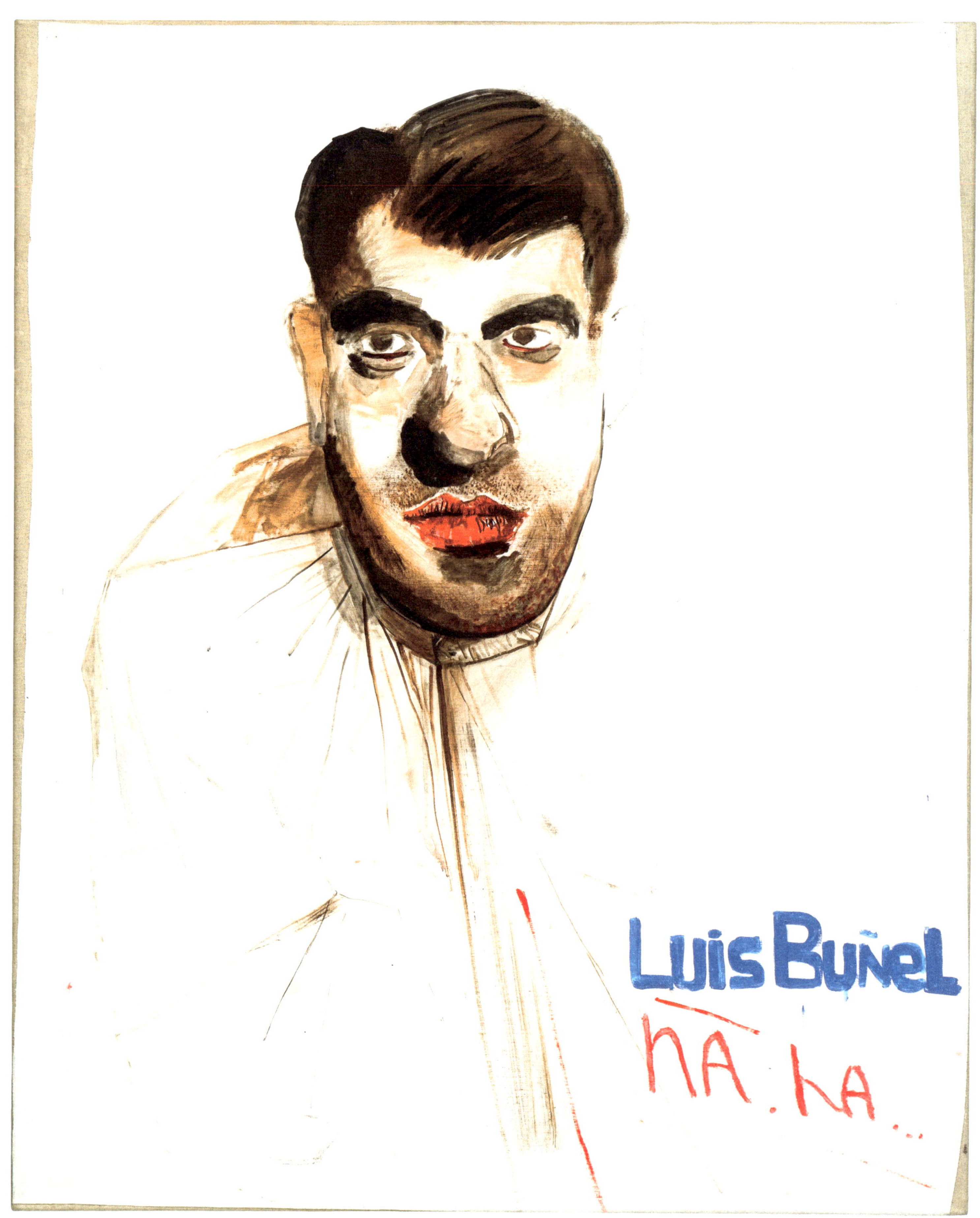


*Luis Buñel ha ha*, c. 1983

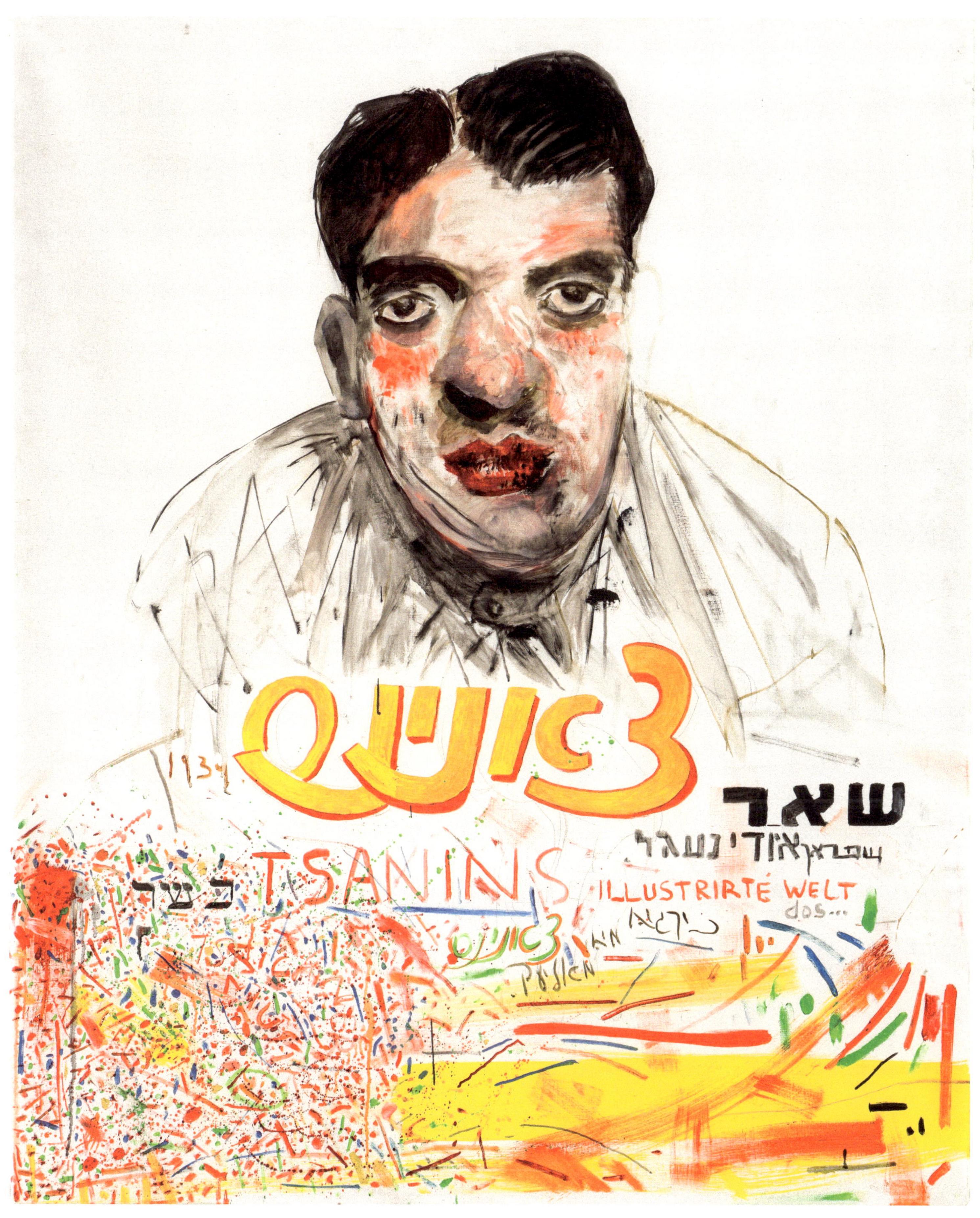


*Quic 3 portrait de Buñuel*, 1983

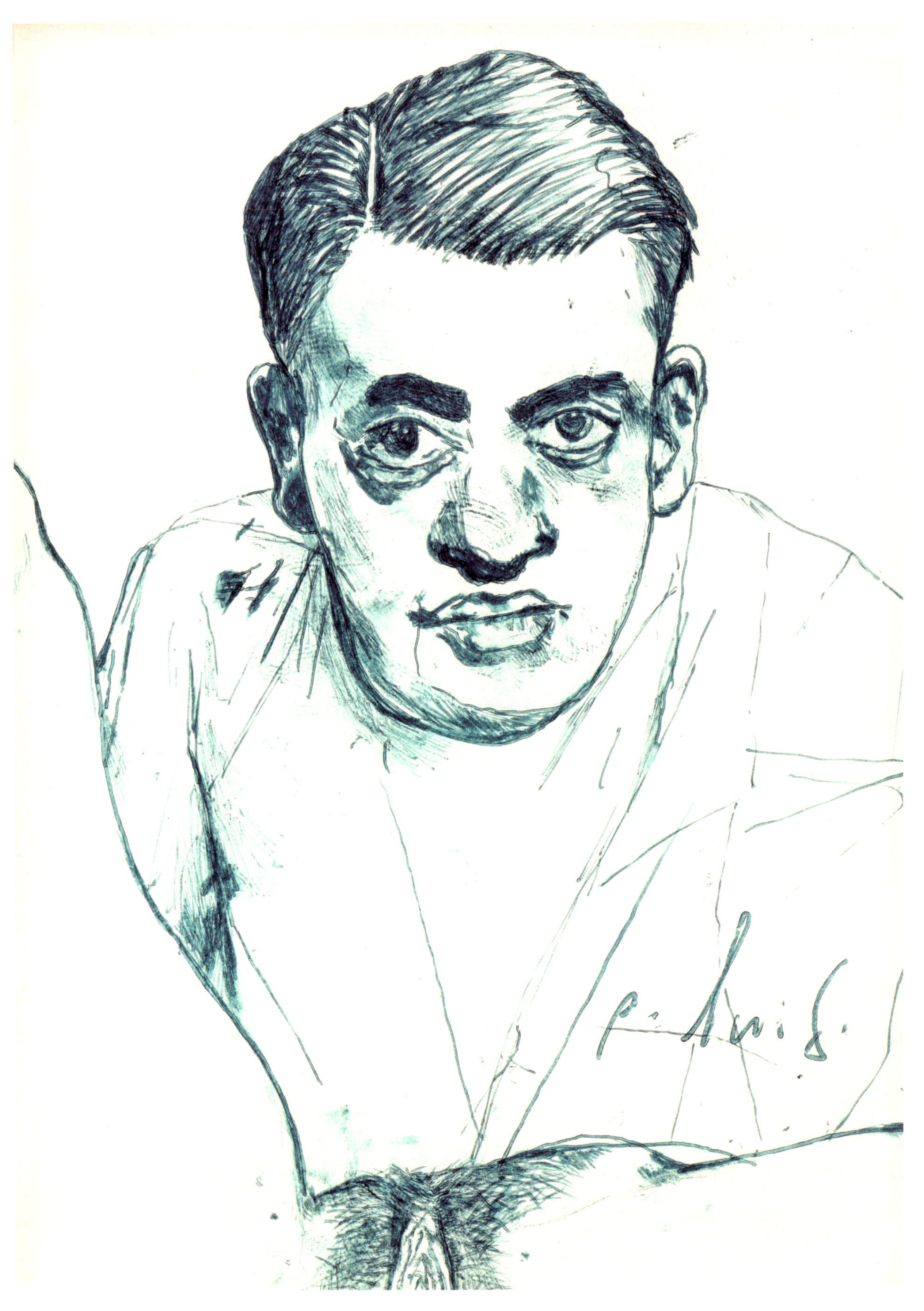

*Luis Buñuel*, 1985

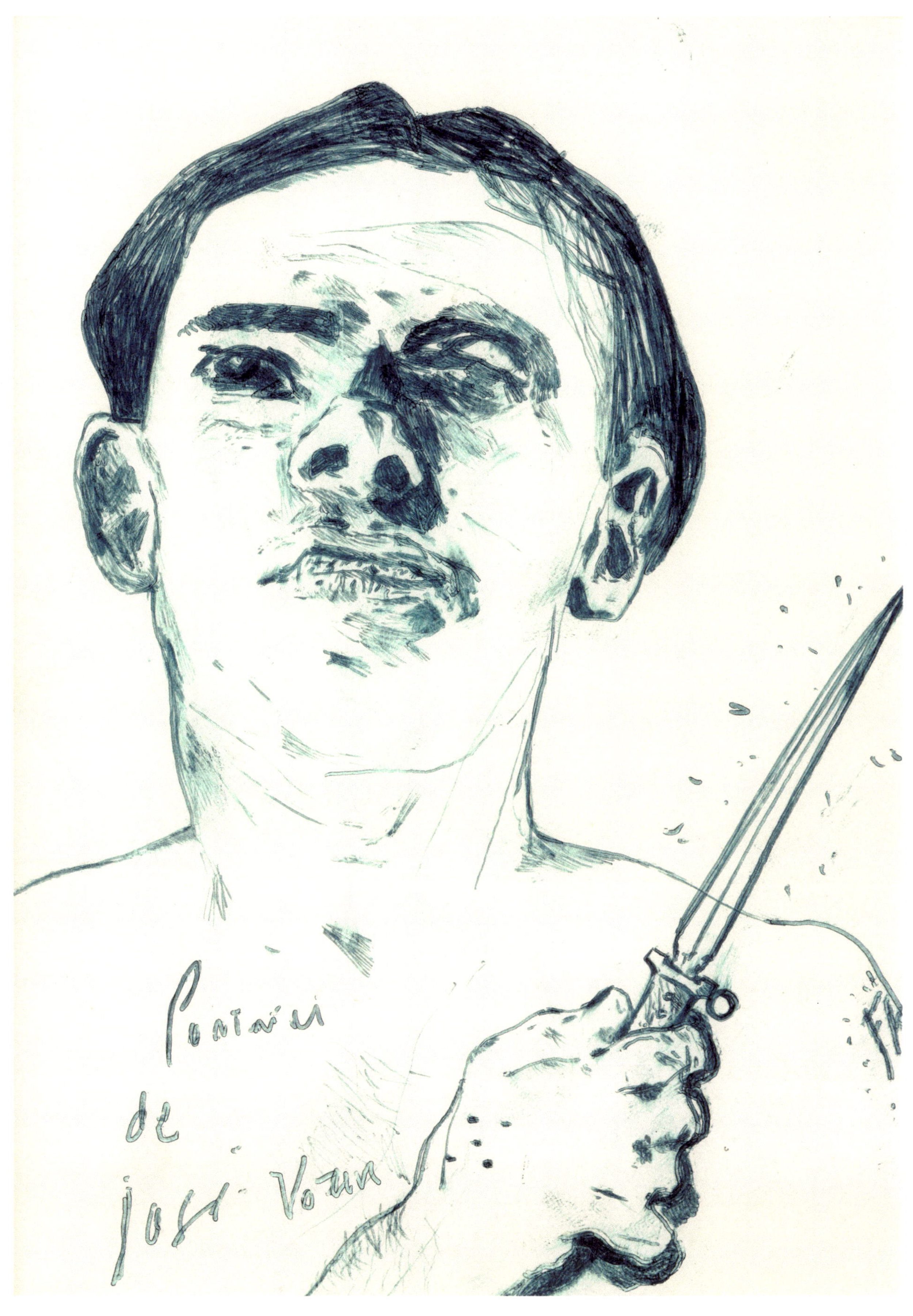


*Portrait de José*, 1985

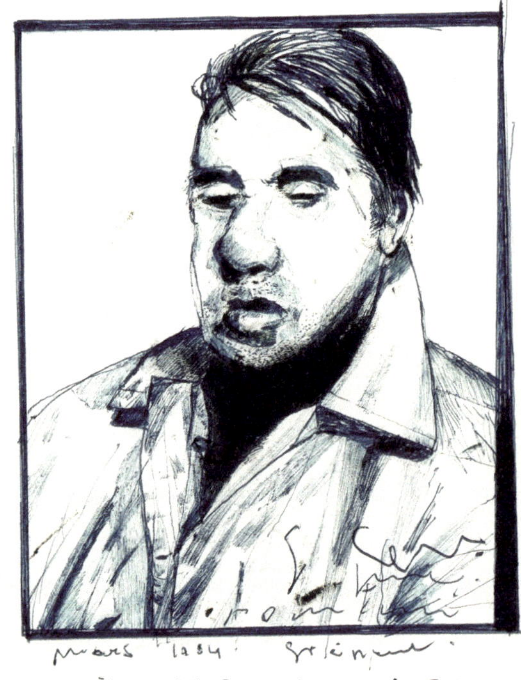

*Portrait of Bacon*, 1984

Stéphane Mardi 24 Juin 1986

Mardi 5 h e 30. à Boitsfort

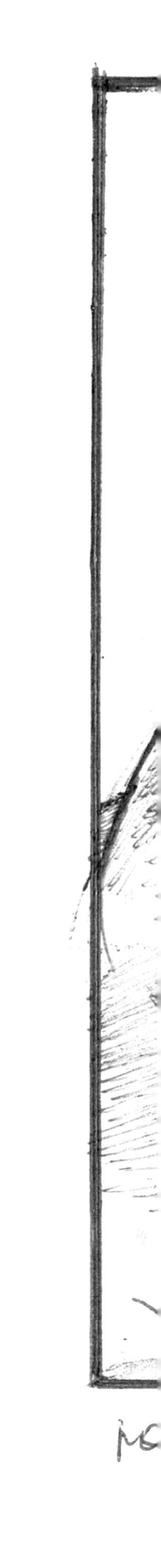

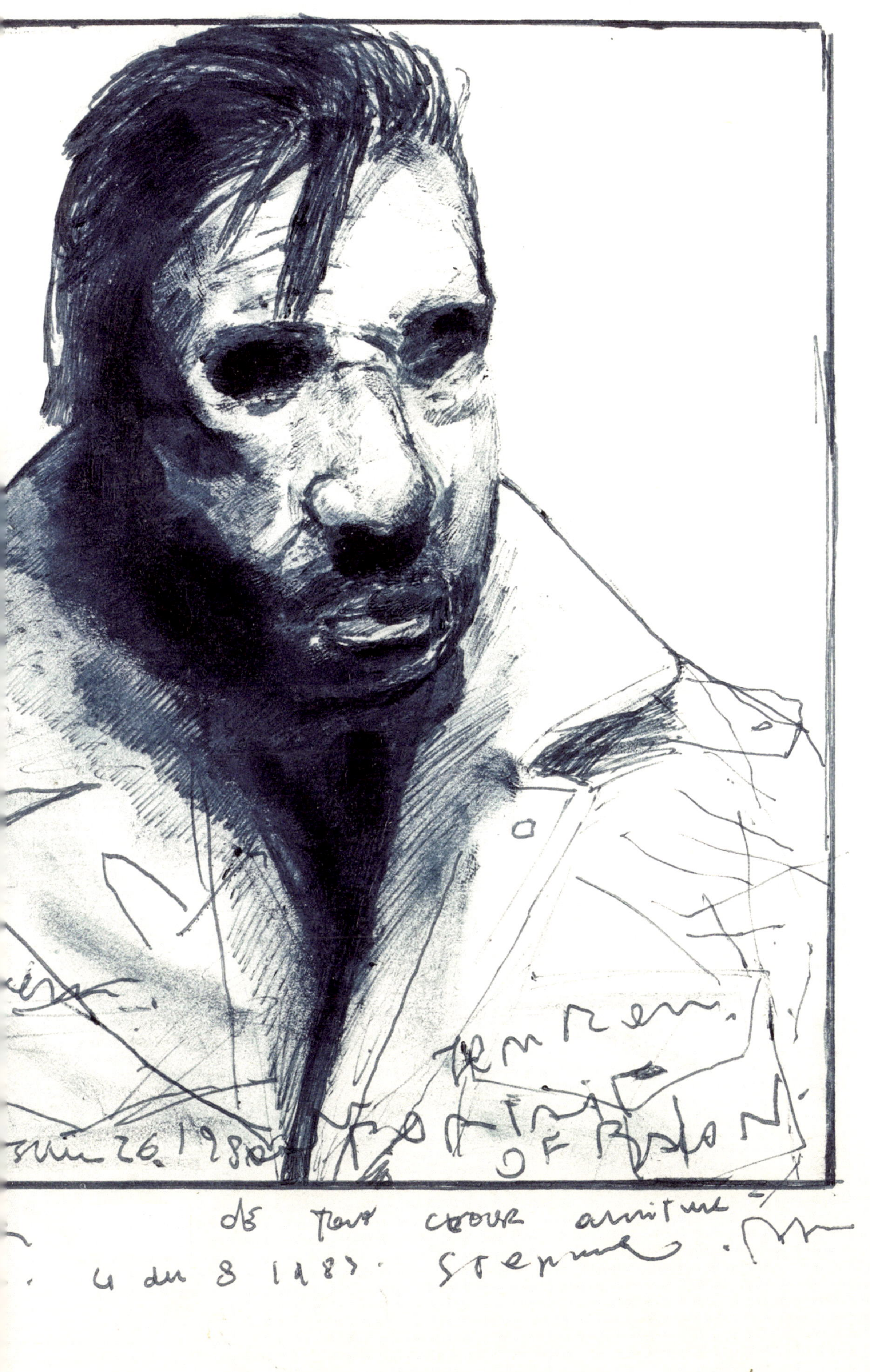

*Portrait of Bacon*, 1980

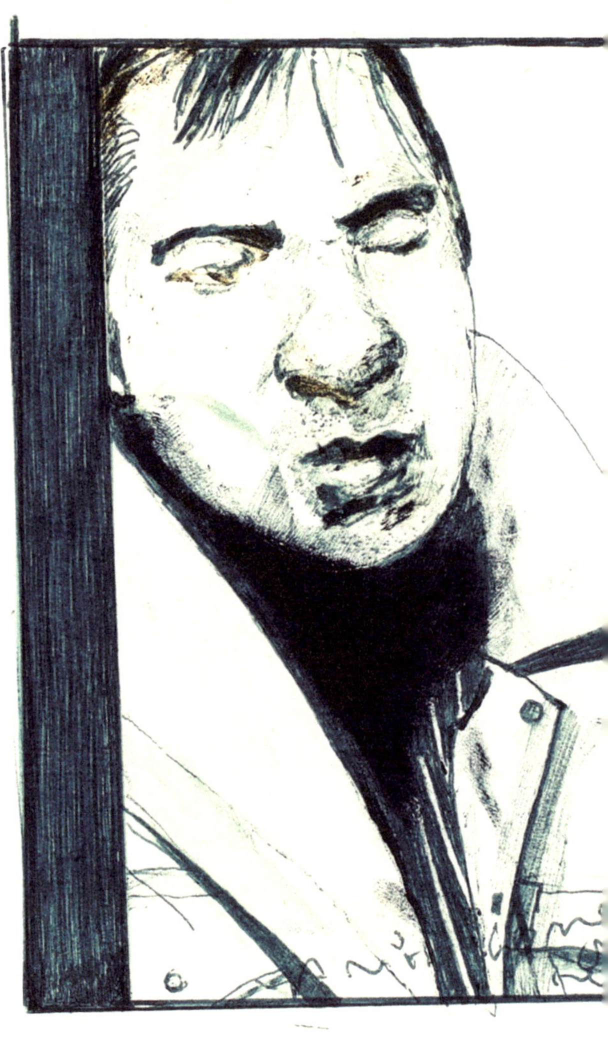

*Francis Bacon*, c. 1980

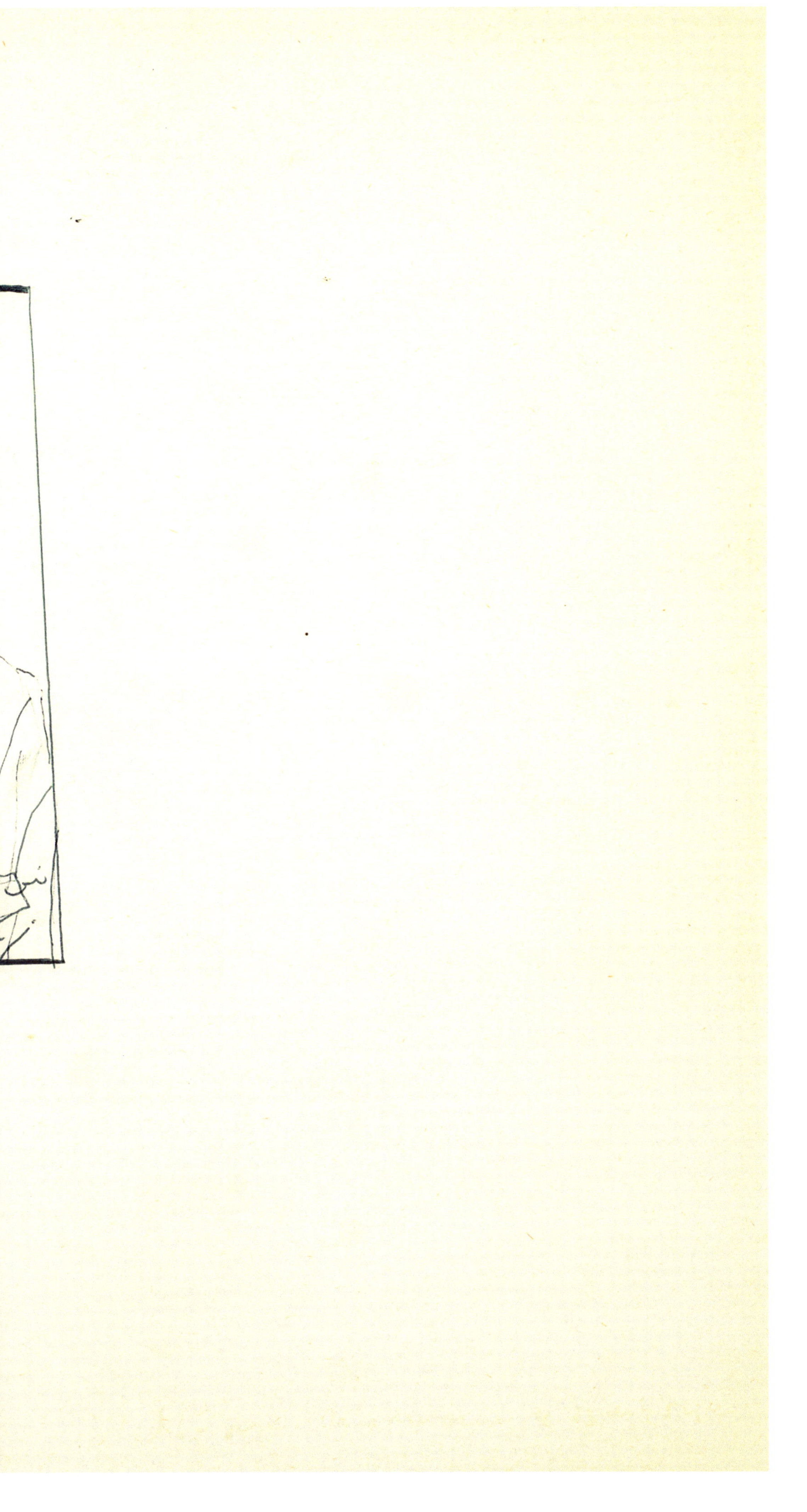

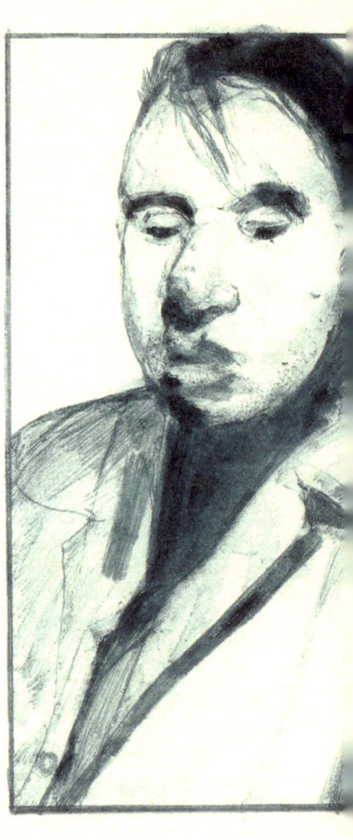

*Francis Bacon*, 1980

Siepmann
mardi 24. Juin 1980.

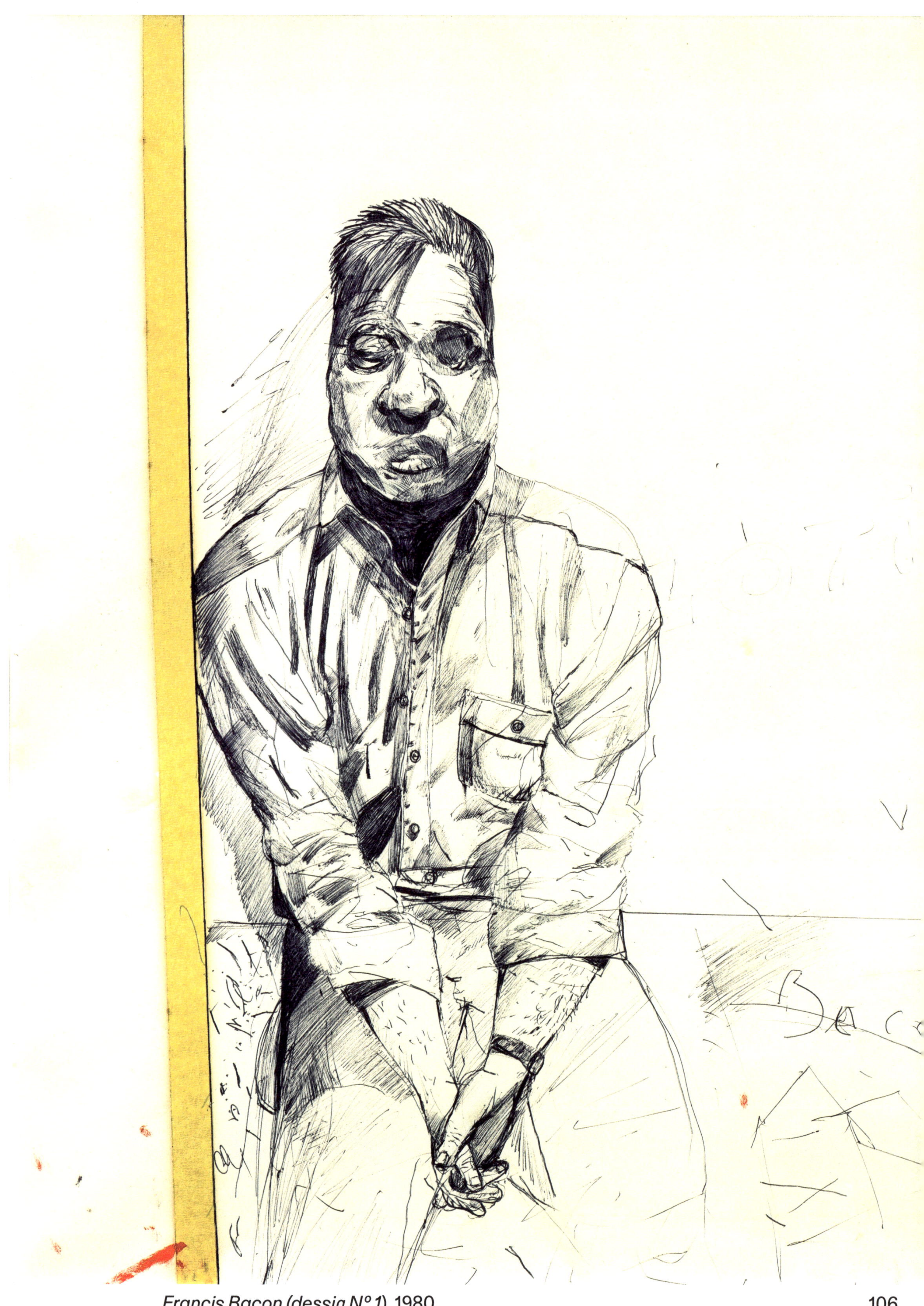

*Francis Bacon (dessin N° 1)*, 1980

DESSIN

NO 1.

No.

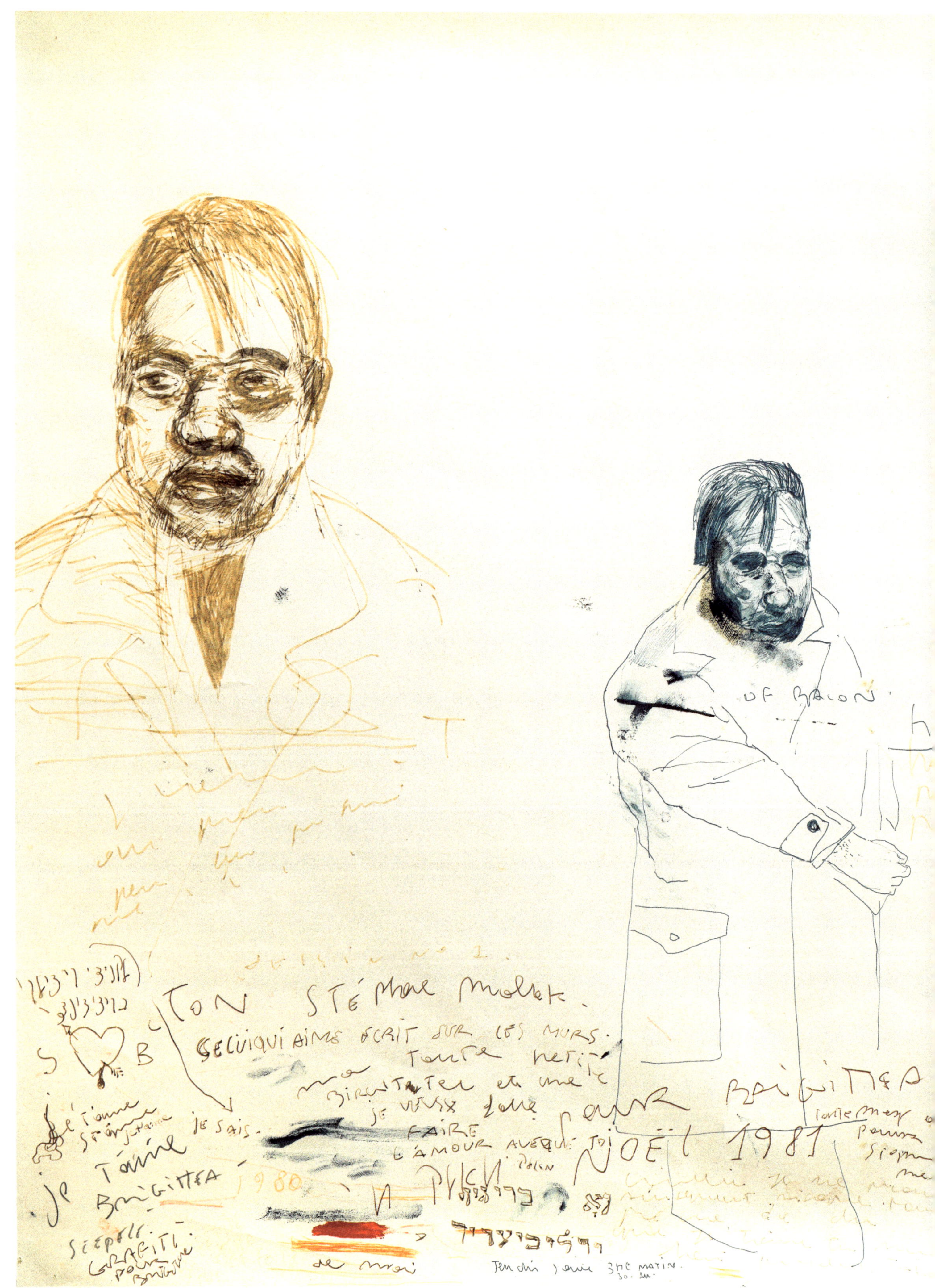

Francis Bacon (Trois portraits), 1981

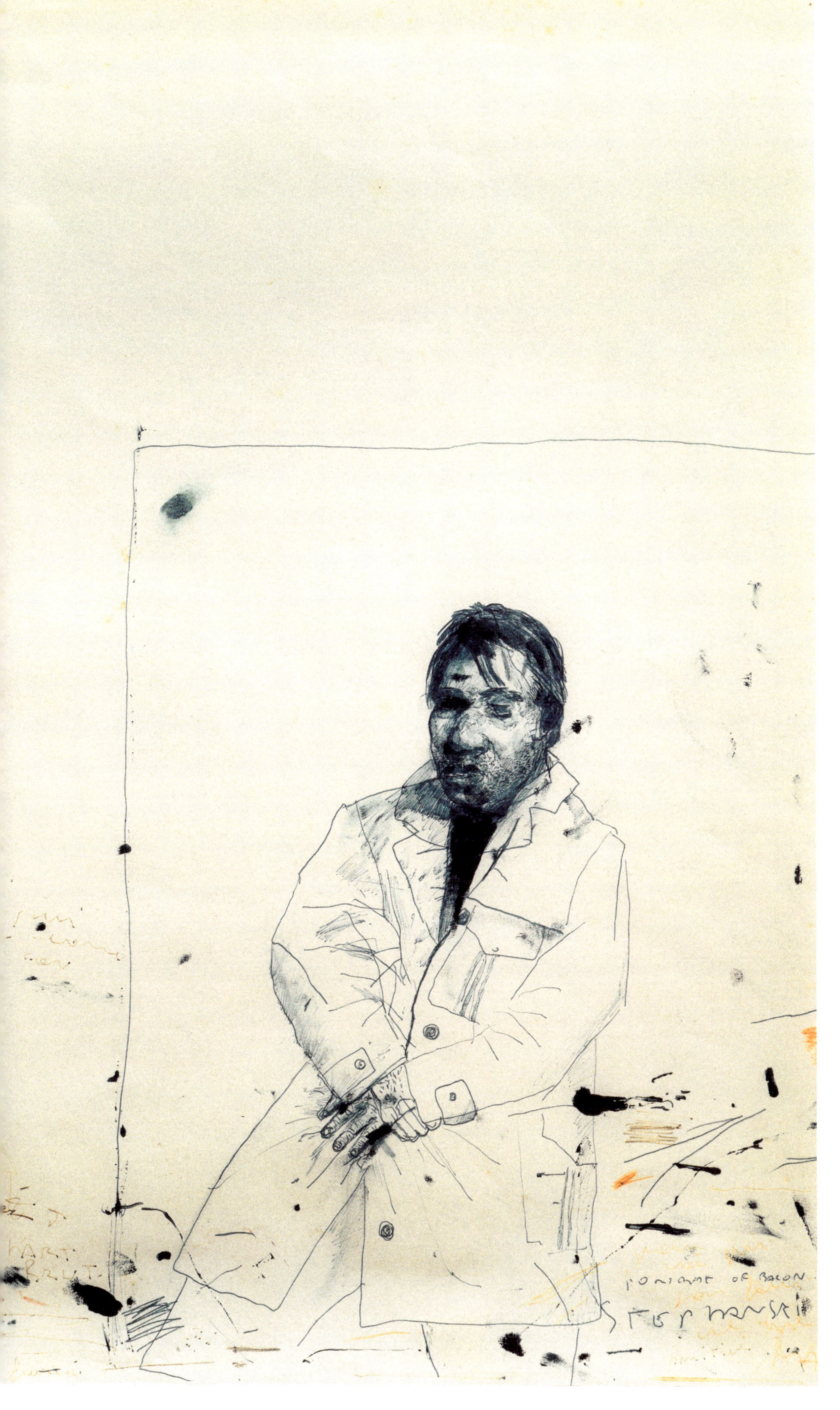

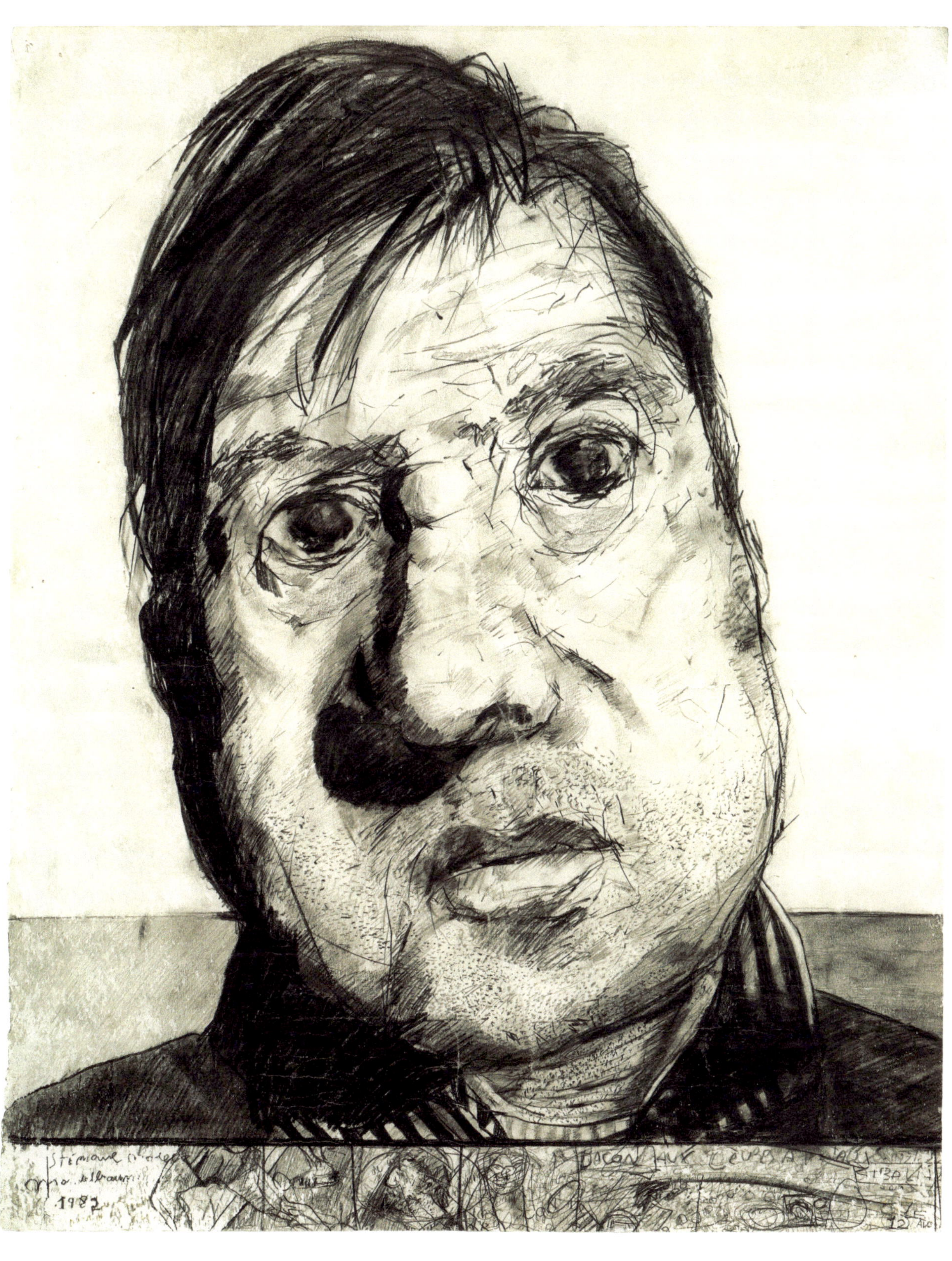

*Bacon et prédelle avec portrait d'Arie*, 1982

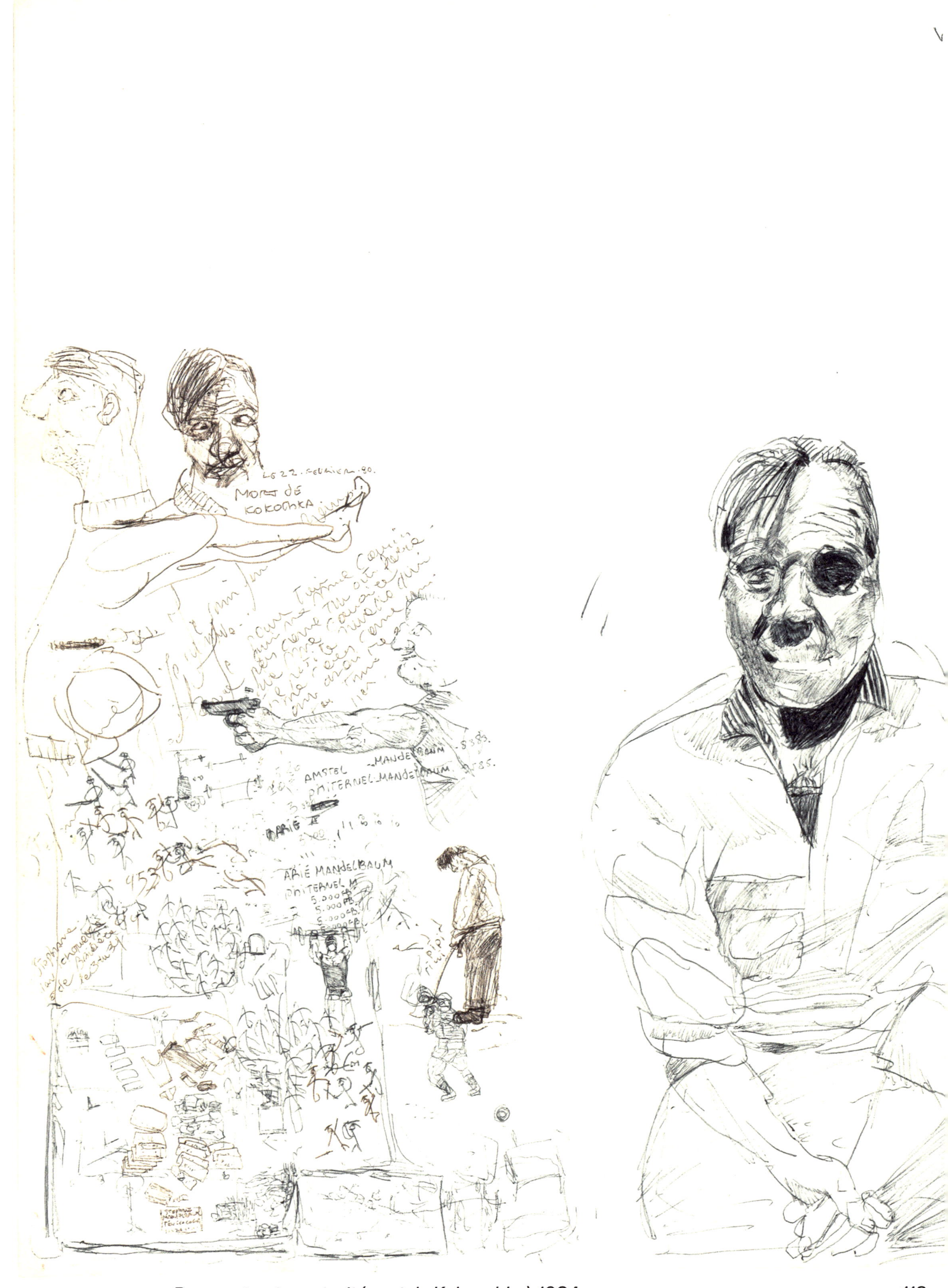


*Bacon et autoportrait (mort de Kokoschka)*, 1984

A AMSTERDAM
LE 26
SAMEDI 12 h
1 2 3 4.

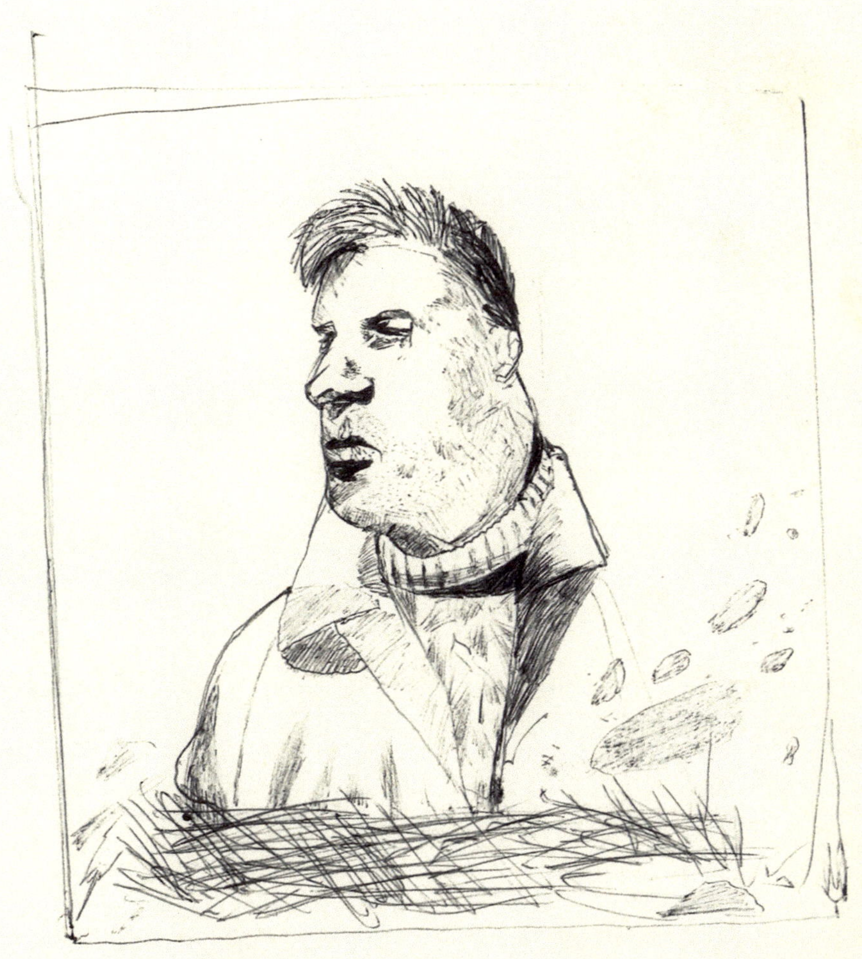

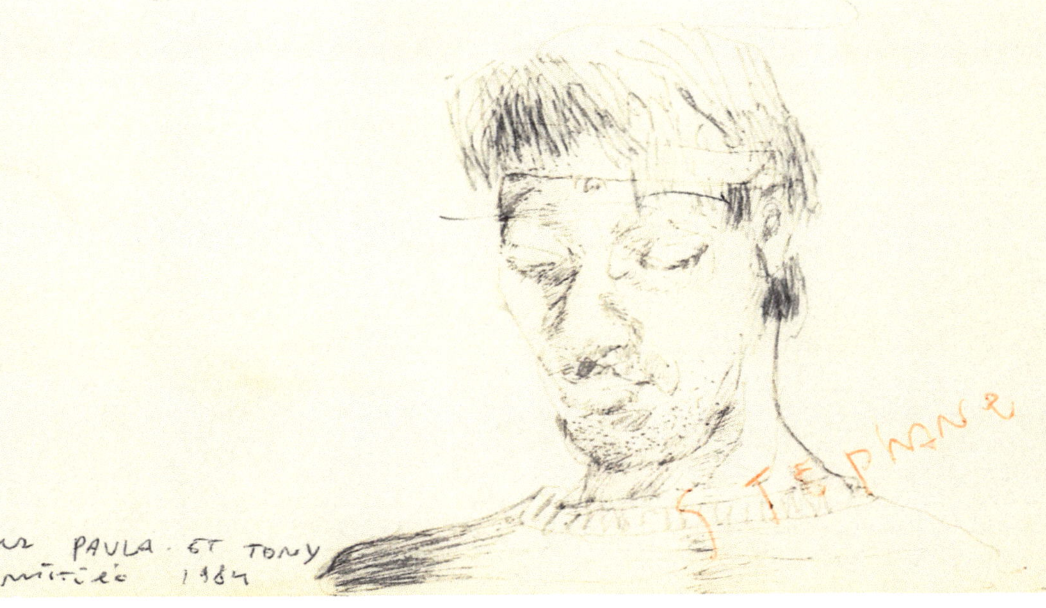
pour PAULA · ET TONY
AMITIÉS 1984
STEPHANE

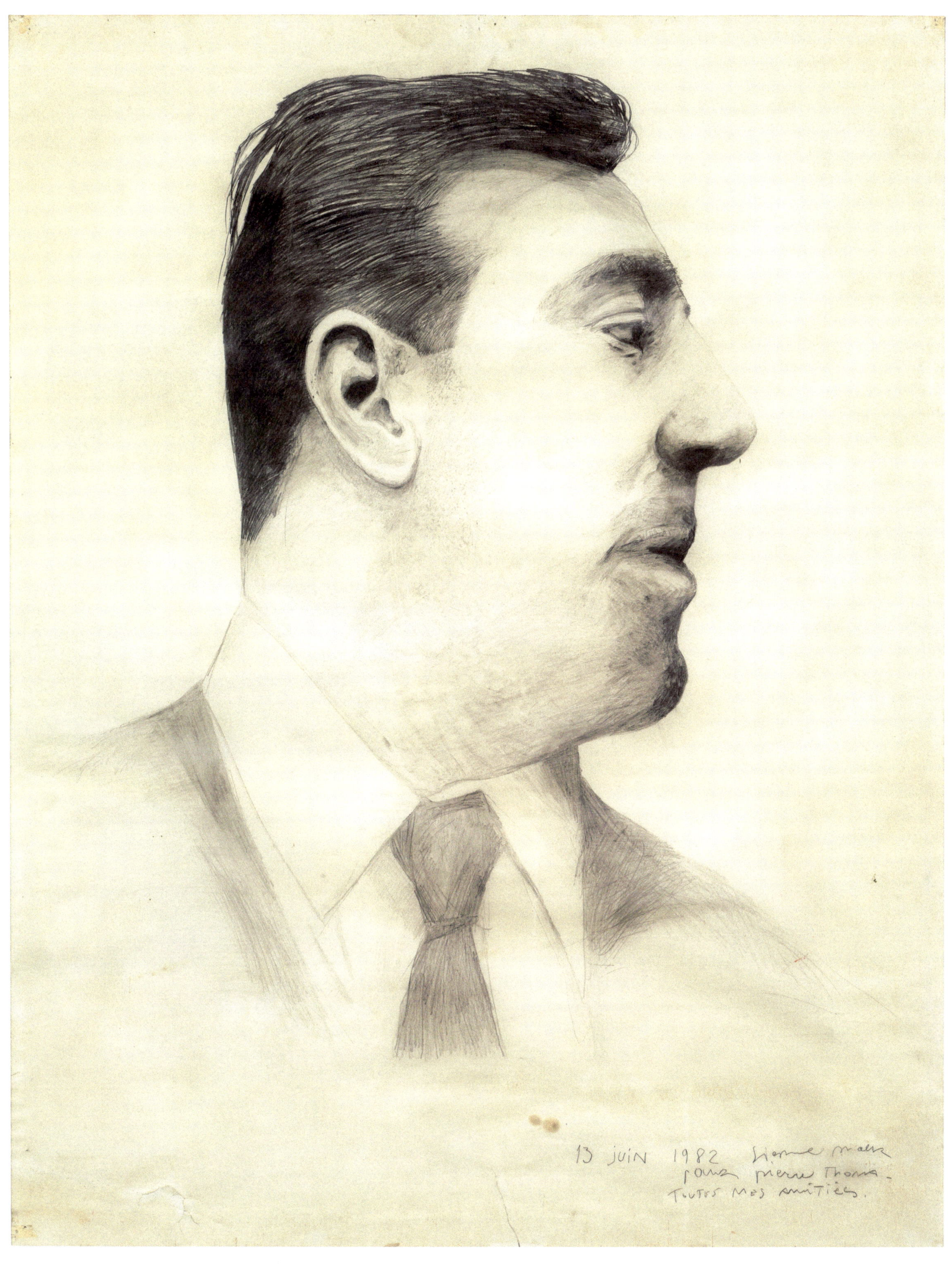


*George Dyer*, 1982

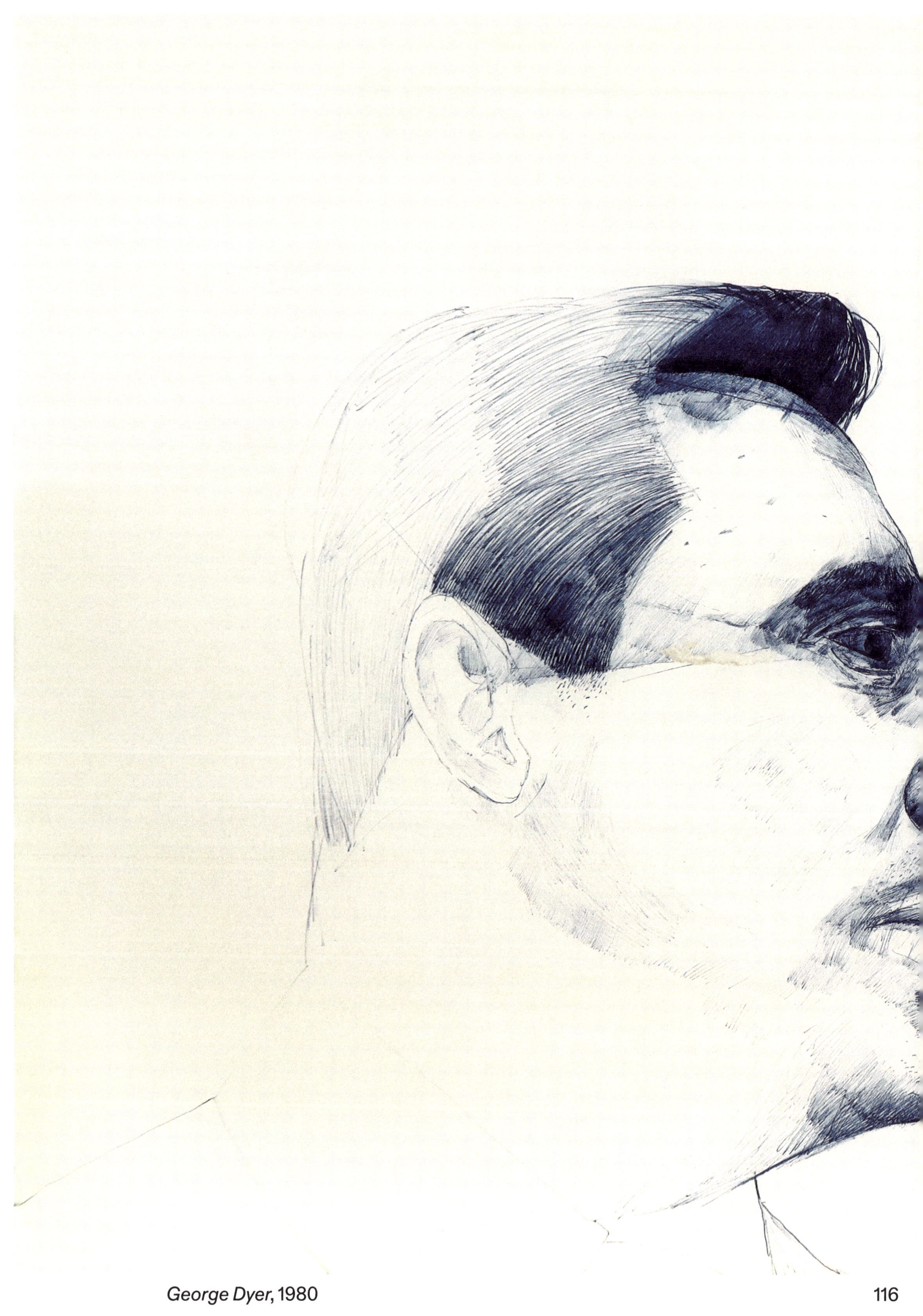

*George Dyer*, 1980

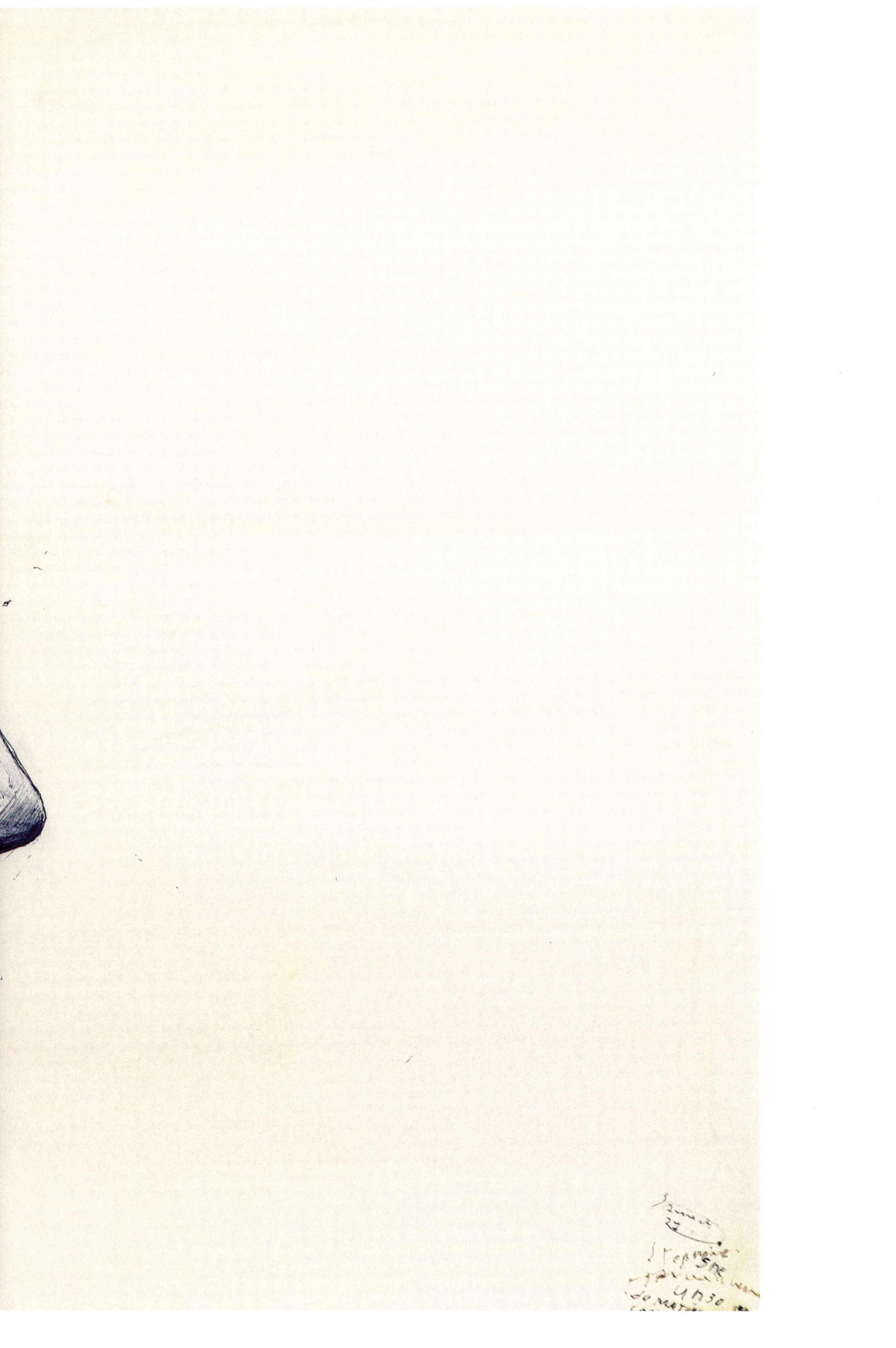

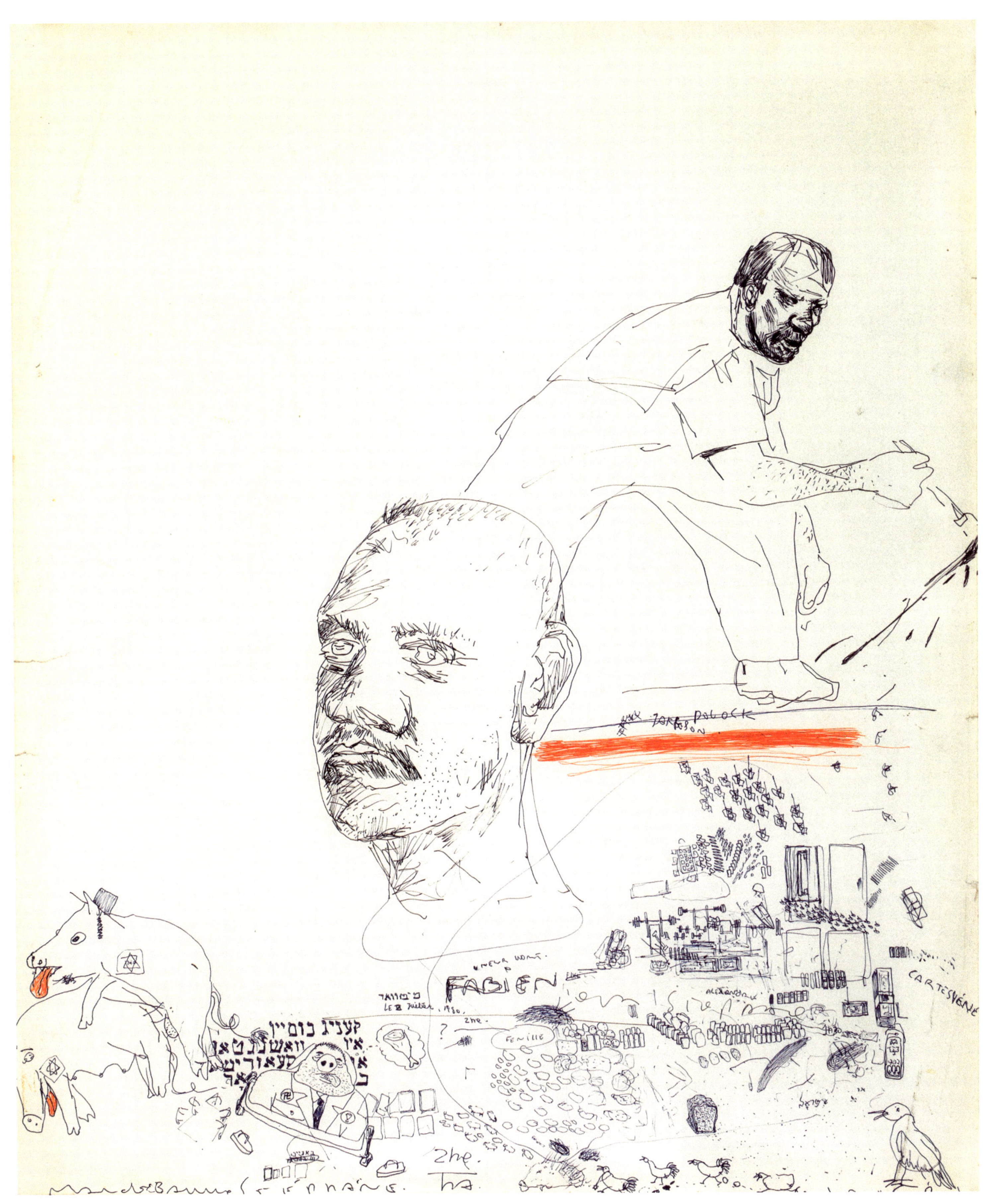


*Pollock et Fabien*, 1980

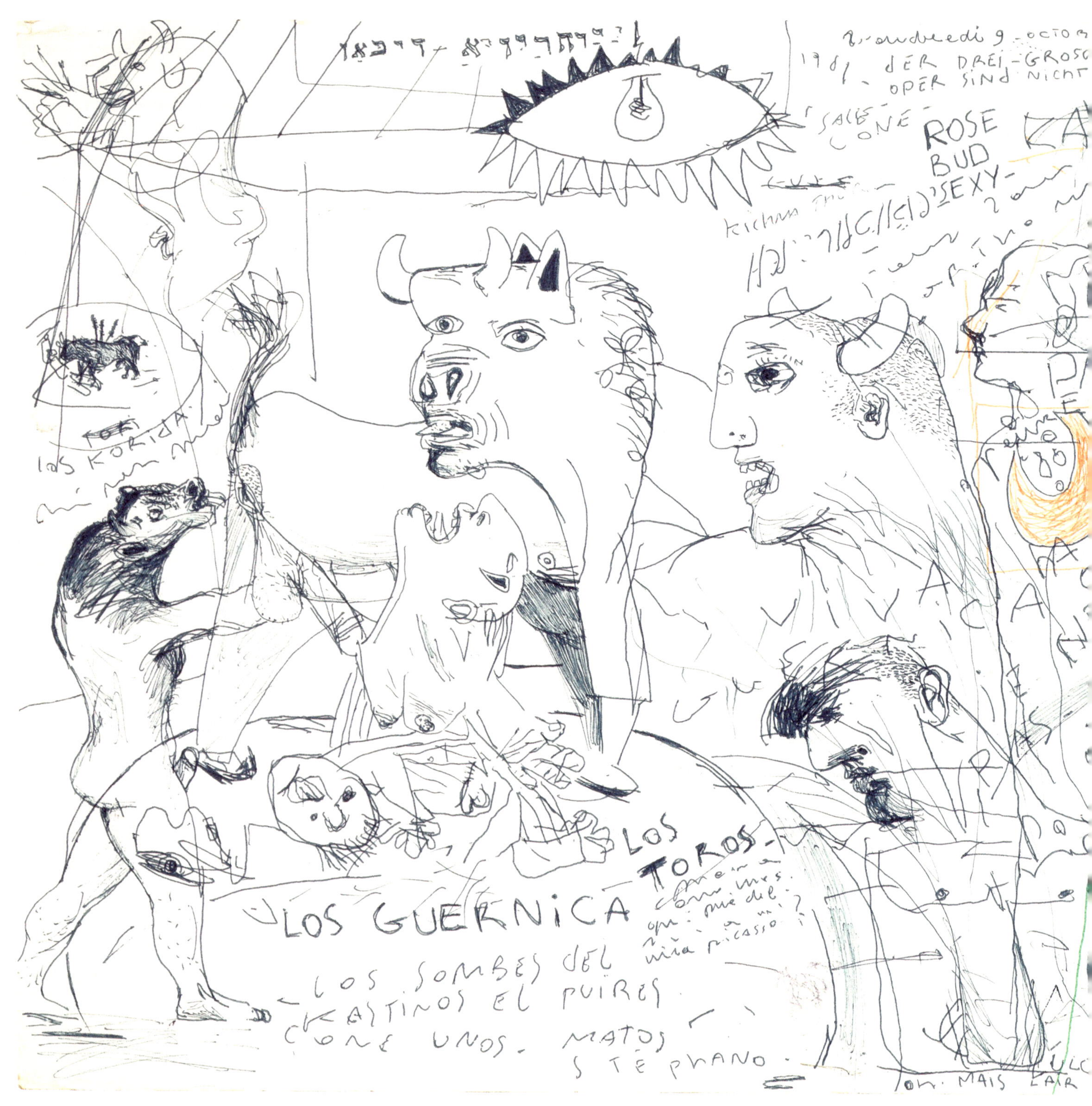


*Composition (Orient)*, 1981

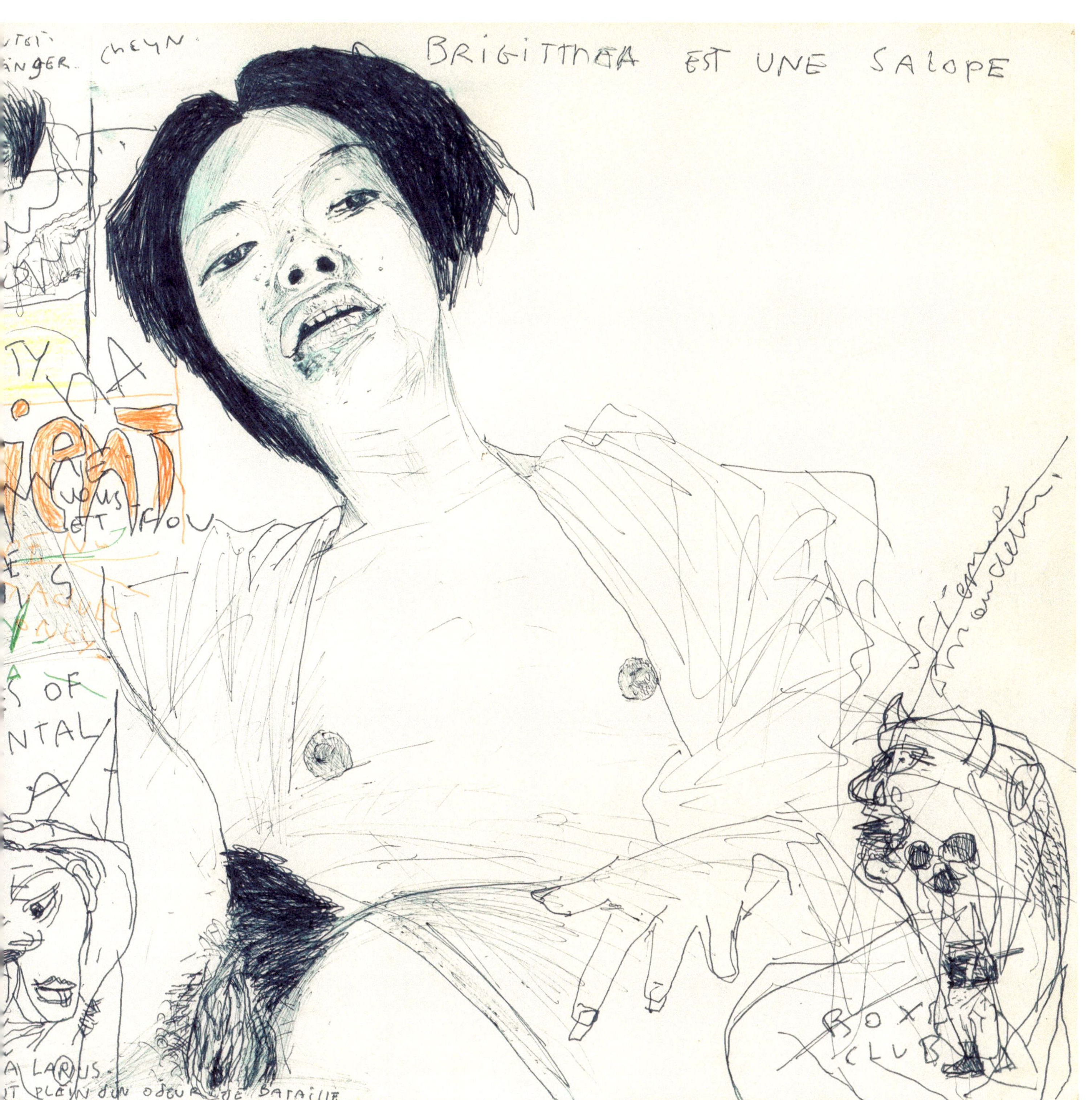
BRIGITTMEA EST UNE SALOPE
BOX CLUB

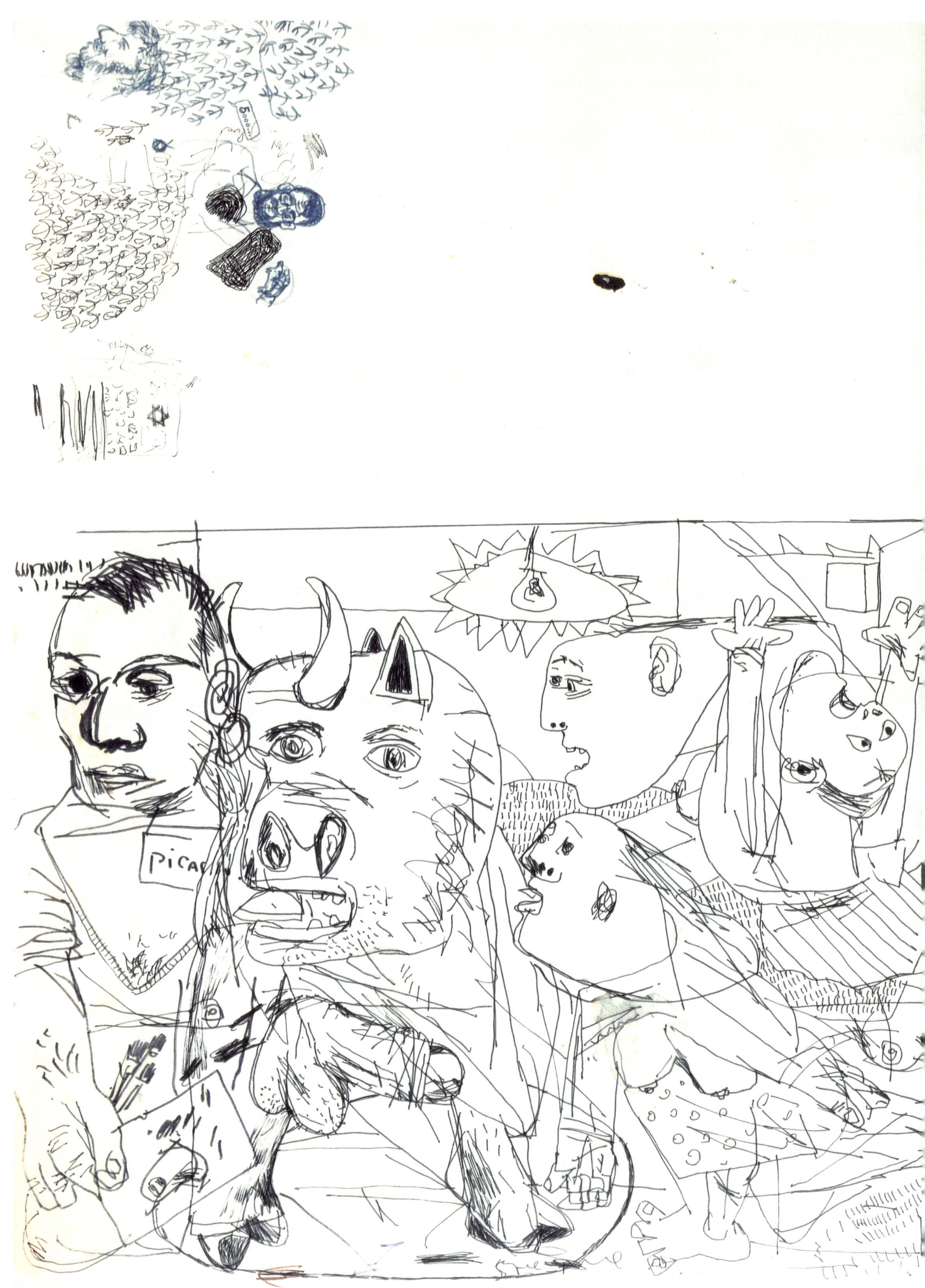


*Picasso, Picador et Guernica*, 1980

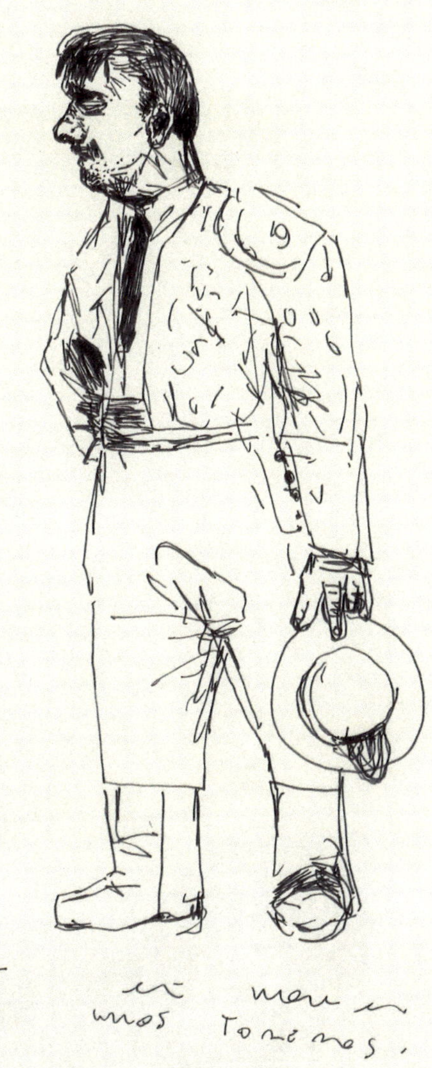

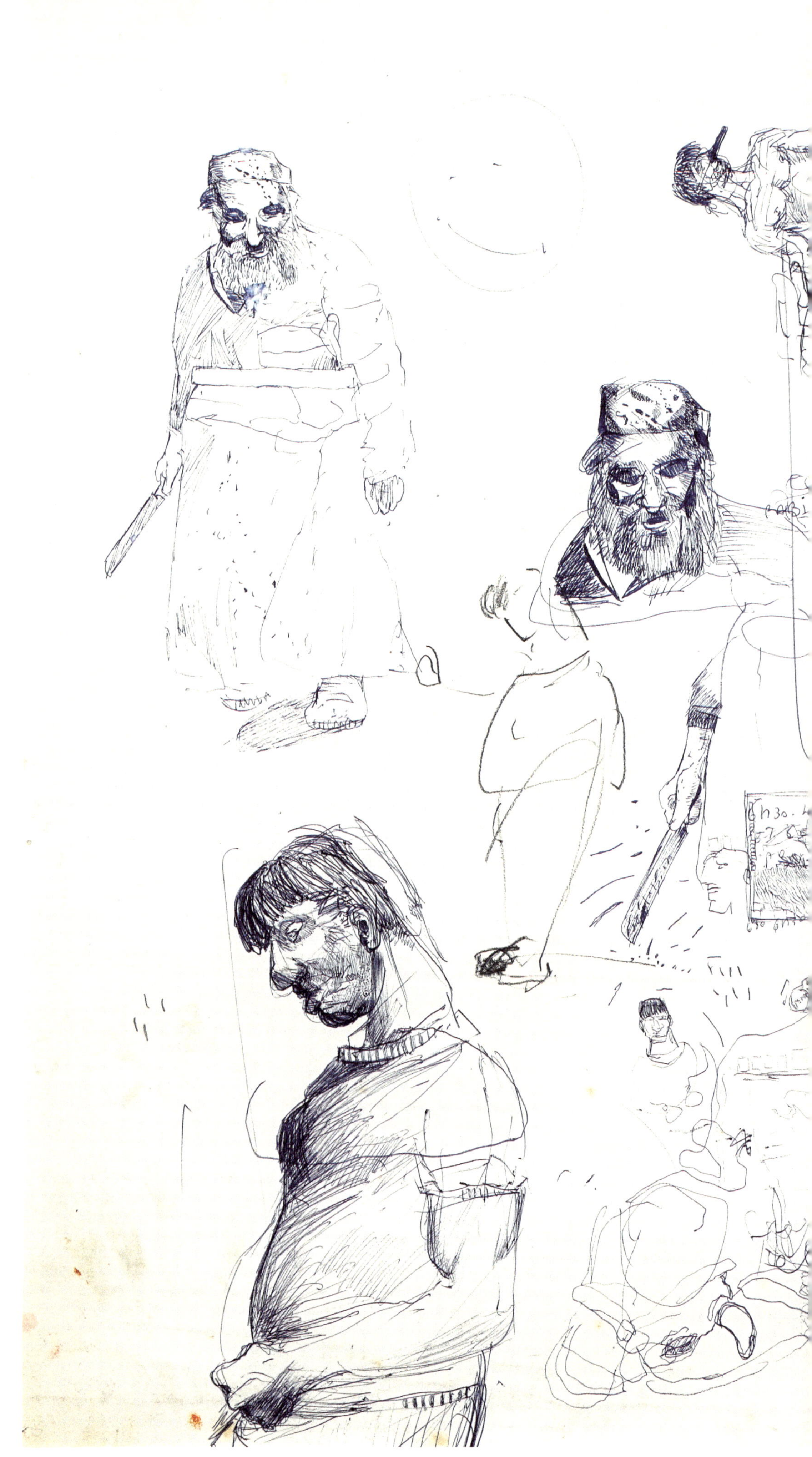

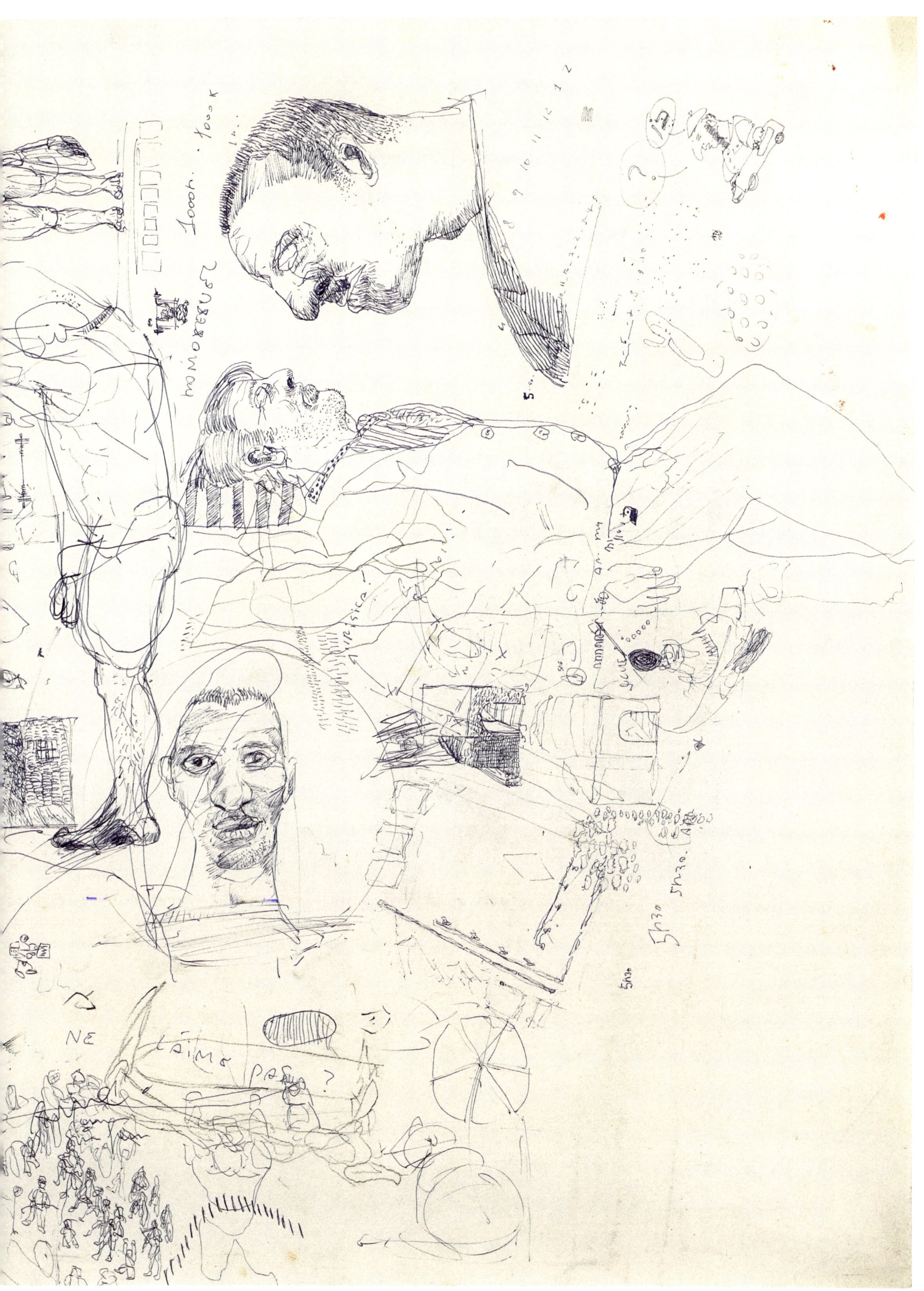

*Composition (Shohet)*, c. 1982

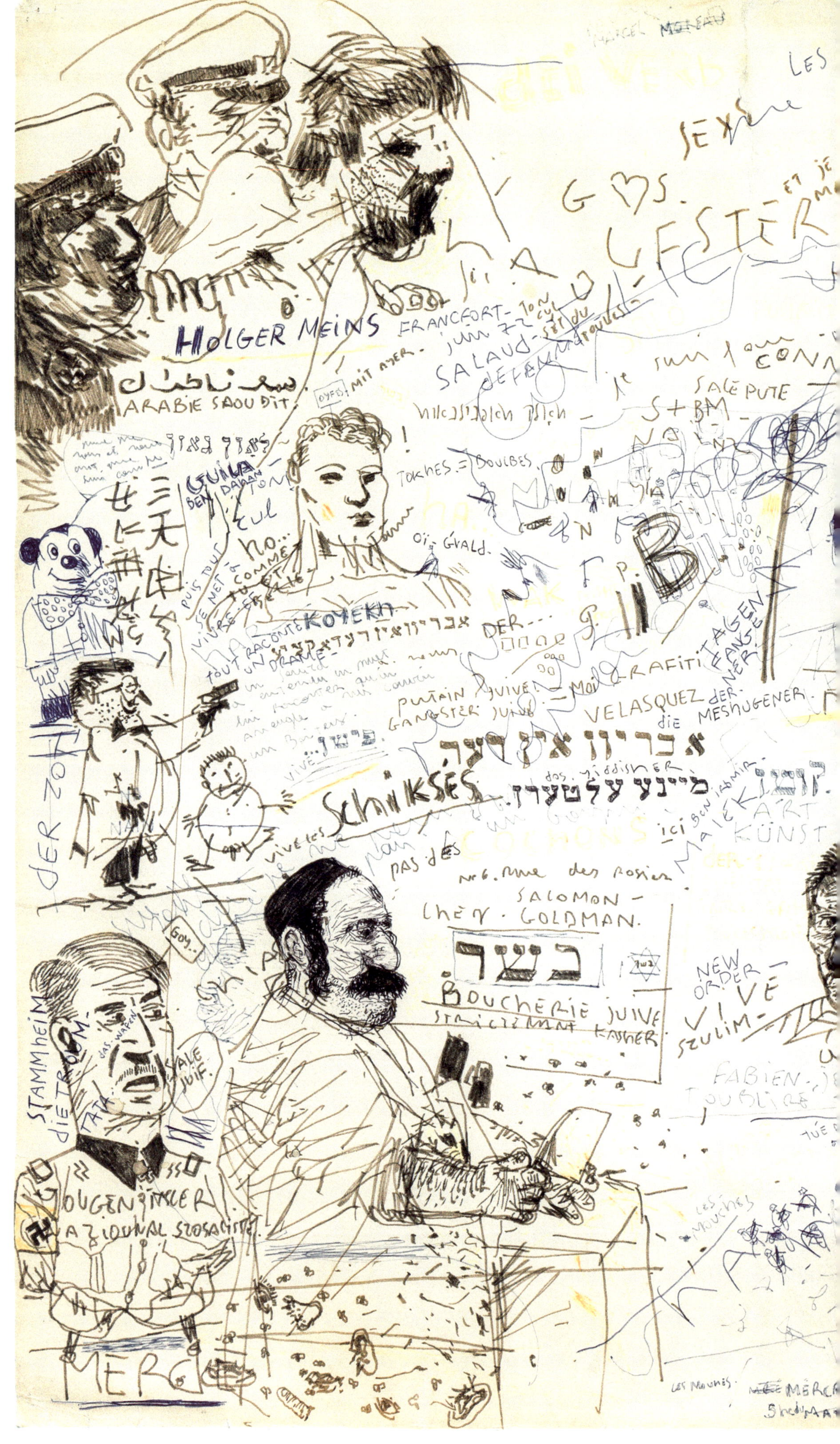

HOLGER MEINS
FRANCFORT - JUIN 72
ARABIE SAOUDIT
SALAUD
SALE PUTE
Tokhes = Doulbes
Oï Gvald
TOUT RACONTE UN DRAME
PUTAIN JUIVE
GANGSTER JUIVE
GRAFITI
VELASQUEZ
die MESHUGENER
Schikses
das Yiddisher
ici BENJAMIN
COCHONS
KÜNST
Nr 6. rue des rosiers
SALOMON - CHEN. GOLDMAN.
בשר
BOUCHERIE JUIVE
STRICTEMENT KASHER
NEW ORDER
VIVE
STAMMHEIM
SALE JUIF
LES MOUCHES
MERC

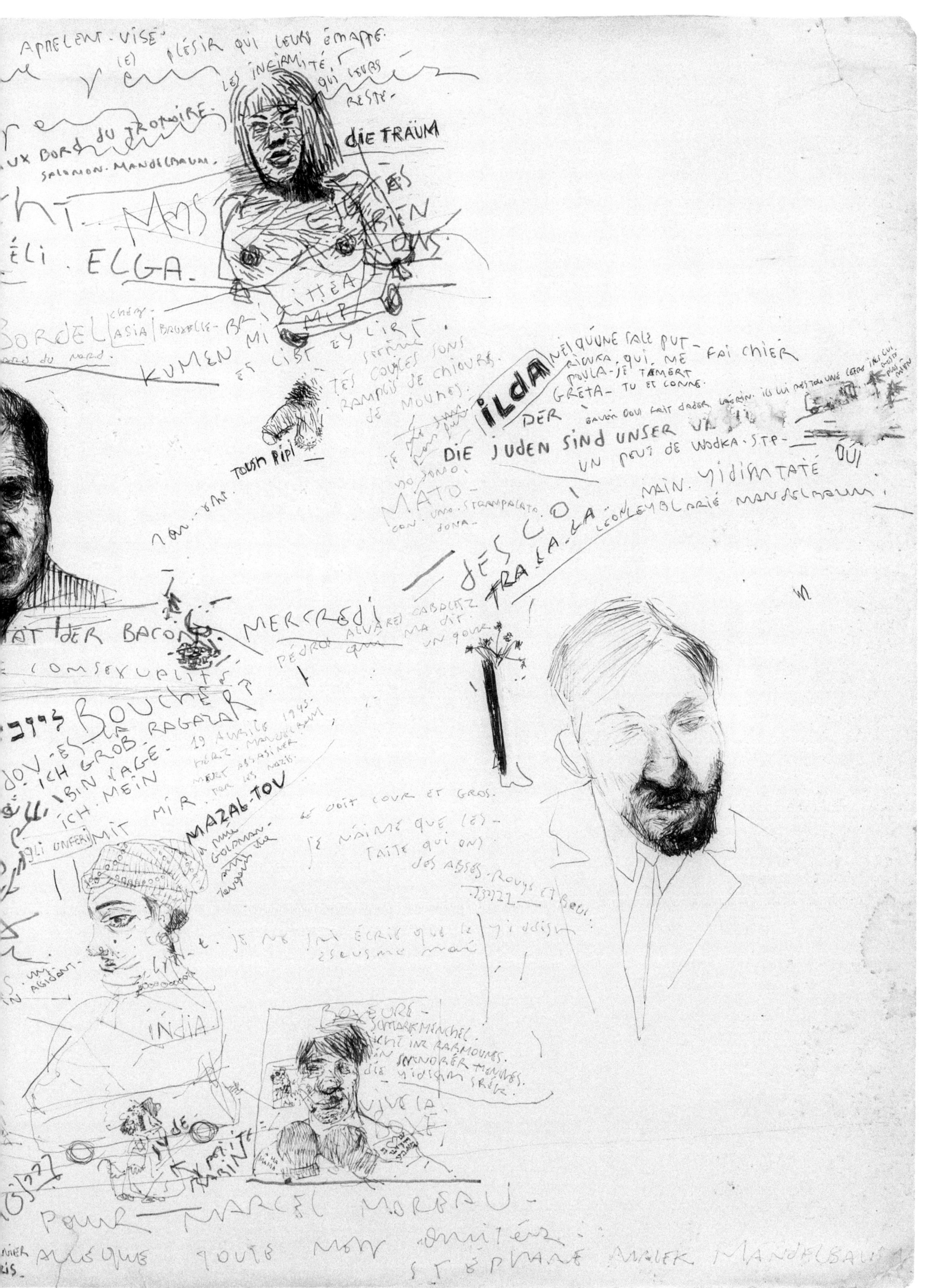


*Composition avec Arié et Bacon (Arrestation de la bande à Baader)*, 1984

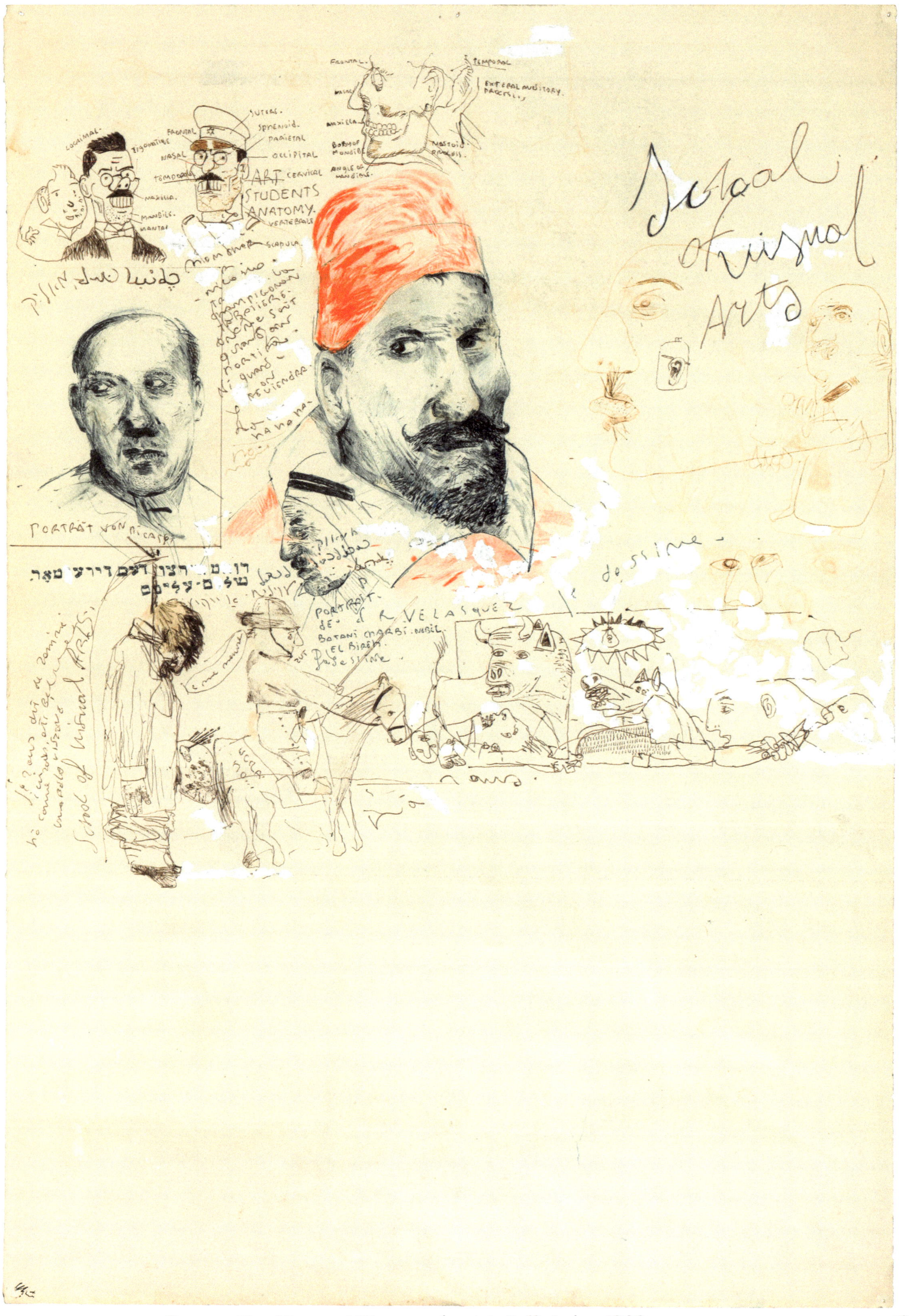


*Composition Picasso Vélasquez (projet d'affiche)*, c. 1983

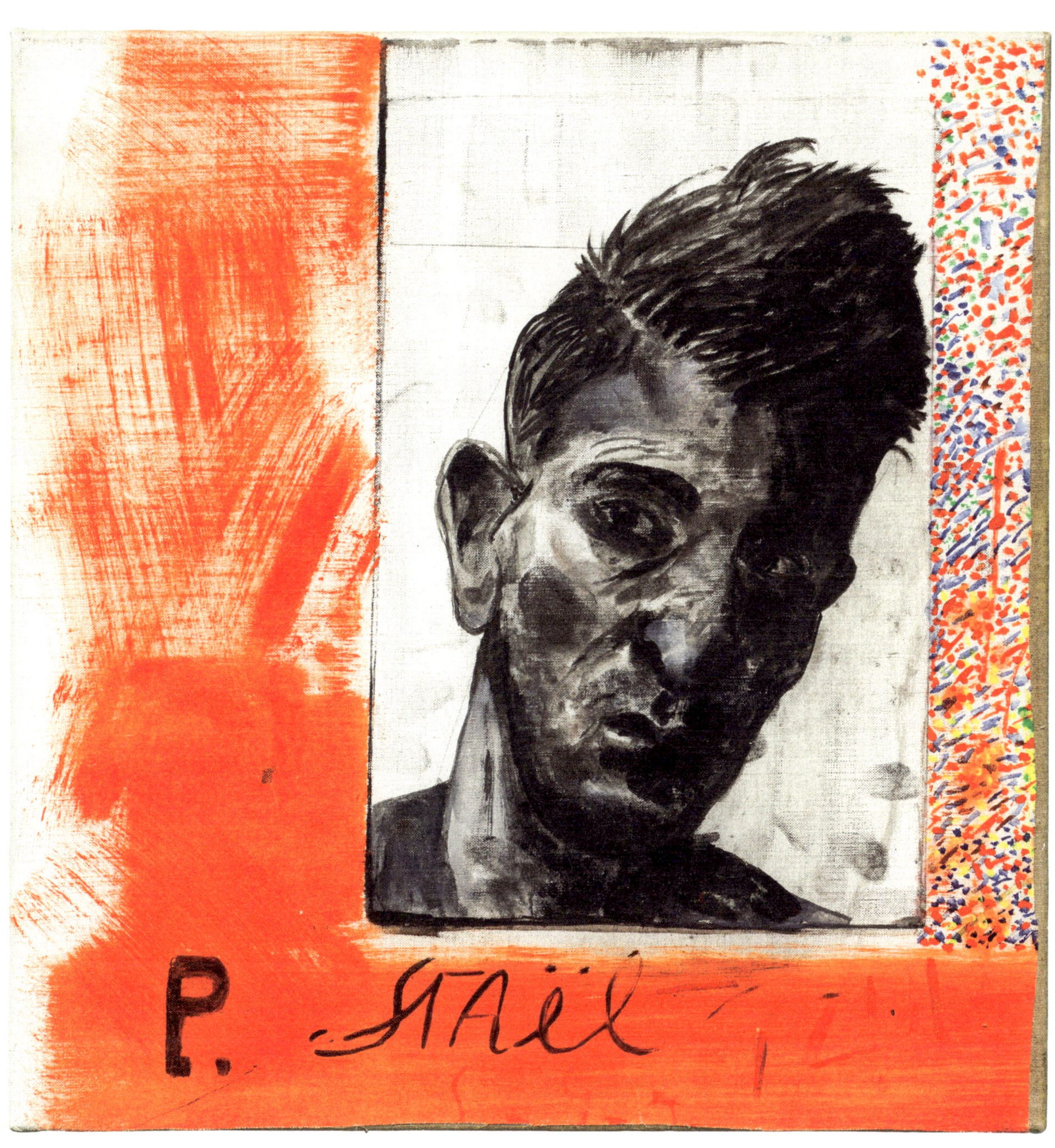

*Portrait de Nicolas de Staël*, 1983

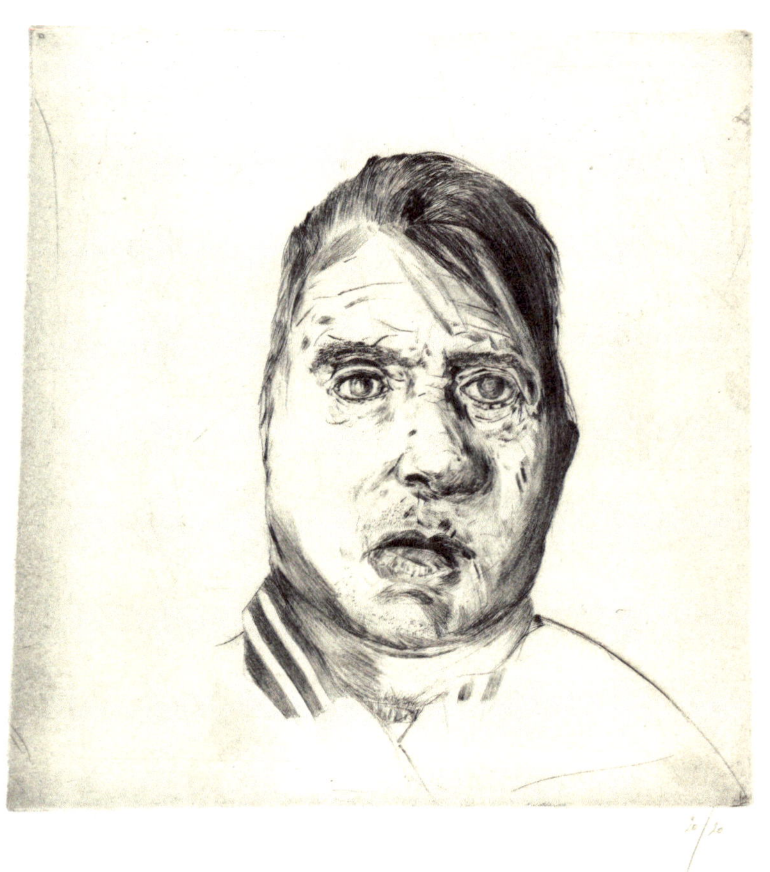

*Francis Bacon II*, 1980

*Autoportrait II*, 1980

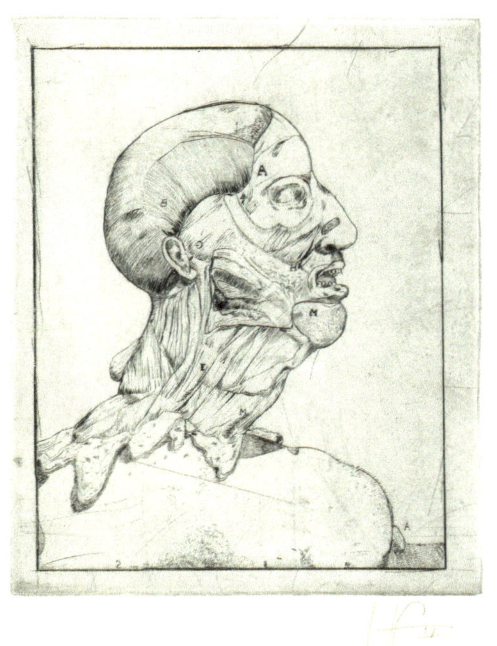

*Écorché II*, 1979

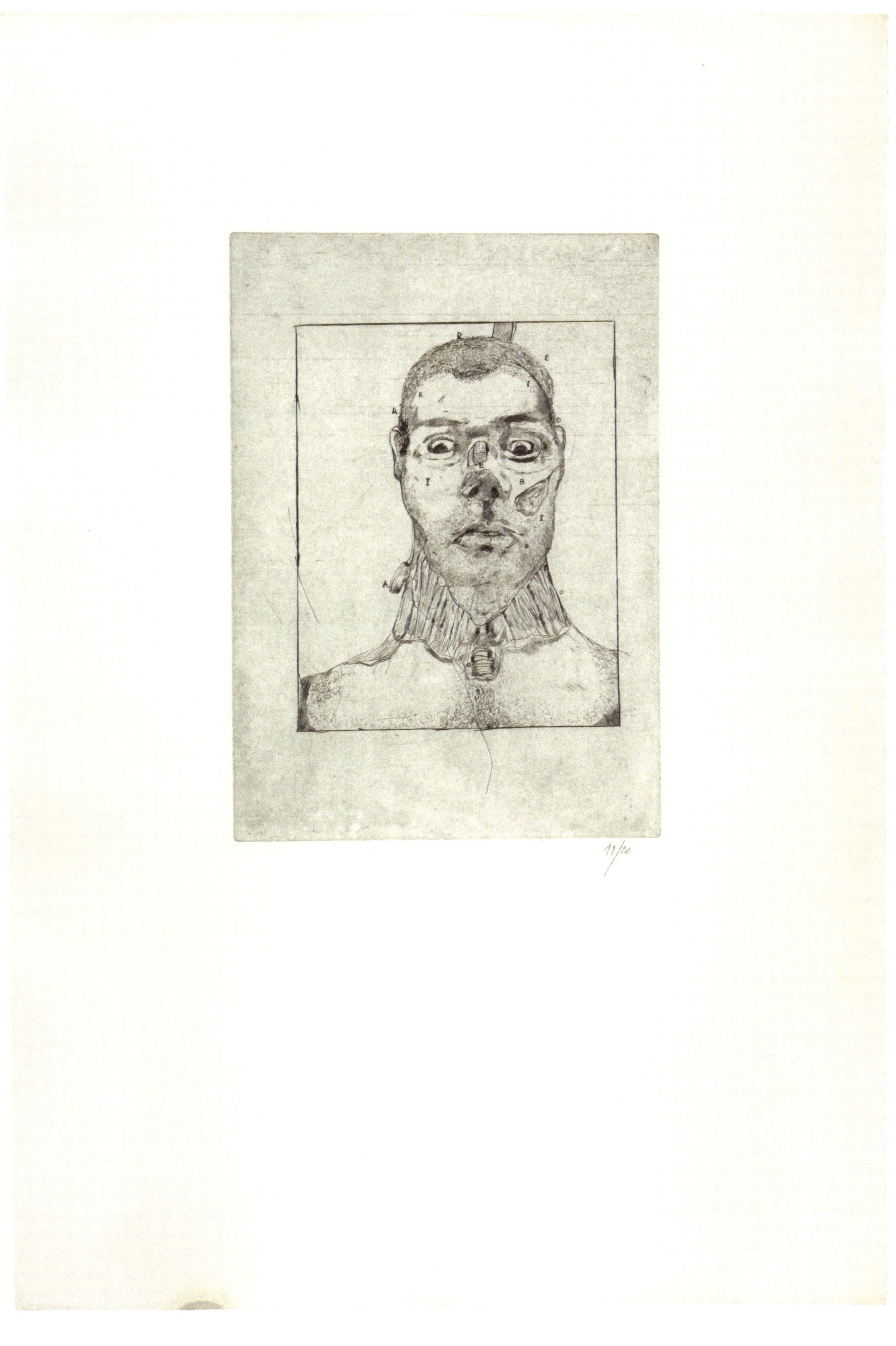

*Écorché III*, 1979

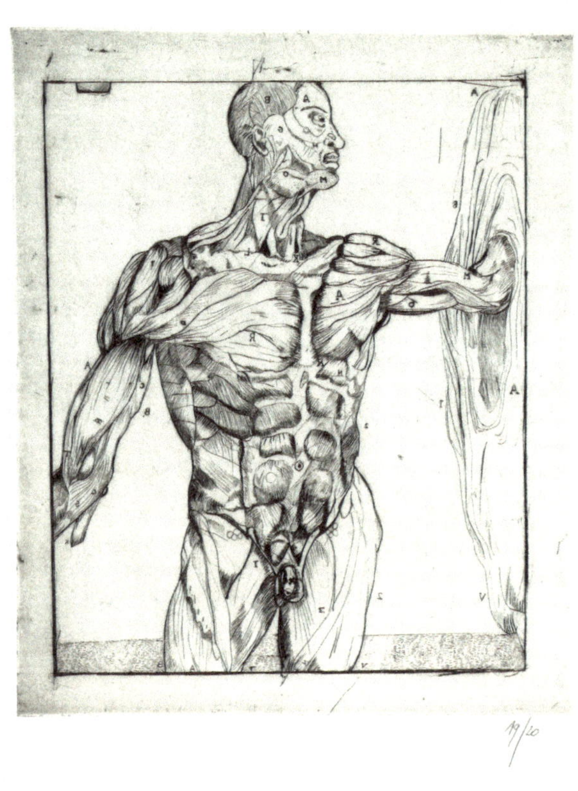

*Écorché I*, 1979

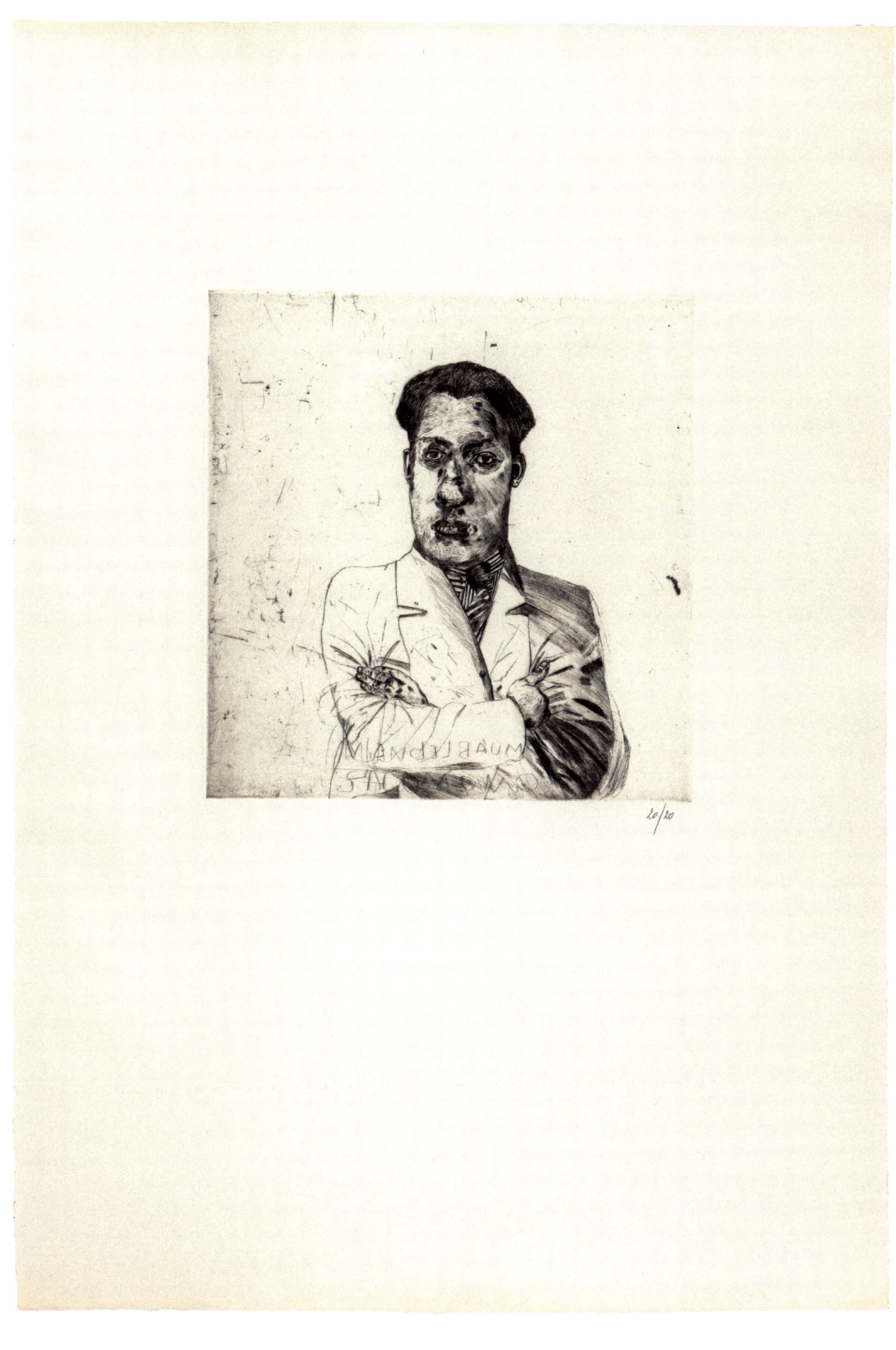

*Szulim Mandelbaum II*, 1980

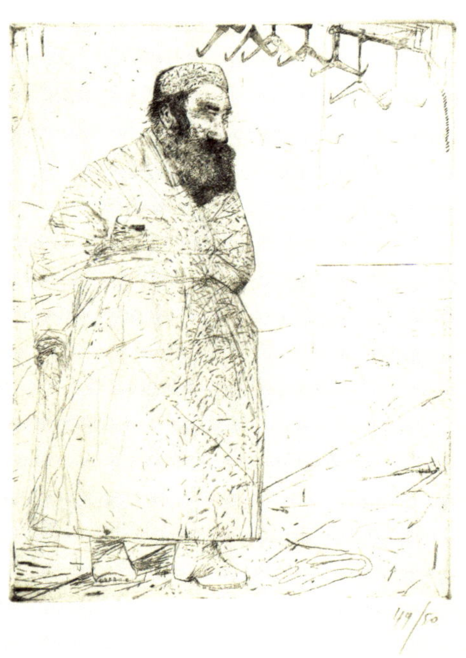

*Shohet*, 1980

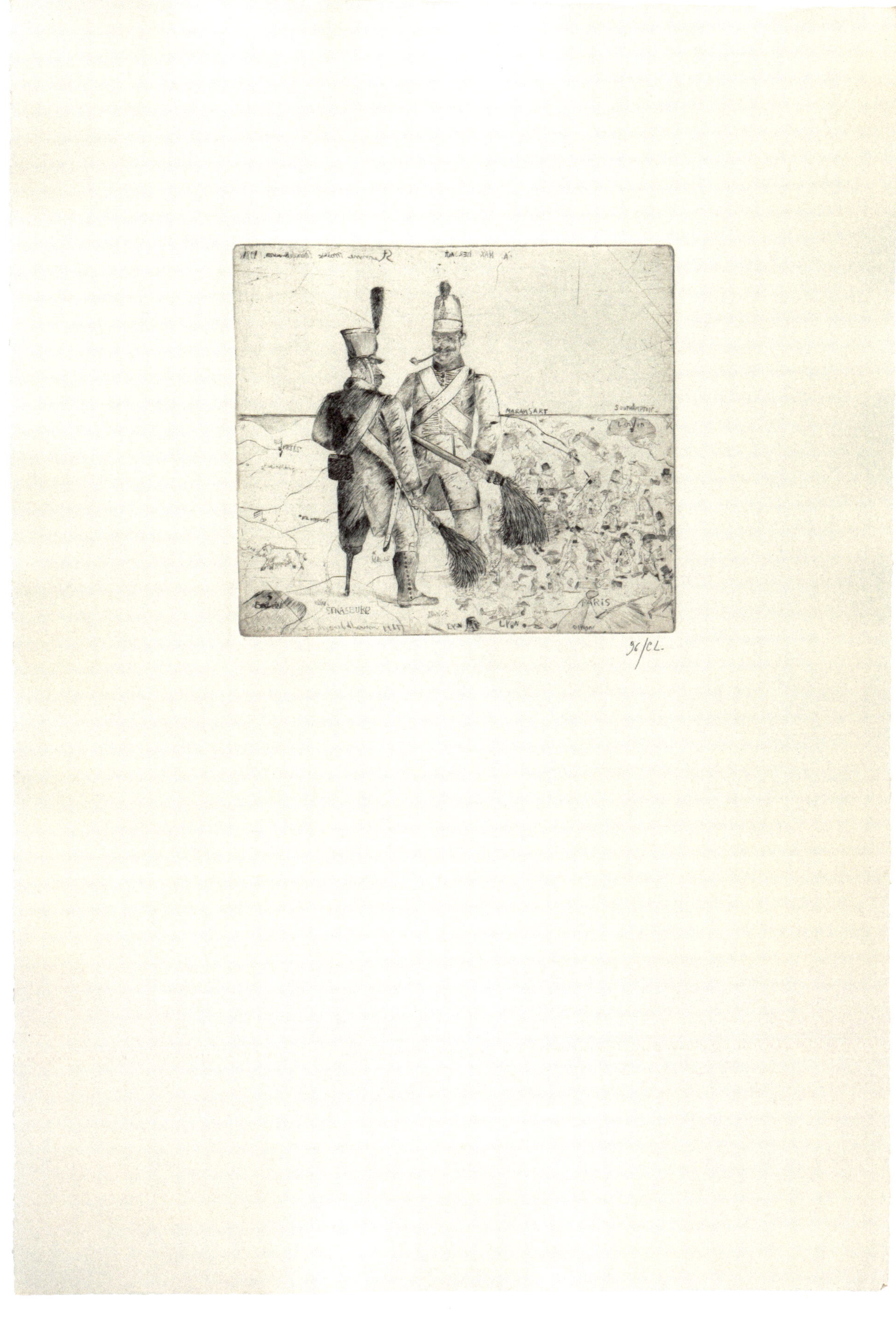


*Champ de bataille*, 1981

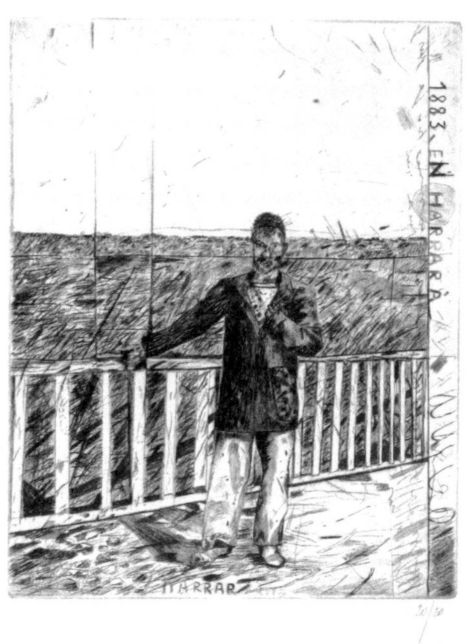


*Arthur Rimbaud I*, 1980

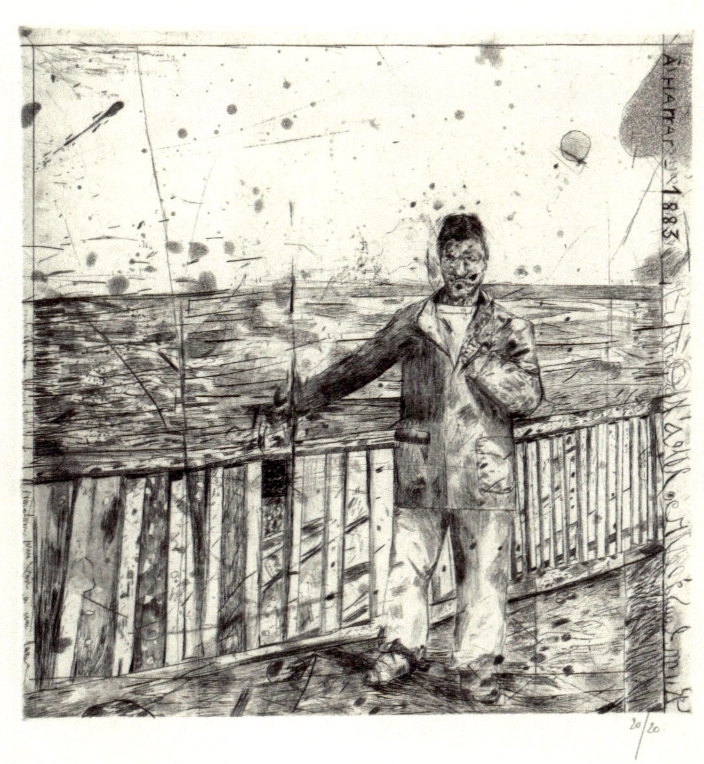

*Arthur Rimbaud II*, 1980

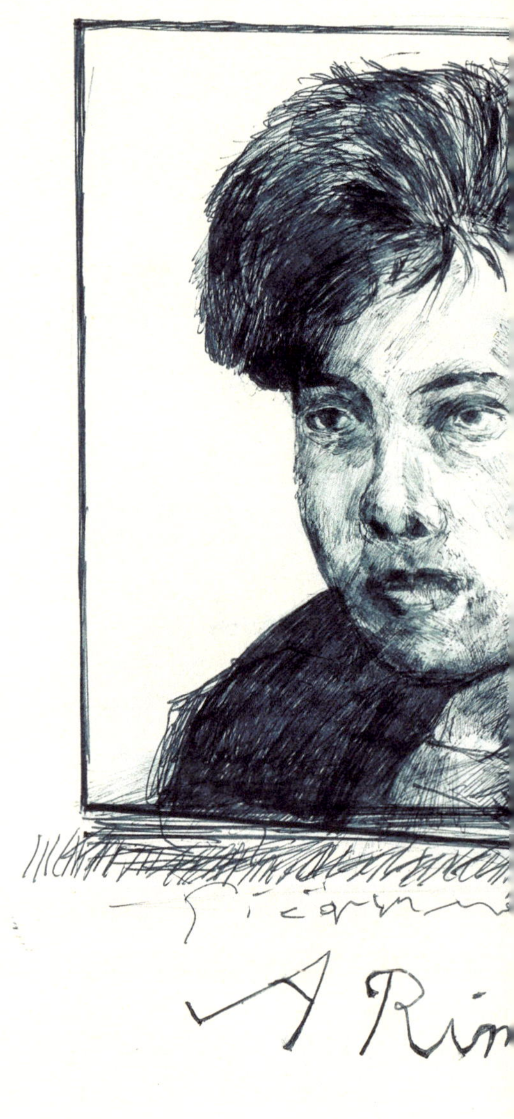

*A. Rimbaud*, 1980

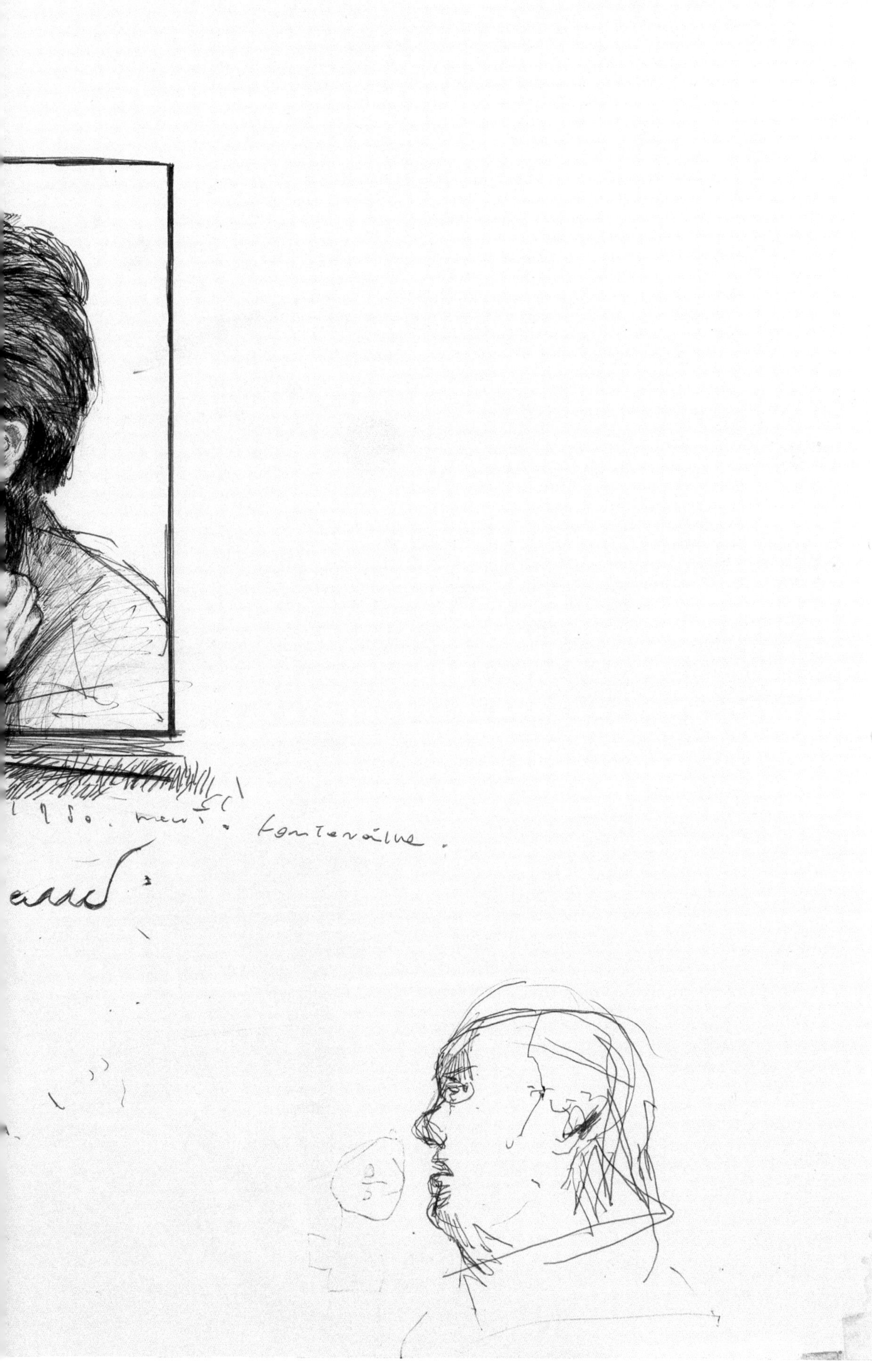

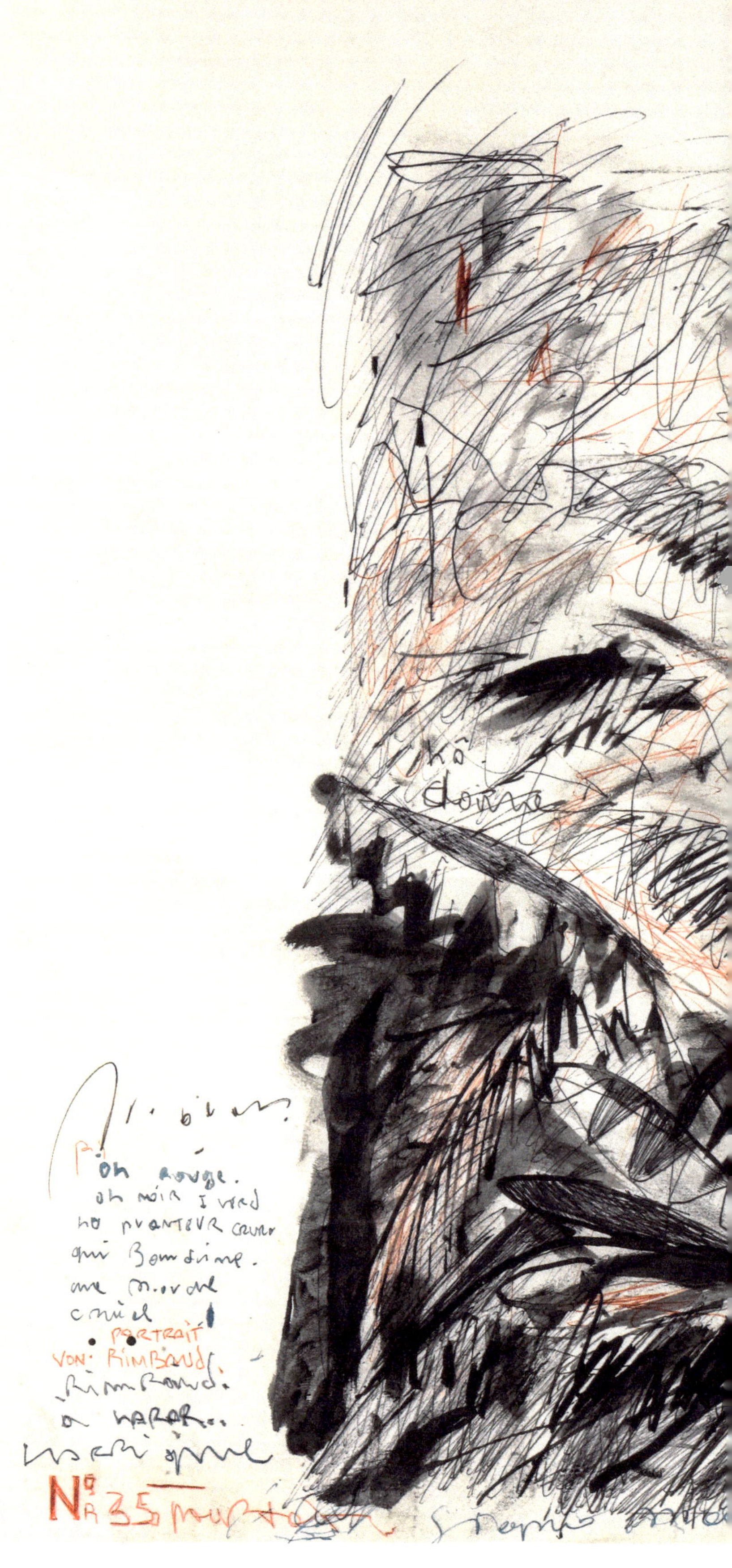

oh rouge.
PORTRAIT
VON: RIMBAUD

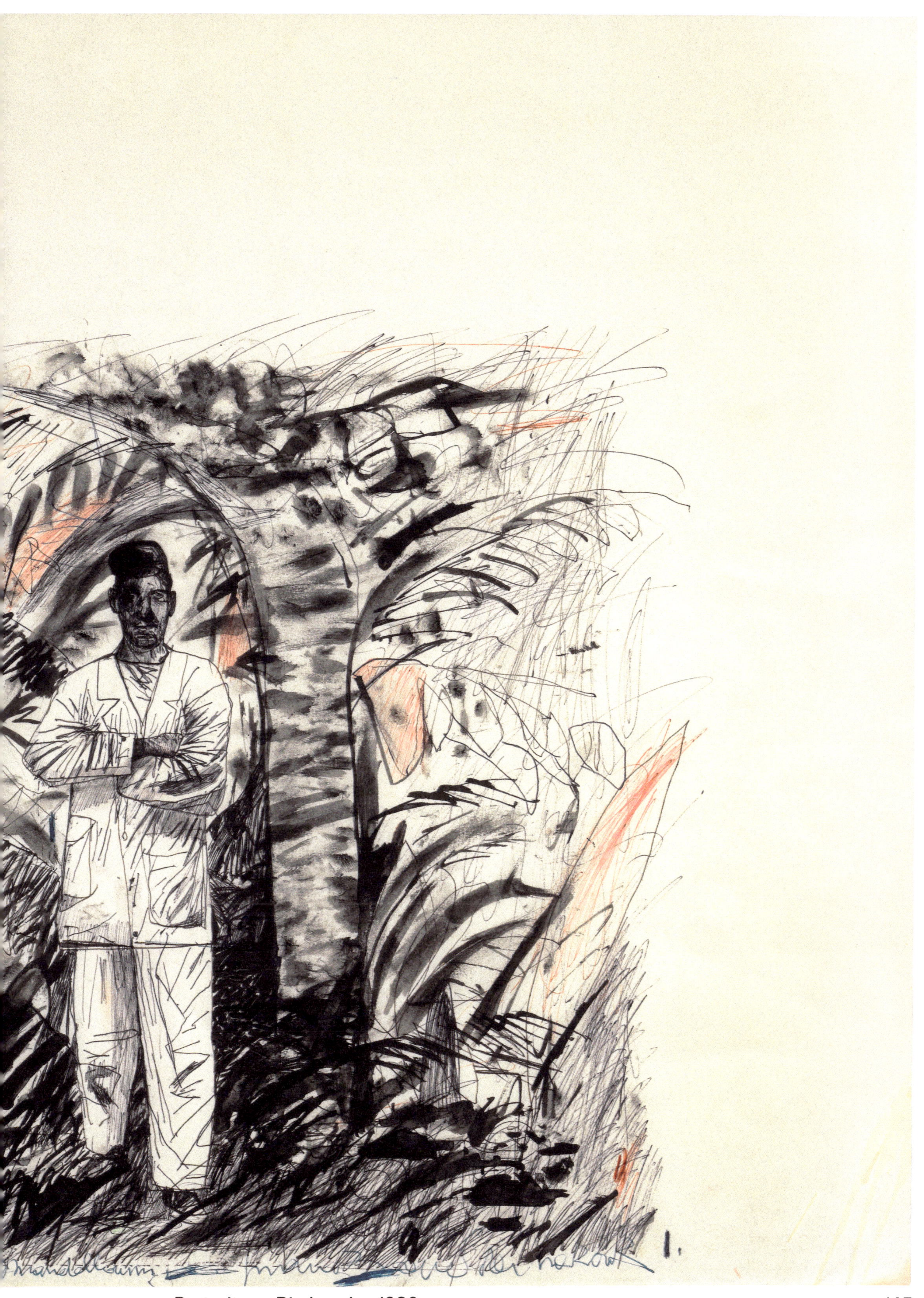

*Portrait von Rimbaud*, c. 1980

DER HAZER
PORTRAIT VON ELMUT CHULBERGER
US.
ATEIRIZ
HOPE
כשר
LIP

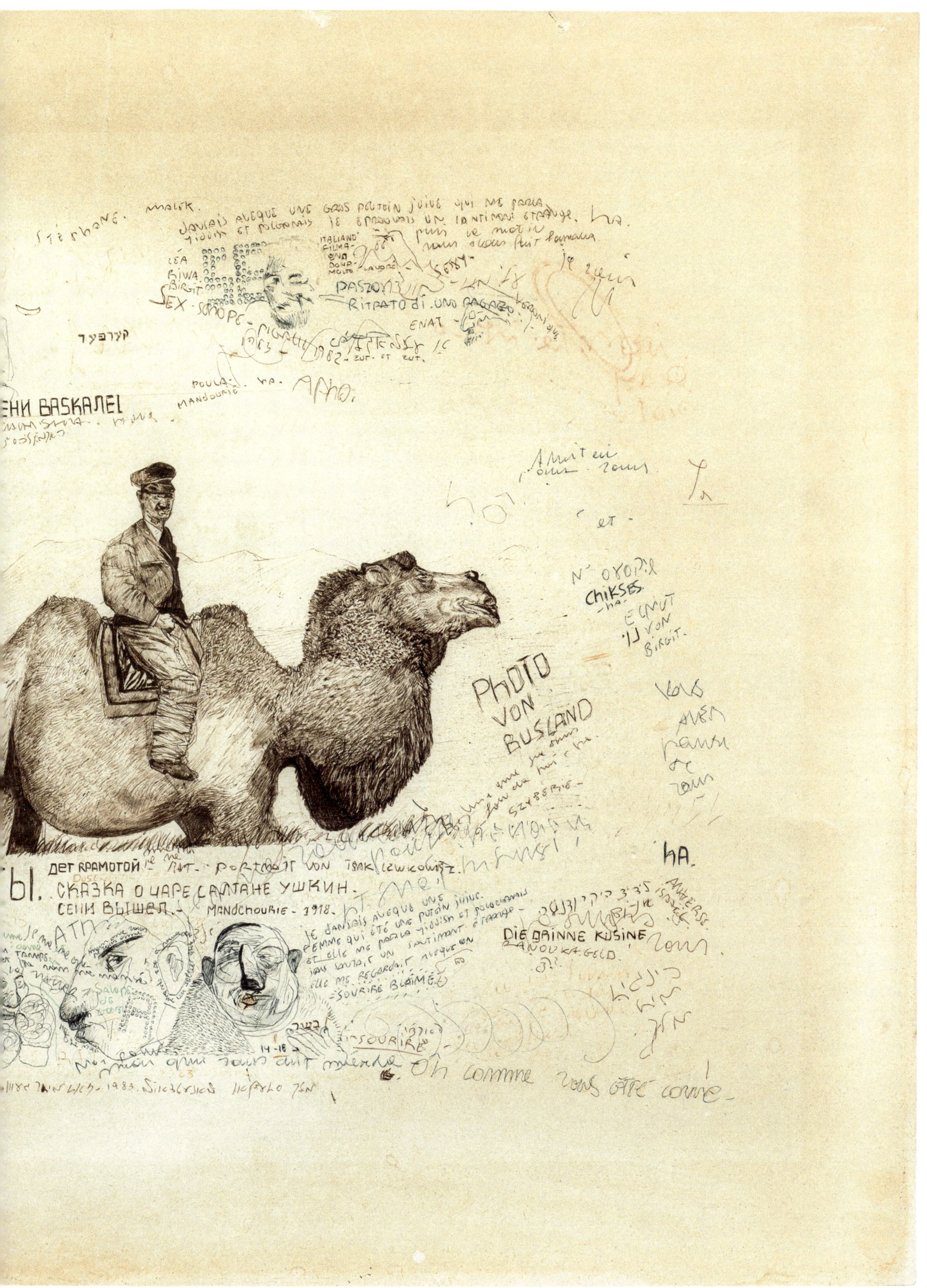


*Composition au chameau*, 1982

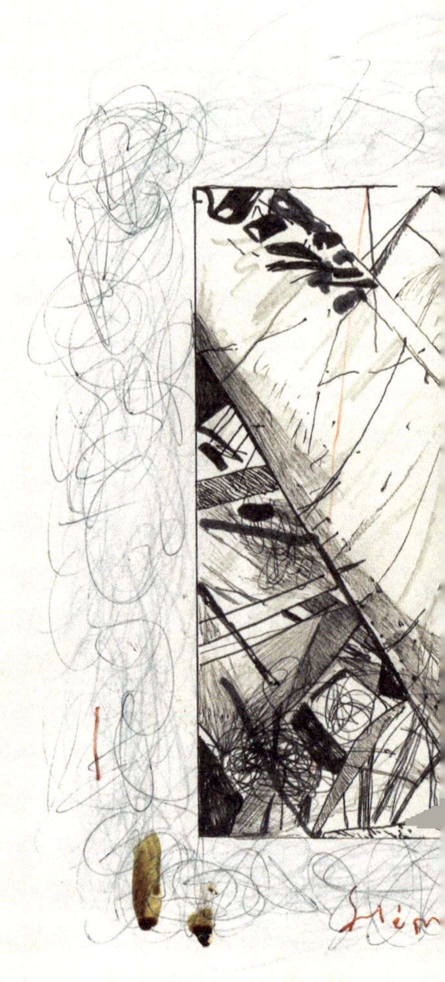

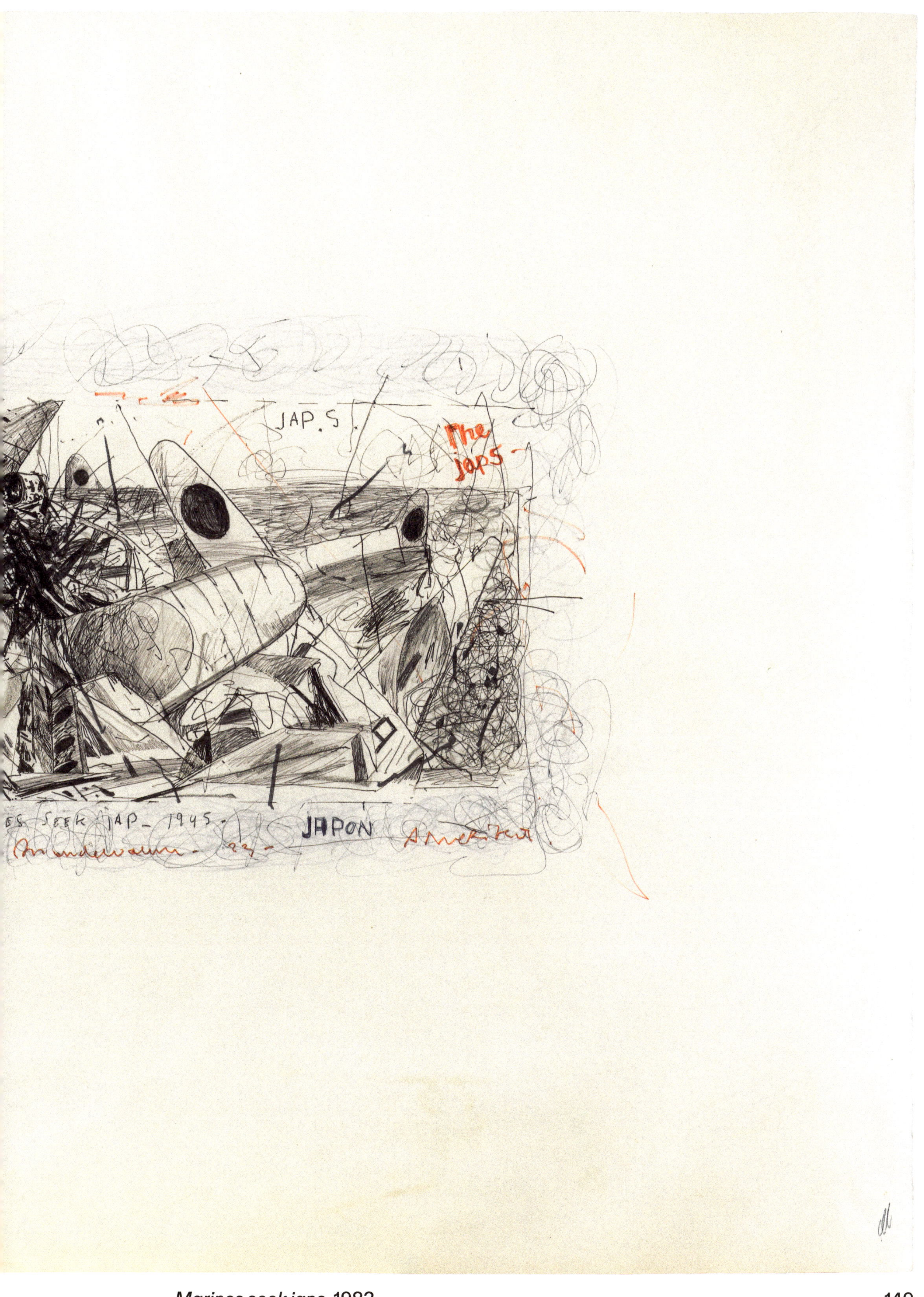


*Marines seek japs*, 1983

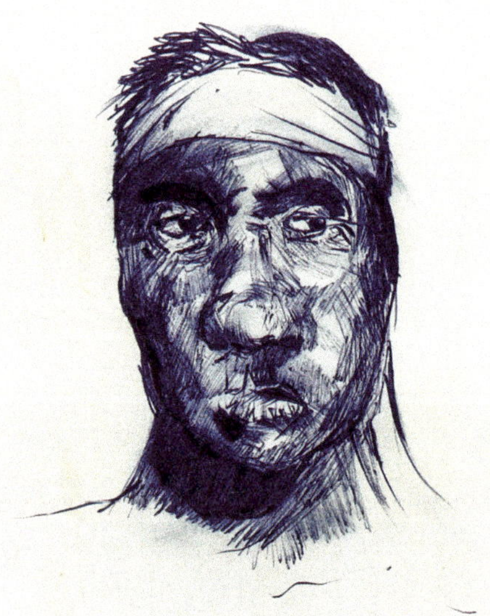

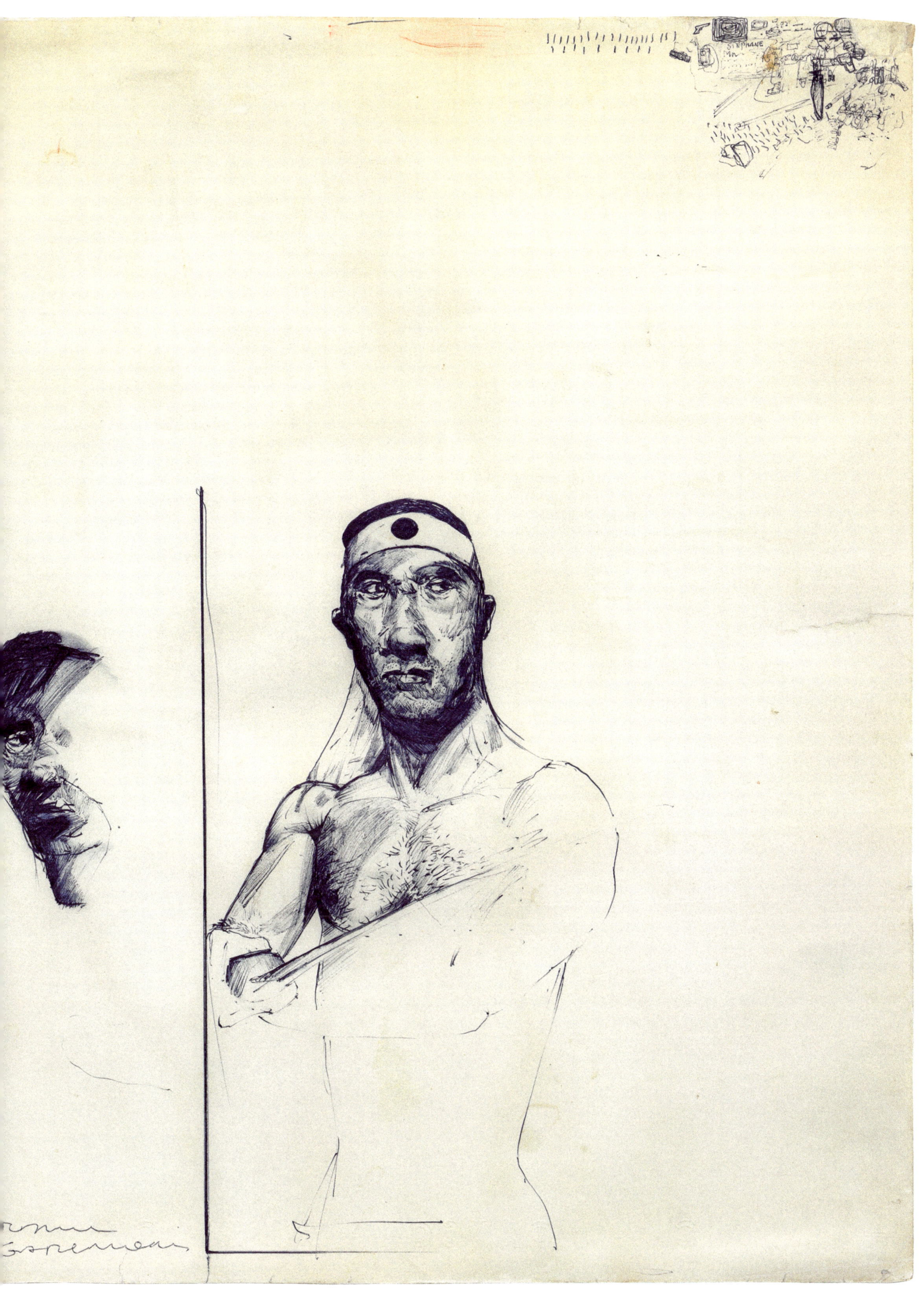

*Mishima et autoportrait*, 1984

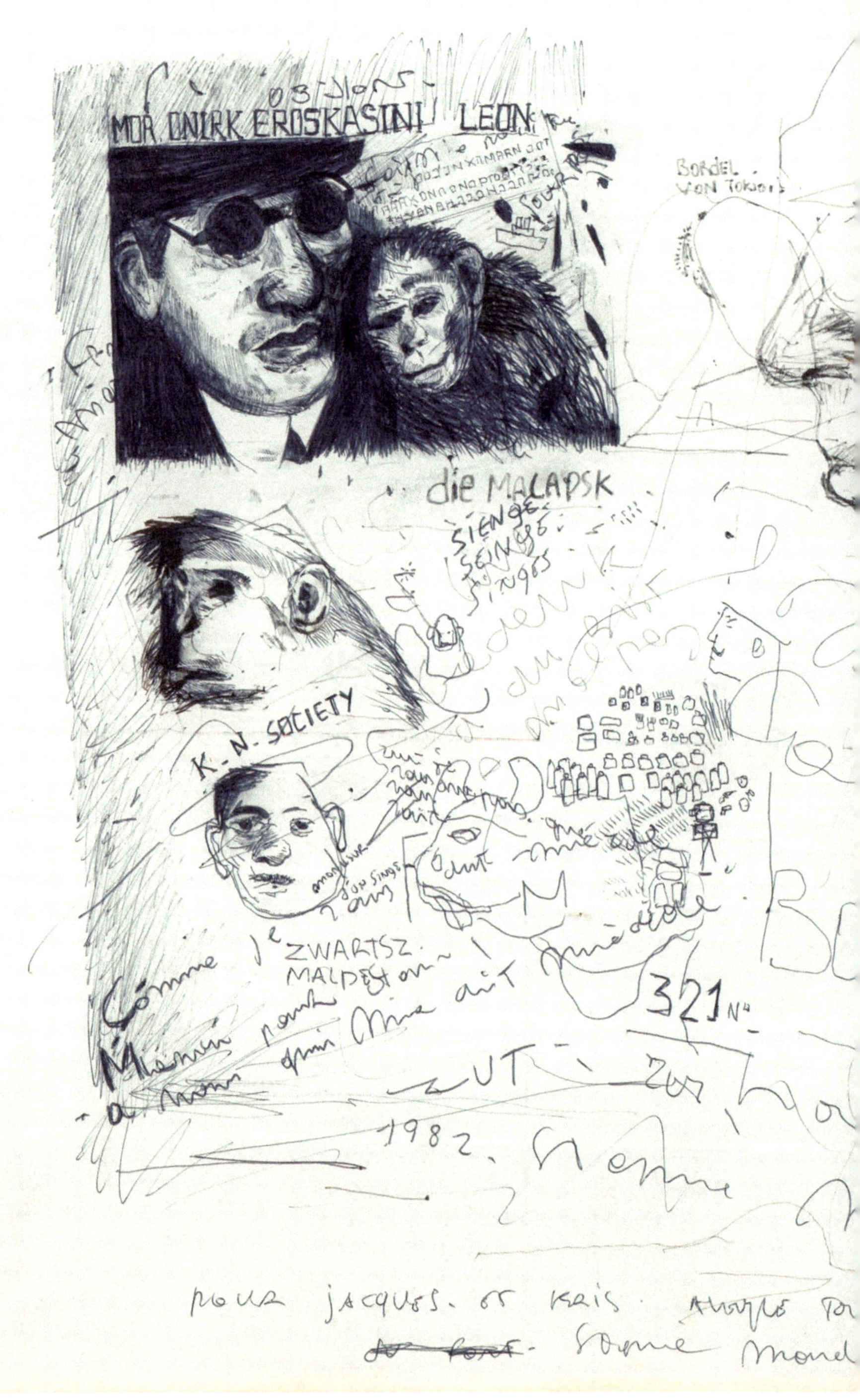


*Composition (L'Homme au singe d'atelier de Bacon)*, 1982

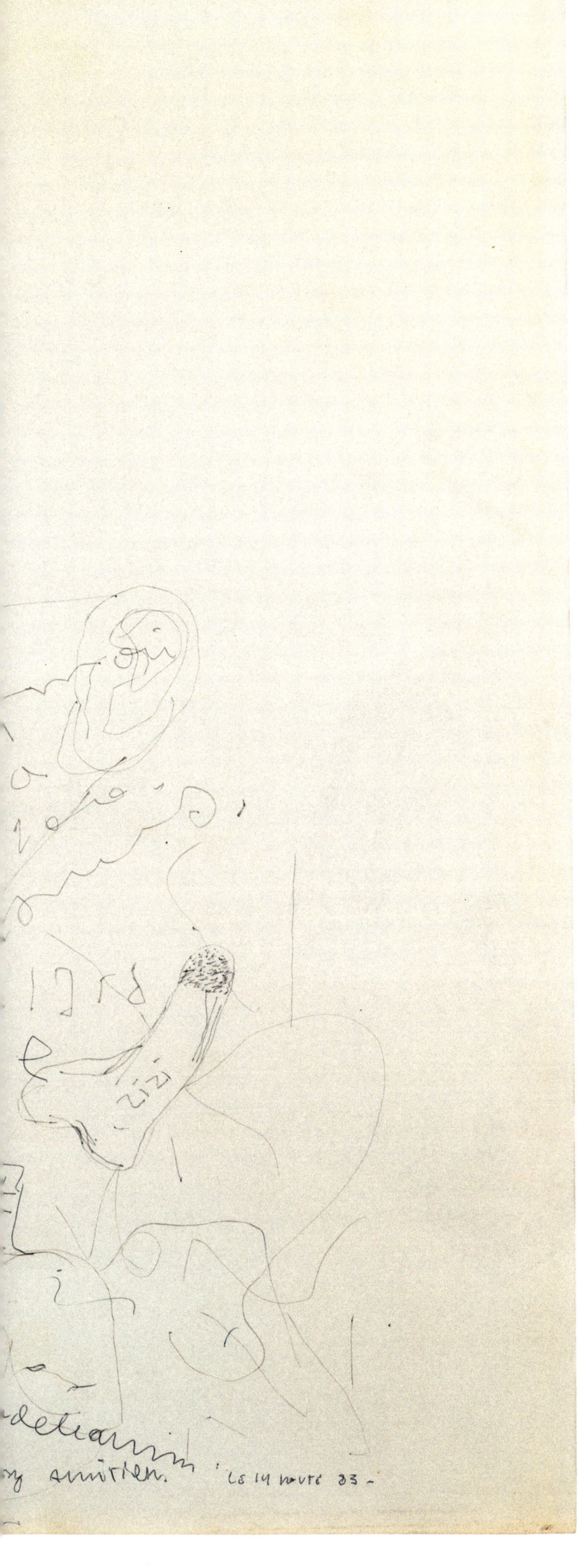

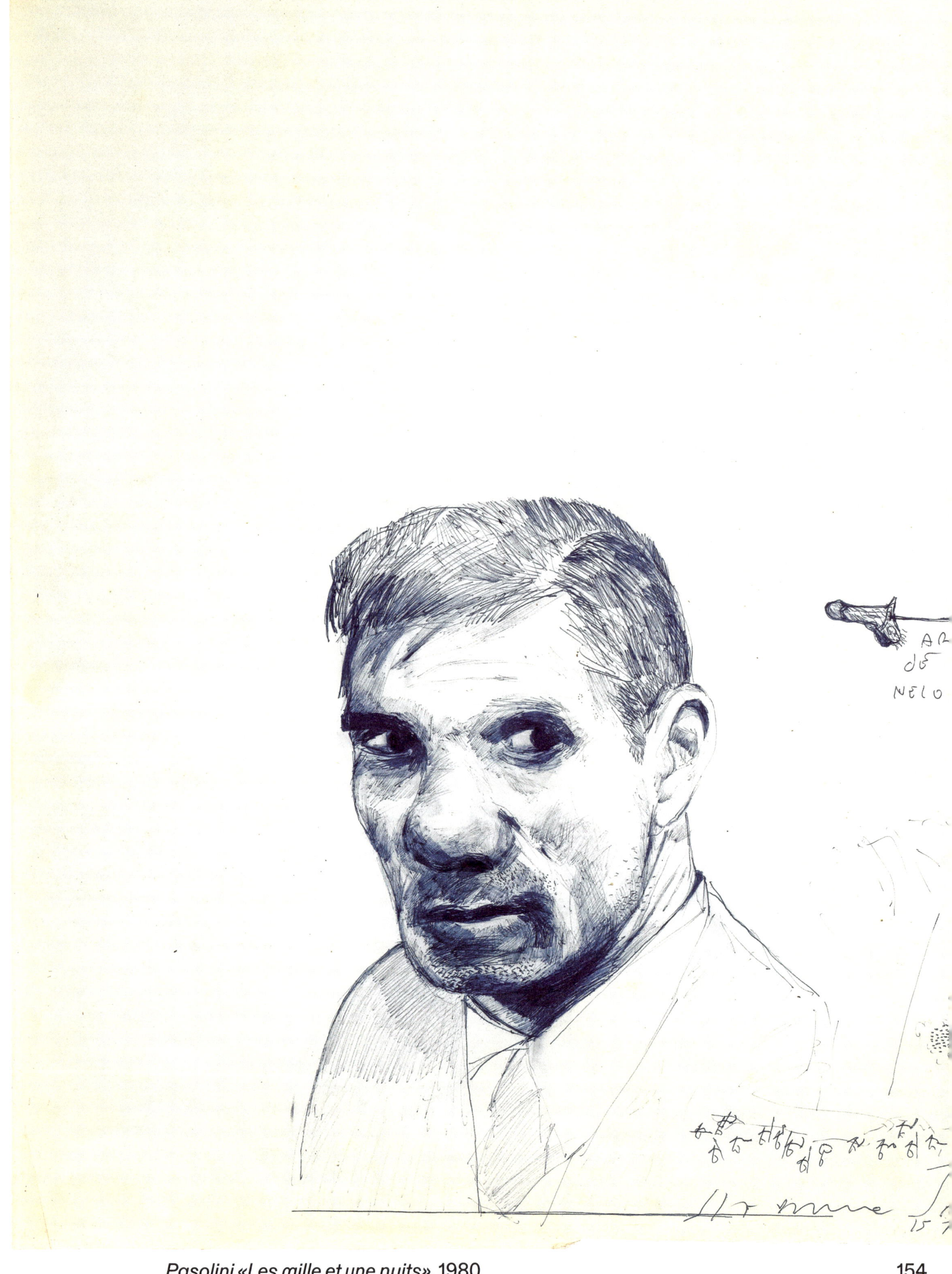

Pasolini *«Les mille et une nuits»*, 1980

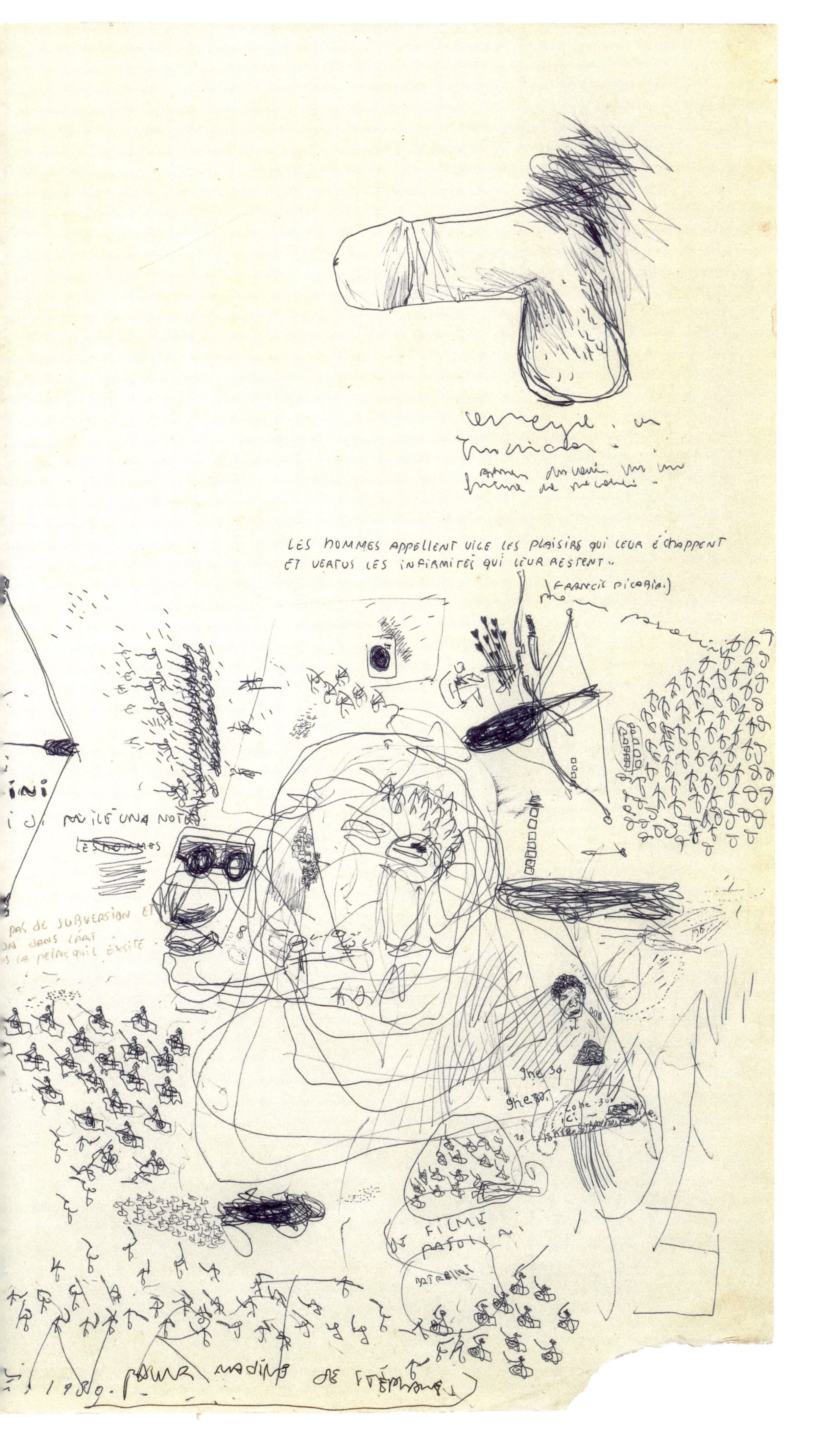
LES HOMMES APPELLENT VICE LES PLAISIRS QUI LEUR ÉCHAPPENT
ET VERTUS LES INFIRMITÉS QUI LEUR RESTENT.
(FRANCIS PICABIA)
LES HOMMES
PAS DE SUBVERSION ET
ON DANS L'ART
S LA PEINE QUIL EXISTE
FILME
PASOLINI
1989.

11h30.

1980.

dimanche
18. mais.
9h30.
matin
1980.

CANE.

SIRO di
TOTUMO. MIAM
CARNICERO.

PASO

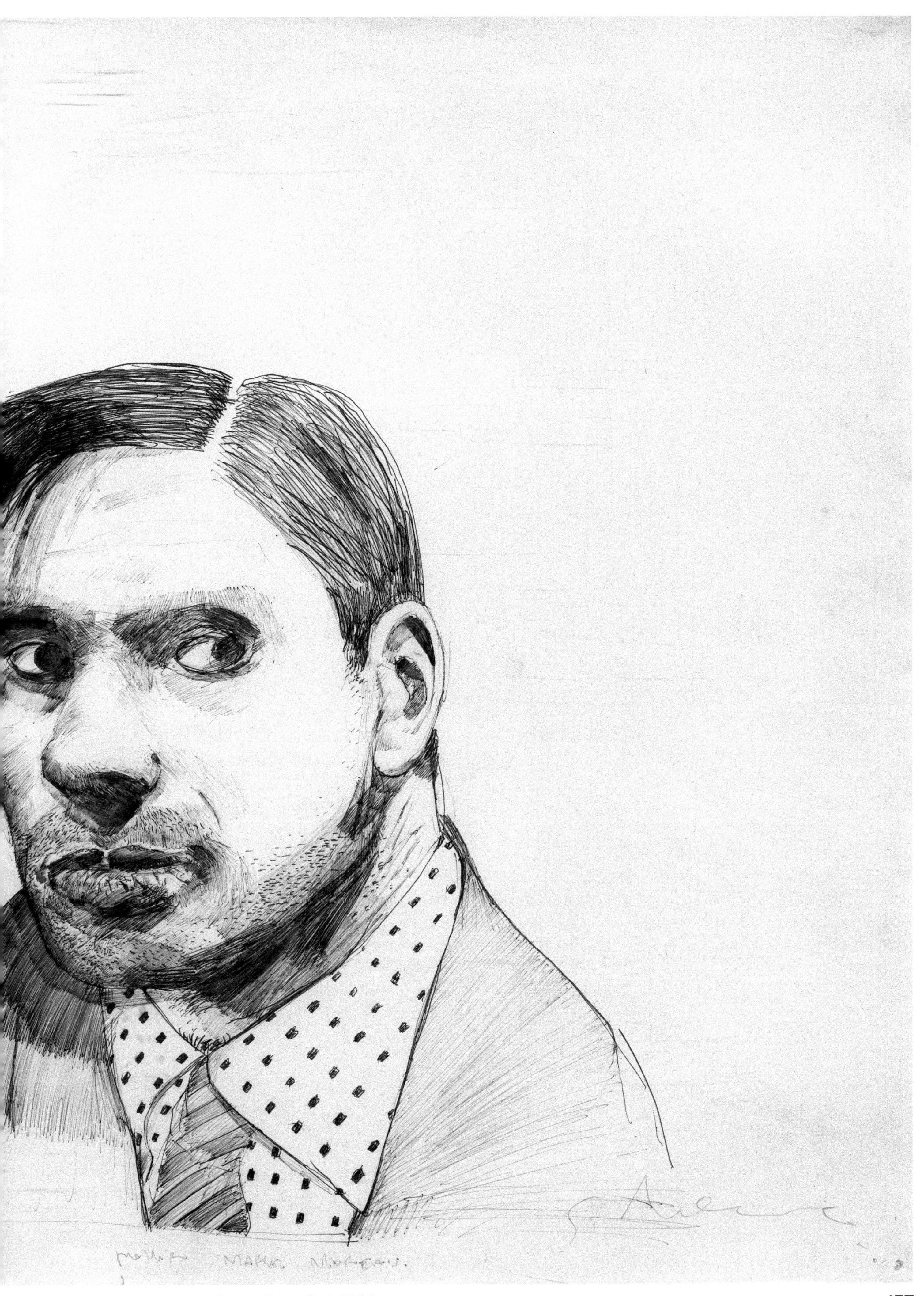

*Pier Paolo Pasolini*, 1980

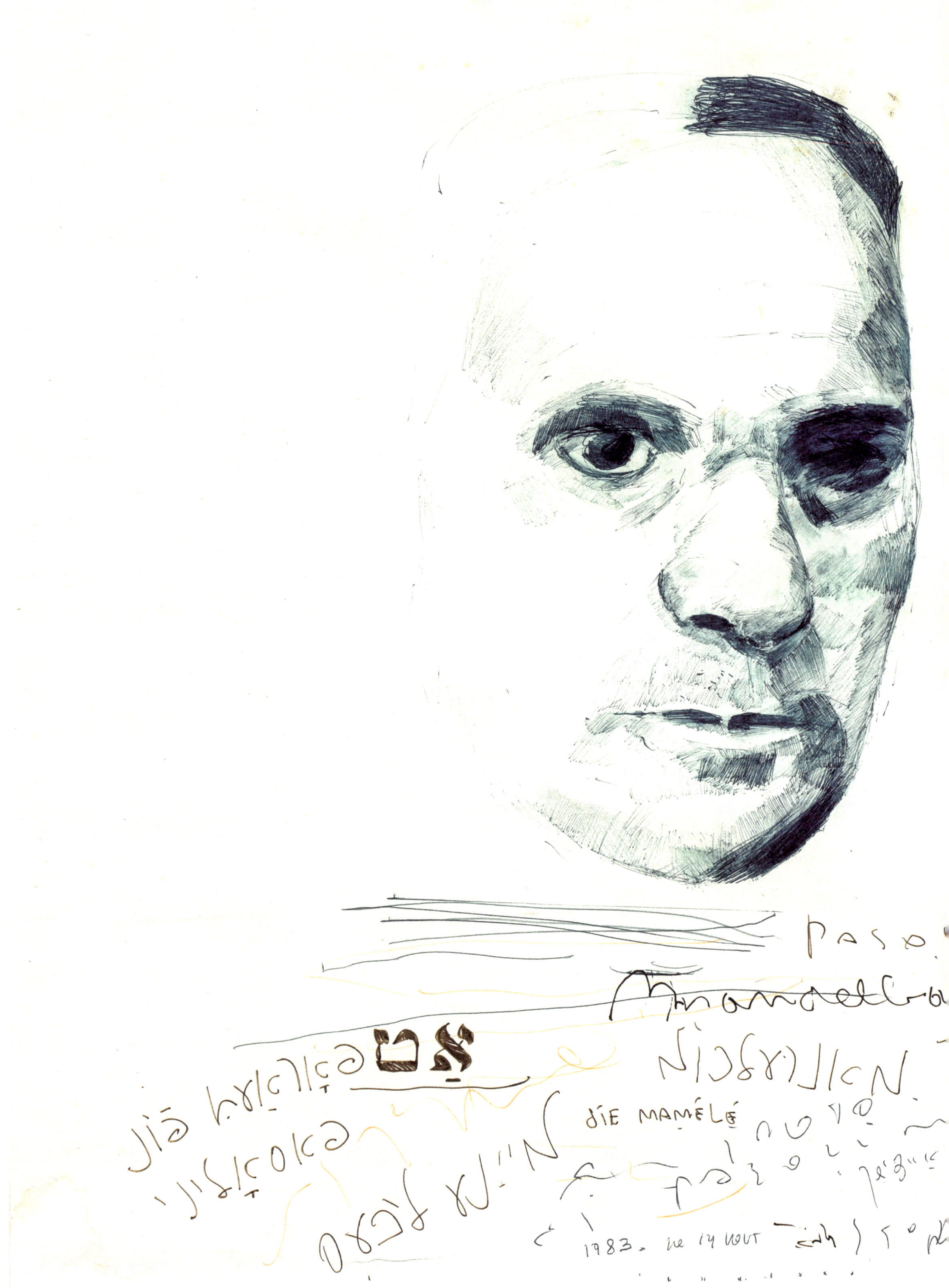


*Pier Paolo Pasolini*, 1980

[illegible]

[illegible] !

[illegible]

[illegible] !

[illegible] et Jacques du fond du [illegible]

Vendredi 6 juin 1950.

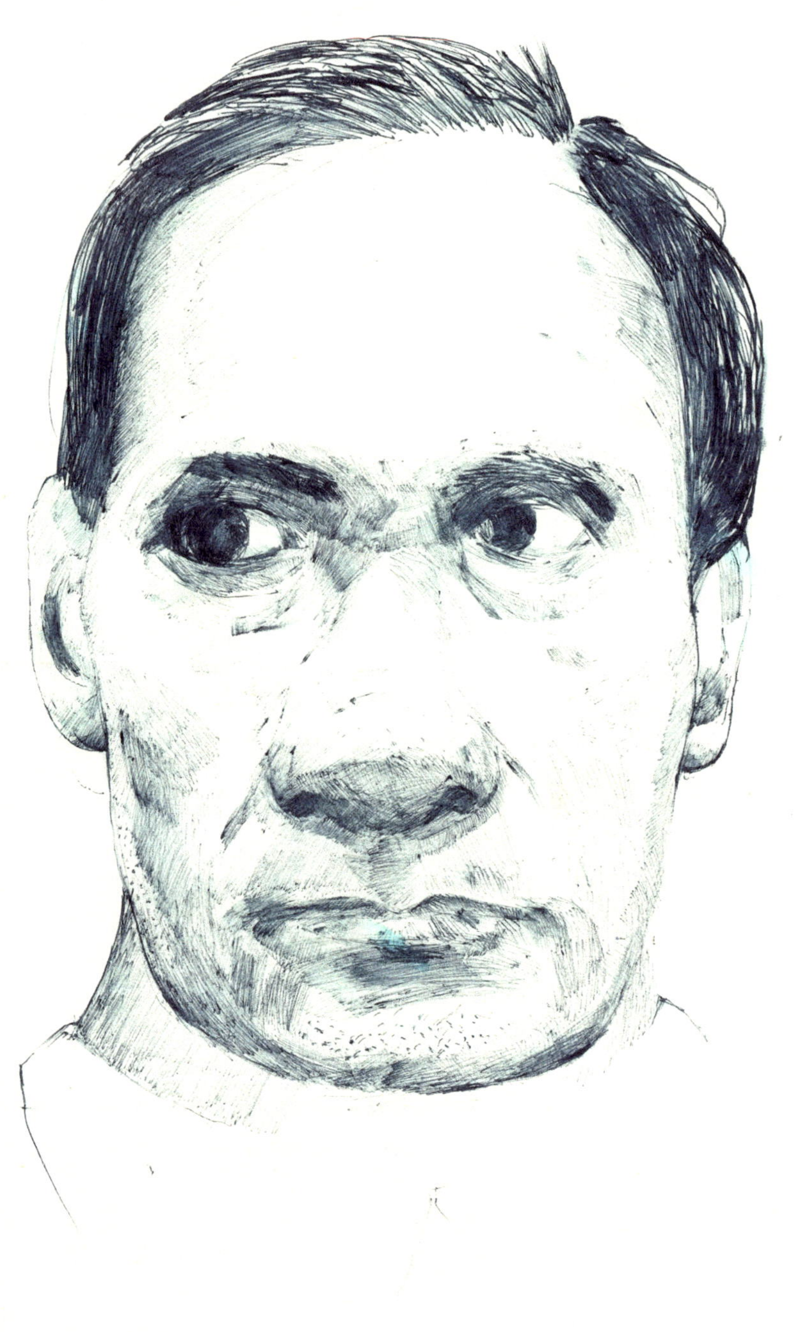

*Pier Paolo Pasolini (Antonello de Messine, 1477–1478)*, 1980

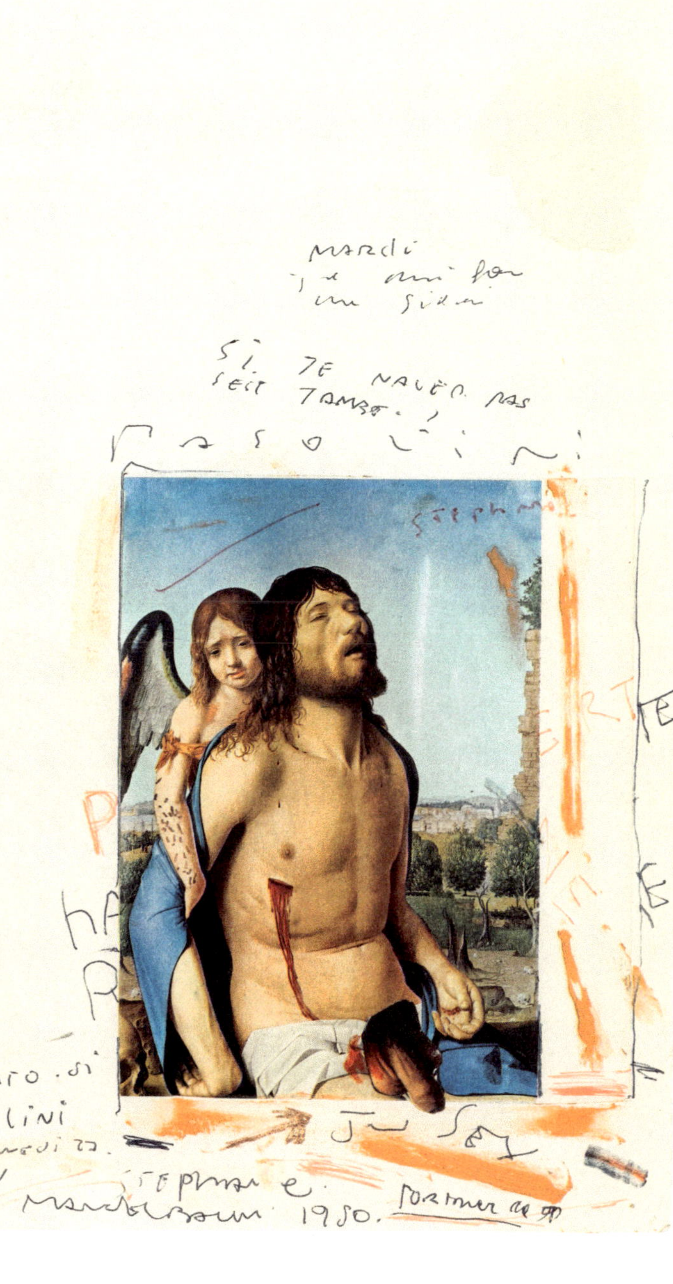

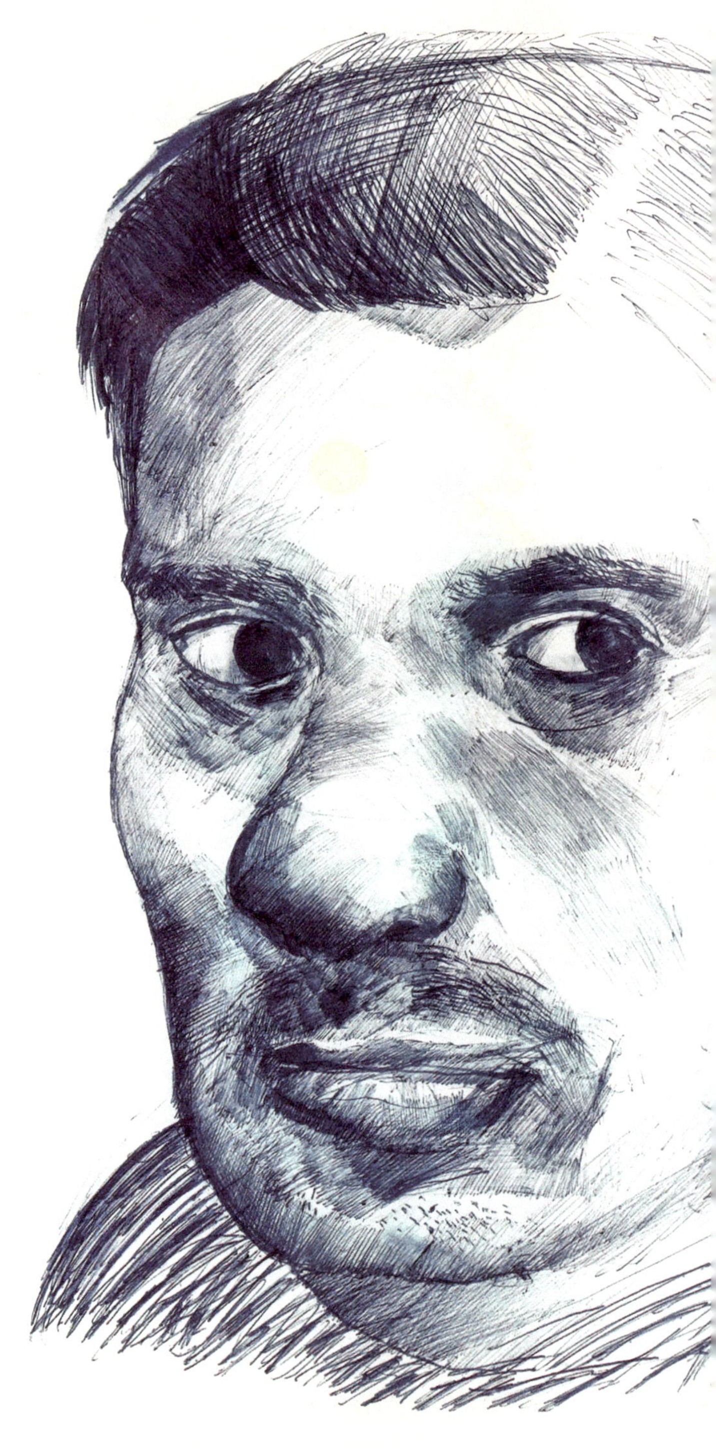

*Pasolini*, 1980

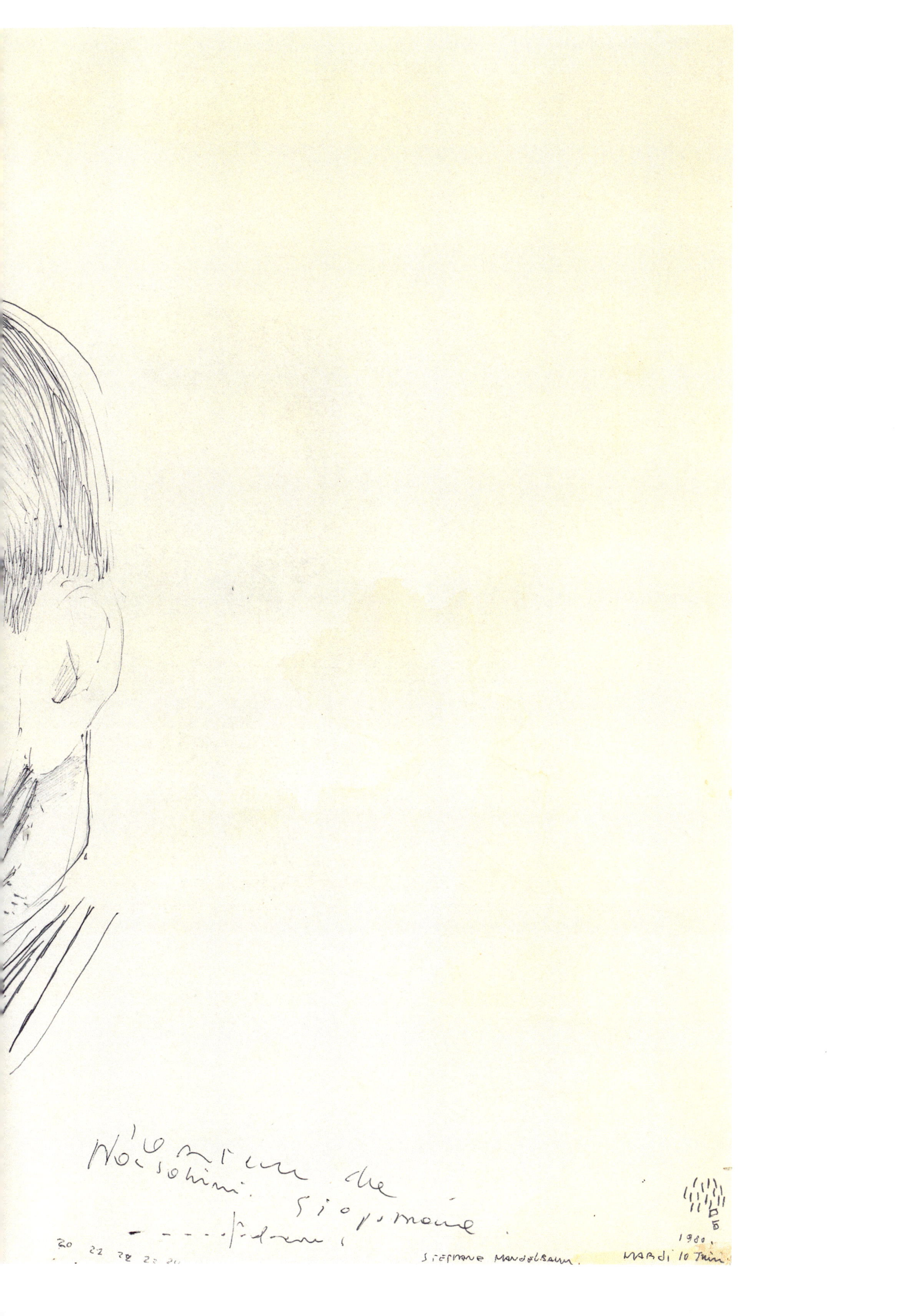

20 22 28 22 20

STEPHANE MANDELBAUM.

1980.
MARDI 10 JUIN.

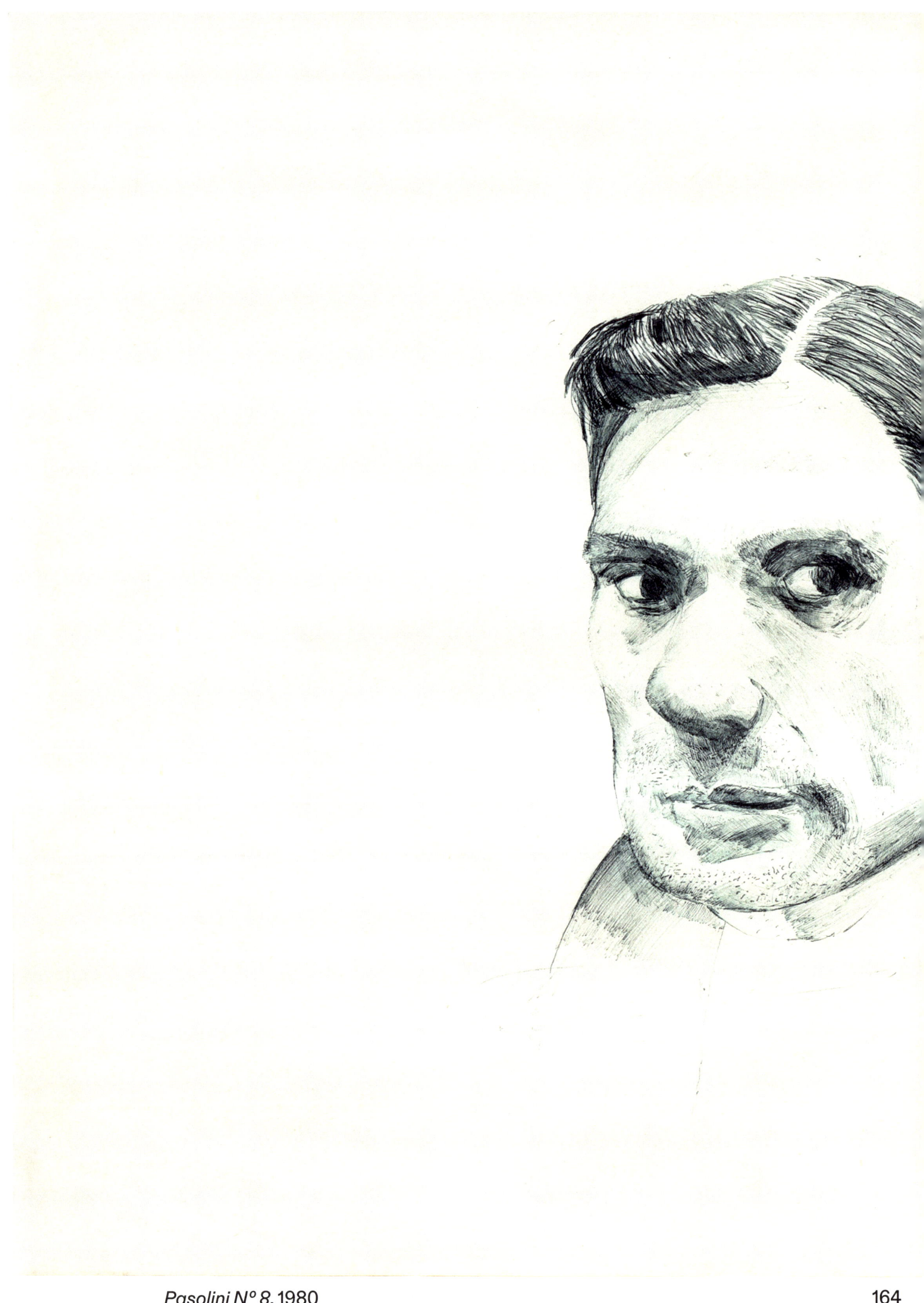

*Pasolini N° 8*, 1980

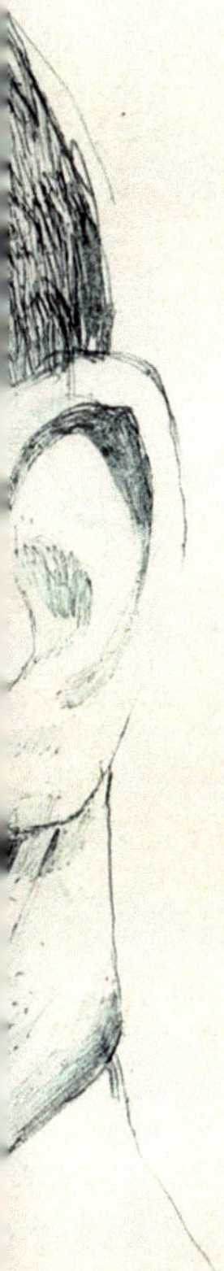

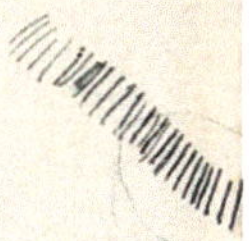

אָ.בֶּ

24 Jenin

Pasolini

Nop-Jessins,

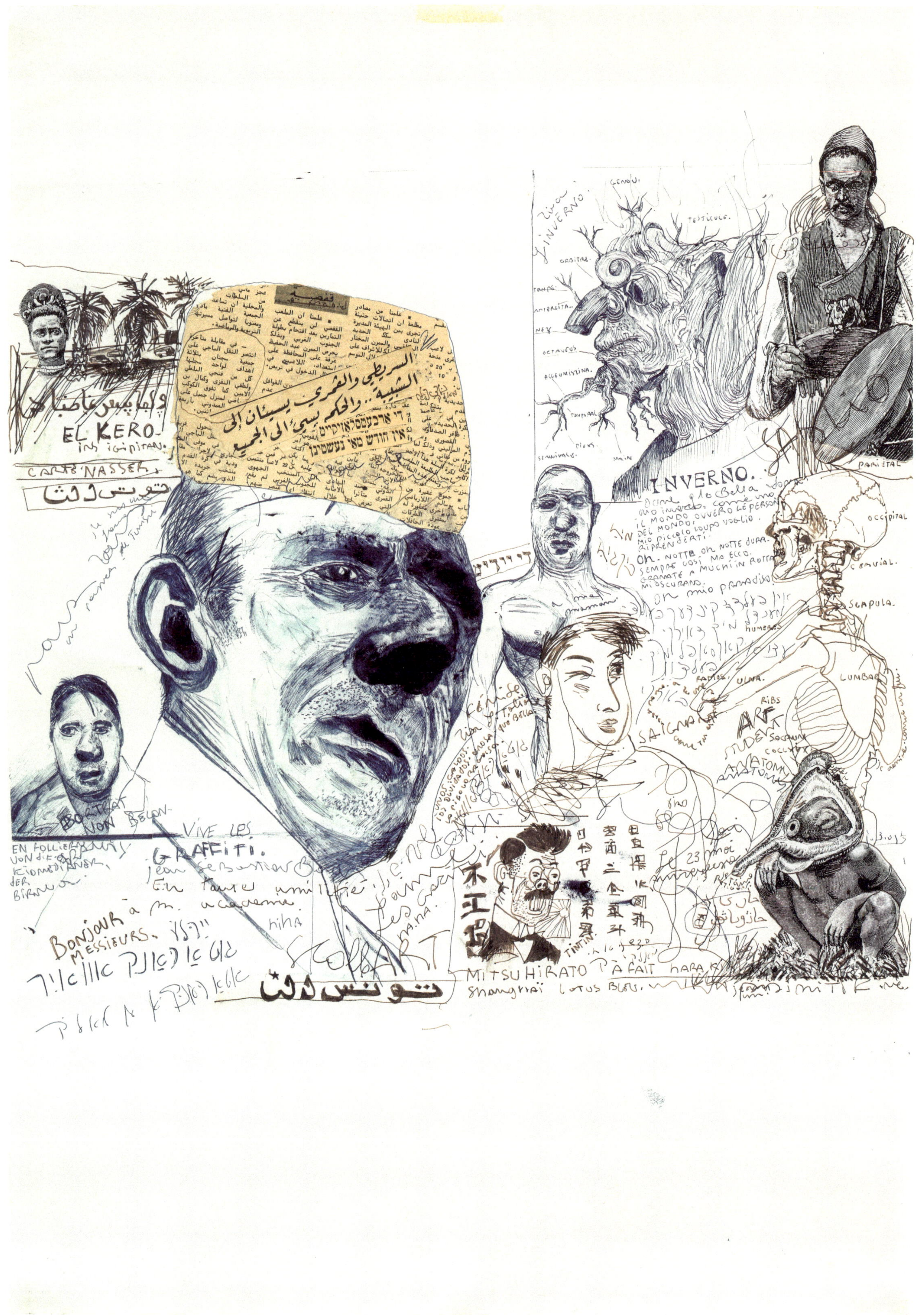

*Composition (El Kero)*, 1981

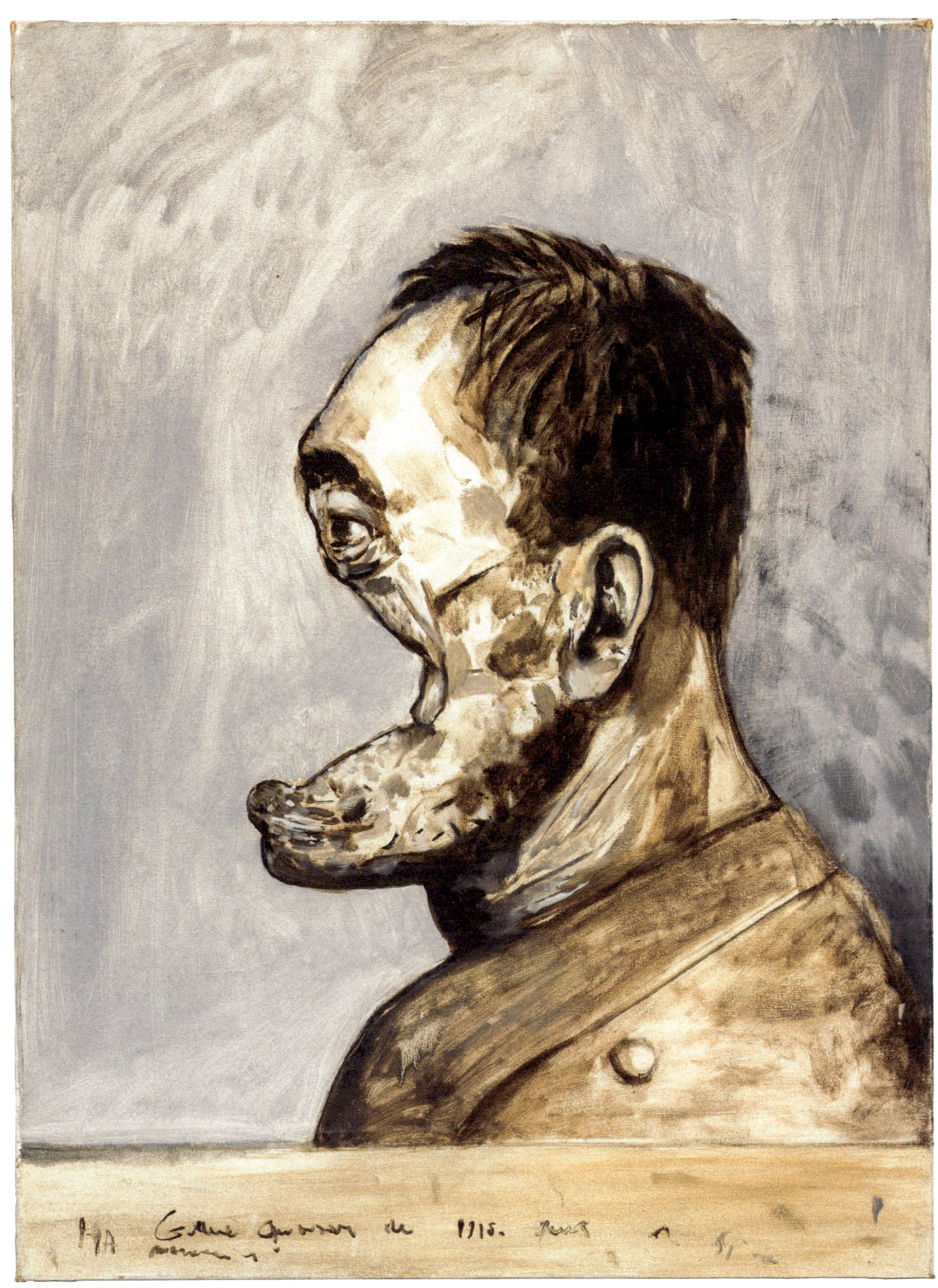

*Gueule cassée*, c. 1980

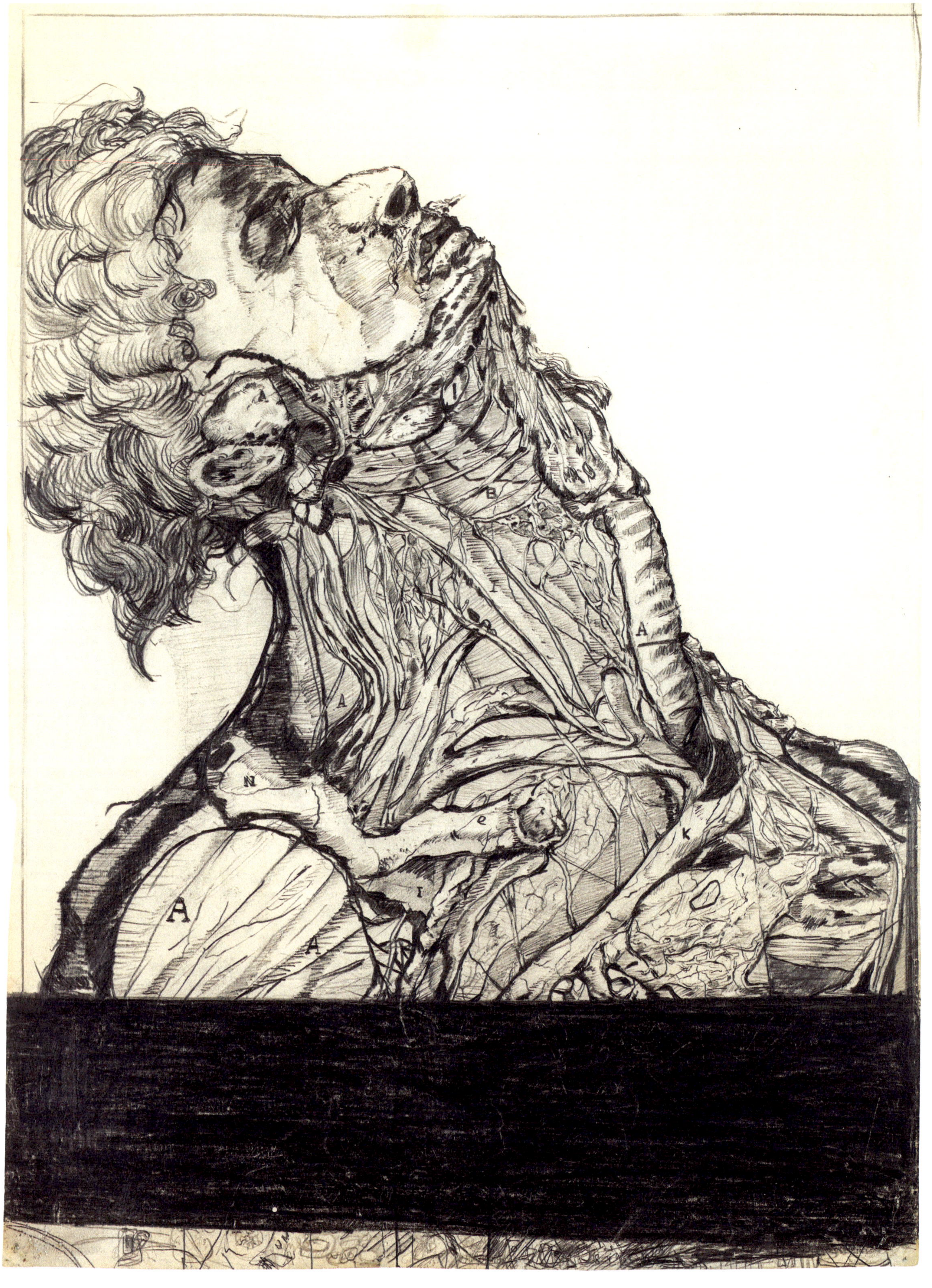

*Écorché*, 1978

# A History of Violence in Europe since the Holocaust, Unfinished
Diedrich Diederichsen

More than half of Stéphane Mandelbaum's works visible today are portraits, and nearly all of them, even those of a different structure or following other artistic genres, contain further collaged, integrated portraits. From 1975 to 1986—the years he was active—that is, there were few artists who believed so strongly in the portrait as a representation and likeness of a specific person. Other formats and media had taken over the task of registering and storing people's unmistakable traces. Even in the (art) photography of the era, between Cindy Sherman and Thomas Ruff, the portrait appears as an aspect of the culture industry and surveillance state, beyond the international reach of the individual artist: stereotypes, stars, and mugshots. And even if Mandelbaum's preferred drawing media and techniques—ink, pencil, charcoal, which were also not very relevant during the first half of the 1980s—were experiencing a revival, for example in the drawings of Raymond Pettibon that were no longer produced just for record covers but also for the art market or in the *Hotel Drawings* of Martin Kippenberger of the late 1980s and early 1990s, in parallel with an international comeback of the underground comic and caricature, few had faith in the portrait as a real reference. It remained a form of the reappropriation of stereotypes, pastiches, and so on that had been worn out by the culture industry. In a sense, people shied away from the visual use of proper and real names.

In Mandelbaum's case, by contrast, it went in the opposite direction. With the same fierceness and directness that he employed for self-portraits and portraits of his father, the famous Belgian artist Arié Mandelbaum, and of his grandfather, Szulim Mandelbaum, a Shoah survivor, he drew portraits of George Dyer and Pier Paolo Pasolini, which were clearly based on press photos and other publicly accessible images, but as if they were people close to him. In his work, Pasolini, who was often depicted in the second half of the 1970s, becomes a personally familiar, elusive character who, in the sum of his portraits by Mandelbaum, becomes a very private, fierce, difficult-to-understand, gruff, but also inimitable person with the gift of sarcastic wit. In all of these portraits as evocations, very much against the contemporary postmodern irony, there are, despite the varied and usually very skillfully employed techniques, strange continuities: a penchant for potato noses, say, which one could understand in the Francis Bacon drawings but which continues in very different faces as an involuntary ungainliness that even the sharpest contours cannot compete with. Even stronger are the gazes that radiate beyond the frame of reference: fixing, desperate, triumphant, and always, above all, shocked looks, for example in *Portrait d'Annie, Homosexuel, Putain juive* (1985 → 36) who is identified in writing as a "homosexuel, putain juive," supplemented by the multilingual inscription: "Mad in Polen." Made? So, made in Poland? Or Maid? Or simply crazy and/or angry? And why "Polen" in German?

He was dyslexic and a draftsman, enthusiastic about points of precision. I don't know whether there is a context, but it seems to me that precision in the details of iconic representation and virtuosic handling of the specific imprecision of symbolic signs (letters) do not go well together. Anyone who has difficulty with symbolic signs sees them as images because he or she cannot remember them as arbitrary signs, so they have to be copied and imprinted visually. (This is where the whole-language method with which reading used to be learned begins). There is nevertheless a lot of text in Mandelbaum's drawings and paintings: notes and games with typography but also, again and again, the use of other alphabets (Cyrillic, Hebrew), words that ultimately—deliberately?—make things unclear no matter whether we are dealing with a sketch, a scrap of paper, or indeed with a composition. And the words written into the images are often massively misspelled, but then again, there are some that, despite their unusual and phonetically counterintuitive spelling, are spelled correctly. It can be assumed that these are words that the dyslexic artist first saw written down rather than hearing them; he remembers them visually. The names of concentration camps and other places where the German murder of European Jews occurred appear on one sheet, and some of the not-so-famous ones are spelled correctly while others clearly derive from a deeper, privately phonetic familiarity and are spelled "incorrectly," based on hearing.

From today's perspective, it is surely puzzling that Stéphane Mandelbaum approached the malice and baseness of the German murder of Jews with artistic means similar to those he used for transgressions (also ethical ones) of a very different kind: radically lived-out sexuality, prostitution, criminal demimonde, slaughterhouses, Joseph Goebbels, and Pasolini all in one drawing style; Ernst Röhm and Brussels' nightlife, with the same fondness for the boorishly bizarre, for the glamorously misplaced. And these are the means that are also employed for the artists that Mandelbaum portrayed again and again: Pasolini, Arthur Rimbaud, Bacon—but then Goebbels, over and over, Goebbels and Ernst Röhm. Many homosexual motifs see in homosexuality above all a transgression, and then there are the primarily grotesque, damaged faces from the demimonde and a milieu whose caricatural outward appearance also seems to vouch for a certain truthfulness.

The mindset from which Mandelbaum decided what interested him can perhaps best be explained based on another hero he clearly admired and often portrayed: the now rather forgotten author, journalist, and *Libération* writer Pierre Goldman. Goldman, who has been called one of the "three Jewish leaders of 1968" (the others would have been André Glucksmann and Daniel Cohn-Bendit), was a radical leftist and anti-fascist activist who was not only game for armed struggle but also and above all for illegal acts in general. In the wake of which the police not only charged him with several robberies that he did not deny but also tried to pin a murder on him, for which he was condemned and imprisoned. That ruling turned out to have been politically motivated, however; Goldman's innocence was established on appeal. A paramilitary terrorist organization named Honneur de la Police, consisting of supporters and members of the GAL (Grupos Antiterroristas de Liberación), a secret police organization that practiced vigilante terrorism in the French and Spanish Basque Country against (real and alleged) members and supporters of ETA (Euskadi Ta Askatasuna), murdered Goldman on a public street in 1979.

Goldman explicitly connected the struggle against bourgeois society and its state with his Jewish identity and appreciated the Jewish solidarity he was shown across political camps. He also connected his Jewish identity with a global anti-bourgeois and anti-racist struggle, said he had chosen to "live as a pariah," fought as a guerrilla fighter in South America, and wrote his impressive book *Souvenirs obscurs d'un juif polonais né en France*[1] in prison while listening to Cuban music on audio tapes that Chris Marker had mixed for him.

Having grown out of the experience of European Jews, this international solidarity of all the opponents of a repulsive Western status quo—which led to intense and existential encounters with other opponents and victims of capitalist bourgeois society and hence also to solidarity and communality with illegals and criminals—seems to have been especially important and formative

1 Pierre Goldman, *Souvenirs obscurs d'un juif polonais né en France* (Paris: Éditions du Seuil, 1975), trans. by Joan Pinkham, *Dim Memories of a Polish Jew Born in France* (New York: Viking Press, 1977).

for Mandelbaum. However, he was from a later generation and was shaped by an artistic (both parents) Belgian family with Jewish-Polish (and Armenian) background and influenced by the late 1970s. His gallery of *transgressive*, tragic, and/or existentialist, and/or heroic male artists—Pasolini, Bacon, Rimbaud, Yukio Mishima, Luis Buñuel, and Nagisa Ōshima—points to the years in which the political reason for a radical opposition to bourgeois society that shrank from any taboo and tried out every drastic measure withdrew after political disappointments and defeats of all kinds to a fetish-like radicality and transgression for their own sakes. The names mentioned also roughly form the canon of an international, post-political, protopunk mood whose voices included Patti Smith around 1976 as well as the West Berlin Foucault fans at the TUNIX meeting of 1978, the leftist French fans of the "heroic" criminal Jacques Mesrine, and the German readers of books published by konkursbuch and the early Matthes & Seitz Verlag. That this cultural atmosphere by no means completely explains Mandelbaum is due, not solely but nevertheless essentially, to his position as a Jew, which he articulated less politically than his hero Goldman had.

Violence and obscenity negotiate in a strange connection this post-left-radical discontent in the culture of the second half of the 1970s. It is no longer political violence that can be discussed in terms of arguments or even strategies—not violence against a much greater one—but merely a violence that floods all other nuances of political experience and that, in the political failure to even attempt to gain a seriously considered opportunity for action, wanders over to depicting and reifying it in art, which raises the problem of obscenity. The specific obscenity of (any?) depiction of the Shoah is an aspect of several works by Mandelbaum, but without revealing any way out, any clear alternative position such as the stance—advocated by Claude Lanzmann—of rejecting on principle any image of the Holocaust at all. Instead, in one Mandelbaum painting, an image of the entrance to a concentration camp, defiled with chaotically distributed spots of red, is hanging on the wall of a fictive room while the image is dominated by an erect red penis in the foreground (*Le Rěve d'Auschwitz*, 1983). Simultaneous despair over the possibility of depicting violence (especially state terrorism) and immersion in that very problem was not solely Mandelbaum's concern at that time. Others among his heroes, such as Pasolini with *Salò o le 120 giornate di Sodoma* (*Salò, or the 120 Days of Sodom*), were also trying to advance by fighting forward.

In Mandelbaum's case, however, one can scarcely speak of fighting, much less any planned direction it could take. Extreme violence is more of a point of departure for someone who, at fifteen, portrayed himself as a bloody body hanging from a meat hook—without any of the self-pity of puberty, but instead in a matter-of-fact and dry manner. Using Pasolini, he explored the tension between an existentially charged portrait of a familiar person and that of a face known only from the media; this disquiet generally turns into a recurring tension in his work between determination and fanaticism, not very far from several of the Goebbels portraits. The path from transgressor to fanatic, from fanatic to perpetrator, and perpetrator to mass murderer, and then back to surprised determination, stuck halfway, and then ultimately to a poor bastard, takes the form of a zigzagging course. There is no opportunity to flee to the security of admiration, even though it is clear that it played a role in many of the portraits—but so did contempt.

In addition to the charged portrait that, despite the dependence of its arrangement on rectangular sheets, seems capable of leaping out of them at any time, there is another basic compositional attitude; the works in question are even titled *Composition*. One could say that it grew out of the occasional integration of portraits into the collages, out of working with original images disseminated by the media in connection with portraits, but really, it is there the whole time. I'm referring to something that I would call "visual lists." Teeming images but, again and again, with homogeneous elements: little piles, weapons, or sunglasses, lying side by side like the symbols from a game, like playing cards or tools for a computer game. But then faces over and over, drawn and sometimes pasted in, small portraits, and then miniaturized soldiers and tanks, as if preparing for strategic scenarios, war games, or a game of Battleships.

All of this is overwhelmingly washed away and vaulted by the cascades of writing: carefully drawn Hebrew words, copied typography, scribbled lists of names and sums of money—all of it always strokes and hatching on the road from iconicity to the registering, enumerating symbol. An uncanny tendency of symbols to mix themselves up and combine their logic and function under the dominance of an artist—this is reminiscent of another practice that moved to the center of visual culture during Mandelbaum's active years: graffiti. Mandelbaum's design principle is not so much the look of the writing that was then spreading internationally but rather the specific allover of its appearance in public. One can more easily imagine endless walls and subway windows functioning as the virtual frames of Mandelbaum's compositions rather than the rectangular sheet or stretcher frame. Not only is there no depth, no receding, and one can always picture something being added, but above all, the juxtaposition of the formulaic, the formless scrawl of legible writing, and executed visual elements are reminiscent of the real public surfaces on which graffiti come together, growing rampantly side by side in reference to one another (sometimes violently) or occupying space unconnectedly. This consorting of visualities happens without constraint and randomly, but it has structure, a structure one can recognize and apply, which Mandelbaum seems to do.

Friends and family have recognized in many of these collages of shopping lists—sums of money (owed, nabbed?), and autobiographical confessions, of favorite motifs, names of obsessions and obscenities—the same stories, sometimes made up, that Mandelbaum also told in other ways; they recognized the names of women the artist claimed to have slept with (or did?), plans for robberies in which he claimed to have participated (and that never happened). Mandelbaum seemed increasingly to be creating a world in which his existentialism, his attempt to get a handle on—I can only speculate about this—the history of violence that pursued him personally, that he experienced and/or inherited, would get an appropriate backdrop. Presumably, the stories were sensed from the demimonde of Brussels, which he did in fact frequent: small and medium thefts but also countless acts that he added to them that never actually occurred. That he was murdered by accomplices with whom he wanted to steal a Modigliani is, of course, a reason to bury his art forever beneath this in every respect monstrous and therefore attractive story. It would, however, also be inappropriate to separate from this biography an œuvre whose artistic meaning is so much determined by autobiographical gestures (more so even than by direct references: traces of intensity as signs of entanglement and involvement). How does the desire for reality in the artistic work relate to the obviously increasing fictionalization of real life? How appropriate is it for posterity to make that relationship the focus of speculation?

These questions become especially relevant for any determination of this œuvre's place in art history. Around 1980, the *scenes*—as they would be called today—of European metropoles were much farther apart than they are now. When we find terms such as Neo-Expressionism, Art Brut, and even Post-Expressionism in the biographies of Mandelbaum now circulating, it seems strange. So-called Neo-Expressionism stood out for its room-filling grand gestures and motifs and above all for painting being its preferred medium, at least amongst its first generation that would perhaps include Georg Baselitz, A.R. Penck, and even Julian Schnabel—at most there is a very distant relationship to Penck. In the second generation, that of Kippenberger and the Oehlen brothers, it was already a reflexive Neo-Expressionism that itself no longer believed in expression and operated from an opposite pole to such existentialism. One can again at best see distant similarities to Werner Büttner or even Walter Dahn. The simultaneity of spontaneous, random composition and a rather obsessive drawing style—of letting oneself go and knowing very precisely where one wants to go—tends rather to inscribe Mandelbaum into a line of eccentric outsiders who derive from their time only in terms of subject matter and experiences without having (yet) found a place artistically; remaining *unfinished*—which here, for once, one can justly say without fear of the usual kitsch about artists.

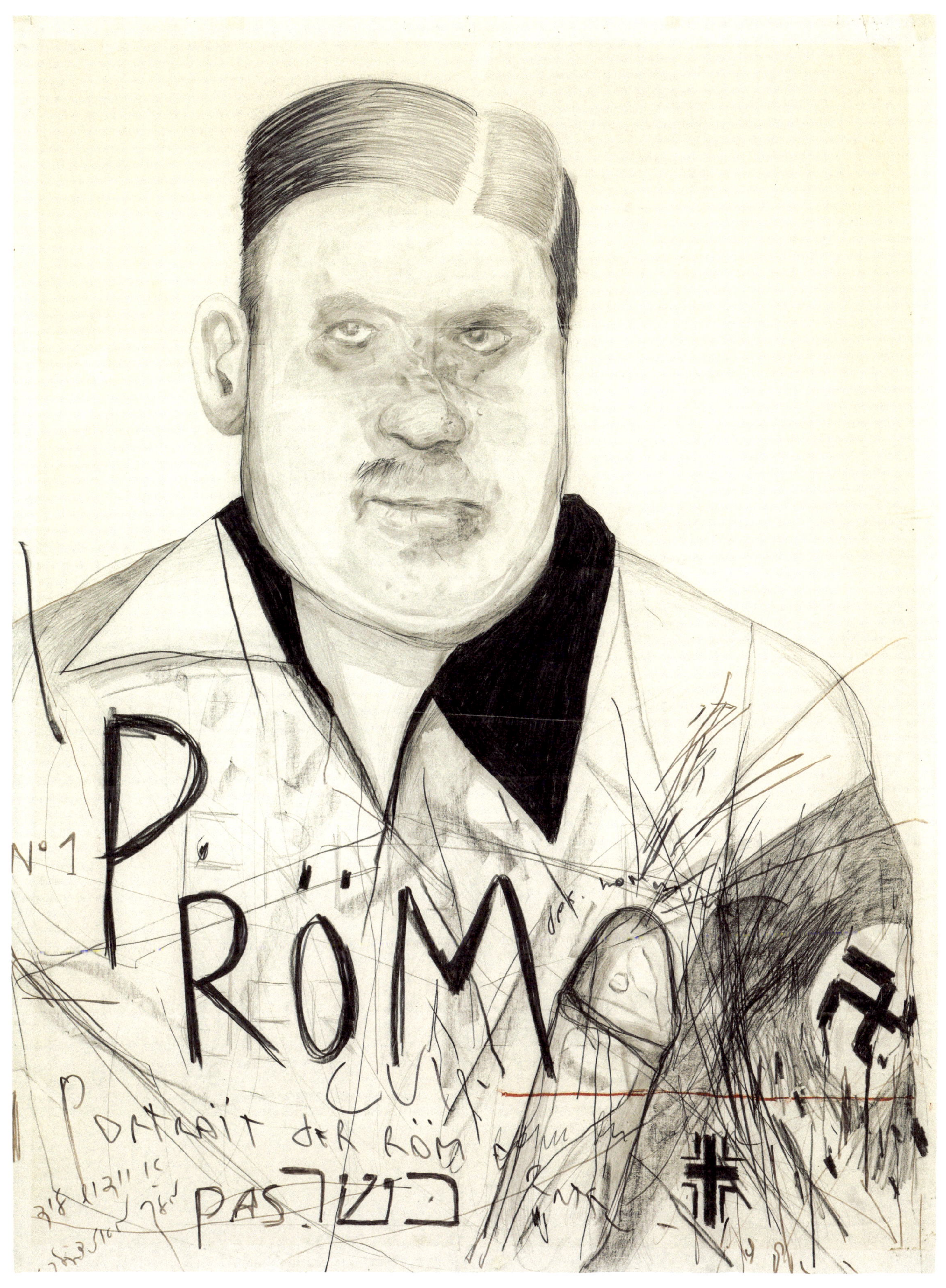


*P. Röm (N° 1 / Portraït der Röm)*, 1981–82

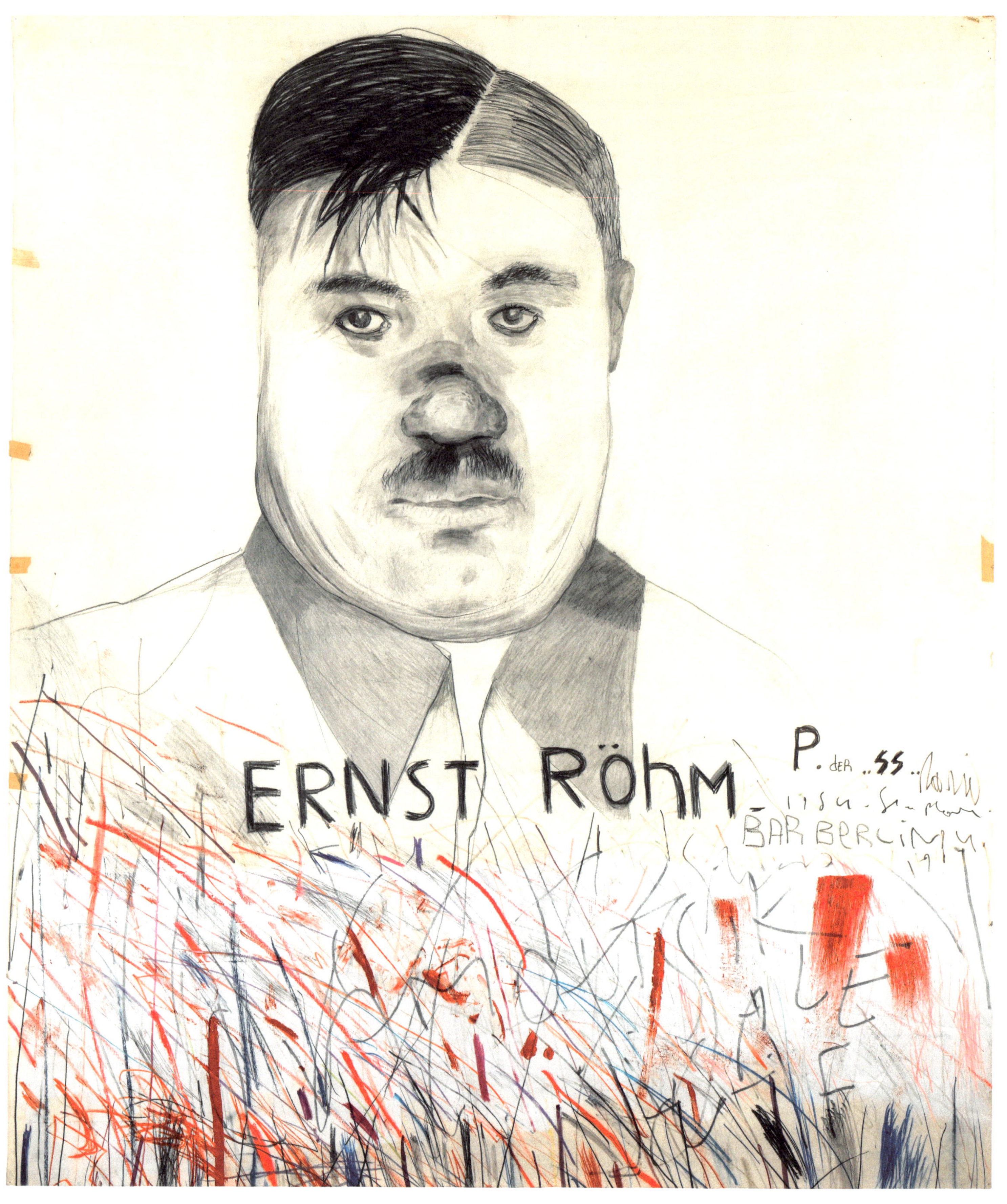


*Ernst Röhm*, 1981

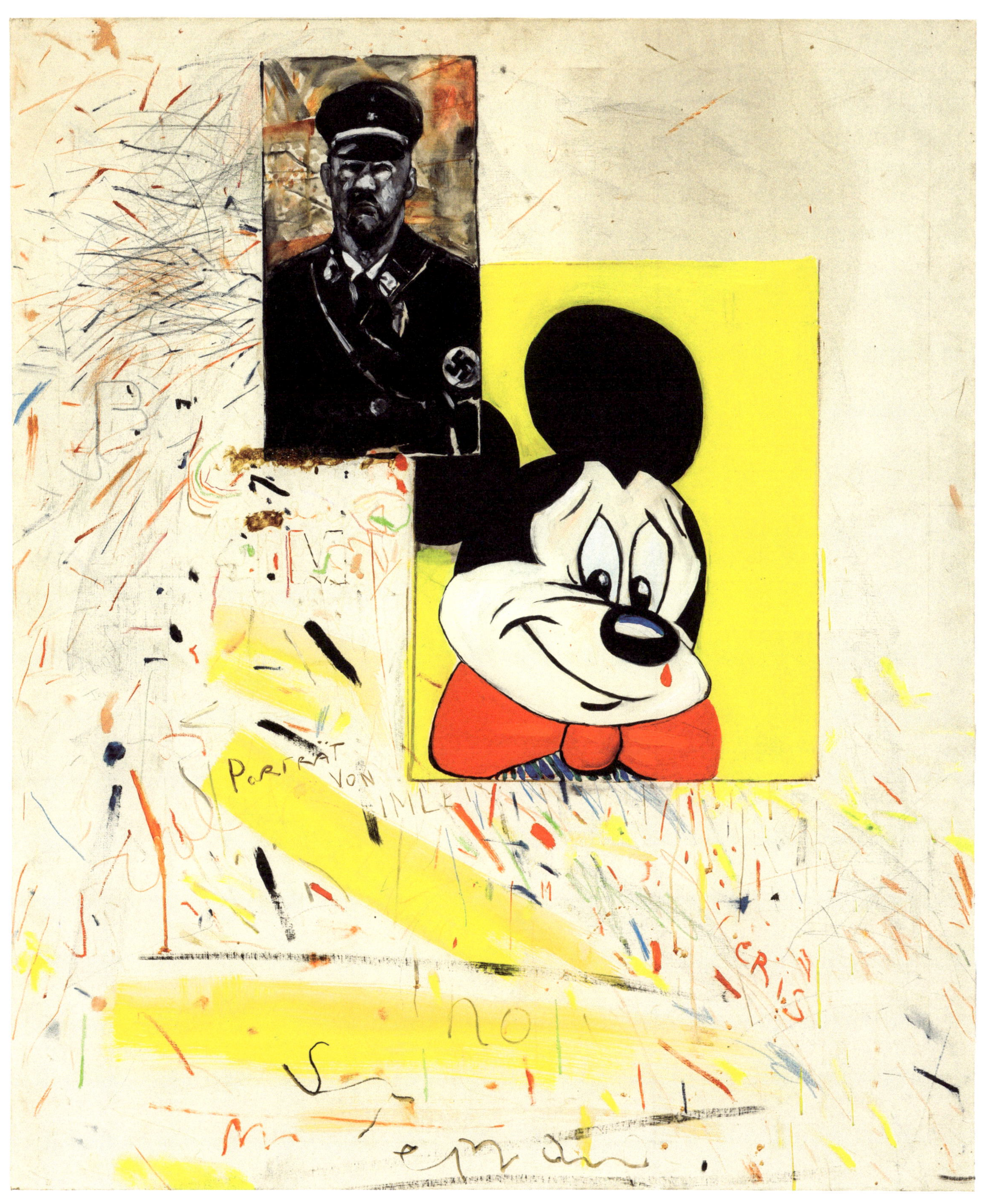


*Mickey et Himmler*, 1983

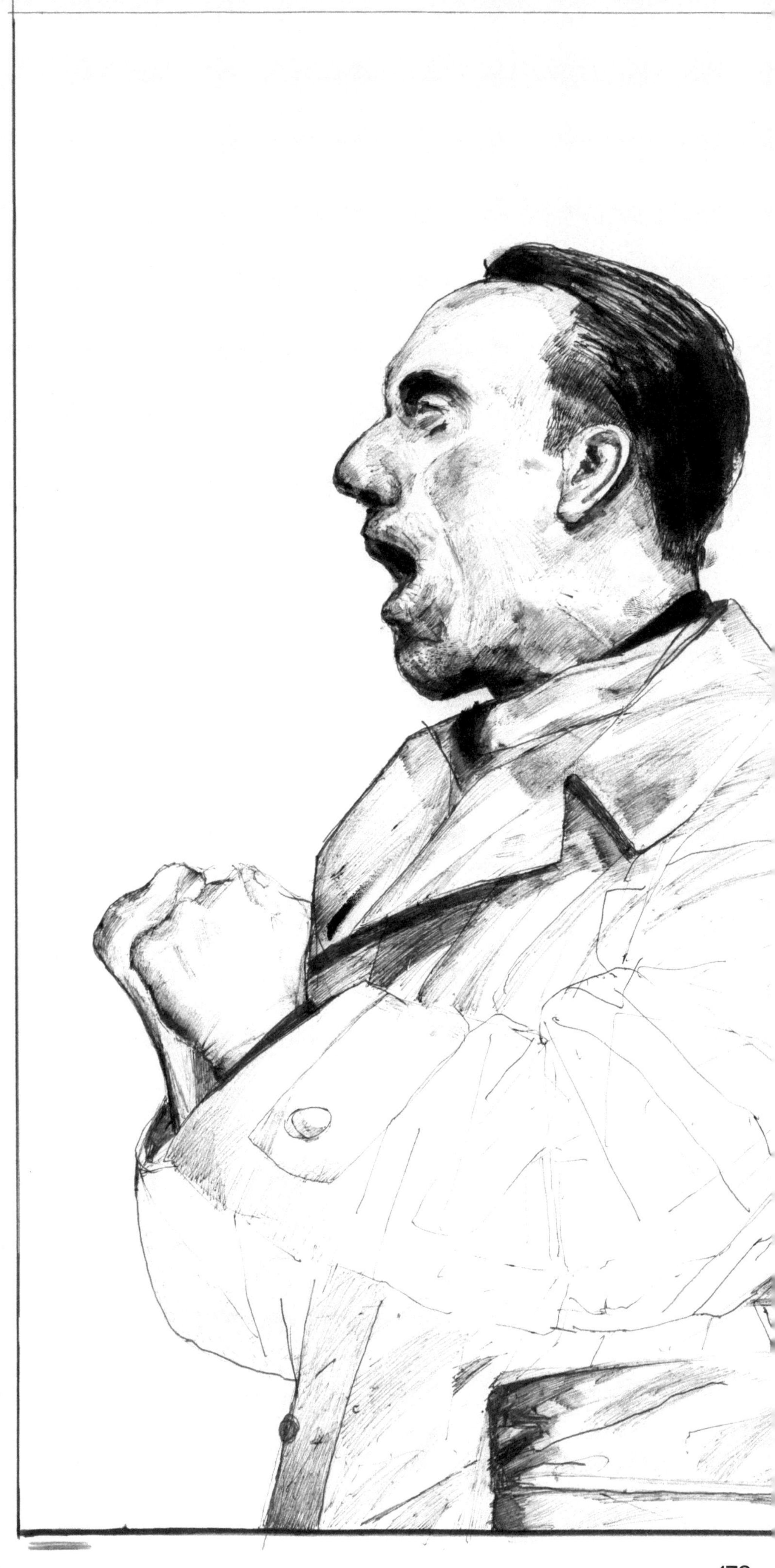

*Goebbels*, 1980

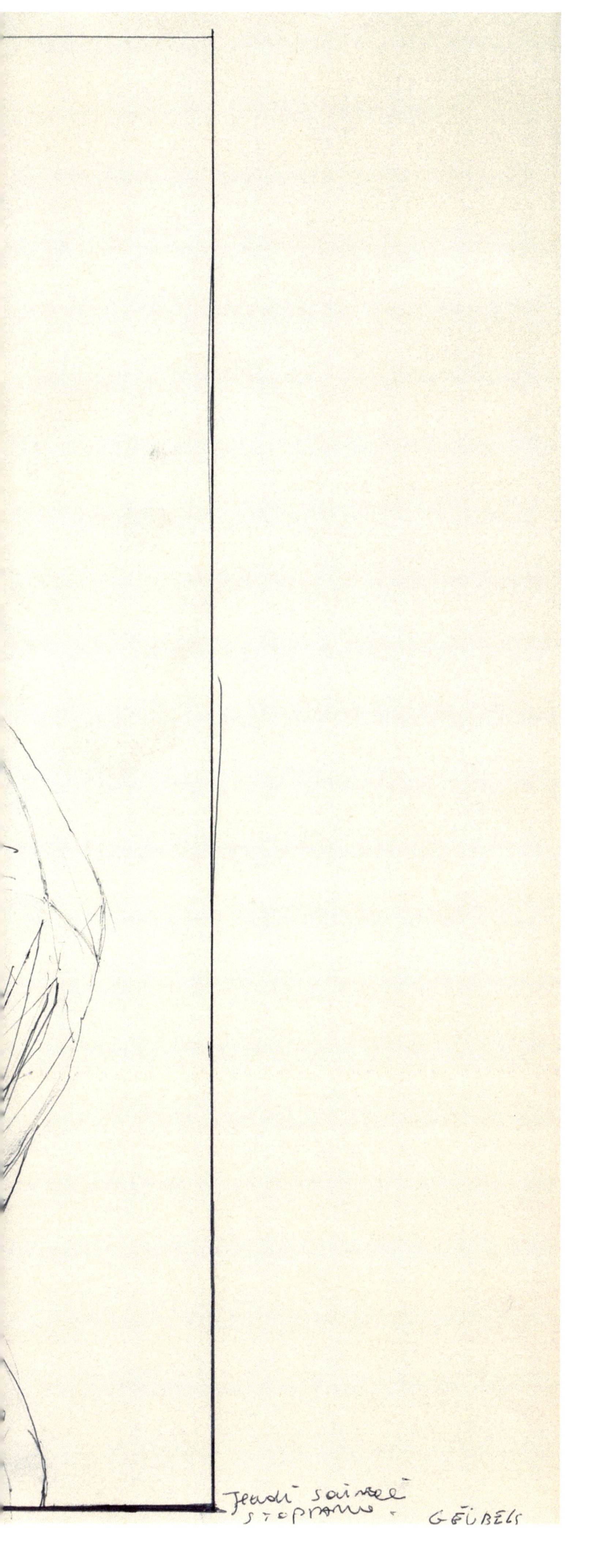
Jeudi soirée

*Goebbels*, 1980

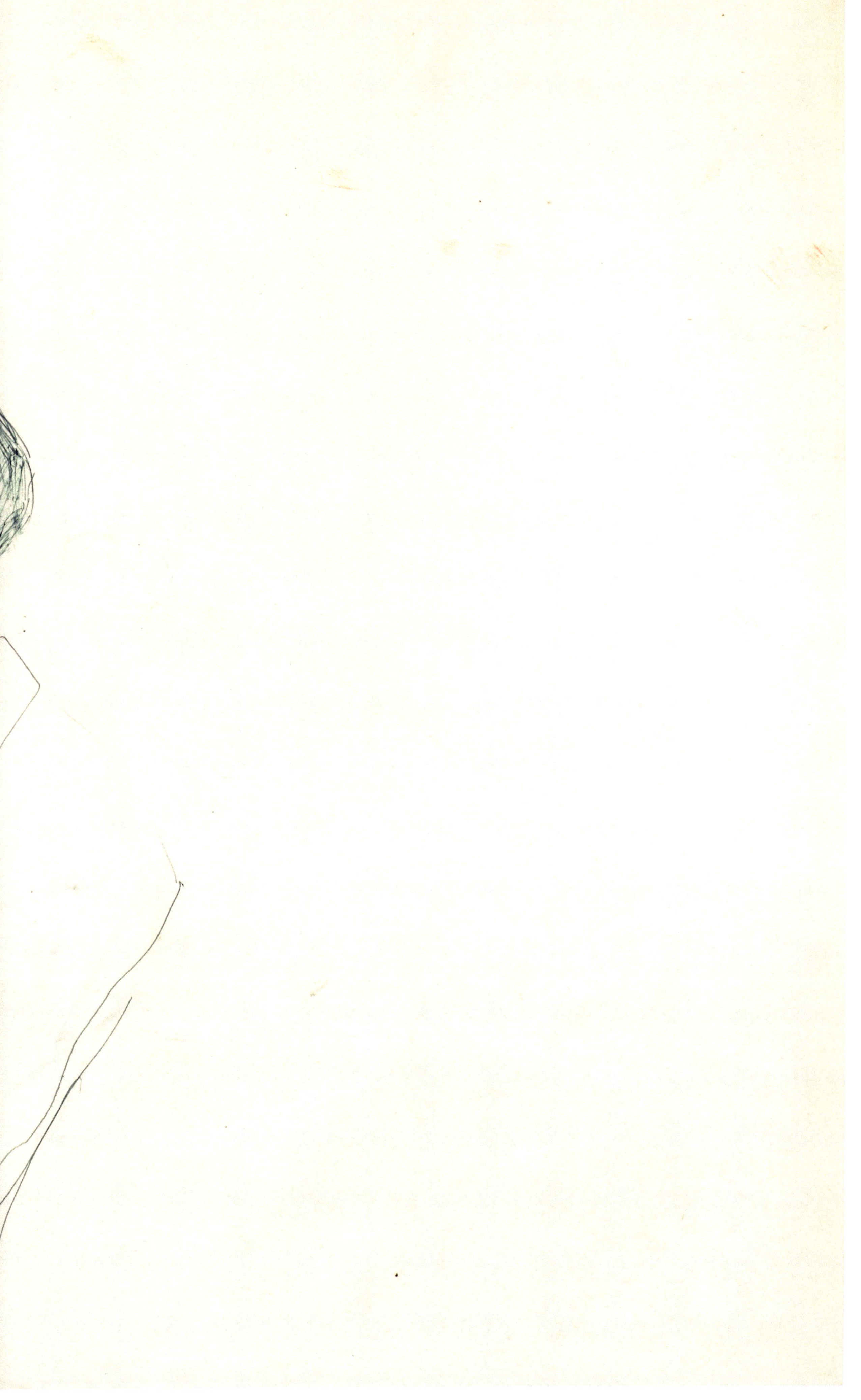

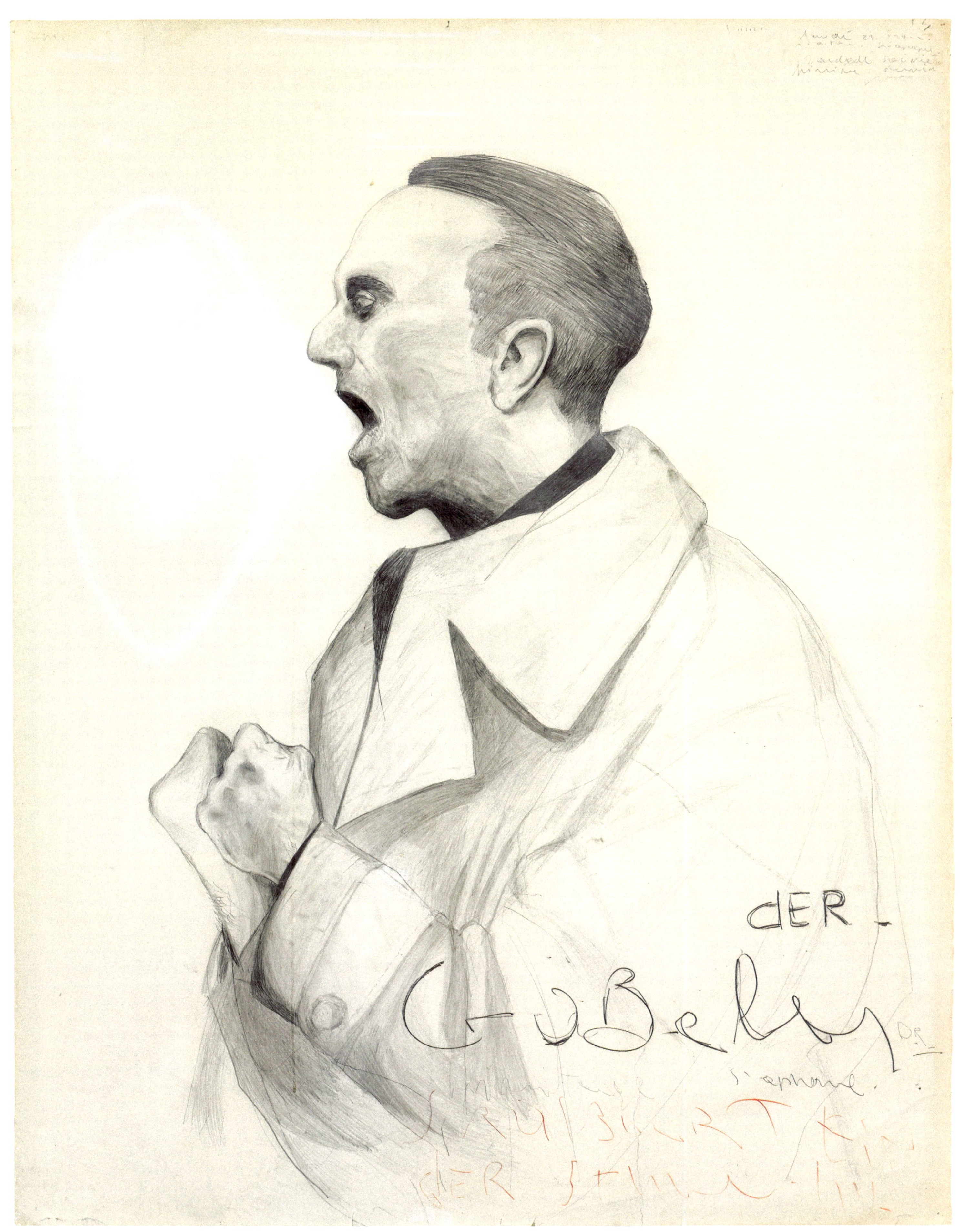


*Der Göbels* [*Goebbels*], 1980

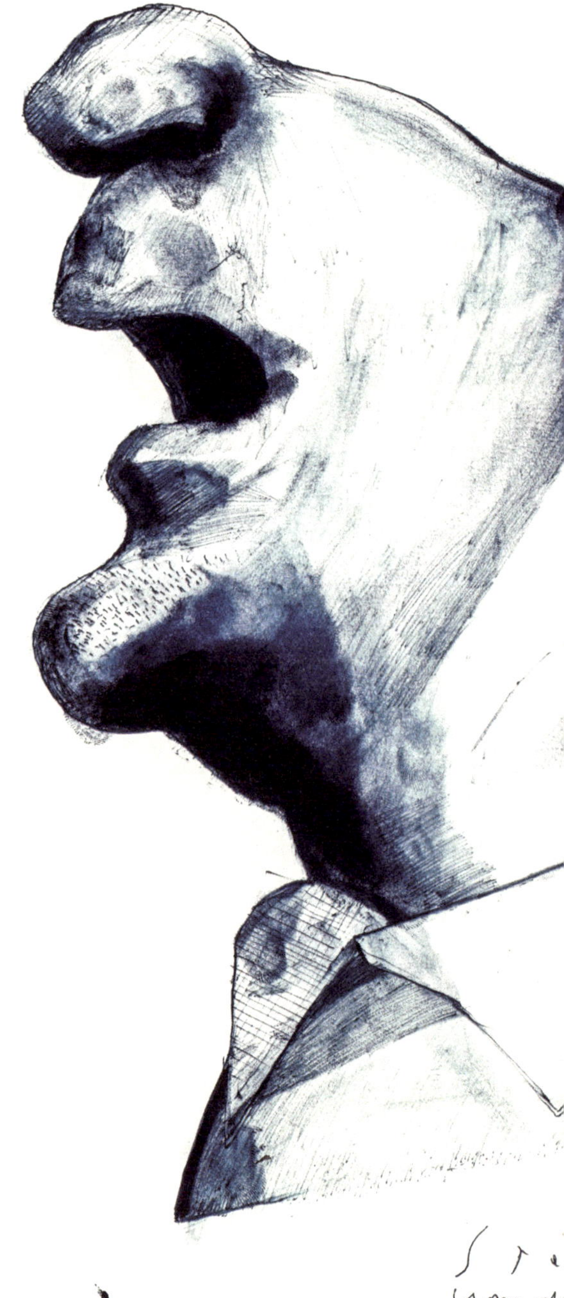

*Composition (Cul-de jatte au brassard à croix gammée)*, 1980

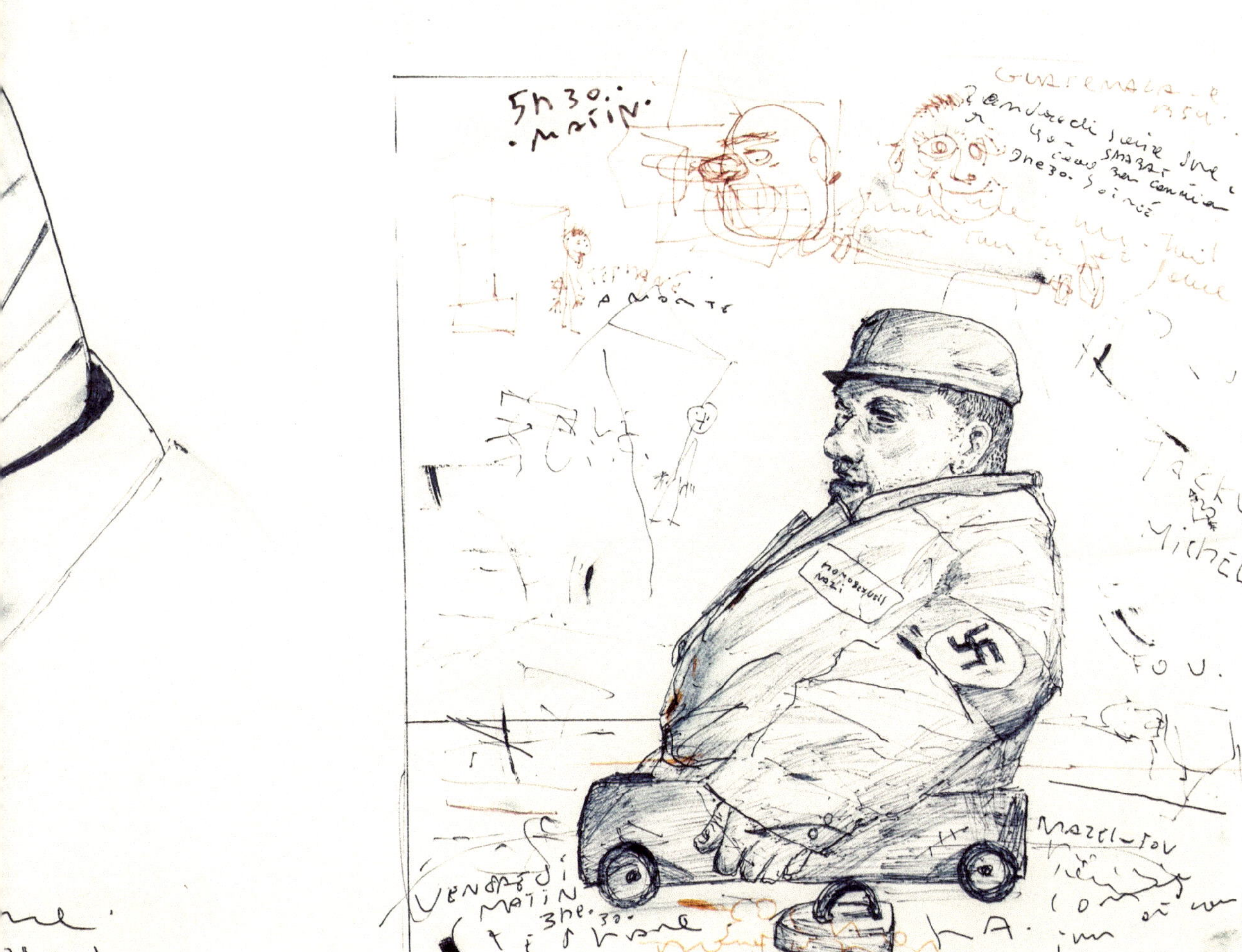
5h30.
MATIN.
AMANTE
Michel
FOU.
MAZEL-TOV
VENDREDI
MATIN
3he.30.

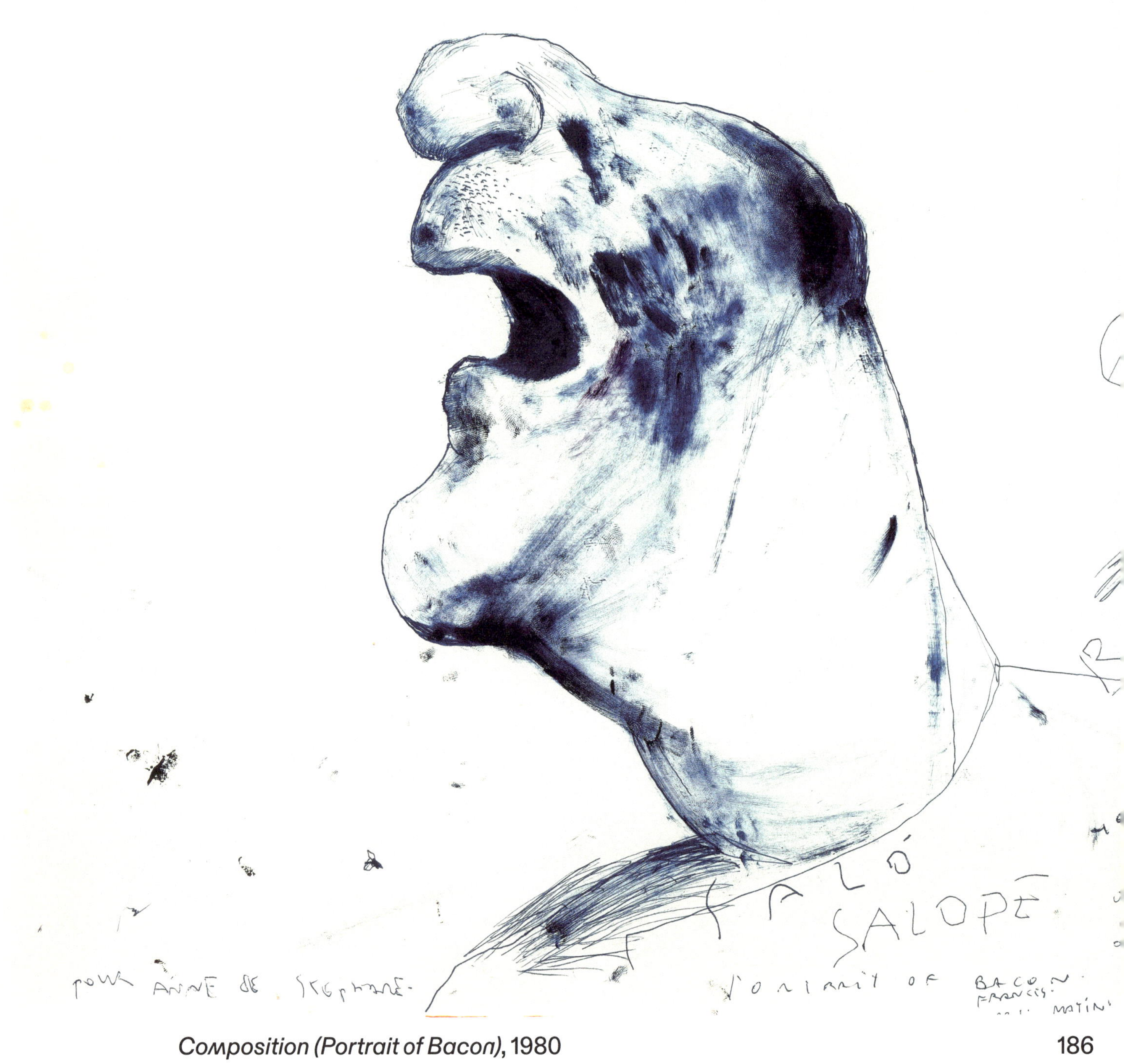


*Composition (Portrait of Bacon)*, 1980

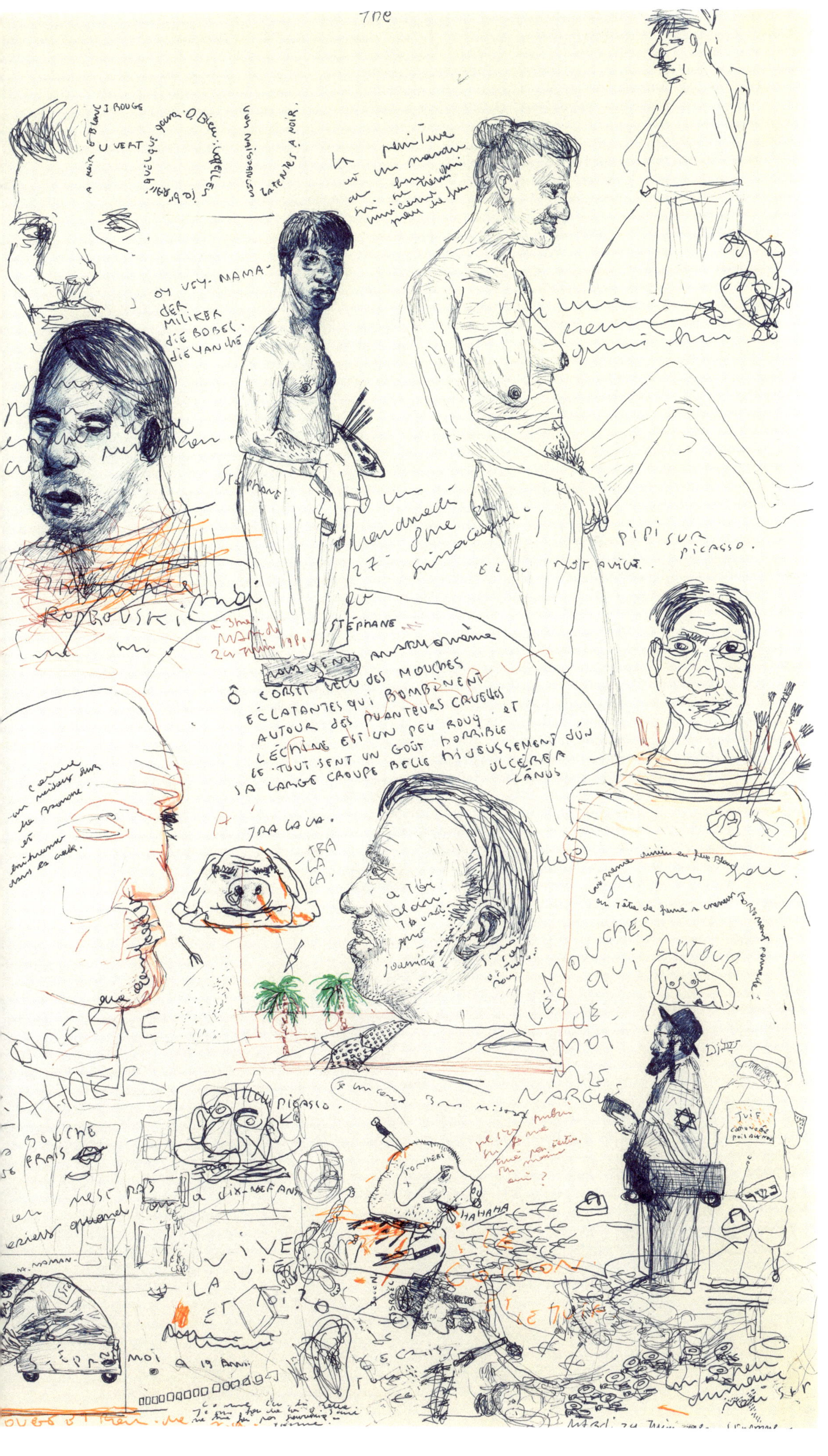

OY VEY- MAMA-
DER
MILIKER
DIE BOBEL
DIE YANCHE
STÉPHANE
RODROUSKI
STÉPHANE
Ô CORSET VELU DES MOUCHES
ÉCLATANTES QUI BOMBINENT
AUTOUR DES PUANTEURS CRUELLES
L'ÉCHINE EST UN PEU ROUG . ET
LE TOUT SENT UN GOÛT HORRIBLE
SA LARGE CROUPE BELLE HIDEUSEMENT D'UN
ULCÈRE A
L'ANUS
PIPI SUR
PICASSO.
TRA LA LA.
TRA
LA
LA
LES
MOUCHES
QUI AUTOUR
DE
MOI
MES
NARGUE
CHÉRIE
PICASSO.
JUIF
HAHAHA
VIVE
LA VIE
ET TOI ?
MOI A 19 ANS

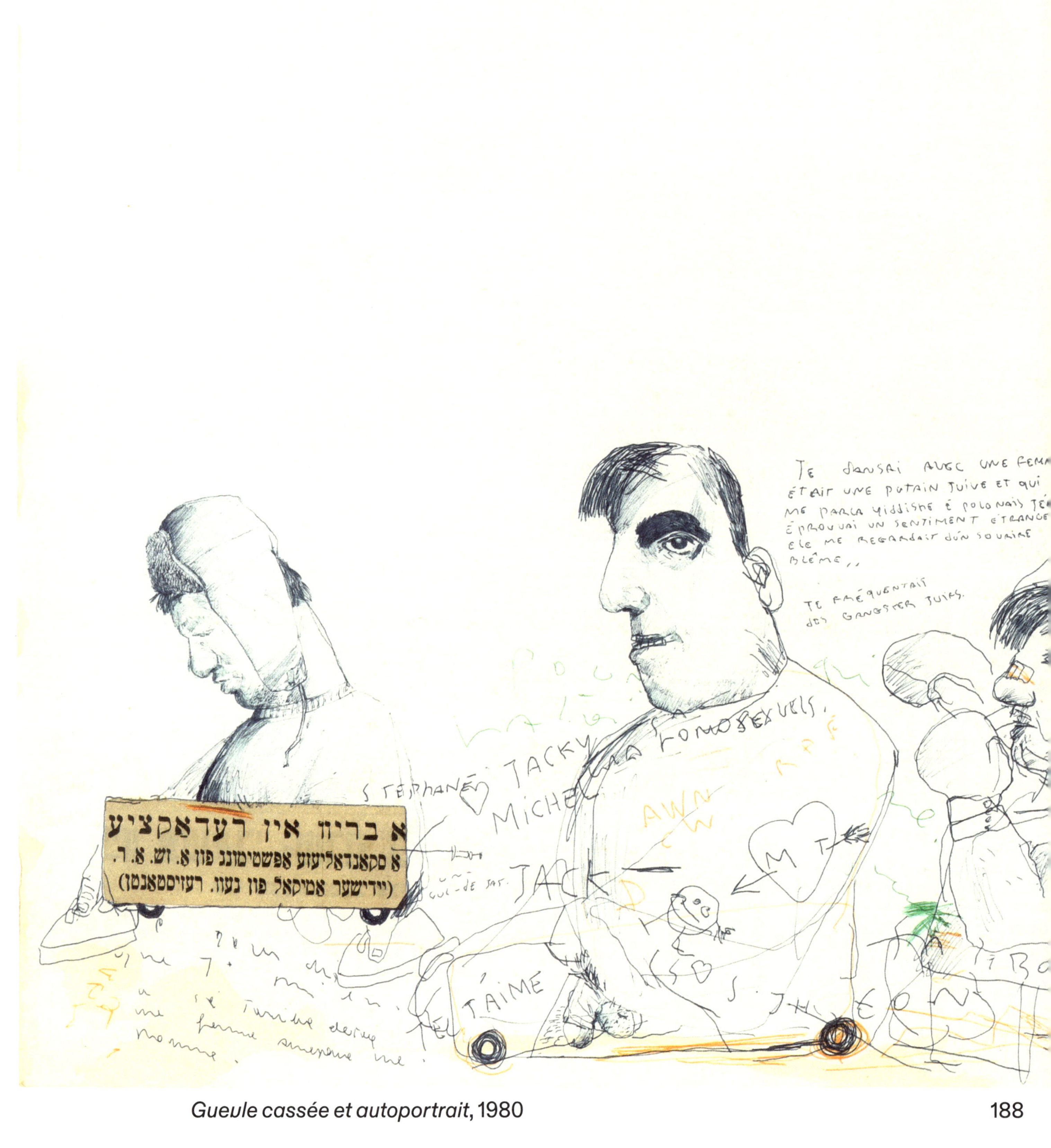


*Gueule cassée et autoportrait*, 1980

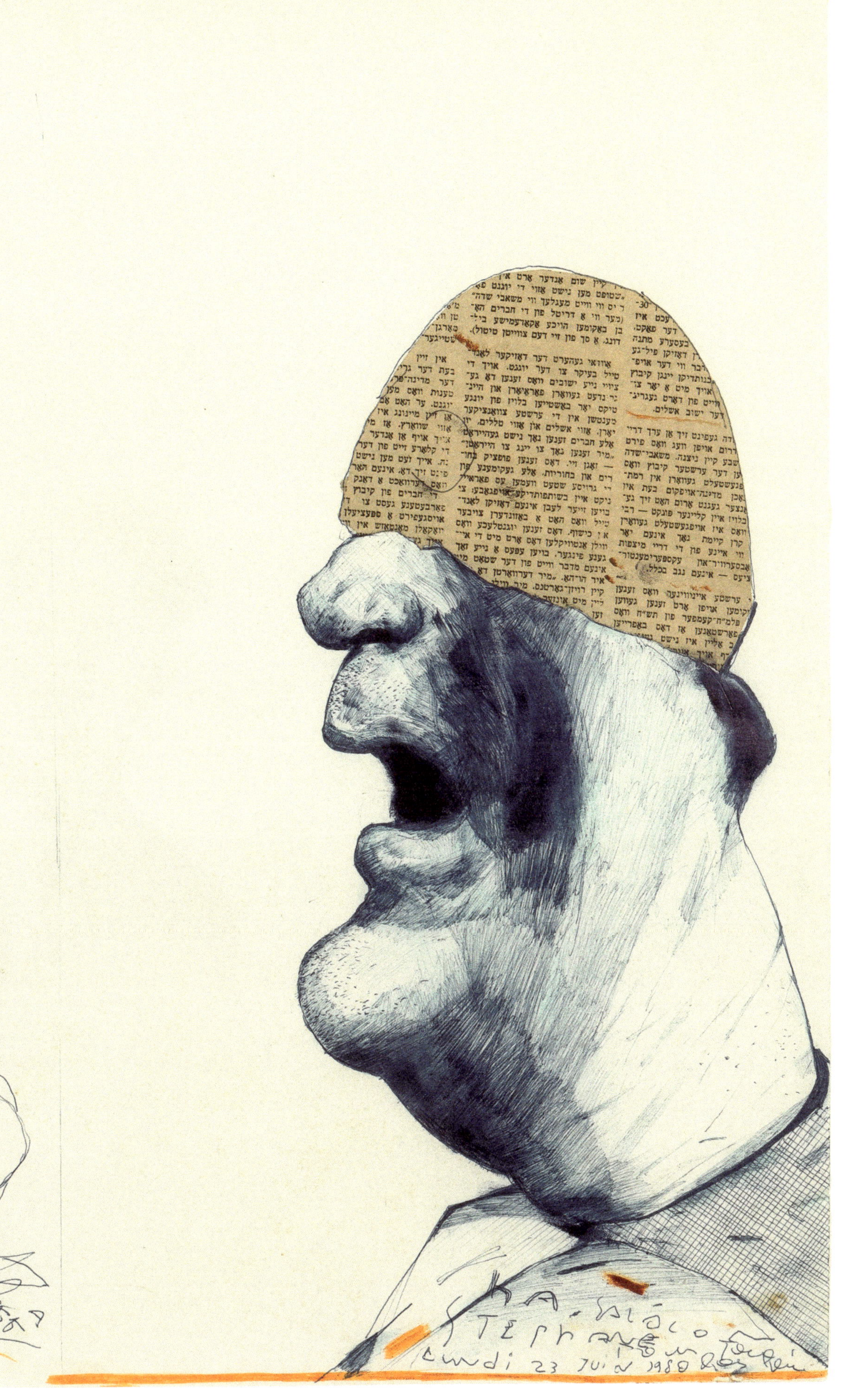
Stephane
23 Juin 1980

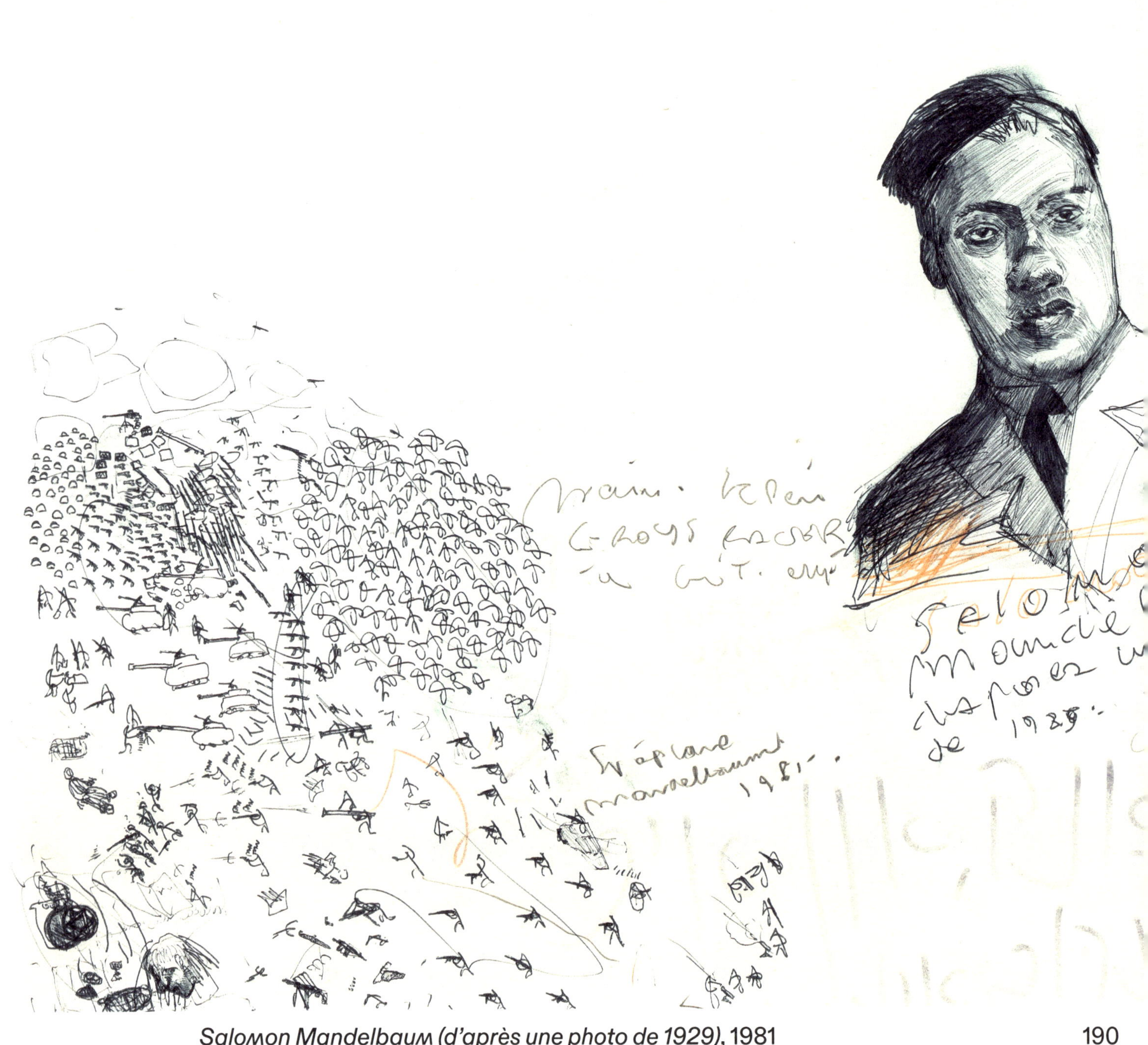

*Salomon Mandelbaum (d'après une photo de 1929)*, 1981

ha....

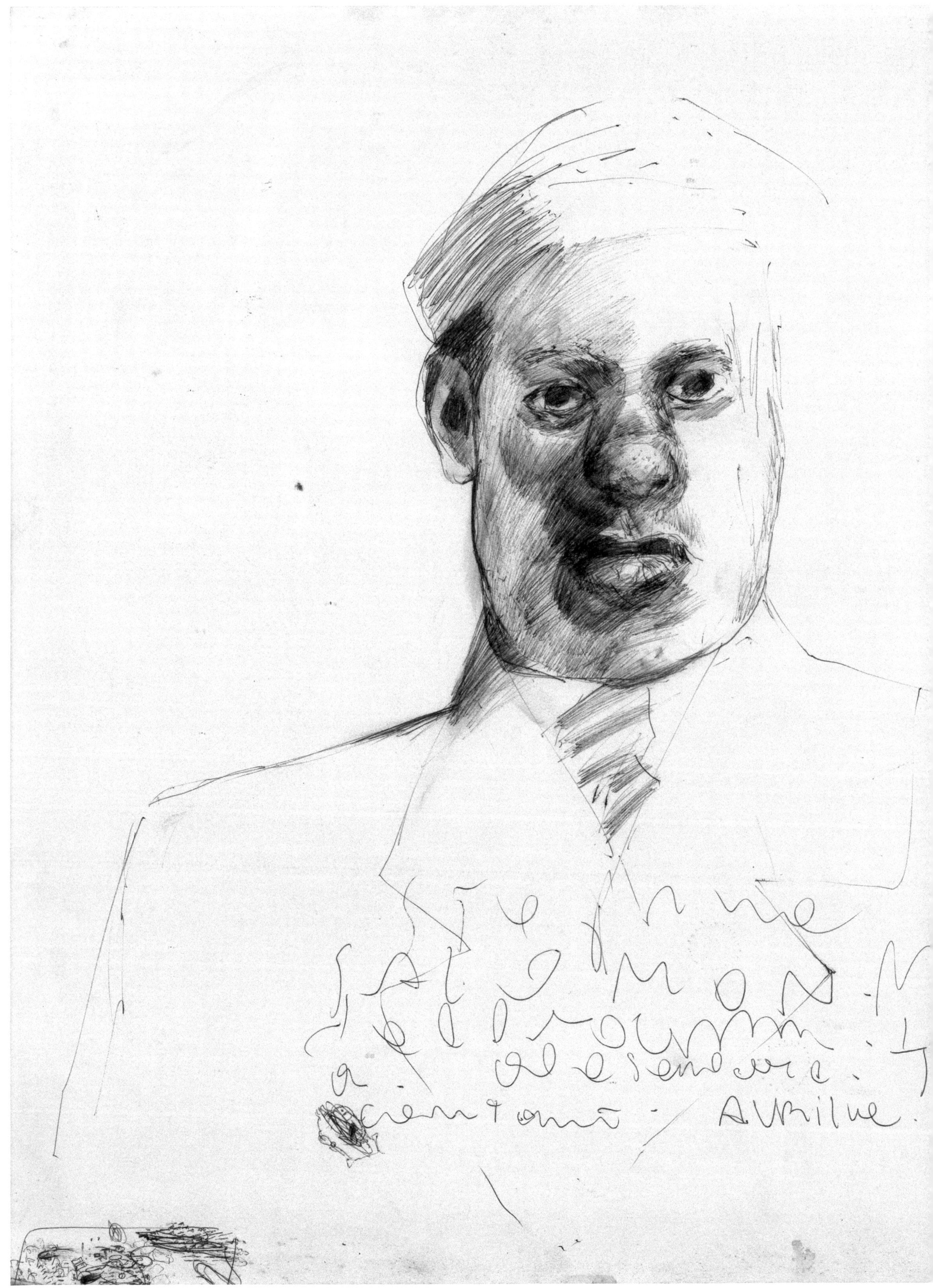

*Salomon Mandelbaum*, 1980

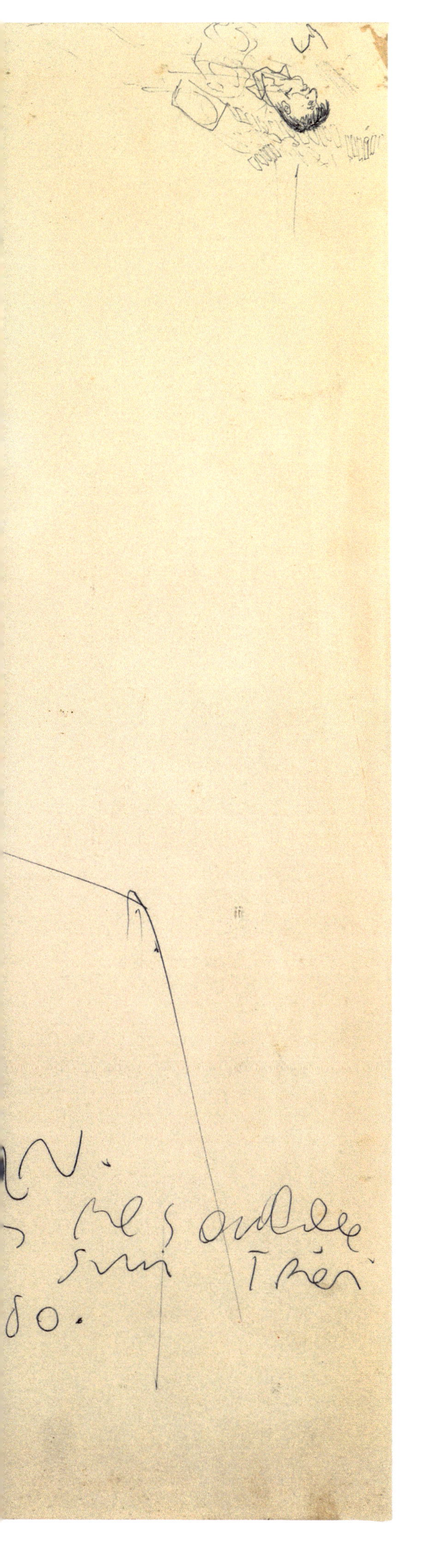

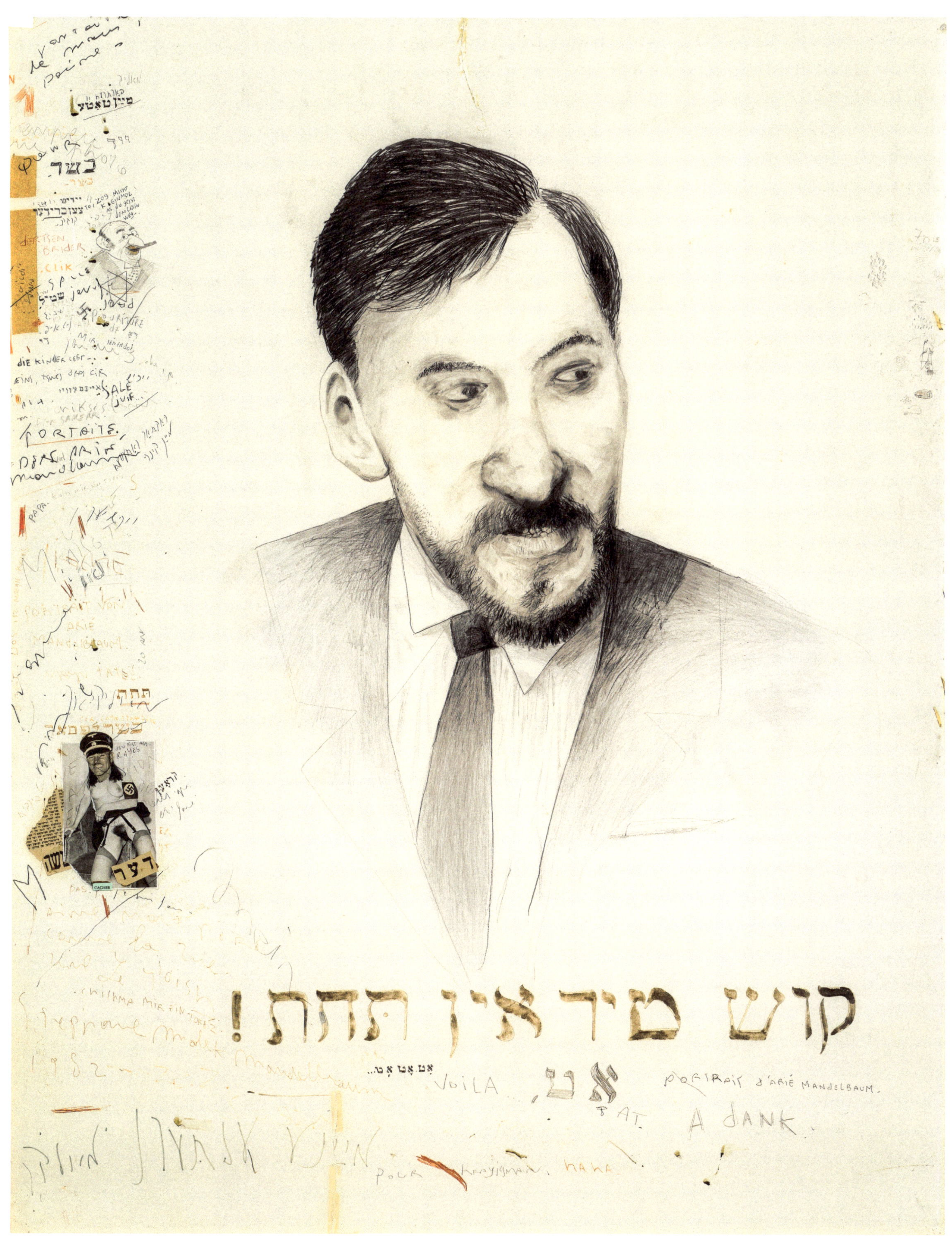


*Kismatores! (Portrait d'Arié Mandelbaum)*, 1982

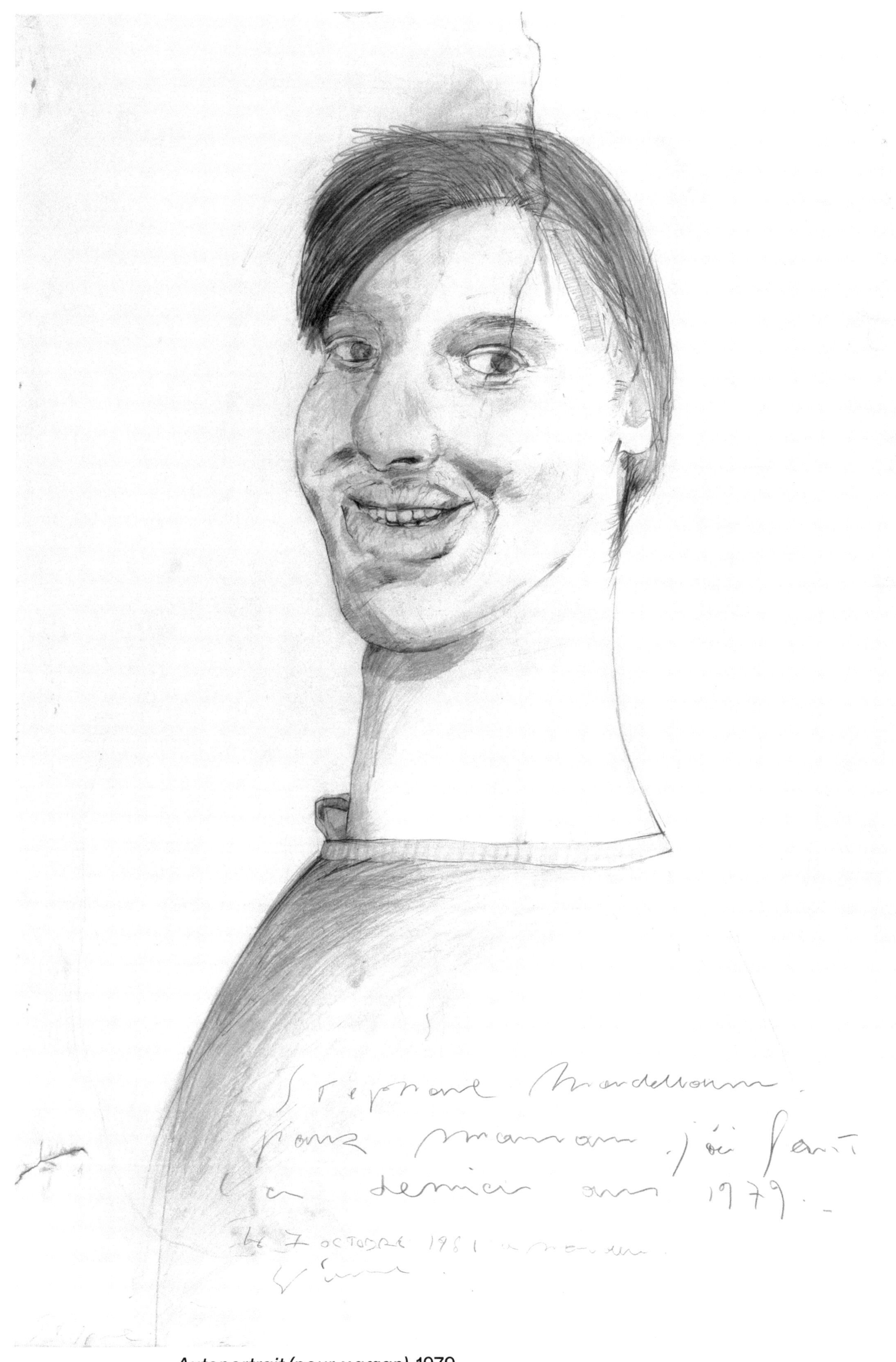

*Autoportrait (pour maman)*, 1979

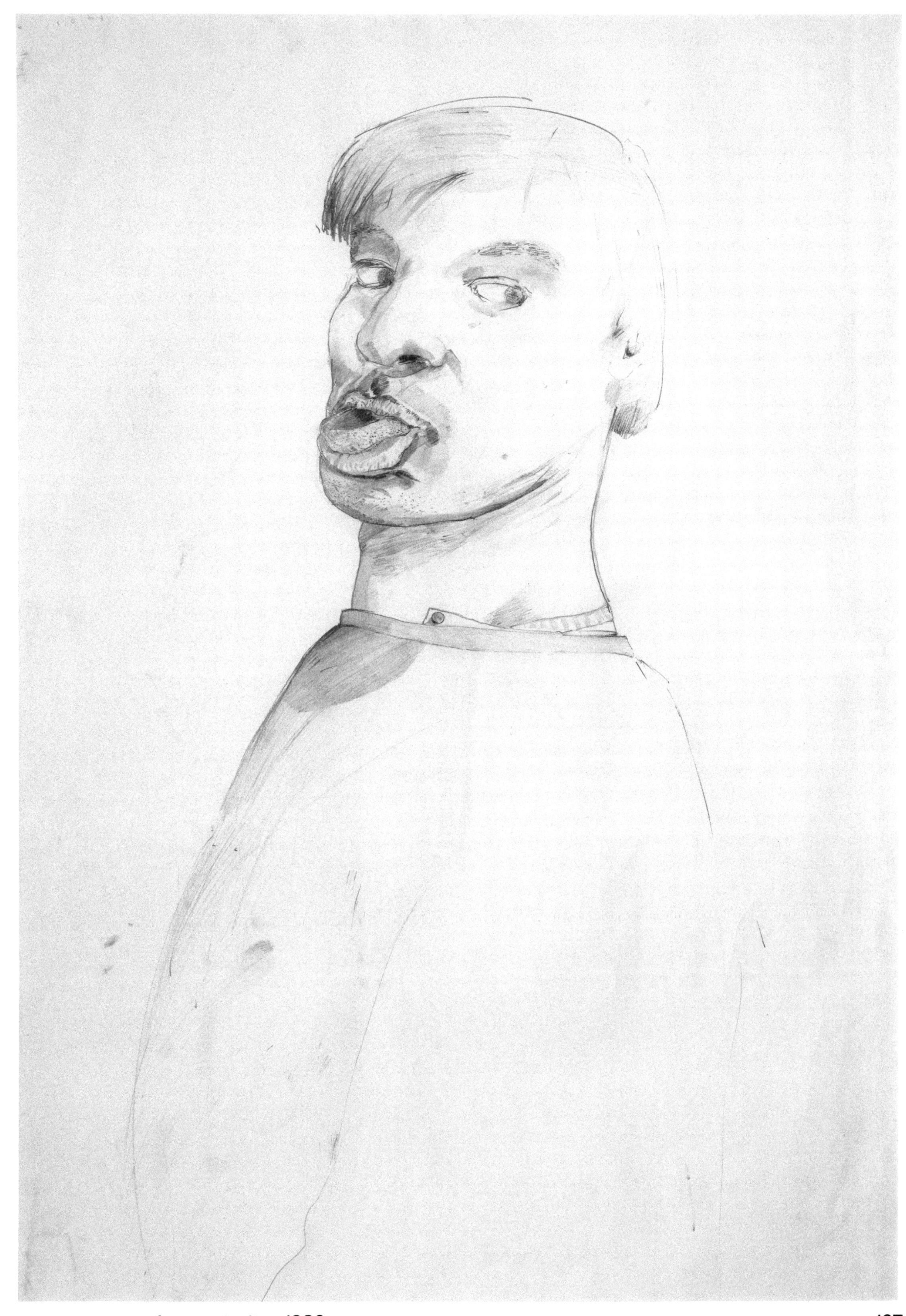

*Autoportrait*, c. 1980

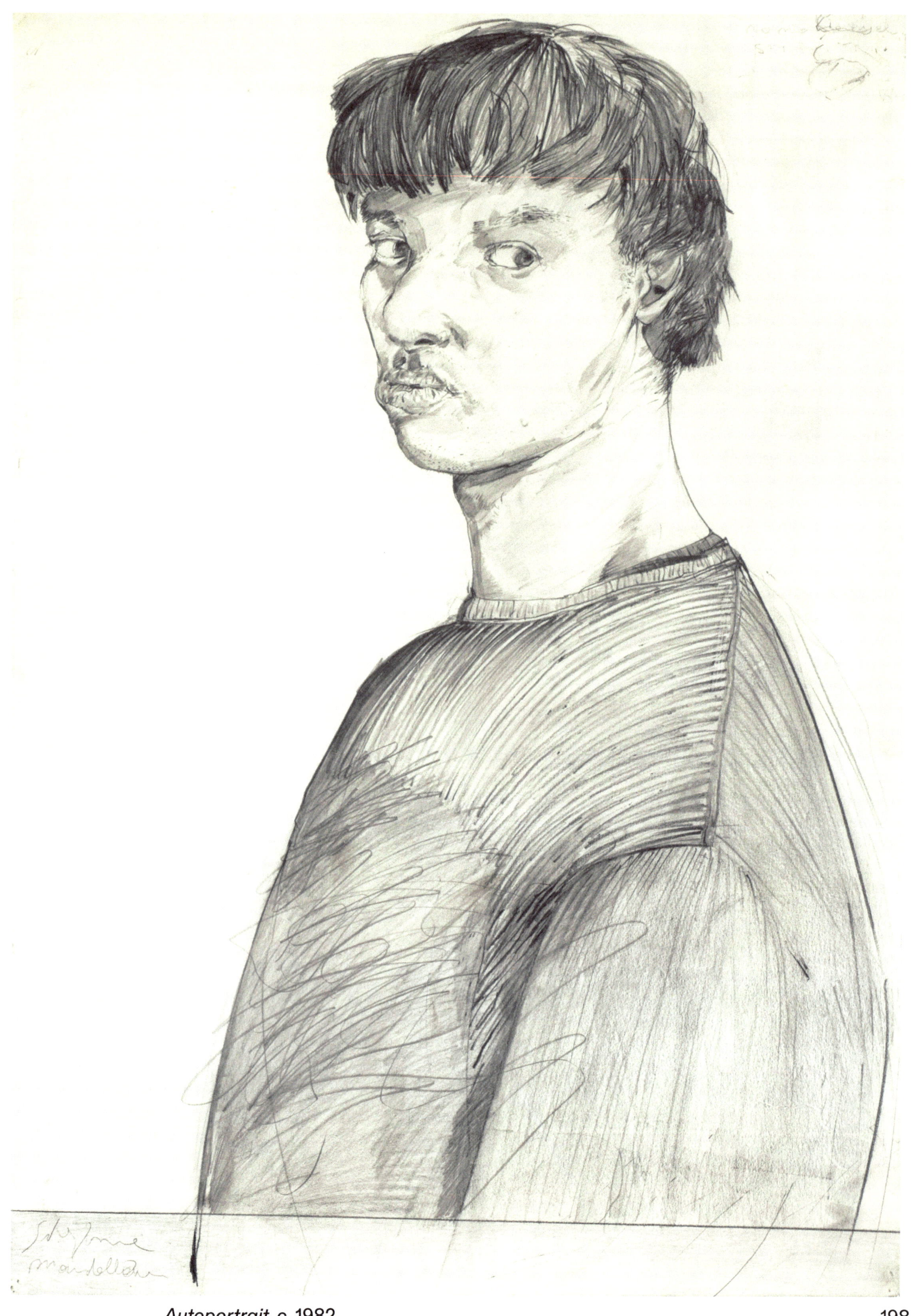

*Autoportrait*, c. 1982

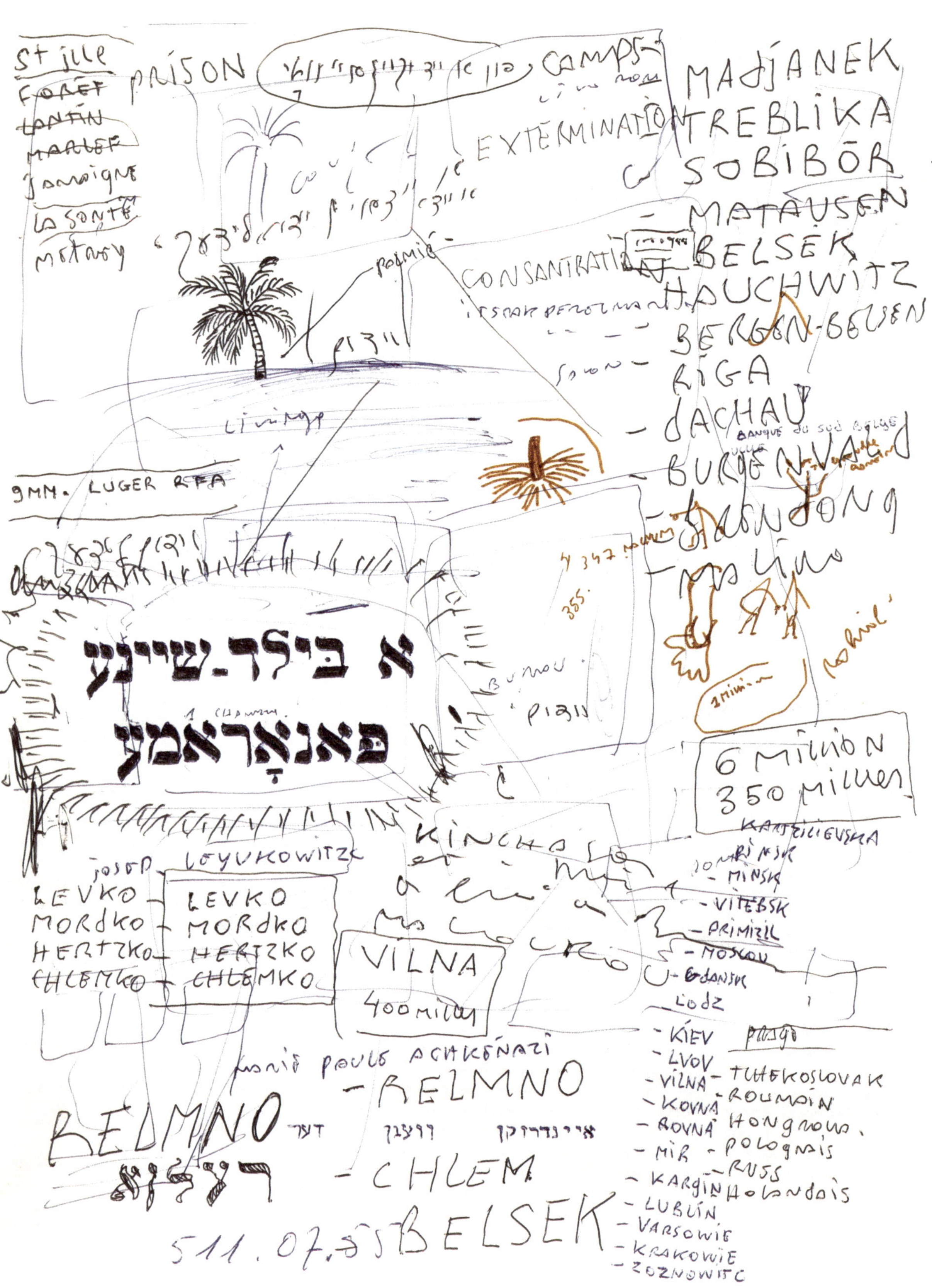

Untitled, 1985–86

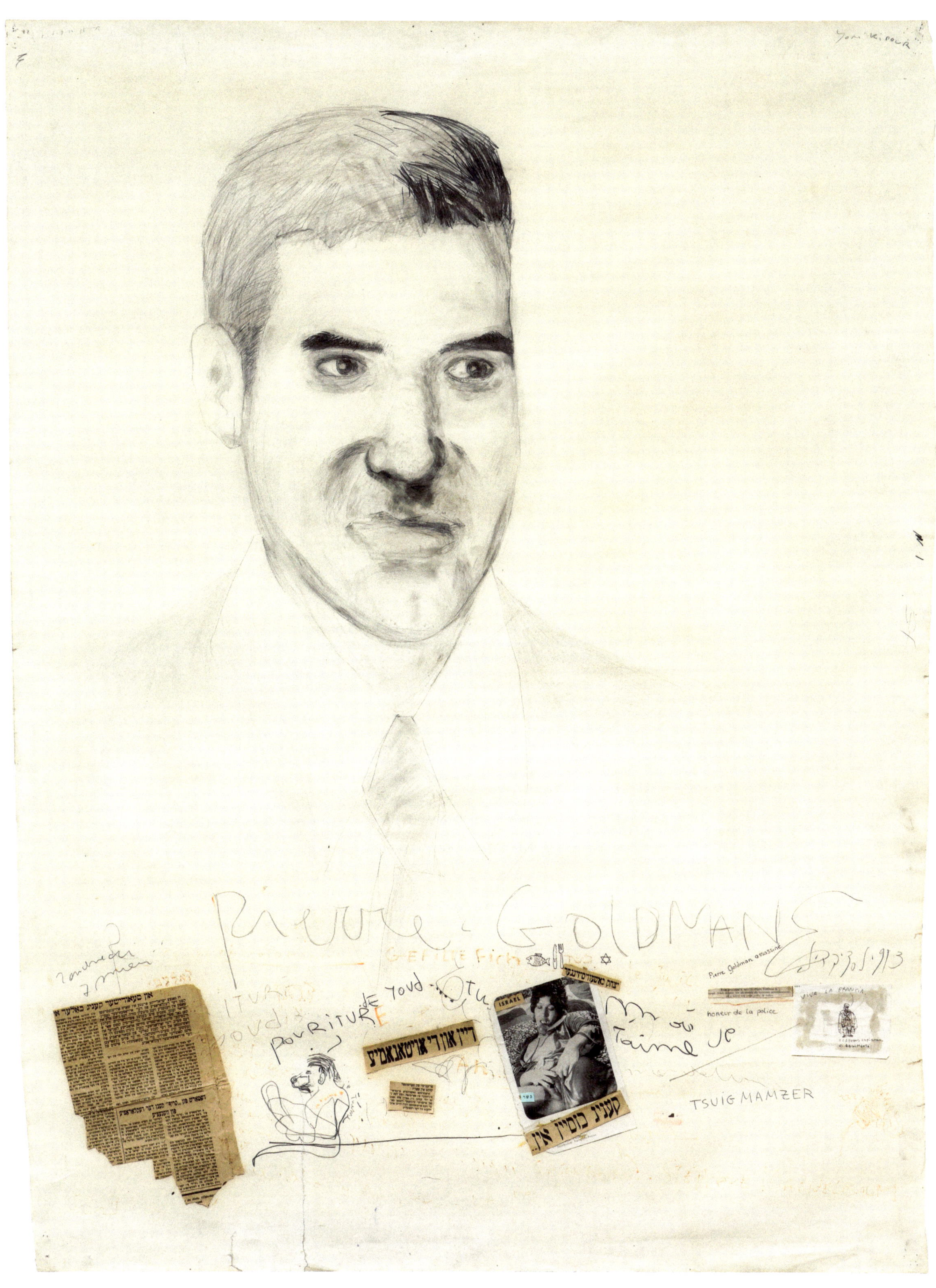


*Pierre Goldman*, 1980

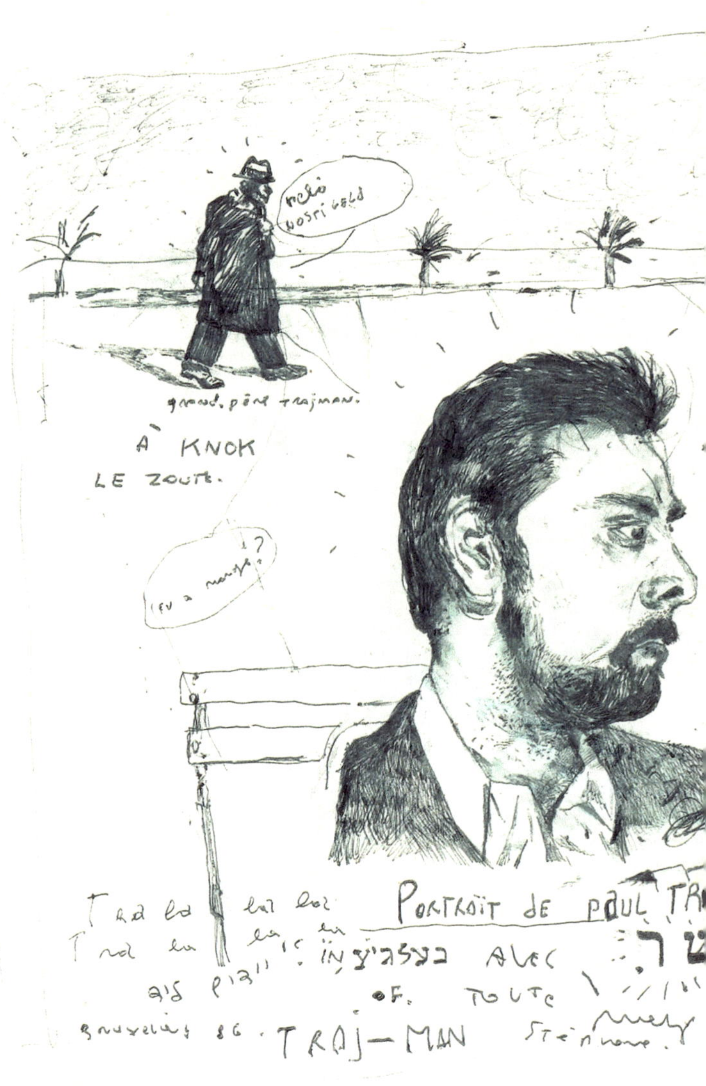


*Portrait de Paul Trajman*, 1986

WINTER - ZOUTE

VEJ

No 1

ITION OF
. PASSOVER
ITE

JE DANSAI AVEC UNE FEMME QU
ME PARLA YIDDISHE É POLONAIS. JÉN
ÉTRANGE, ELLE ME REGARDAIT DÚN S

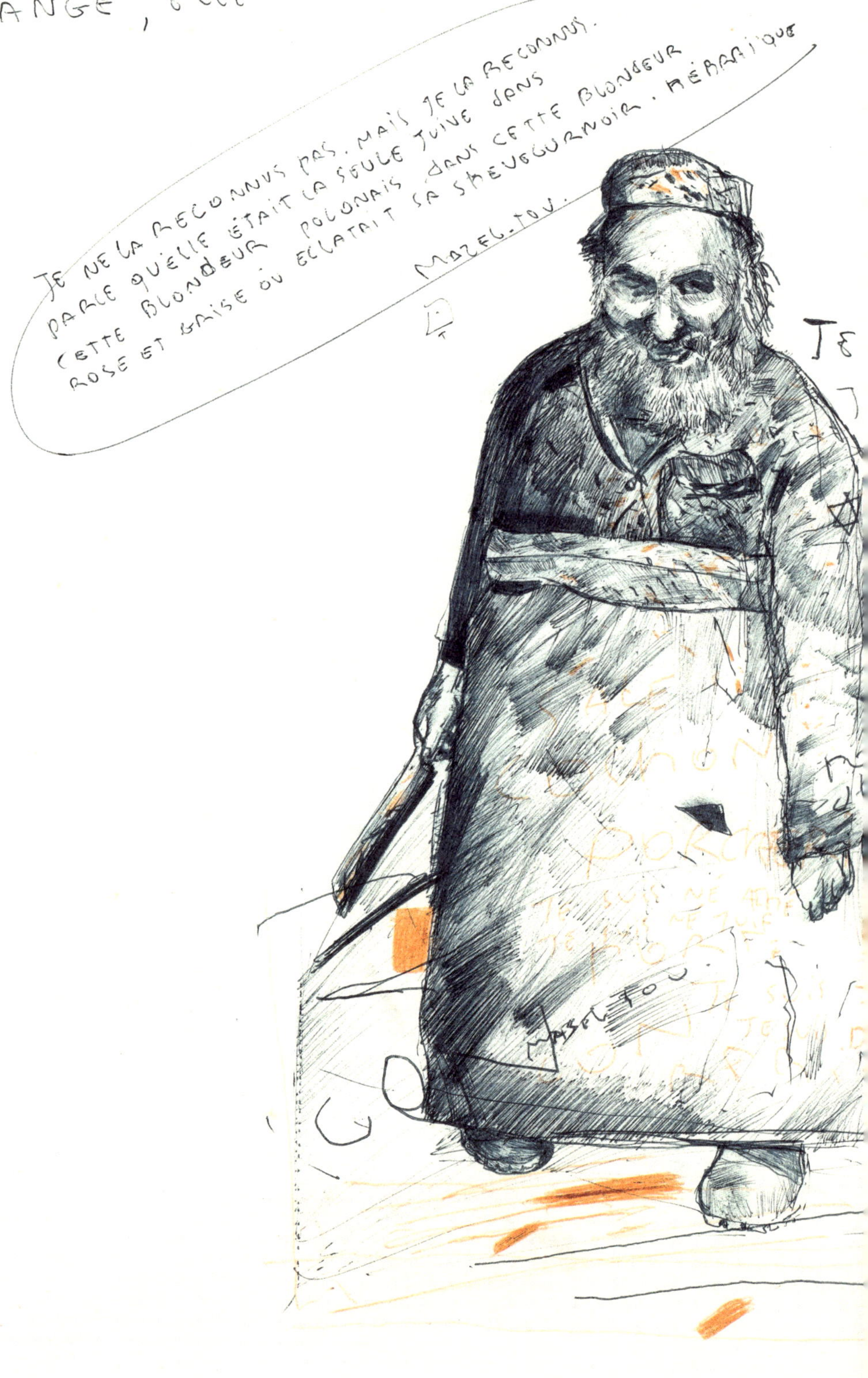


*Shohet*, 1980

ÉTAIT UNE PUTAIN JUIVE ET QUI
UVAI UN SENTIMENT
E BLÊME,

NIRS OBSCURS D'UN JUIF POLONAIS
FRANCE.

NÉ JUIF. JE SUIS D'ORIGINE JUIVE ET JE SUIS JUIF.
NÉ JE SUIS NÉ DE L'OMBRE ET MON DÉSIR
LONGTEMPS QU'ON NE M'ARRACH PAS A L'OMBRE OU JE SUIS

ILS ME RESTAIT CINQ ANS A VIVRE.

JE DANSAI AVEC UNE FEMME QUI ÉTAIT UNE PUTAIN JUIVE ET QUI ME PARLA YIDDISHE & POLONAIS. J'EN ÉPROUVAI UN SENTIMENT ÉTRANGE ELLE ME REGARDAIT D'UN SOURIRE BLÊME.

IN
AIT DU
UTRE AU
UN.

T JUIF.

JUIVE
SUIS JUIF

JE FRÉQUENTAIS
DES GANGSTERS JUIFS.

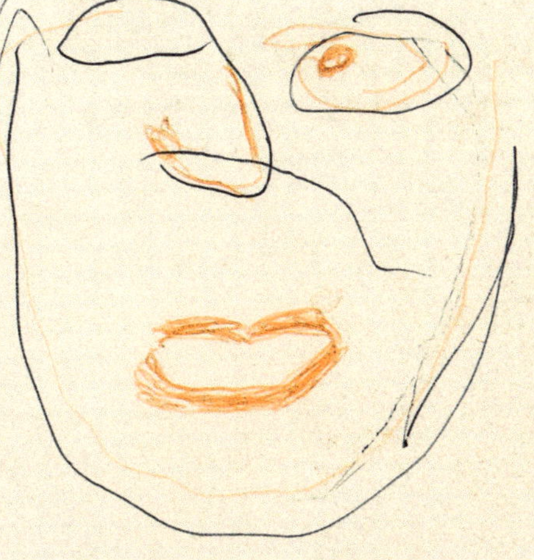

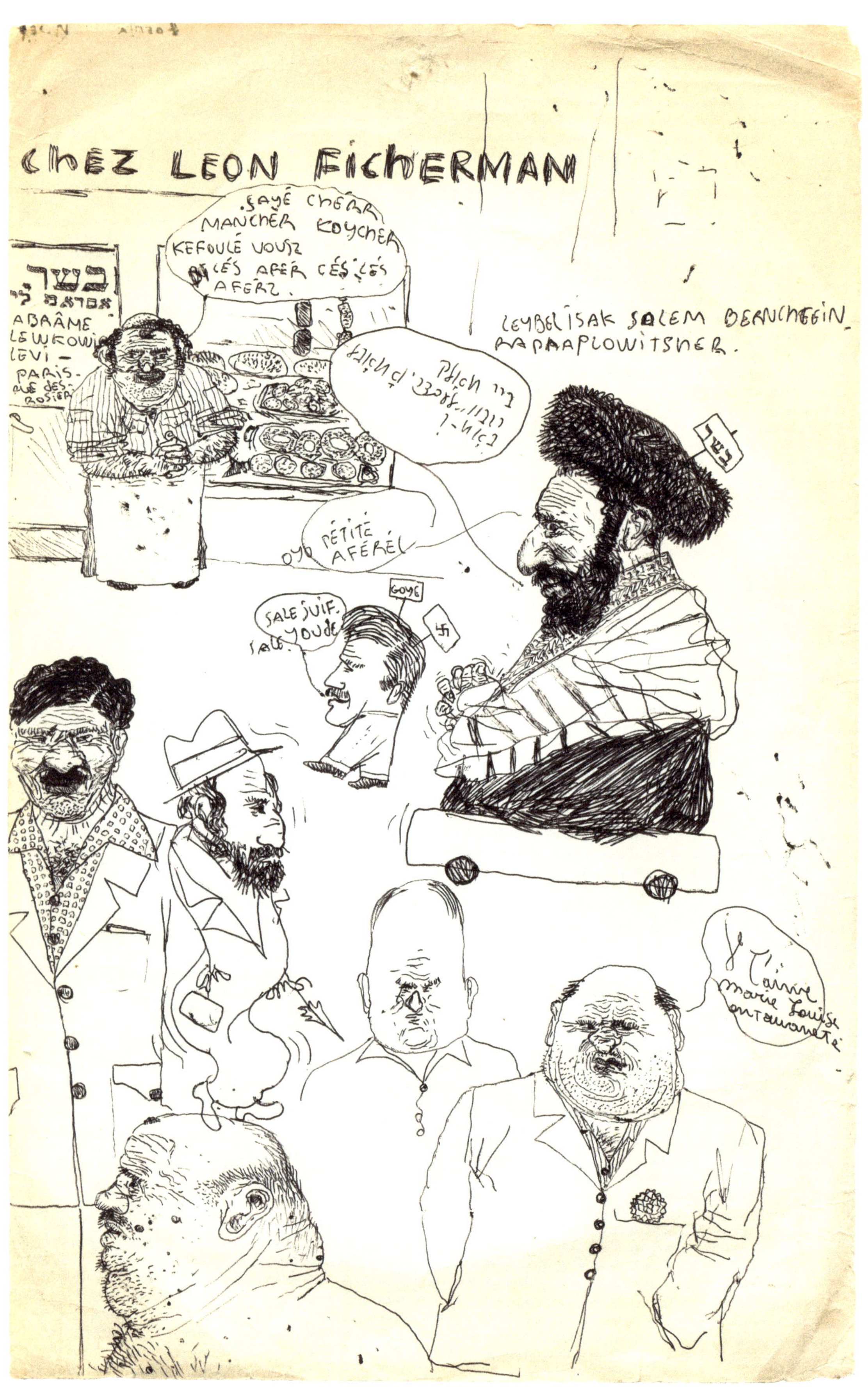


Chez Leon Ficherman, 1985

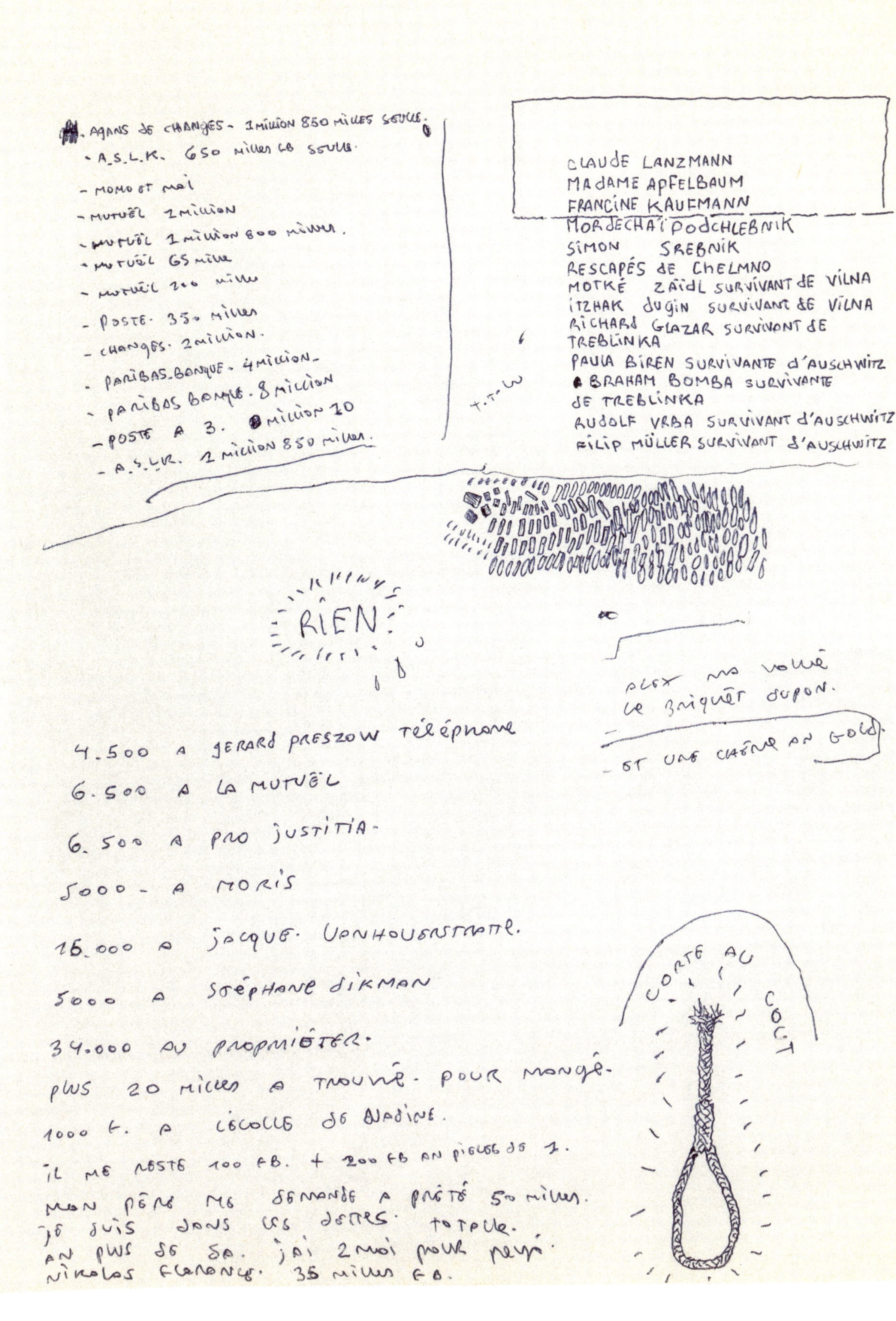


Untitled, 1985–86

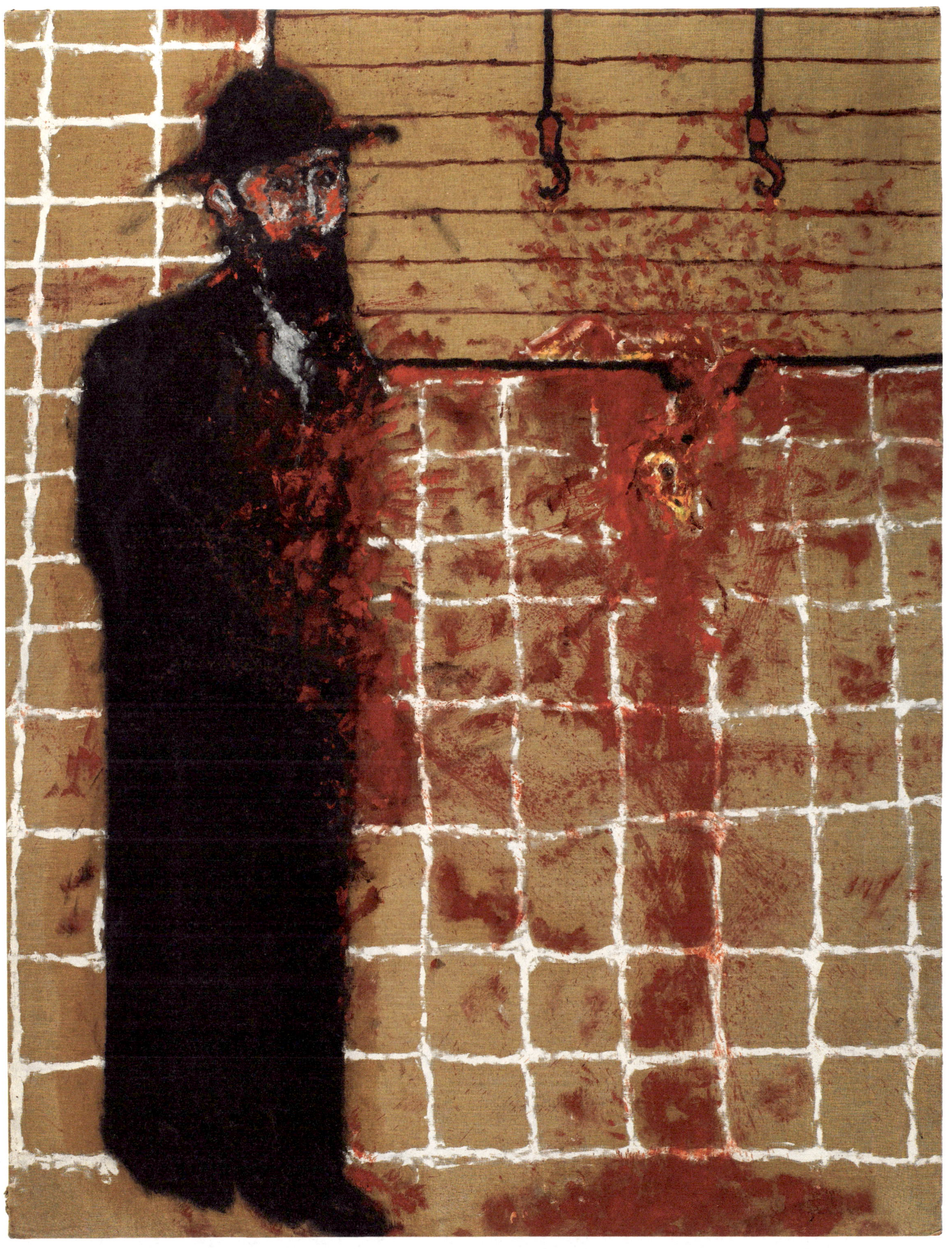

*Rabbin aux abattoirs*, 1977

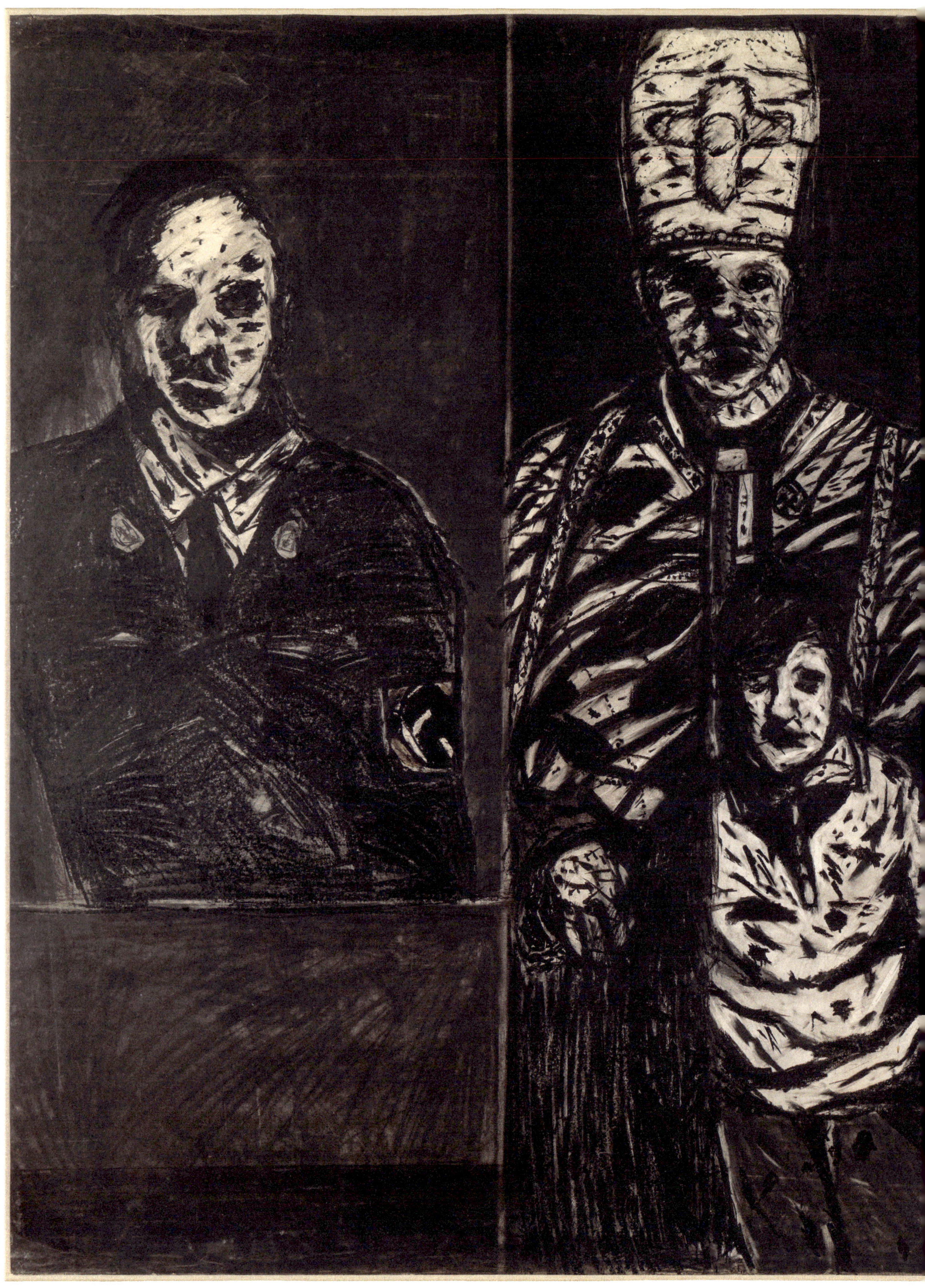

*Le Nazi, saint Nicolas, les frères et la grand-mère*, 1978

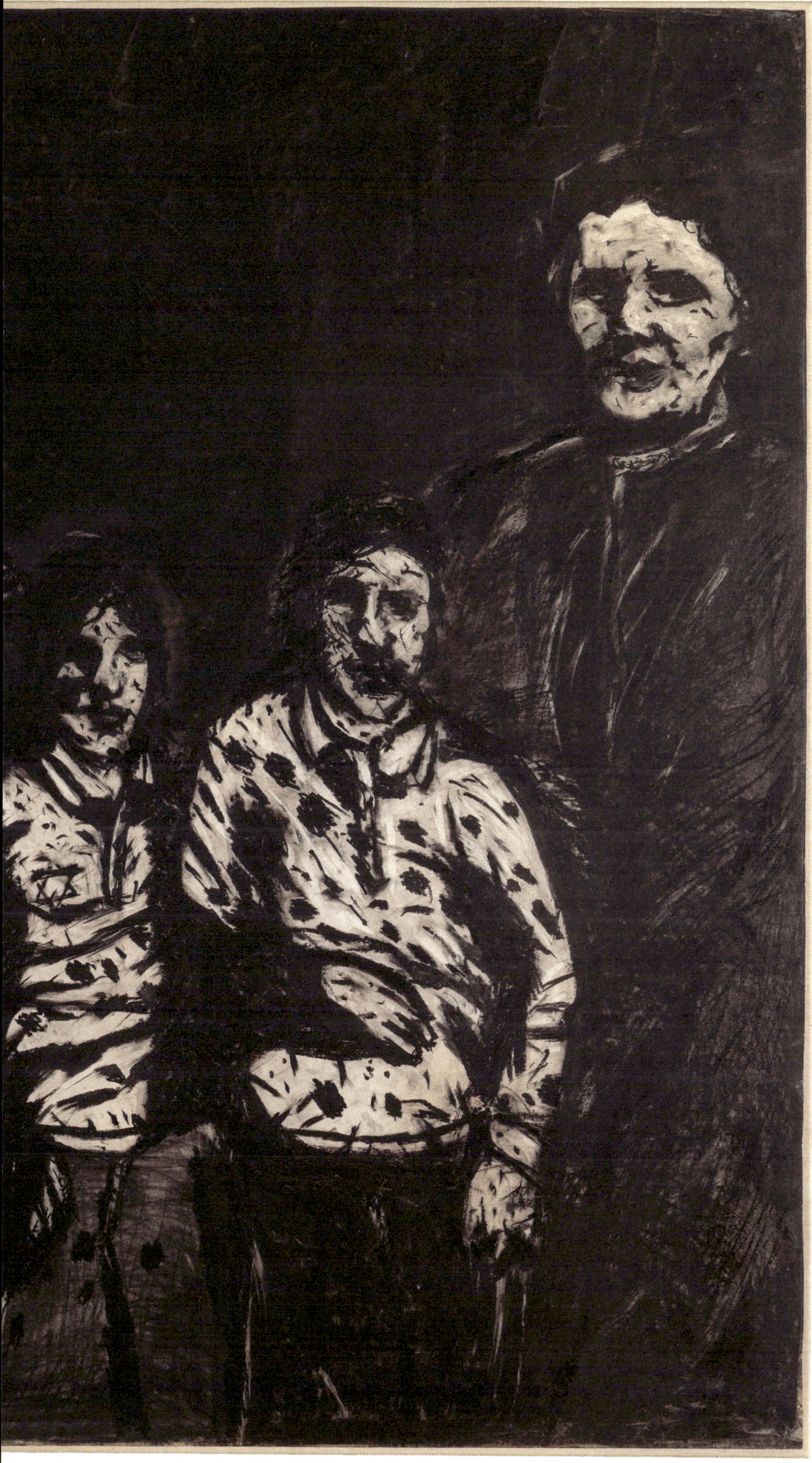

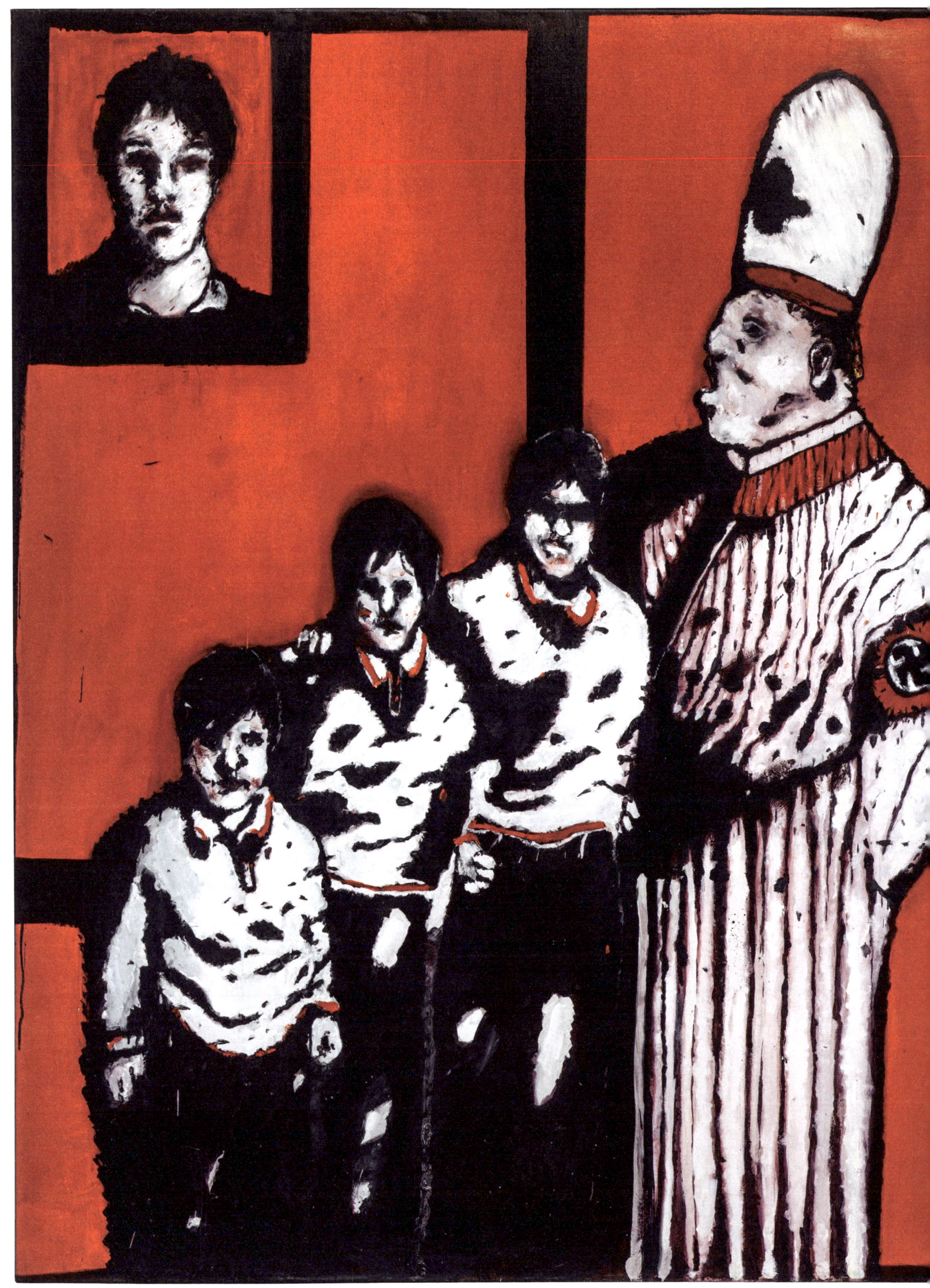

*Saint Nicolas*, 1979

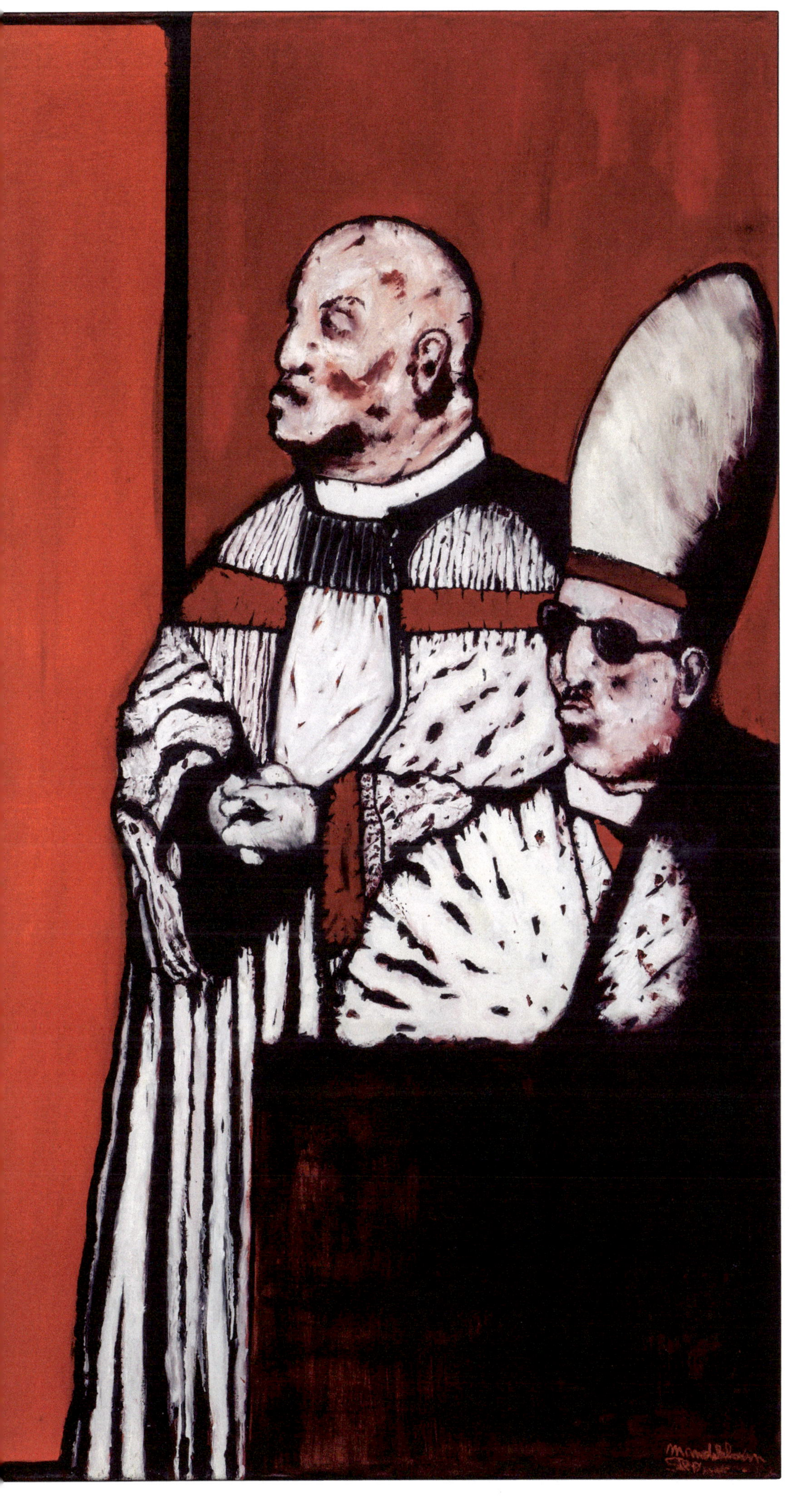

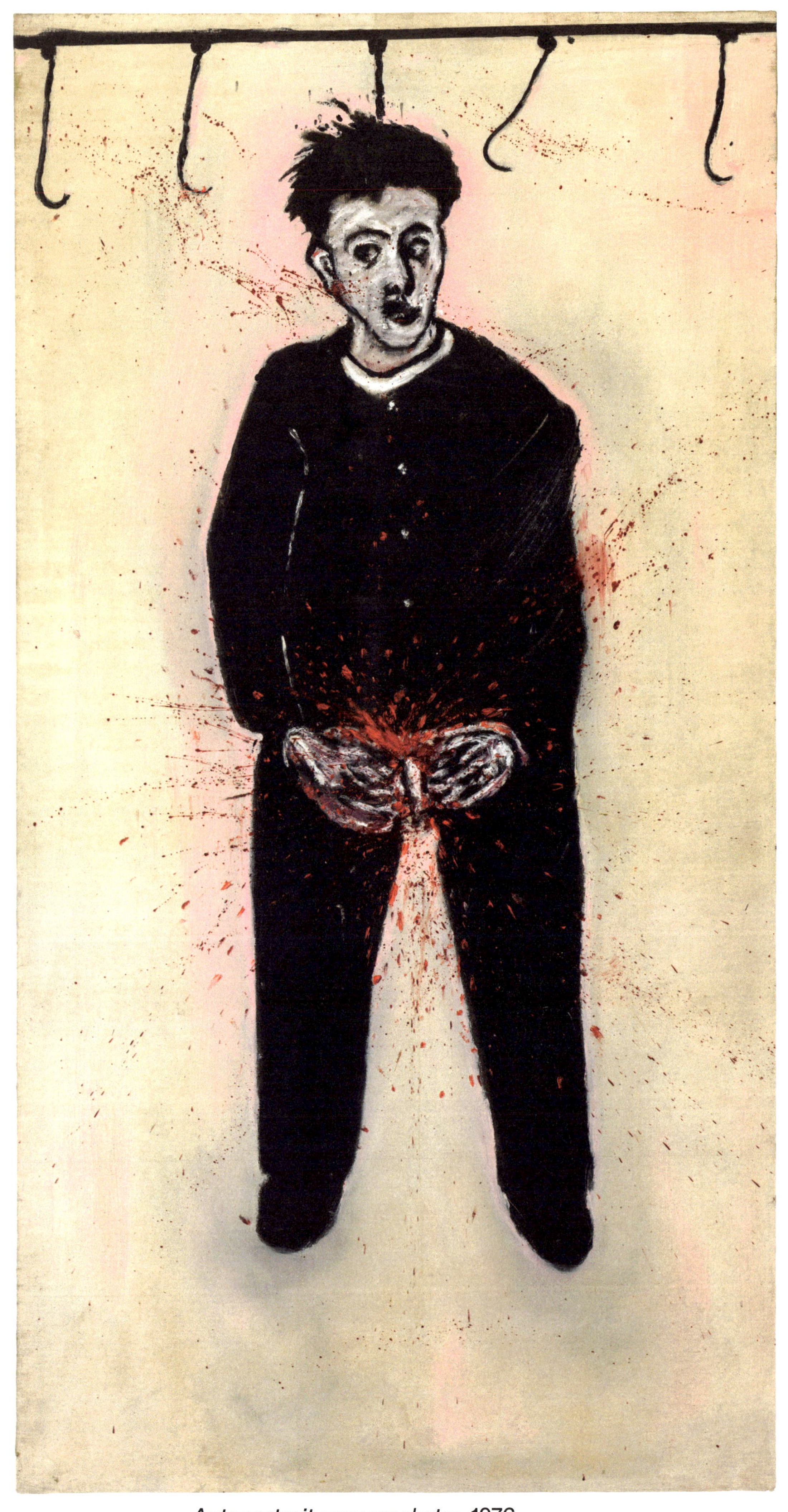

*Autoportrait «aux crochets»*, 1976

Bitter as a Beacon[1]
Ralf Marsault

> [...] io mi trovo alla rabbia, come un giovane
> che di sé non sa altro che è nuovo,
> e si accanisce contro il vecchio mondo.
> E, come un giovane, senza pietà
> o pudore, io non nascondo
> questo mio stato: non avrò pace, mai.[2]

Stéphane Mandelbaum's work, a kind of *Portrait of the Artist as a Young Man*, was created over a period of only ten years, but it leaves no one unmoved. The esthetic challenge and the density of the questions that his images set in motion are such that it is difficult to classify them in pre-established artistic currents, be that in the form of Neo-Expressionism or even the compulsive figuration of an obsessive work of Art Brut. This work is as much a sense of grip as it is reminiscent of an escape.

Beyond any reference, it materializes above all the singular political emergence of a movement whose hidden, even forgotten force would suddenly have no time or any other alternative but to emerge, to give itself to be understood and felt, and then to manifest itself in all the violence of its exit from the frame. His production, consisting of a few paintings and engravings but primarily drawings, potentiated the raw and dynamic expression of a return of the repressed due to its brevity: "There is not a moment when I don't remember when he wasn't drawing. All the time."[3] It is as if an urgency forced Stéphane Mandelbaum to invent, in the sense of discovering, the cartography of a subtle territory, or even the score of a *petite musique* (little music) or *ritournelle* (ritornello) in a Deleuzian sense, where he could recapture and constitute himself as a subject, determine the limits, and exercise his power in his relationship to the world. In this work, the perceptible tension is the sensitive expression of a Gordian knot, stretched between the impulse of a young man seeking to assert himself sexually but also as a singular being, and a zeitgeist where the order of discourse is beginning to show the hollowness of its epistemological flaws. In fact, and as it seems, what this work reveals to us are probably already the premises of the whole problematic that still preoccupies us today. When it is not so much a question of knowing "what should I do," but rather of "what can I do"[4] in order to exist as an individual and find one's place among others, in the face of the duplicity of normative injunctions and other discursive formations of the instances of power that culturally govern our existence.

To approach, if not truly understand, Stéphane Mandelbaum's work, it is necessary to briefly recall the context of its emergence. Not that this context is the explanation or the provider of meaning, but in that it allows us to put his esthetic production into perspective, as well as the interactions or interdependencies that we

1 "Je pense beaucoup au rêve amer qui me tourmente" (I think a lot about the bitter dream that torments me), confession of Stéphane Mandelbaum, quoted from Gilles Sebhan, *Mandelbaum ou le rêve d'Auschwitz* (Paris: Les Impressions Nouvelles, 2019), p. 9. In French, the adjective *amer* also has a substantive form that expresses something bitter, and not only a kind of beer; it can refer to the warning sign of a beacon too. All translations are by the author unless referenced otherwise.

2 "La rabbia," 1961, quoted from Pier Paolo Pasolini, *La religione del mio tempo* (Milan: Garzanti, 2018), p. 167: "I find myself in anger, like a young man / who knows nothing of himself but that he is new / and rages against the old world. / And, like a young man, without pity, / or modesty, I do not hide / this state of mind: I will never have peace."

3 Interview with Stéphane's brother, Ariéh Mandelbaum, and Gérard Preszow, a documentary film writer and filmmaker, who confirms the facts of this statement some time later. See the film by Stéphane Collins, *Mad in Polen: Portrait de Stéphane Mandelbaum* (FR, 2000).

4 See Reiner Schürmann, *Se constituer soi-même comme sujet anarchique* (Paris: Diaphanes, 2021), p. 35.

can sense. After all, some of his paintings and drawings are portraits that look to the left, to the past, and to History; this may be a methodology where the search for sources helps to bring the present into focus.

Stéphane Mandelbaum was born in Brussels on March 8, 1961, to a painter father, Arié Mandelbaum, and an illustrator mother, Pili Mandelbaum, at the heart of what is known in francophone Europe as the *trente glorieuses*—that is, 30 years of economic growth (1945–75). This ambiguous period, which was positivist and even in search of social well-being, but also cynical in the ambiguity of its recycling of a war economy, took on the task of making people forget the misery and disasters of the past conflict to rebuild a "modern," if not new, management of exchanges between people. This was the moment when a hierarchical organization of work, by definition, its objectives,[5] was put in place: when the producer remains free to choose the means to be used for his project, but in fact becomes the manager and the only person responsible for his being in the world. If the exercise could give the illusion of a certain improvement in living conditions, it was at the price of a paradigm shift. As a result of a forced reindustrialization, prewar Europe's mainly agricultural societies, which were centered on their intimate relationship with nature, had to be rethought. And its *Weltanschauung* of a culture of mass production for a society of consumption and immediate satisfaction of desires took on the task of buying social consent through contentment. Henry Miller had already denounced the malaise in 1945 with his book *The Air-Conditioned Nightmare*.[6] For even if this concept of progress could seduce for a time, it was not without entropy, the cruelest one being that which began to atomize human beings, putting them in competition, one with another.

The Beat movement, which emerged at around the same time, produced a set of critical reflections on the loss of meaning and community. This rush towards the commodification of the world, where the paradigms of asepsis and, underhandedly, of purity and orderliness, could well carry with them a danger of uniformization and segregation. Whether through the writings and poetry of Jack Kerouac, William S. Burroughs, or Allen Ginsberg, these bitter questionings extended in their own way to Sigmund Freud's dark intuition in *Civilization and Its Discontents*,[7] twenty years earlier. This cultural movement particularly tried to propose a different beat, a different *rhythm*. Apparent in literature, it was also present in the work of Jackson Pollock, whom Stéphane Mandelbaum quotes in one of his drawings (*Pollock et Fabien*, 1980 → 119) by reproducing one of Hans Namuth's most famous photographs of the painter in a "dance" performance of his drippings. A ritual seeking to produce or rediscover, metaphorically, the place of the body in its relationship to the environment, and which echoed and affected Pollock's fascination with the Indigenous cultures on the verge of extinction. The perception of an inherited responsibility in the

5 "Discipliner les femmes et les hommes en les considérant comme de simples facteurs de production et dévaster la Terre, conçue comme un simple objet, vont de pair." (Disciplining women and men as mere factors of production, and devastating the Earth as a mere object.), quoted from Johann Chapoutot, *Libres d'obéir. Le management du nazisme à aujourd'hui* (Paris: Gallimard, 2020), p. 141.

6 Henry Miller, *The Air-Conditioned Nightmare* (New York: New Directions, 1945).

7 Sigmund Freud, *Civilization and Its Discontents* (London: Penguin, 2002), German original: *Das Unbehagen in der Kultur* (The Uneasiness in Civilization, Vienna: Psychoanalytischer Verlag, 1930).

genocide perpetrated by the immigrants who dispossessed the Indigenous peoples of their land and their intimate relationship with it is as much a part of Jackson Pollock's early paintings as it is of a Beat poet like Gary Snyder. This extermination of Indigenous cultures[8] charges the American ethos with a heavy guilt. It still makes explicit today its fascination with violence and the use of weapons, the latent permanence of its racial problem. Several of Stéphane Mandelbaum's drawings portray figures of Indigenous people from the Amazonas region, whose culture is also constantly threatened (*Indigène et predelle*, 1979; *Indigène au collier*, 1979; *Indigène à la tresse*, 1983; *Indigène au collier*, 1983; *Indigène à l'oreille perçée*, 1983; *Indigène aux peintures*, 1984). In this way, they mark a recurrent question in his work. And one wonders if this evoked genocide could not be like the reminiscence, or even the metaphor, of another.

The 1960s confirmed the first questions about the real value of this religion of progress confronted with its own entropy. The philosopher Herbert Marcuse published his essay on the ideology of advanced industrial society, *One-Dimensional Man*, in 1964.[9] This was the moment when the hippy movement tried, in reaction, to defend peaceful ideals, contest authority, and propose attempts at an alternative life liberalization—a liberalization of sexuality. The weekly magazine *Actuel* widely disseminated these ideas, images, and texts in French-speaking European societies. The Woodstock and Isle of Wight music festivals gave the illusion of a possible subversive and collective body through the crowds they mobilized. Pili Mandelbaum, Stéphane's mother, can thus say, looking at a photograph, "The seventies [...] the hippies, when we believed in them very strongly."[10] The question remains: what did they believe in? What did this cultural phenomenon promise to bring them? Emancipation, as a subject, through the liberation of sexuality? Wasn't this already a trap, the avatar of hedonism under the control of neoliberalism, which was to sound the death knell of postwar fraternity and good intentions? Many individuals were in fact no longer part of a community or a family, as they were already experiencing a social force that pushed them to become isolated, narcissistically disconnected from others.

Stéphane Mandelbaum grew up in this universe and suffered from extreme dyslexia, which made him give up the traditional school curriculum. His parents entrusted him to an alternative school, the Snark in Charleroi, Belgium, inspired by the self-managed pedagogical project of Alexander Sutherland Neill, the Libres enfants de Summerhill. One of his friends said: "The Snark [...] we wanted something else; at the beginning, it was a complete mess."[11] Then he went to the Academy of Fine Arts in Watermael-Boitsfort, Belgium, because he discovered a passion for drawing. The painter Pierre Thoma, his friend at the Academy, tells how they deepened their knowledge in museums but also on the spot in the slaughterhouses of Brussels:

8 See the four-part experimental documentary film series by Raoul Peck, *Exterminate All the Brutes* (USA, 2021).

9 Herbert Marcuse, *One-Dimensional Man* (Boston: Beacon Press, 1964).

10 An interview with Stéphane Mandelbaum's mother, Pili Mandelbaum, in the family house in Fontenoille, quoted from Collins, *Mad in Polen*.

11 Jean Nicolas Craps (sculptor and teacher at the École des Arts d'Uccle, Belgium), quoted from ibid.

> Stéphane had already immersed himself in [Chaïm] Soutine's work [...] we looked at how it was done, how it exuded flesh, life. Our obsession was with meat and death. [...] You only have to look at Stéphane's écorchés to understand that it's no longer an anatomical plate; it's really flesh ... *in pictura carne* ... you'd have to invent the formula.[12]

Very early on in his production, paintings thus reveal the violent world of slaughterhouses: the evocation of blood by the projection of red stains on the tiled walls, as a centrifugal explosion on an aseptic grid with its lines of butcher's hooks, points to the rationalism of this Taylorism in the management of death that progress brings. One can speak of a form of fascination or repulsion in the painter: "Stéphane could not stand violence; he would make a face as soon as he saw a brutal scene. This is what happened when we went to visit the slaughterhouses. After that, that was all he drew."[13]

The slaughterhouse, however, remains an emblematic place of contemporaneity: it concentrates the questions affecting the dichotomy and, at the same time, the interdependence between the conceptions we have of the animal world.[14] But in our way of practicing anthropic violence, the slaughterhouse above all highlights the paradoxes in a singular relationship to existence, more particularly in the face of what is designated as otherness and its capacities for resistance. Between all that we want to cherish and all that we imagine we are entitled to exploit—one being unthinkable without the other—human rationality has set up devices and rituals by proxy, ruthlessly efficient, with no possibility of escape. By extension, the vision of the slaughterhouse thus gives rise to reflection on the nature of the economy of exchanges between humans. Stéphane Mandelbaum seizes upon this and summons a ghost that could well be that of the Shoah (*Rabbin aux abattoirs*, 1977 → 209). However, at the heart of the 1970s, this vision shows above all how a political economy, still in essence fundamentally patriarchal, was able to exert its violence on the bodies it discredited through the prism of the agreed ethos of its peremptory vision.
All these bodies that contradict the legitimacy and supremacy of its power are precisely those that Mandelbaum challenges, whether they are feminine, racialized, or singular in their own way. These bodies must fight against the self-evidence of a culture that seeks to keep them in subjection, to repress them, to exploit them, and even to lead them to their ruin, for lack of being able to completely recycle them. For these misfits that he draws, embodying the stigmatization that is made of them, serve as witnesses and beacons to orient himself and understand himself in his own situation. Their looks are filled with doubt and circumspection, sometimes almost flabbergasted. This is already apparent in the portraits of Pier Paolo Pasolini, Francis Bacon, or Pierre Goldman, but is amplified later in other drawings (*Bar l'Asia B N° 1*, 1984 → 32; *Portrait d'Annie, Homosexuel, Putain juive*, 1985 → 36; *L'Albertine Bar (Beautiful*

12 Pierre Thoma, "Entrevue" (interview with Bruno Jean in July 2018), in: Anne Montfort, *Stéphane Mandelbaum*, exh. cat. (Paris: Édition Dilecta / Centre Pompidou, 2019), pp. 121–22; *Stéphane Mandelbaum* exhibition at the Centre Pompidou (Cabinet d'arts graphiques), 6.3.–20.5.2019.

13 Ibid., p. 123.

14 Charles Stépanoff, *L'animal et la mort: Chasses, modernité et crise du sauvage* (Paris: La Découverte, 2021), p. 10.

*Deception C.)*, 1986 → 13; *Portrait de Meknil*, 1985 → 9). These glances, lost in some elsewhere (in his drawing *Shohet*, 1980 → 204–05), Stéphane Mandelbaum quotes Pierre Goldman evoking "a pale smile") testify in their own way to this violence in the maximization of profit and performance as an ethic, which overwhelms them. The feeling of a loss of self in a world where human relationships have become commercial. It looks like a challenge and seems to say: What can I do then, to be neither the victim nor the oppressor in this equation?

Stéphane Mandelbaum devotes at least one drawing to Rainer Werner Fassbinder (*Rainer (Portrait de Rainer Werner Fassbinder)*, c. 1984 → 28), the inspiration for which seems to come from an image taken from the film *Fox and His Friends*.[15] The director is also the author of *In a Year with 13 Moons*,[16] which was released when Stéphane Mandelbaum was seventeen years old. In it, Elvira Weishaupt, a transgender woman who questions gender assignment in a scene shot against a slaughterhouse chain on which carcasses of oxen are paraded before her, ponders her existence. Two years later, Fassbinder filmed the epilogue to his adaptation of Alfred Döblin's novel *Berlin Alexanderplatz*,[17] which he called *Epilogue: My Dream of the Dream of Franz Biberkopf*.[18] In this film, the main character, Biberkopf (this is also Max's family name in *Fox and His Friends*), sees his friend Mieze in a dream that plays out inside a slaughterhouse with high-hanging butcher's hooks, the tiled walls splattered with blood; her belly is stained with blood, and she ends up sticking a knife into it. This frightening scene is strangely like one Stéphane Mandelbaum had painted a few years earlier in *Autoportrait «aux crochets»* (1976 → 214). Fassbinder and Mandelbaum did not know each other, so they could not have inspired each other, but nonetheless, both artists' works contribute to generating the symptom of an era in the expressiveness of their creations. One of the questions that stands out in *Berlin Alexanderplatz* is: "Wie soll man leben, wenn man nicht sterben will [...] Ich will ja anständig sein."[19]

Some years later, Stéphane Mandelbaum painted the *écorchés* (flayed), (*Écorché I*, *II*, *III*, 1979 → 134–36), which, as Pierre Thoma pointed out, are flesh made image. But perhaps this flesh evoked is not so much what constitutes bodies as a "Visibility, this generality of the Sensible in itself."[20] One senses that the accumulation of representations, which confront and challenge each other in order to deconstruct themselves in the manner of Robert Rauschenberg's *Combines*, participates in a kind of dance whose choreography is not noted in advance but constructed in the practice of its interactions. Bodies again, but only in such a way as to produce a figure through a movement that puts them in relation.

Of these bodies, we note in particular the necks that Stéphane Mandelbaum draws—strong, thick, and wide.[21] Although massive, they seem, paradoxically, to be tight-throated, as if bursting with a desire to cry out while holding back tears in a strangled malaise, to make a noise about the injustices. Something

15 Rainer Werner Fassbinder, *Fox and His Friends* (*Faustrecht der Freiheit*, BRD, 1975).

16 Rainer Werner Fassbinder, *In a Year with 13 Moons* (*In einem Jahr mit 13 Monden*, BRD, 1978).

17 Rainer Werner Fassbinder, *Berlin Alexanderplatz* (BRD, 1980), a fourteen-part mini-series broadcast by the WDR Westdeutscher Rundfunk, Cologne. The eponymous novel by Alfred Döblin was published in 1929 by S. Fischer Verlag in Berlin.

18 Rainer Werner Fassbinder, *Epilogue: My Dream of the Dream of Franz Biberkopf* (*Epilog: Mein Traum vom Traum des Franz Biberkopf*, BRD, 1979/80).

19 "How is One to Live if One Doesn't Want to Die? [...] You swore [...] to stay decent.", https://www.fassbinderfoundation.de/movies/berlin-alexanderplatz-197980/?lang=en, accessed October 16, 2024.

20 Maurice Merleau-Ponty, *The Visible and the Invisible: Followed by Working Notes*, ed. by Claude Lefort, trans. by Alphonso Lingis (Evanston: Northwestern University Press, 1968), p. 139.

21 Stéphane Mandelbaum's mother noticed that her son had "un long cou [...] une forme de tête tout à fait spéciale" (a long neck, a very special head shape), quoted from Collins, *Mad in Polen*.

that has accumulated and has not passed. These suppressed cries, however, are reminiscent of those that Francis Bacon or Pablo Picasso fully express in their paintings. One thinks, for example, of Bacon's fascination with the scream represented in Nicolas Poussin's painting *Le Massacre des Innocents* (*The Massacre of the Innocents*, c. 1628). Despite their silence and internalized power, the figure of Mandelbaum's swallowed cries fully participates in the type of *gueuloir* (yelling) that Flaubert needed to ensure the accuracy of his writing.[22] The experience of denouncing the unbearable is uncontrollable, an inevitably necessary extreme to meet expressive relevance. Perhaps also to begin to "heal" oneself of the suffering undergone, if one thinks of its staging in rituals of mourning.[23]

Several cries are nevertheless evident (*Composition (Portrait of Bacon)*, 1980 → 186–87; *Gueule cassée*, c. 1980 → 167), and their expressiveness resonates not only with Francisco Goya's *Los Desastres de la Guerra* (*The Disasters of War*) engravings (c. 1810–14) and Otto Dix's print series *Der Krieg* (*The War*, 1924) but also with the more than 100 sketches that Zoran Mušič began to paint 25 years after he was liberated from Dachau concentration camp in the series *Non siamo gli ultimi* (*We Are Not the Last*, 1971–74).[24]

While what Mandelbaum is trying to say to us in his work is not explicit, it perhaps evokes an affliction, linked to his parents' deep disillusionment with their own expectations, that he seeks to express. *The Limits to Growth*[25] and the effects of the oil crises of 1973 and 1979 destabilized the ideological matrix of the social contract. The terrorist activities of the far-left Red Army Faction in Germany[26] and the Red Brigades in Italy locked the European democracies' fragility into a reflex of fear and repression, identified by the poisoned air and the dystopian image of the "leaden years." The guilt felt in the face of forgetting the horrors of the war, which one senses could return, encourages the last witnesses and all those who do not want to resign themselves to the worst to put back on the job a question that no analysis has ever succeeded in unraveling: that of the persistence of evil, even in a society of progress.

Stéphane Mandelbaum shares this guilt according to Thoma: "I then saw a radical change in Stéphane's drawing with the 'Pasolini' series, etc. There was no longer the noise of Auschwitz. There was silence and flesh."[27] Thus, Mandelbaum turned to these figures of doubt and intellectual awareness as navigational beacons: Pasolini, Goldman, Bacon, and Fassbinder, among others. With his father, he discovered Pasolini's films *Pigsty*[28] and *Salò, or the 120 Days of Sodom*,[29] and he saw the film *Shoah*[30] by Claude Lanzmann, the published screenplay of which he kept. In Paris, he saw Francis Ford Coppola's *Apocalypse Now*.[31]

In these same years, Fassbinder released two more films: *Why Does Herr R. Run Amok?*[32] and *The Marriage of Maria Braun*,[33] which, just as much as Pasolini's *Pigsty*, sharply denounced the legacy and implicit reproduction of the ideology of the Third

22 Gustave Flaubert was known to declaim his own texts aloud to check their impact and rhythm. See Michael Fried's novel, *Flaubert's "Gueuloir": On Madame Bovary and Salammbô* (New Haven: Yale University Press, 2012).

23 See Ernesto De Martino, *Mort et pleurs rituels: De la lamentation funèbre antique à la plainte de Marie*, trans. by Marcello Massenzio (Paris: EHESS, 2022).

24 See Marco Goldin, *Zoran Mušič*, exh. cat. Palazzo Attems Petzenstein, Gorizia (Conegliano: Linea d'ombra libri, 2003).

25 Dennis Meadows et al., *The Limits to Growth: A Report for the Club of Rome's Project on the Predicament of Mankind* (New York: Universe Books, 1972).

26 Stéphane Mandelbaum clearly refers to the Rote Armee Fraktion (Red Army Faction) in his drawing *Composition avec Bacon et Arié (arrestation de la bande à Baader)*, 1984.

27 Thoma, "Entrevue," p. 122.

28 Pier Paolo Pasolini, *Pigsty* (*Porcile*, IT/FR, 1969).

29 Pier Paolo Pasolini, *Salò, or the 120 Days of Sodom* (*Salò o le 120 giornate di Sodoma*, IT/FR, 1975).

30 Claude Lanzmann, *Shoah* (FR, 1985).

31 Francis Ford Coppola, *Apocalypse Now* (USA, 1979).

Reich in the *weltanschauung* of the German economic miracle. Samy Szlingerbaum's Yiddish film *Bruxelles-transit* (BE, 1980) evokes the return of the Jews to postwar Belgium, while Liliana Cavanis' film *The Night Porter*[34] was indicative of a malaise felt in the face of the creeping eroticization of power relations. The releases of the films *Christiane F.*[35] and *In the Realm of the Senses*[36] did not escape anyone. One also thinks of Viennese Actionism, particularly the latest work of the Austrian artist Günter Brus,[37] the work of Gina Pane, and the body art performances, which Stéphane Mandelbaum had also learned about at the Academy. All these works evoke the expression of malaise, deep dissatisfaction, or incompleteness, which Nina Hagen termed *Unbehagen* (unease) in an album she released with her band at the end of the 1970s.[38] Stéphane Mandelbaum co-opts a few quotations from this period, the seminal birthplace of the punk movement and its DIY esthetic composed on a field of semiotic ruins, in his portraits: the mockery of the Nazi ideology's thurifers (*Mickey et Himmler*, 1983 → 177), associating the specter of the Reichsführer-SS with the Disney character's distressed rictus in a thick provocational[39] scrawl (or *scraboutcha*,[40] as he called them), or *Der Göbels* [*Goebbels*] (1980 → 183), whose overlay of a flat area of white gouache seems to occult the belching of a discourse in order to better signify its vacuity.[41] Two or three portraits evoke the personality of the SA[42] leader (*Ernst Röhm*, 1981 → 174; *P. Röm (Nº 1/Portraït der Röm)*, 1981–82 → 173), gratifying him with a disillusioned mimicry and the absent air of someone who has been cheated and whose certainties have been broken. Two portraits (*Portrait von punk türk (Hugo)*, 1984 → 44; *Ernst Cön (portrait von Ernst Cön, eïne Punk)*, 1984 → 45) refer to characters that Stéphane Mandelbaum may have met in Berlin, since the city is apparent: the German flag, a waitress with beer mugs, and a photograph of a woman uncovering her sex are all depicted. The scrambled and proliferating aspect of this esthetic echoes the blurring of codes that punk fanzines make immoderate use of. The coupling of two pigs amidst a chaos of signs, which Stéphane Mandelbaum shows in at least two of his drawings (*Pollock et Fabien*, 1980 → 119; *Composition (Shohet)*, c. 1982 → 124–25), is reminiscent of the cover of the London punk fanzine *Chainsaw*.[43]

The figure that appears in *Shohet* (1980 → 204–05) is presumably his grandfather Salomon, with whom Mandelbaum reconnects with the Jewish tradition and the communal experience of the family uniting across generations. The character in *Shohet* holds a knife that participates in the ritual covenant by rupture (the Brit Milah or Circumcision), and one can well imagine, in this young man busy "living and writing with ardour,"[44] that this is Stéphane Mandelbaum, moreover, drawing subjects in which sexuality and death collide. The artist is aware that death and death confront each other (*Picasso, Picador et Guernica*, 1980 → 122–23)[45] and that this quest for a rite of passage is part of his understanding of the world. He seeks to represent a self that experiences things in a sensory way.

32 Rainer Werner Fassbinder and Michael Fengler, *Why Does Herr R. Run Amok?* (*Warum läuft Herr R. Amok?*, BRD, 1970).

33 Rainer Werner Fassbinder, *The Marriage of Maria Braun* (*Die Ehe der Maria Braun*, BRD, 1978).

34 Liliana Cavani, *The Night Porter* (*Il portiere di notte*, IT, 1974).

35 Uli Edel, *Christiane F.* (*Christiane F. – Wir Kinder vom Bahnhof Zoo*, BRD, 1981).

36 Nagisa Ōshima, *In the Realm of the Senses* (*Ai no korīda / L'empire des sens*, JP/FR, 1976).

37 Günter Brus, *Zerreißprobe*—this was the artist's last Actionist performance, shot on 16-mm color film on June 19, 1970, in Munich.

38 Nina Hagen Band, *Unbehagen* (CBS Records, 1979).

39 "If there is no subversion and contestation in art there is no need for it to exist" is the phrase reproduced in Stéphane Mandelbaum's drawing, *Pasolini «Les mille et une nuits»*, 1980 (→ 154–55).

40 Recounted by Gérard Preszow, quoted from Collins, *Mad in Polen*.

41 Funnily enough, what this flake of white paint hides is the baseline humor of a scribble that reads "Jef, j'ai soif" (Jef, I'm thirsty), which is an attempt at ridiculing Goebbels' eructation.

It is through the body that he interprets his relationship to reality, as, for example, when visiting Rome in 1978, he insisted on sleeping on the beach at Ostia, where Pasolini was murdered.[46] Of the testimonies that can be read, all attest to the son's affection for his parents: the portrait he made of his father (*Kismatores! (Portrait d'Arié Mandelbaum)*, 1982 → 195) is at once imbued with an acute perception of the complexity of the feelings that run through the character and with an irreverent humor that has free rein. The oil painting entitled *La Prothèse, portrait de Pili* (1977), important in its format and seminal in its choice of a ternary spectrum of color, expresses no cruelty towards his mother;[47] the object symbolizes an articulation to the world through the experience of the body. In one of his notebooks, he writes, "[...] in my last drawings, I have only the memory of my smell, my perspiration, that of my wife and my lovers [...]. I have a disgust for what I have done and also a respect; it empties me of my whole body, like when I ejaculate."[48]

If Stéphane Mandelbaum, inevitably, is of his time and of the culture he shapes in his confrontation with the figures that serve as his references, his work cannot be reduced to time and place completely. A form of escape remains implicit in it; it is this escape that crosses time and comes to take us. What interests Stéphane Mandelbaum is the gesture of painting, the freedom, the dynamics, and the choreography of this movement. In this is expressed one of the major lines of flight that run through his work. Faced with the misery of the world, he does not oppose a defense or an illustration of the instinct of life; he engages the figure of speech of a movement. Everything is very mobile in his drawings. In his quotation from Pollock's work, he figures the throwing of dripping paint. His drawings of accumulated lines, marks, and signs materialize the movement of his hands. They enter a form of trance that is inspired by the American painter's dance. If Mandelbaum tries to redefine himself through an orchestrated chaos of cohorts of signs, battalions of erasures, quotations, interjections, reported insults, and so on, it is perhaps because he has a poor grasp of the grammar of the order of discourse. But, above all, it is because he is trying to say and express something else. Thus, he gets rid of the trivial jumble of contingency that makes up the background of his drawings, and we find it piled up in the layout, defiantly swept into a corner, into a margin, sometimes even highlighted with a strip of adhesive paper, or parked in the box of a comic-book window. For Stéphane Mandelbaum is compelled to make room for the advent of this other truth that really concerns him. His guilt about the Shoah, the expression of a survivor's syndrome, and the melancholy of his condition as a stigmatized person. He shares it in a mirror image with the figures Pasolini reveals in his films: "[I]f the 'body' lives a 'life unworthy of being lived' (a Black, a Sardinian, a Bohemian, a Jew, an invert, a wretch), it is also manifestly revolutionary [...]. A poor person, an unhappy person are always, by themselves, heroic, either by resigning themselves or rebelling—and also by carrying out

42 The SA, or Sturmabteilung, was the Nazi paramilitary "Storm Detachment."

43 *Chainsaw*, no. 5 (November/December 1977), in: Vincent Bernière and Mariel Primois, *Punk Press: L'histoire d'une révolution esthétique, 1969–1979* (Paris: Éditions de La Martinière, 2012), p. 128.

44 "Vivre et créer en rut," quoted from Rainer Maria Rilke, *Lettres à un jeune poète et proses* (Paris: Le Livre de Poche, 1989), p. 44.

45 The picador with an erection in Stéphane Mandelbaum's drawing observes an evocation of Picasso's painting.

46 Montfort, *Stéphane Mandelbaum*, p. 33.

47 The object is his mother's prosthesis.

48 See the film by Gérard Preszov, *La Sainteté Stéphane (1961–1986)* (BE, 1993).

delinquent actions—which are always without any real alternative."[49] He therefore knows that he is close to the young thugs and to the destiny of Pierre Goldman.[50] He is at once an outcast but, above all, a bandit. He identifies with these figures in reality as much as in a phantasm, such as when one likes to tell stories. And in all the drawings in which he precisely lists all his feats of arms and his many sexual conquests, he shares the aura that these crimes, real or figurative, give him all the pleasure to sate him: "[...] one steals for the pleasure of the risk that it represents. You feel like you are outside of the others; you live another life than the others."[51] Finally, he no longer suffers the stigma; it is he who orchestrates reality and leads the dance. This turbulent life will end tragically, probably more because of an unfortunate chain of circumstances than in the clear line of a promised destiny. The fact remains that the matrix of his work as a visual artist never ceases to touch the heart. Through this sharp look at the human condition, a great affection is revealed: the words *je t'aime* are recurrent in the accumulation of signs.
But above all, it is this setting in motion—the kinetics of "what can I do?"—that impresses. The lesson that Stéphane Mandelbaum retains from Francis Bacon is that of the gradual shift of form and the evanescence of its plasticity, reminiscent of the myth of the Golem, a spectral and unfinished form that serves to protect him. And to embrace representation, the stammering language takes shape from the zone of bodily unconsciousness through which he communicates with the world in, for example, *Autoportrait II*, 1980 (→ 133); *Composition (El Kero)*, 1981 (→ 166); and *Portrait de José*, 1985 (→ 10). Stéphane Mandelbaum neither forces the line nor offers caricatures; his creative gestures are never more than a seminal praxis giving access to the invisible in forms: "When deformed, faces and bodies, far from revealing their irreducibility to their biological texture, disappear into this texture itself, thus revealing that they have never been anything other than contingent forms of life."[52] This trance—a liberation from the bitterness that torments him as much as formative in respect of the beacons that guide his adventure—is the self-generated energy in the poiesis of his inaugural creative gesture, when he knows, intuitively, that his line will be the substance, the flesh of his hopes.

49 "Le bon sauvage n'est pas un mythe," Pier Paolo Pasolini interviewed by Tommaso Anzoino, in: Pier Paolo Pasolini, *Entretiens (1949–1975)* (Paris: Éditions Delga, 2019).

50 Pierre Goldman was a French left-wing intellectual (b. 1944) who had been convicted of several robberies and was assassinated in mysterious circumstances in Paris in 1979, possibly by the Spanish state's death squads known as the GAL (Grupos Antiterroristas de Liberación).

51 *Jacques Mesrine, L'instinct de mort* (Paris: Flammarion, 2008 [1977]), p. 14.

52 Catherine Malabou, "From Deconstruction to Plasticity: Morphing Francis Bacon," in: *Francis Bacon: Painting, Philosophy, Psychoanalysis*, ed. by Ben Ware (London: EFB Publishing and Thames & Hudson, 2019), pp. 86–87.

## À bout de souffle

Tal Sterngast

> The wanderer's country is not truth, but exile; he lives outside, on the other side which is by no means a beyond, rather the contrary. He remains separated, where the deep of dissimulation reigns, that elemental obscurity through which no way can be made and which because of that makes its awful way through him.[1]—Maurice Blanchot

1 Maurice Blanchot, *The Space of Literature*, trans. by Ann Smock (Lincoln: University of Nebraska Press, 1982), p. 238.

The concise body of work of Stéphane Mandelbaum appears as an outcome, or the residue, of an implosion—an adolescent, self-stimulating life—that triggered, sparked, and galvanized itself until it was extinguished like a flame. Mandelbaum opted for an imagined mythology that was an idiosyncratic mixture of several bohemian traits and indulged by taking pleasure in transgression, including in the form of pain. His life was shaped by the conviction of being true to one's own obsessions, and in that sense, true to radicality.

In this life, which was cast against a post-Second World War Western European prosperous middle class (aspiring to the bourgeoisie), criminal activity was perceived as a means of rebellion or social critique, and terrorism was seen as a form of liberation. Brussels, where Mandelbaum lived, studied art, and worked, was the junction between Flemish- and French-speaking cultures, and it was a meeting point between Western Europe and Africa. Among Mandelbaum's artistic precedents, whose lives also set ablaze in Brussels, were Vincent van Gogh, who briefly stayed in the city in 1878; Arthur Rimbaud (see Mandelbaum's portraits *A. Rimbaud* → 142–43; *Arthur Rimbaud I* → 140; *Arthur Rimbaud II* → 141; *Portrait von Rimbaud*, all 1980 → 144–45); and *Portrait de Rimbaud*, c. 1983), who was shot by his friend and lover Paul Verlaine in 1873; and Charles Baudelaire, who had left Paris for Brussels three years before his untimely death in 1867. This cohort nourished a corresponding myth about Brussels itself, which must have consumed Mandelbaum before his murder at the age of 25.

In his earliest painting, the large-scale self-portrait *Autoportrait «aux crochets»* (Self-portrait with hooks, 1976 → 214), Mandelbaum depicts himself suspended from a row of slaughterhouse hooks, his clothed body set against a glowing rosy-white background. Blood-red paint splashes from his groin and spreads across the canvas. At age fifteen, Mandelbaum portrays himself as a hanging piece of meat, circumcised and castrated, being born and put to death at the same time. Soon afterwards, Mandelbaum abandoned painting in favor of drawing with graphite, colored pencil, and ballpoint pen on paper, at times on an unconventionally large scale. Paradoxically, the colorless, sketchy nature of the drawings offered Mandelbaum a more incisive means of creation than painting, which seemed to better suit his bold, contrarian disposition. Mostly portraits, the drawings are rough and on the verge of caricature, with exaggerated and hypertrophied features like potato noses and overtly thick necks.[2] They are instantaneous and direct but remain ever unraveled, on the move, never fully done. These will become Mandelbaum's main innovation.

The protagonists who populate Mandelbaum's work—family members, friends, politicians, alongside "cursed" artists, such as Pier Paolo Pasolini, Francis Bacon, or Arthur Rimbaud, or infamous Nazis like Joseph Goebbels or Ernst Röhm[3]—all drawn from photographs or reproductions create a web of magnetic coordinates. In this inventive landscape which is as internal as it is external, Mandelbaum's identifications, fascinations, and repulsions mirror each other in a painterly treatment that is evidently egalitarian. There is no implicit correlation in the work between subject matter and a particular style, or an apparent distinction between evil and glory, or any sort of ethical stance. More than an attempt to create a likeness, the contours of bodies, organs, and faces in Mandelbaum's drawings appear to gush out of an impulse to outline the movement of a transient hidden essence. It seems that his portraits aim at dismantling or rediscovering something that lies beneath the face of his figures.

The short life of Mandelbaum was modeled after a succession of selected father figures, most of whom he repeatedly depicted and referred to in his works, a genealogy of pariah predecessors that he used to nurture his own self-mythology. They are an elective family of damned and doomed who were consumed till death by societal defiance, self-destruction, or illness, at least two of whom, like Mandelbaum, were murdered or assassinated.[4] Moreover, they share an inherent sense of exile and banishment that necessitates simultaneously being in different societies or life circumstances. This is an intrinsic precondition for his body of work. Mandelbaum incorporates the designation of being an outsider and transforms it into an inner drive.

In his book on Francis Bacon, Gilles Deleuze distinguishes between the figurative and—the Figure ("figural"). While figurative work is illustrative, narrative, and signifying (it represents an object or narrates a story), the Figure is something like pure form. He writes: "There are two ways of going beyond figuration (that is, beyond both the illustrative and the figurative): either toward abstract form or toward the Figure."[5] Internalizing a distortion projected from the outside, Mandelbaum attains a deviant, deformed Figure that is almost like a morphological sum of this ancestry of pariahs. His work is as particular as it is symptomatic. It refers to an explicit collective syndrome, and it originates in a certain existence (mostly Jewish but not exclusively) between two epochs, with one foot firmly planted in complete assimilation (as a Jew in a gentile society) and the other foot continuing to nurture the memory of unimaginable being. Mandelbaum was clearly influenced by Chaïm Soutine and by Bacon, the two consecutive masters of a

2 Mandelbaum's evidently versatile drawing skills testify to his choice of a rough style. For example, in *Composition (Masques Nô)*(1983 → 66–67) a small collage-like composition, the crowded group of figures are drawn with free-flowing and cartoonish lines.

3 Stéphane Mandelbaum dedicated at least two works to Ernst Röhm, a wounded First World War soldier, who was openly homosexual, and led the ruthless paramilitary SA (Sturmabteilung). Röhm and the SA were instrumental in Adolf Hitler's rise to power but were gotten rid of by him in the Night of the Long Knives in 1934. Röhm was assassinated for alleged sedition.

4 The circumstances of Stéphane Mandelbaum's murder in 1986 are obscure, although it was most likely the result of a criminal deal that went wrong in an attempt to steal a (fake) painting by the Italian artist Amedeo Modigliani. It is interesting to think of Mandelbaum's drawings in relation to Modigliani—another "doomed" bohemian artist who died young—famous for his paintings of idealized women with swan-like necks and perfect oval faces.

5 Gilles Deleuze, *Francis Bacon: The Logic of Sensation*, trans. by Daniel W. Smith (London: Continuum, 2003), p. 34.

distorted figuration. He was guided by their experience but also in the way he absorbed being labeled—as an outcast or as a Jew—and in the way he identified with this labeling. The uncertainty of Mandelbaum's sexuality (although he was married to a woman) and his attraction to the Brussels underworld, in his work and in his lifestyle, are part of this dialectic between internalization and transgression.

Within this genealogy of father figures, a special place is reserved for the radical French intellectual Pierre Goldman (1944–1979). Indeed, it is almost as if Mandelbaum sought to become Goldman in his own life. Sketched portraits of Goldman reoccur in Mandelbaum's compositions, as does his name; occasionally his name and portrait are accompanied by a pistol or the word "Juif," or newspaper snippets about Goldman's trial and murder. The son of Polish Jews residing in France who were communist resistance fighters, Goldman was a charismatic left-wing activist and author who reached a degree of mythic fame in France. Alongside André Glucksmann and Daniel Cohn-Bendit, he became one of the three Jewish leaders of the student revolt in May 1968.[6] Goldman had visited Cuba and fought with guerillas in Venezuela; later he was convicted of several robberies as well as murders for which he was sentenced even though he maintained his innocence. Acquitted, he was assassinated in broad daylight in Paris in 1979, just outside his apartment, an act claimed by an alleged far-right group called Honneur de la Police (Honor of the Police). The Pierre Goldman affair split French society and manifested its political chasms.[7]

Despite major differences, most profoundly in Goldman's radical politics that Mandelbaum did not seem to share, Mandelbaum and Goldman were both possessed by death and haunted by a history (the extermination of the European Jews) to which they felt they were submitted. Goldman noted in his memoir: "My long obsession with death [...] had its source in my first breath. [...] Doubtless I know I had come from death, and I was hardly alive before I was preparing to return to it. I lived in this (biblical) expectation."[8] Consciously or not, Mandelbaum and Goldman seemed to be committed to a past that they did not experience firsthand. They were fully invested in the violence that occurred before they were able to confront it and driven by a quest to attain a history they could neither reach nor of which they could get ridden. Their lives revolved around the reality of Auschwitz's existence and a particular Jewish being that was cast in its shape. Theirs was an ongoing attempt to compensate in the form of violence for the fact that they lived after the Shoah.[9] Recalling his youth, Goldman wrote: "In Poland I was seized with a taste for action, overcome by the dream of, the desire for, history, and I wanted it to be [a] history of violence, in which I could free myself from the pain of being a Jew."[10] Mandelbaum's association with gangsters and criminal activities can also be thought of in relation to his longing to act within history itself, driven by a quest to give tangible form to the primordial curse he sensed he bore by being a "Jew."

6 See Diedrich Diederichsen, "A History of Violence in Europe since the Holocaust, Unfinished," in this volume.

7 Among Pierre Goldman's vocal supporters were the philosopher Jean-Paul Sartre, the actress Simone Signoret, the playwright Eugène Ionesco, the politician Pierre Mendès France, and the artist and filmmaker Chris Marker who, as Goldman acknowledges in his memoir, recorded Cuban music for him to listen to while he was in jail. See the acknowledgments in Pierre Goldman, *Dim Memories of a Polish Jew Born in France*, trans. by Joan Pinkham (New York: Viking Press, 1977), n. p., French original: *Souvenirs obscurs d'un juif polonais né en France* (Paris: Éditions du Seuil, 1975).

8 Goldman, *Dim Memories*, p. 10.

9 Uncanny analogies between Pierre Goldman's and Stéphane Mandelbaum's biographies stand out: a sensitivity towards the oppressed, the discriminated against, and almost any kind of victim; violence as a way of life; and death by murder. Both also had African wives, perhaps following Charles Baudelaire's lifelong relationship with Jeanne Duval.

10 Goldman, *Dim Memories*, p. 8.

The large portrait, *Pierre Goldman* (1980 → 201), is similar in scale and composition to *Kismatores! (Portrait d'Arié Mandelbaum)* (1982 → 195), a portrait made two years later of the artist's father Arié Mandelbaum, himself a painter and the director of the Académie royale des Beaux-Arts in Brussels. Mandelbaum depicts both men in half-profile, wearing a jacket and tie, with indistinct expressions captured in pencil strokes and smears. Goldman's name is written like a signature in the lower edge; the drawing only vaguely resembles his fervent appearance. Other details in the portrait refer to the murder of Goldman. A piece of newspaper in French reads (translated into English): "Anyone could kill him, and Pierre Goldman knew it, last Thursday his shot and perforated body was raised from the pavement in the 13th arrondissement." Written in pencil next to the clipping are the phrases "Pierre Goldman assassiné" and "Honeur de la police."

Both portraits feature a scattered collage of writing, sketches, and newspaper clippings in a mixture of languages. Notably, the imagery includes a pornographic image of a female figure with spread legs. In *Pierre Goldman*, the woman is on the phone, touching herself, and cut-out words are pasted onto the photo: "כשר" (kosher), "Israel," and "יצחק באַשעוויס זינגער" (Isaac Bashevis Singer). In the neatly confined margin of *Kismatores! (Portrait d'Arié Mandelbaum)* (1982 → 195), the head of the half-naked woman is replaced with the head of a smiling SS officer and a swastika is stuck on her arm. Instead of a name, the portrait of Arié Mandelbaum is adorned with gleeful profanity in agile block letters "קיש מיר אין תָּחַת!"[11] Grotesque and obnoxious, this is an expression of adolescent defiance, with the word "Tores" (buttocks) endowing the painting with a sense of lasciviousness. Among the multitudes of obscenities and curse words filling Mandelbaum's drawings, the word "kosher"—a hallmark, certification, or indicator of purity—reappears in various forms and languages, placed next to swastikas (like in *P. Röm (N° 1/ Portraït der Röm)*, 1981–82 → 173) or on top of pornographic imagery, inverted and discharged in a rebellious gesture.

Both portraits of father and father-figure resemble each other not only in their melancholy and the contrarian juxtaposition of authority with pornography but also in Mandelbaum's efforts to consolidate them together into a Figure.

Within this attempt, the heads in Mandelbaum's drawings rise out of a dense foundation from the neck up, almost as if they were placed on a pedestal made of signatures and inscriptions, abstract drawings, ornaments and patterns, graphic signs, and collaged elements: newspaper snippets, reproductions of paintings, and photographs. Against the rather airy heads, the jammed, compressed edges are confined by lines (seen or unseen), and they are pulled down or to the sides as if submitted to their own weight and gravity. These constant tensions between center and margin, between overflow and blankness, activate the work and keep the drawings as completed as they are preliminary.

11 The title of the work translates to "kiss my ass."

Letters and words in his works act first as visual signs. In this way, they register as a graphic line, a pattern, an ornament, or a grid; their form and position on the surface overwhelming any sense of fixed meaning. The margins in the drawings both serve and disrupt the image's legend or title. Mandelbaum stretches the connection between language and reality, and words and things. In the small sketch *Untitled* (from the series *L'œuvre intime*, 1985–86 → 200), for example, the margin takes over the figure completely, epitomizing Mandelbaum's play with the bond between words and figures. The words "א בילד שיינע פאנאראמע" (a picture of a beautiful landscape), drawn in bold letters with ballpoint pen, are surrounded by a cartoonish halo.[12] In a brief twist on René Magritte's painted phrase "Ceci n'est pas une pipe" (This is not a pipe),[13] Mandelbaum ostensibly shows that this *is* a pipe, but it lacks the figure. The A4-sized sheet of paper is otherwise filled with names and numbers: Eastern European cities, numbers of Jewish victims murdered by the Nazis, and a list of extermination camps, such as Majdanek, Treblinka, Sobibor, Auschwitz. A sketched palm tree is the only recognizable figurative element.

The artist's focus on Yiddish, a language he learned from his grandfather Salomon Mandelbaum, is like a play with an internal, secretive language. But more importantly, it serves a major role in the identity Mandelbaum nurtured. Within the pastiche of contemporary references like pop, punk, and politics in the Middle East, Yiddish—the language of the extinguished Eastern European Jewish diaspora—stands out because its immediate daily usage had been rendered obsolete. In Israel, Yiddish was rejected in favor of modern Hebrew as part of the Zionist attempt to establish a new sense of "nativeness" as an antidote to diasporic existence. By using pieces from daily newspapers published in Yiddish (and not Hebrew) discussing political affairs in Israel, Mandelbaum knowingly made himself outdated, celebrating an imaginary diasporic realm.

In a pair of colorful portraits, *Quic 3 portrait de Buñuel* (1983 → 95) and *Gamal Abdel Nasser* (1983 → 93), the delineated heads of the Spanish Surrealist film director (one of Mandelbaum's heroes) and of the Egyptian president and champion of Pan-Arabism—celebrities of completely different orders—lean on a bright bold logo reading "צאנינס" (Tsanin's). The logo alluded to "צאנינס אילוסטרירטע וועלט" (Tsanin's Illustrated World), a popular illustrated magazine published by Mordechai Tsanin in Israel in the 1970s with sensationalist covers that blended politics, news, art, and gossip. Mandelbaum reinforces this Yiddish post-Second World War universe as one with a transgressive potential. The handwritten logo emerges from overflowing bottom margins of red and yellow lines that mimic brush strokes and fill this condensed space by cartooning a painting.

Both Goldman and Mandelbaum rejected Zionism as the answer to the question of Jewish being. Despite the vagueness of Mandelbaum's politics, it seems he saw Israel as an unwanted arrival at a destination that inherently contradicted the

12 Stéphane Mandelbaum borrowed the typeface from fonts used in Yiddish newspapers, a modernized font from the nineteenth century that resembled the early square typeface used since the sixteenth century in prayer books and in the Talmud.

13 This phrase is painted on René Magritte's *Treachery of Images* (1928–29), which is in the collection of the Los Angeles County Museum of Art.

Jewish restless nomadic destiny.[14] For Goldman, being Jewish was an existential state, a condition, rather than a content: "What Jews can bring to civilization is stateless wandering, the feeling of non-belonging. I believe in the Jewish values that the anti-Semites hate. I believe in nihilism, in negativity. I believe in the libertarian Jew who exists as a dissolvent principle of positive values, because he is neither the man of one land nor the man of one country, nor the man of one nation."[15]

In this interview, Goldman also talks about the Jewish talent for "all that is international" (being as "'gifted' at capitalism as at communism"), a trait perceived as uncanny by right- and left-wingers alike that fueled anti-Semitism.[16] At the same time, he describes how anti-Semitism contributes to maintaining a Jewish reality. Goldman outlines in this interview a dynamic dialectic of projection and introspection that reinforce and even constitute each other. Mandelbaum shares a philosophical and mystical vision of exile, an outcome of a persistent movement between worlds without truly belonging to any of them.

According to Maurice Blanchot, Franz Kafka could also not envision for himself a cure through Zionism. He saw himself excluded from Zionism as a remedy, yet at the same time, he profoundly wanted this reconciliation. "Magnificent, all that, except for me, and rightly so," Kafka wrote in his *Diaries*.[17] Art, or what Blanchot relates to as literature's "space," is described as exile or banishment, an errancy that signifies a new relation to "truth." Kafka "already belongs to the other shore," Blanchot writes, "and his wandering does not consist in nearing Canaan, but in nearing the desert, the truth of the desert."[18] For Blanchot, there is a truth and a vocation in exile, and the idea of division and separation is inscribed within its nomadic movement in contrast to paganism. According to Blanchot, to be pagan is to be fixed ("to plant oneself in the earth"[19]). The Jew "relates to the origin not by dwelling but by distancing himself from it, thus saying that the truth of the beginning is in separation," Blanchot contends.[20] The artist-writer wanders in the desert, like Kafka, far from Canaan, too weak to collaborate in the active concerns of competent men. Instead, the desert is a privileged zone of freedom and solitude. If art is exiled from the world of valuable achievements, it is also exempt from the world's demands. Or it would be, were the desert a place one could actually reach.[21]

In the *First Diasporist Manifesto*, R.B. Kitaj, the Jewish American painter expatriated in London, coined the term Diasporism in order to define his own school of art. Kitaj ends his *Manifesto* with Blanchot's Kafka. He outlines Diasporism as a seed that is passed down through generations. It is something instinctive to one's culture that enters into one's art and can even be seen in work that has been assimilated into modernism. Like Mandelbaum, Kitaj populated his paintings with images of friends, enemies, heroes, and monsters and dedicated his life and work to what he defined as

14 Evidence of Mandelbaum's interest in this subject can be found in his works with pasted texts that refer to Israeli politics. For example, *Pierre Goldman* features snippets of Yiddish newspaper reports of the Venice Declaration in 1980, the first European acknowledgment of the Palestinian right to self-definition and the critique from Crif (Conseil représentatif des institutions juives de France / Representative Council of French Jewish Institutions).

15 Catherine Chaine, "Goldman the Foreigner," interview with Pierre Goldman, originally published in French in *Le Monde* (30.9.1979); published online in English (trans. by Mitchell Abidor): https://www.marxists.org/history/france/pierre-goldman-affair/foreigner.htm, accessed October 2, 2024.

16 Ibid.

17 Blanchot, *Space of Literature*, p. 68.

18 Ibid., p. 71.

19 Maurice Blanchot, "The Indestructible," in: *The Infinite Conversation*, trans. by Susan Hanson (Minneapolis: University of Minnesota Press, 1993), p. 125.

20 Ibid., p. 126.

21 Blanchot, *Space of Literature*, p. 11. See Franz Kafka, *Diaries* (28.1.1922), quoted from ibid., p. 69. The original quotation reads: "Indeed, my situation is something like the wandering in the desert in reverse, with continual

his obsessions. The surfaces in Kitaj's works, as in Mandelbaum's, are fragmented and divided. They serve as a collage that integrates different motifs, styles, and materials, including newspaper clippings, texts, and photographs. Both artists cultivated personas that navigated their work through the violence and disasters of the twentieth century. They used figurative painting and drawing to exclude themselves and to reject the illusions of modernity, especially as these were projected onto abstract painting.

Kitaj avoids solid definitions of identity like race, ethnicity, nationality, religion, or culture, and describes instead the contemplation of a transience in paint, which is an outcome of one's "restlessness, un-at-homeness and groundlessness."[22] According to Kitaj, Diasporist art is marked by exile and its discontents "as subtly and unclearly as pictures painted by women or homosexuals are marked by their inner exilic discontents."[23] He asks whether Jewishness can be an attribute of art: "A Diasporist painting is one in which a pariah people, an unpopular, stigmatized people, is taken up, pondered in their dilemmas, as unsurely as Impressionists ponder the dilemmas of light in nature or as Cubists take up perspectival and planar dilemmas."[24] He claims Diasporist art is contradictory at its heart and argues it is both universal and particular. For the Diasporist, the diaspora can be anything outside of ordinary standards (some are diaspora Jews, and some may wander in a sexual diaspora); the Diasporist lives and paints in two or more societies at once. Finally, Kitaj describes the formation of his object ("the Jews," for example) that oscillates between external and internal forces, projection and transgression: "My own Diasporist mode resists (gently) the absolute wisdom of assimilationism in art. I would rather find the energy to do for Jews at least what Morandi did for jars."[25]

In Mandelbaum's ballpoint drawing *Pollock et Fabien* (1980 → 119), Jackson Pollock is drawn after the *Life* magazine feature on the painter published in 1949. Its title both asks and pronounces, "Is he the greatest living painter in the United States?" Pollock was portrayed in the article like no artist before him, a Marlon Brando–James Dean-like rebel, rugged, intense, and soiled, with a cigarette hanging from the corner of his mouth. Even more than the text, the photographs incarnated Pollock as a mythic figure and a star of mass media. In addition, by focusing on the man in the act of painting, the photographs shifted the focus from the paintings to the process of artmaking. In his drawing, Mandelbaum positions himself in relation to Pollock, not only as an artist embodying Abstract Expressionism and masculinity but as one mastering the physical language and choreography of paganist trance and ritual. Notably, this is one of a few cases where Mandelbaum depicts a full body, even though it is lightly sketched. In the cartoon-like drawing of a drip painting being made, Mandelbaum distances himself not only from this kind of painting but also from this mode of being an artist. In the lower part of the drawing, Mandelbaum scribbled a

approaches toward the desert and childish hopes (particularly concerning women): 'Perhaps I shall keep in Canaan after all?' And in the meantime, I have been in the desert for a long time, and these are only visions born of despair, especially at the moments when, out here too, I am the most miserable of men and Canaan necessarily offers itself as the sole Promised Land, for there is no third land for men."

22 R. B. Kitaj, *First Diasporist Manifesto* (New York: Thames and Hudson, 1989), p. 31.

23 Ibid., p. 97.

24 Ibid., p. 99.

25 Ibid., p. 43.

cartoon with anti-Semitic motives: two pigs with a star of David, one with *payot*, the other with breasts, crouch on top of each other with their orange tongues sticking out. Next to them is a pig in a Nazi uniform surrounded with the text "קעניג כוסיין אין וואשינגטאן" (King Hussain in Washington).

The drawings of Mandelbaum, who never outlived his adolescence, remain representative and always confrontational despite an inner disruption or even deconstruction. Whereas the well-reasoned work of Kitaj—a "good bad boy" in his own words (unlike the bad bad boy Mandelbaum)—lasted over five decades and is saturated, referential, and academic. Yet the paradoxical Figure at the heart of the work of both Kitaj and Mandelbaum shares a morphology and a psychology of malformation. It is rendered by a perception from the outside that distorts what it regards and incorporates the designation of a new kind of Degenerate Art.

Living in the Imagination
Susanne Pfeffer

[…] I wanted to write my life in life.[1]
—Pierre Goldman

[…] when you are painting somebody, you know that you are, of course, trying to get near not only to their appearance but also to the way they have affected you, because every shape has an implication.[2]—Francis Bacon

How to live when your own history exists before you are born? How to live when millions died—like sheep to the slaughter, as it states in the Psalm? What to become when the past doesn't point to a future? How to die as an individual?

What links Arthur Rimbaud, Pier Paolo Pasolini, Francis Bacon? Being lost, freedom, and anarchy? Being different, doing things differently, thinking new things, full of intensity and passion? Someone trying to live their own life?

Stéphane Mandelbaum was a Belgian Jew, born in Brussels in 1961. His father was a painter, his mother an illustrator. Mandelbaum started drawing at a tender age, an activity that he would perform for hours and days on end. At the age of fifteen he completed his first oil painting: The work *Autoportrait «aux crochets»* (Self-portrait with hooks, 1976 → 214) depicts the artist himself hanging from a meat hook. Blood spurts from his penis all over the canvas. Multiple hooks to his left and right, similar to those in *Rabbin aux abattoirs* (Rabbi in the slaughterhouses, 1977 → 209), show that he is hanging in a slaughterhouse. The slaughterhouses of Brussels were locations that he often revisited. The violence contained within the painting is shocking—just as shocking as the atrocities of the Nazi era.

As the grandson and son of Holocaust survivors, Stéphane Mandelbaum explored his history specifically and Judaism in general at an early point in his life. He learned Yiddish, became acquainted with Yiddish customs, and remained in close contact with his grandfather. Rabbis, the butchers known as Katzoffs, Yiddish words, characters in the Hebrew alphabet, his grandfather, his father, as well as contemporary and historical Jewish figures all appear in his imagery. One in the latter category is Pierre Goldman, whose autobiography *Dim Memories of a Polish Jew Born in France* recounts a story that had a deep impact on Mandelbaum in his youth. Goldman was a French intellectual who was born in Lyon in 1944, the son of French underground resistance fighters. After the war, his parents separated and his mother returned to Poland, while Goldman grew up with his father in Paris. He initially worked as a journalist until he himself went underground in the 1960s. In 1970, he was arrested for several robberies. Four years later he was sentenced to

1 Pierre Goldman, *Dim Memories of a Polish Jew Born in France*, trans. by Joan Pinkham (New York: Viking Press, 1977), French original: *Souvenirs obscurs d'un juif polonais né en France* (Paris: Éditions du Seuil, 1975).

2 Francis Bacon, quoted from David Sylvester, *The Brutality of Fact: Interviews with Francis Bacon* (London: Thames & Hudson, 1975), p. 130.

life imprisonment not only for these crimes, to which he pleaded guilty, but also for two murders during the robberies that he had not in fact committed. It was in prison that he wrote his autobiography, which was published in 1975. After numerous petitions his case was reviewed and the miscarriage of justice was cleared up. Goldman's conviction for murder was overturned and he was released early on October 5, 1976. In 1979 he was shot and killed in a street, allegedly by the right-wing extremists, the Honneur de la Police (Honor of the Police). To this day, the case has not officially been solved.

Mandelbaum's fascination with the underground, gangster milieu, and subcultures emerged when he was still a teenager. The fact that he soon positioned himself on the margins of society as an artist testifies to his enormous admiration for free-spirited mavericks bent on creative renewal. Arthur Rimbaud swiftly came to occupy a key role in his life and art, symbolizing exactly this kind of free spirit and true individual. The few photographs of Rimbaud in existence repeatedly crept into Mandelbaum's work as source material. His was not the only figure to have been inspired by Rimbaud to undertake a radically subjective exploration of their own constitution and their own life via modern art. Rimbaud experienced and described his journey within himself and what he had become as *A Season in Hell*,[3] and the same could be said about Mandelbaum's visual explorations of his own life.

Francis Bacon reflects the deformation and decay of someone's spirit caused not only by their being but also by the mundanity and violence of their surroundings, invoking the tattered mobility of his subjects' bodies in works that have their own unique logic of visual sensation. Rimbaud's constituted subject seems to have been literally blown apart, driven almost to the point of unrecognizability by the abstraction.

Vulnerability and sensitivity, alongside rawness and the depths to which anyone can lapse and fall, are also themes addressed by Pier Paolo Pasolini in his films and writing. Always questioning the motives and depths of what is supposedly the human condition, Pasolini uses his reduced landscapes and social structures to look for movements that ultimately stand in the way of goodness, then allows them to reappear in art in the face of all kinds of adversity.

Pasolini questions societal, social, and political taboos to see what lies behind them, and skillfully presents moral contradictions and general hypocrisy, seeking to rescue a social and natural beauty that is based on more than just esthetics. Whether in his prose texts, poems, or journalistic statements on contemporary issues, in what were known as his *scritti corsari* or "pirate writings," or in his documentary and feature films, Pasolini created a unique and complex œuvre that never lacks attitude, even when it is erroneous. Mandelbaum draws the portrait of the filmmaker over and over again, as if he wants to epitomize Pasolini's exuberant creative urge, his intensity, and the uncompromising nature of his work. Here,

3 Arthur Rimbaud, *A Season in Hell & Illuminations* (Rochester, New York: BOA Editions, 1991), French original: *Une saison en enfer* (Brussels: Alliance Typographique, 1873).

too, he uses familiar photographs, which he presents in a manner that recalls Francis Bacon's approach, as if they came from a personal encounter. The intense eye contact that the subjects seem to make with us, the viewers, lets us create a direct personal relationship with them.

Alongside the figures who left a deep impression on Mandelbaum on account of their art, and thus entered his own works and reappeared time and again to a greater or lesser extent, depicted either exhaustively or like a strip cartoon, there are the nightmarish mass murderers from history who similarly find their way into his imagery.

The face of Joseph Goebbels during his speech on May 1, 1933, on Tempelhofer Feld in Berlin, which subsequently led to mass arrests and the torture and murder of trade union officials, left-wing intellectuals, and manual workers, is included in Mandelbaum's work as part of his research on the expressive capacity of people's physiognomy. Goebbels' face is projected at us, screaming and spitting—and here, too, Mandelbaum is horrifically successful at creating a highly personal depiction. In a technique similar to that used for the portraits of Rimbaud, Bacon, and Pasolini, he repeatedly draws the Nazi propaganda minister in the same pose, but in very different formats.

The proximity and contingency of sexuality and violence that are addressed in Pasolini's œuvre also feature in many of Mandelbaum's works. He depicts Ernst Röhm, the leader of the SA—the thuggish stormtroopers of the NSDAP—whose homosexuality was an open secret, in uniform and with an erect penis (*P. Röm* (*N° 1 / Portraït der Röm*), 1981–82 → 173), thereby creating an almost unbearable closeness through sexualized intimacy. Mandelbaum confronts violence, horror, and Eros even more drastically and transgressively in his two depictions of Auschwitz (*Le Rêve d'Auschwitz* and *Le Rêve d'Auschwitz II*, both 1983), which also present an erect penis in the foreground.

In his final works before he was murdered by his clients in 1986 at the age of 26, deemed an uncontrollable risk after his theft of a fake Modigliani, Mandelbaum depicts sex as a commodity. The red-light district in Brussels had long been a place where he felt alive and at home on the fringes of society. Barmaids, sex workers, pimps, homeless people, gamblers, fences, drug dealers, and criminals all cast a spell over the artist. He created huge portraits and small scribbled sketches of them. All of his subjects were real people he knew from the nightlife scene; none of them were merely the product of his imagination. And yet, during this period, his imagination seems to have increasingly started shaping his day-to-day existence, when the boundaries between reality and imagination seemed to dissolve even more than before. Rather than the characters he portrayed being the transgressive criminals, it was him, dreaming of fast money, designer clothes, and a fast-paced luxurious lifestyle. He committed the kind of robberies that he had admired Pierre Goldman and Jaques Mesrine for as a teenager. He traveled to the Democratic Republic of the Congo with a view to dealing in traditional African art. He depicted burglaries that he had not actually committed as if they were his own and drew masks, clothes, and weapons that he had never owned. It seemed as if his imagination was the only way out of an unbearable past and the exhausting mundanity of the present—and that living in the imagination would be the inevitable step.

## List of Works

p. 3
*Portrait de Max*, 1984
Graphite pencil on paper
150 × 118 cm
MUSEUM MMK FÜR MODERNE KUNST, Frankfurt am Main
Acquired with the generous support of the partners of the MMK
Inv. No. 2022/96

p. 9
*Portrait de Meknil*, 1985
Graphite pencil on paper
170 × 130 cm
Private Collection

p. 10
*Portrait de José*, 1985
Graphite pencil on paper
160.5 × 134 cm
Collection Antoine de Galbert, Paris

p. 11
*Portrait de Max*, 1985
Graphite pencil, colored pencil, and felt pen on paper
147 × 109 cm
Private Collection

p. 13
*L'Albertine Bar (Beautiful Deception C.)*, 1986
Charcoal and graphite pencil on paper
150 × 115 cm
Private Collection, Paris

p. 14
*Papa Franco «Mama zaïroises»*, 1985
Charcoal and graphite pencil on paper
149.5 × 122 cm
Private Collection

p. 15
*Portrait de Ousman*, 1985
Graphite pencil on paper
175 × 134 cm
MUSEUM MMK FÜR MODERNE KUNST, Frankfurt am Main
On permanent loan from the MMK Foundation
Inv. No. 2022/110L

p. 16
*Bar Albertine Bruxelles Nord*, 1985
Graphite pencil on paper
148 × 126 cm
Collection Graffe

pp. 18–19
*Porträit of Changaÿ Park*, 1984
Colored pencil, felt pen, oil pastel, ballpoint pen, and graphite pencil on paper
81.5 × 88.5 cm
Musée Juif de Belgique—Joods Museum van België, Brussels

pp. 20–21
*Portrait de Mama Pauline*, 1984
Ballpoint pen and felt pen on paper
46 × 48 cm
Collection Simone and Arthur Benzaquen, Paris

pp. 22–23
*Bordel de la vie (Jerard Preszow)*, 1986
Ballpoint pen on paper
53 × 70 cm
Collection Paul Trajman, Gary Trajman & Romy Trajman

p. 24
*Lolita les gros lolo au Mambo Club*, 1985
Ballpoint pen on paper
29 × 21 cm
Collection Gil Weiss, Brussels

p. 25
*Rovné (Henri Gerro Rosita Londner au Mambo Club)*, 1985
Ballpoint pen on paper
29 × 21 cm
Collection Gil Weiss, Brussels

p. 26
*Blue Note*, 1985
Ballpoint pen on paper
29 × 21 cm
Collection Gil Weiss, Brussels

p. 27
*Mambo Club soirée (Portrait de Delval Mambo)*, 1985
Ballpoint pen on paper
29 × 21 cm
Collection Gil Weiss, Brussels

p. 28
*Rainer (Portrait de Rainer Werner Fassbinder)*, c. 1984
Graphite pencil, charcoal, colored pencil, and gouache on paper, mounted on canvas
148 × 108.5 cm
Private Collection, Belgium

p. 31
*Cadre dans un café rose*, 1984
Graphite pencil on paper
150 × 109 cm
Private Collection, Antwerp

p. 32
*Bar l'Asia B N° 1*, 1984
Graphite pencil on paper
150 × 120 cm
Collection C. J. J., Brussels

p. 35
*Pierre et José*, 1985
Graphite pencil on paper
175 × 129.3 cm
Private Collection

p. 36
*Portrait d'Annie, Homosexuel, Putain juive*, 1985
Graphite pencil on paper
149 × 114 cm
Private Collection, Belgium

p. 38
*Portrait de Chan*, 1985
Graphite pencil on paper
167 × 140 cm
Private Collection

p. 39
*Buñuel*, c. 1985
Graphite pencil on paper
182 × 142 cm
Private Collection R. C., Belgium

pp. 40–41
*Portraït von Bill*, 1982
Graphite pencil, colored pencil, and ballpoint pen on paper
121 × 127 cm
Collection Jérôme Herbaut, Belgium

pp. 42–43
*Composition (Der libé fon Berlin West)*, 1984
Ballpoint pen, felt pen, colored pencil, and graphite pencil on paper
51.3 × 67.5 cm
Collection E. Crochet, Brussels

p. 44
*Portrait von punk türk (Hugo)*, 1984
Felt pen, colored pencil, graphite pencil, and collage on paper
148.5 × 119 cm
Collection Gil Weiss, Brussels

p. 45
*Ernst Cön (portrait von Ernst Cön, eïne Punk)*, 1984
Pencil, oil, felt pen, and colored pencil on paper
141.5 × 112.5 cm
Collection Antoine de Galbert, Paris

pp. 46–47
*Composition à la figure rouge*, c. 1984
Ballpoint pen, felt pen, and gouache on paper
46 × 61 cm (recto)
Collection Graffe

pp. 48–49
*Composition à la figure rouge*, c. 1984
Ballpoint pen, felt pen, and gouache on paper
46 × 61 cm (verso)
Collection Graffe

pp. 50–51
*The Fabulous*, 1984
Felt pen and colored pencil on paper
46 × 60 cm
Private Collection, France

p. 53
*Portrait d'un con*, 1984
Graphite pencil and felt pen on paper, mounted on canvas
126 × 109 cm
Collection Nadine Rizele Mandelbaum

p. 55
*L'Empire des sens*, 1983
Graphite pencil on paper
138 × 115 cm
Collection MK2 Kréations

pp. 56–57
*Composition (Goldman, L'Empire des sens, Guernica)*, c. 1980
Ballpoint pen on paper
50 × 70 cm
Collection Thierry de Valeriola, France

pp. 58–59
*Composition (Hokusaï, Le Rêve de la femme du pêcheur, 1814)*, 1983
Ballpoint pen on paper
46 × 61 cm
Private Collection
Courtesy Galerie Zlotowski, Paris

pp. 60–61
*Tango*, 1984
Ballpoint pen on paper
45 × 59 cm
Collection Serge Goldszal

pp. 62–63
*Composition (Mishima, Bacon...)*, 1980
Ballpoint pen on paper
16.7 × 23.5 cm
Private Collection, Luxembourg

pp. 64–65
*Composition (Figure au masque)*, c. 1981
Ballpoint pen, colored pencil, and graphite pencil on paper
27 × 37 cm
Collection Ariéh Mandelbaum

pp. 66–67
*Composition (Masques Nô)*, 1983
Ink, colored pencil, and ballpoint pen on paper
48 × 72 cm
Collection Éric Decelle, Brussels

pp. 68–69
*Paris, c'est Pigalle (Têtes de caractère, Franz Xaver Messerschmidt)*, c. 1985
Ballpoint pen and felt pen on paper
46 × 61 cm (recto)
Collection Nicolas Jaquet, Geneva

p. 71
Untitled, 1985–86
from the series *L'œuvre intime*
Ballpoint pen on paper
29.5 × 21 cm
Private Collection

p. 72
*Masque japonais* [*Masques Nô*], 1985–86
Ballpoint pen on paper
27 × 20.5 cm
Collection E. Crochet, Brussels

p. 73
Untitled, 1985–86
from the series *L'œuvre intime*
Ballpoint pen on paper
29.5 × 21 cm
Private Collection

p. 74
Untitled, 1985–86
from the series *L'œuvre intime*
Ballpoint pen on paper
29.5 × 21 cm
MUSEUM MMK FÜR MODERNE KUNST, Frankfurt am Main
Acquired with the generous support of the partners of the MMK
Inv. No. 2022/95

p. 75
Untitled, 1985–86
from the series *L'œuvre intime*
Ballpoint pen on paper
29.5 × 21 cm
Private Collection

p. 76
Untitled [*Mama Ngaï*], 1985–86
from the series *L'œuvre intime*
Ballpoint pen on paper
29.5 × 21 cm
Collection Dario Preszow

pp. 78–79
*Fétiches africains*, 1984
Ballpoint pen on paper
46 × 60.5 cm
Private Collection

pp. 80–81
Untitled, 1985–86
from the series *L'œuvre intime*
Ballpoint pen on paper
29.5 × 21 cm
Courtesy Galerie Zlotowski, Paris

pp. 83–88
Untitled, 1985–86
from the series *L'œuvre intime*
Ballpoint pen on paper
29.5 × 21 cm
Private Collection

pp. 90–91
*Stalin*, c. 1985
Ballpoint pen on paper
20.8 × 27 cm
Collection Cristina Ngo, Belgium

p. 93
*Gamal Abdel Nasser*, 1983
Oil on canvas
85 × 65 cm
Collection Gil Weiss, Brussels

p. 94
*Luis Buñel ha ha*, c. 1983
Oil on canvas, mounted on canvas
130 × 118 cm
Courtesy Galerie Zlotowski, Paris

p. 95
*Quic 3 portrait de Buñuel*, 1983
Oil on canvas
120 × 100 cm
Collection Romy Trajman

p. 96
*Luis Buñuel*, 1985
from the series *Les cartes postales*
Ballpoint pen on paper
14 × 10.5 cm
MUSEUM MMK FÜR MODERNE KUNST, Frankfurt am Main
Acquired with the generous support of the partners of the MMK
Inv. No. 2022/91

p. 97
*Portrait de José*, 1985
from the series *Les cartes postales*
Ballpoint pen on paper
14 × 10.5 cm
MUSEUM MMK FÜR MODERNE KUNST, Frankfurt am Main
Acquired with the generous support of the partners of the MMK
Inv. No. 2022/92

pp. 98–99
*Portrait of Bacon*, 1984
Ballpoint pen on paper
47 × 69 cm
MUSEUM MMK FÜR MODERNE KUNST, Frankfurt am Main
Acquired with the generous support of the partners of the MMK
Inv. No. 2022/93

pp. 100–01
*Portrait of Bacon*, 1980
Ballpoint pen on paper
25 × 26.5 cm
Private Collection, France

pp. 102–03
*Francis Bacon*, c. 1980
Ballpoint pen on paper
30 × 40 cm
Collection Karim Hoss, Meudon

pp. 104–05
*Francis Bacon*, 1980
Ballpoint pen on paper
50 × 70 cm
Collection Ariéh Mandelbaum

pp. 106–07
*Francis Bacon (dessin N° 1)*, 1980
Ballpoint pen and adhesive tape on paper
48.5 × 64.5 cm
Collection Gil Weiss, Brussels

pp. 108–09
*Francis Bacon (Trois portraits)*, 1981
Ballpoint pen on paper
50 × 70 cm
Private Collection, France

p. 111
*Bacon et prédelle avec portrait d'Arie*, 1982
Graphite pencil on paper
59.6 × 48.3 cm
Collection Paula Hauser, Brussels

pp. 112–13
*Bacon et autoportrait (mort de Kokoschka)*, 1984
Ballpoint pen on paper
36 × 55 cm
Collection Paula Hauser, Brussels

p. 115
*George Dyer*, 1982
Graphite pencil on paper
150 × 120 cm
Collection Lucien Bilinelli, Milan

pp. 116–17
*George Dyer*, 1980
Ballpoint pen on paper
51 × 70.5 cm
Collection Antoine de Galbert, Paris

p. 119
*Pollock et Fabien*, 1980
Ballpoint pen on paper
70 × 60 cm
Collection M. Bucquoit, Paris

pp. 120–21
*Composition (Orient)*, 1981
Ballpoint pen and felt pen on paper
32 × 70 cm
Private Collection

pp. 122–23
*Picasso, Picador et Guernica*, 1980
Ballpoint pen and felt pen on paper
48.7 × 69.5 cm
Collection Bernard Prévot, Brussels

pp. 124–25
*Composition (Shohet)*, c. 1982
Ballpoint pen on paper
54 × 73 cm
Collection Gil Weiss, Brussels

pp. 126–27
*Composition avec Arié et Bacon (Arrestation de la bande à Baader)*, 1984
Ballpoint pen on paper
50 × 70 cm
Private Collection, Belgium

p. 128
*Composition Picasso Vélasquez (projet d'affiche)*, c. 1983
Ballpoint pen, felt pen, and Tipp-Ex on paper
65 × 46 cm
Collection Ariéh Mandelbaum

p. 131
*Portrait de Nicolas de Staël*, 1983
Oil on canvas
42 × 42 cm
Private Collection, Belgium

p. 132
*Francis Bacon II*, 1980
Drypoint etching on zinc
33.2 × 33 cm
Ed. 20/20
Family Collection Mandelbaum

p. 133
*Autoportrait II*, 1980
Drypoint etching on zinc
14.7 × 13.9 cm
Ed. 19/20
Family Collection Mandelbaum

p. 134
*Écorché II*, 1979
Drypoint etching on zinc
24.4 × 20.8 cm
Ed. HC IV
Family Collection Mandelbaum

p. 135
*Écorché III*, 1979
Drypoint etching on zinc
35.6 × 26.1 cm
Ed. 19/20
Family Collection Mandelbaum

p. 136
*Écorché I*, 1979
Drypoint etching on zinc
29.4 × 29.4 cm
Ed. 19/20
Family Collection Mandelbaum

p. 137
*Szulim Mandelbaum II*, 1980
Drypoint etching on zinc
29.7 × 29.7 cm
Ed. 20/20
Family Collection Mandelbaum

p. 138
*Shohet*, 1980
Drypoint etching on zinc
24.7 × 19.7 cm
Ed. 49/50
Family Collection Mandelbaum

p. 139
*Champ de bataille*, 1981
Drypoint etching on zinc
and copper engraving
22.7 × 26.6 cm
Ed. 96/150 [CL]
Family Collection Mandelbaum

p. 140
*Arthur Rimbaud I*, 1980
Drypoint etching on zinc
24.6 × 19.9 cm
Ed. 20/20
Family Collection Mandelbaum

p. 141
*Arthur Rimbaud II*, 1980
Drypoint etching on zinc
25.5 × 29.5 cm
Ed. 20/20
Collection Ariéh Mandelbaum

pp. 142–43
*A. Rimbaud*, 1980
Ballpoint pen on paper
50 × 70 cm
Collection Arié Mandelbaum,
Fontenoille

pp. 144–45
*Portrait von Rimbaud*, c. 1980
India ink, ink, ballpoint pen,
and colored pencil on paper
50 × 70 cm
Collection Lucien Bilinelli, Milan

pp. 146–47
*Composition au chameau*, 1982
Sepia ink and pencil on cardboard
41 × 56 cm
Dr. André-Jaque Neusy and
Collection Jacob Lifshin
(wedding present, 1983)

pp. 148–49
*Marines seek japs*, 1983
Graphite pencil, ballpoint pen,
and colored pencil on paper
48 × 62 cm
Collection Gil Weiss, Brussels

pp. 150–51
*Mishima et autoportrait*, 1984
Ballpoint pen on paper
49.5 × 64.5 cm
Collection Antoine de Galbert,
Paris

pp. 152–53
*Composition (L'Homme au singe d'atelier de Bacon)*, 1982
Ballpoint pen on paper
50 × 60 cm
Collection Ariéh Mandelbaum

pp. 154–55
*Pasolini «Les mille et une nuits»*,
1980
Ballpoint pen on paper
50 × 70 cm
Private Collection, Belgium

pp. 156–57
*Pier Paolo Pasolini*, 1980
Ballpoint pen, graphite pencil,
and adhensive tape on paper
51 × 68 cm
Private Collection, Brussels

pp. 158–59
*Pier Paolo Pasolini*, 1980
Ballpoint pen and felt pen
on paper
50 × 70 cm
Collection Robert Combas

pp. 160–61
*Pier Paolo Pasolini (Antonello de Messine, 1477–1478)*, 1980
Ballpoint pen, felt pen,
and collage on paper
51.7 × 71.2 cm
Collection E. Crochet, Brussels

pp. 162–63
*Pasolini*, 1980
Ballpoint pen on paper
50 × 70 cm
Collection Graffe

pp. 164–65
*Pasolini Nº 8*, 1980
Ballpoint pen on paper
47.5 × 67 cm
Collection C. J. J., Brussels

p. 166
*Composition (El Kero)*, 1981
Ballpoint pen, felt pen,
and collage on paper
69.5 × 49.5 cm
Collection Antoine de Galbert,
Paris

p. 167
*Gueule cassée*, c. 1980
Oil on canvas
79.5 × 60 cm
Collection Ariéh Mandelbaum

p. 168
*Écorché*, 1978
Graphite pencil on paper
60 × 40 cm
Private Collection, France

p. 173
*P. Röm (Nº 1 / Portraït der Röm)*,
1981–82
Charcoal on paper
152 × 115 cm
MUSEUM MMK FÜR MODERNE
KUNST, Frankfurt am Main
Inv. No. 2023/1

p. 174
*Ernst Röhm*, 1981
Graphite pencil, gouache, felt pen, and colored pencil on paper
139 × 120 cm
Collection Lucien Bilinelli, Milan

p. 177
*Mickey et Himmler*, 1983
Oil, felt pen, and colored pencil on canvas
100 × 85 cm
Collection Félix

pp. 178–79
*Goebbels*, 1980
Ballpoint pen on paper
47 × 55 cm
Private Collection

pp. 179–80
*Goebbels*, 1980
Ballpoint pen on paper
50 × 70 cm
Collection Antoine de Galbert, Paris

p. 183
*Der Göbels* [*Goebbels*], 1980
Graphite pencil and gouache on paper, mounted on canvas
152.5 × 122.8 cm
Centre Pompidou / Le Musée national d'art moderne—Centre de création industrielle, Paris

pp. 184–85
*Composition (Cul-de jatte au brassard à croix gammée)*, 1980
Ballpoint pen on paper
50 × 70 cm
Collection Antoine de Galbert, Paris

pp. 186–87
*Composition (Portrait of Bacon)*, 1980
Ballpoint pen and felt pen on paper
50 × 70 cm
Collection Graffe

pp. 188–89
*Gueule cassée et autoportrait*, 1980
Ballpoint pen and collage on paper
50 × 70 cm
Private Collection, Belgium

pp. 190–91
*Salomon Mandelbaum (d'après une photo de 1929)*, 1981
Ballpoint pen on paper
50 × 70 cm
Collection Graffe

p. 192
*Salomon Mandelbaum*, 1980
Ballpoint pen on paper
54 × 58 cm
Collection Ariéh Mandelbaum

p. 195
*Kismatores! (Portrait d'Arié Mandelbaum)*, 1982
Graphite pencil, colored pencil, and collage on paper
150 × 118 cm
Private Collection, Brussels

p. 196
*Autoportrait (pour maman)*, 1979
Graphite pencil on paper
95 × 65 cm
Collection Pili Mandelbaum

p. 197
*Autoportrait*, c. 1980
Graphite pencil on paper
77 × 48 cm
Collection Éric Decelle, Brussels

p. 198
*Autoportrait*, c. 1982
Graphite pencil on paper, mounted on canvas
91.5 × 62.2 cm
Collection MK2 Kréations

p. 200
Untitled, 1985–86
from the series *L'œuvre intime*
Ballpoint pen, felt pen on paper
29.5 × 21 cm
MUSEUM MMK FÜR MODERNE KUNST, Frankfurt am Main
Acquired with the generous support of the partners of the MMK
Inv. No. 2022/94

p. 201
*Pierre Goldman*, 1980
Graphite pencil and collage on paper
150 × 110 cm
Collection Bernard Prévot, Brussels

pp. 202–03
*Portrait de Paul Trajman*, 1986
Ballpoint pen on paper
50 × 70 cm
Collection Paul Trajman

pp. 204–05
*Shohet*, 1980
Ballpoint pen, felt pen on paper
50 × 70 cm
Collection Graffe

p. 206
*Chez Leon Ficherman*, 1985
Ballpoint pen on paper
33.3 × 21.5 cm
MUSEUM MMK FÜR MODERNE KUNST, Frankfurt am Main
Acquired with the generous support of the partners of the MMK
Inv. 2022/97

p. 207
Untitled, 1985–86
from the series *L’œuvre intime*
Ballpoint pen on paper
29.5 × 21 cm
Private Collection

p. 209
*Rabbin aux abattoirs*, 1977
Oil on jute
150 × 118 cm
Collection Ariéh Mandelbaum

pp. 210–11
*Le Nazi, saint Nicolas, les frères et la grand-mère*, 1978
Charcoal and oil pastel on paper, mounted on canvas
152 × 206 cm
Collection Ariéh Mandelbaum

pp. 212–13
*Saint Nicolas*, 1979
Oil on canvas
208 × 280 cm
Collection Maurice Verbaet, Antwerp

p. 214
*Autoportrait «aux crochets»*, 1976
Oil on cancas
165 × 88 cm
Collection Dario Preszow

Printing plate for *Bacon I*, 1980
Copper
19 × 20 cm
Collection E. Crochet, Brussels
(not illustrated)

Printing plate for *Francis Bacon II*, 1980
Zinc
33 × 33.5 cm
Collection E. Crochet, Brussels
(not illustrated)

Printing plate for *Arthur Rimbaud II*, 1980
Zinc
30 × 30 cm
Collection E. Crochet, Brussels
(not illustrated)

Printing plate for *Szulim Mandelbaum II*, 1980
Zinc
30 × 30 cm
Collection E. Crochet, Brussels
(not illustrated)

Colophon

This catalog is published on the occasion of the exhibition

*Stéphane Mandelbaum*
MUSEUM MMK FÜR MODERNE KUNST
TOWER MMK
April 14, 2022–January 1, 2023
Curator: Susanne Pfeffer

Catalog
Editor: Susanne Pfeffer
Authors: Diedrich Diederichsen, Ralf Marsault, Eileen Myles, Susanne Pfeffer, Tal Sterngast
Translations: Steven Lindberg (Diederichsen), Ralf Marsault (Marsault), Nicola Morris (Pfeffer)
Managing Editors: Regina Barunke, Julia Eichler
Copyediting and Proofreading: Margherita Foresti, Amanda Gomez, Martin Hager, Lu Pahl, Jana Pfort, Tina Wessel
Graphic Design: Dan Solbach, Berlin
Printing, Binding, and Color Separation: DZA Druckerei zu Altenburg GmbH

Printed in Germany.

Copyrights
© 2025, The family of Stéphane Mandelbaum for the artist
© 2025, MUSEUM MMK FÜR MODERNE KUNST, the authors, and Verlag der Buchhandlung Walther und Franz König, Cologne
© 2025, VG Bild-Kunst, Bonn

Photo Credits
All photographs by Axel Schneider, except: Frédéric Dehaen: pp. 160–61, 186–87, 190–91, 204–05; Marc Lavand'homme: pp. 24–27, 124–25; Jean-Louis Losi: pp. 62–63, 68–69, 78–81, 179–80; Bertrand Michau: pp. 50–51, 100–03, 119, 168; Philippe Migeat: pp. 11, 18–19, 22–23, 38, 46–49, 53, 64–67, 71–76, 83–88, 90–91, 108–09, 112–13, 120–23, 128, 132–45, 148–49, 152–55, 162–63, 174, 192, 196–97, 202–03, 207, 209–11; Alberto Ricci: p. 198; Arthur Toqué: pp. 115, 184–85; Courtesy Galerie Zlotowski: pp. 60–61 / photo: unknown.

Cover: Stéphane Mandelbaum, *Buñuel*, c. 1985 → 39

Acknowledgments
Our sincere thanks go to all the lenders, who with their generous loans made the exhibition possible: Simone and Arthur Benzaquen, Paris; Lucien Bilinelli, Milan; Myriam Bucquoit, Paris; Robert Combas; Emmanuel Crochet and Cristina Ngo, Brussels; Éric Decelle, Brussels; Marc Félix; Antoine de Galbert, Paris; Hugo Godderis, Veurne; Alain Graffe, Brussels; Paula Hauser, Brussels; Karim Hoss, Meudon; Jean-Claude Jadot, Brussels; Nicolas Jaquet, Geneva; Arié Mandelbaum, Fontenoille; Ariéh Mandelbaum, Brussels; Léa Mandelbaum, Belgium; Nadine Rizele Mandelbaum, Rijkevoort; Pili Mandelbaum, Belgium; MK2 Kréations, Paris; Musée Juif de Belgique—Joods Museum van België, Brussels; Musée national d'art moderne—Centre Pompidou, Paris; Dr. André-Jaque Neusy and Jacob Lifshin, Israel; Dario Preszow, Sint-Genesius-Rode; Bernard Prévot, Brussels; Paul Trajman, Gary Trajman & Romy Trajman, Brussels; Thierry de Valeriola, France; Maurice Verbaet, Antwerp; Gil Weiss, Brussels; Galerie Zlotowski, Paris; as well as all lenders who wish to remain anonymous.

Our deepest gratitude goes to the family of Stéphane Mandelbaum, and to Bruno Jean.

Published by
Verlag der Buchhandlung Walther und Franz König
Ehrenstraße 4, 50672 Köln, Germany

Bibliographic information published by the Deutsche Nationalbibliothek:
The Deutsche Nationalbibliothek lists this publication in the Deutsche Nationalbibliografie; detailed bibliographic data are available on the Internet at https://dnb.dnb.de

Distribution
Europe:
Buchhandlung Walther König
Ehrenstraße 4
50672 Köln
Germany
T +49 221 2059653
verlag@buchhandlung-walther-koenig.de

UK & Ireland:
ART DATA
12 Bell Industrial Estate
50 Cunnington Street
London W4 5HB
United Kingdom
T +44 (0)208 747 10 61
F +44 (0)208 742 23 19
orders@artdata.co.uk

Outside Europe:
D.A.P. / Distributed Art Publishers, Inc.
75 Broad Street, Suite 630
New York, NY 10004
USA
T +1 (0)212 627 1999
orders@dapinc.com

ISBN 978-3-7533-0724-4

MUSEUM MMK FÜR MODERNE KUNST

Director: Prof. Susanne Pfeffer
Deputy Director / Head of Administration: Karolin Loh
Curator: Julia Eichler
Head of Collection / Curator: Lukas Flygare
Curatorial Assistants: Haris Giannouras, Leon Jankowiak, Lu Pahl
Scientific Trainee Collection / Exhibitions: Louise Knafla
Digital Matter and Archives: Nadine Hahn (Head, parental leave), Margherita Foresti (Parental leave replacement)
Photo Archive: Thomas Schröder
Head of Publications: Regina Barunke
Press and Public Relations: Samet Belhoche, Berkant Bengil, Ai Vi Bui, Lea Handon
Art Education: Marie Fiedler, Hanna Franke, Nele Imbescheid, Dalwin Kryeziu, Katharina Mantel, Isabel Monroy Moreno (Head), Sharleen Waibel
Head of Cultural Management: Katja Schmolke
Administration: Stefan Koczwara, Alexandra Leue, Melanie Petry
Head of Library: Antje Gegenmantel
Friends of MMK: Lilli Beckers (Managing Director), Laura Metz, Saskia Wagner
Head of Exhibition and Production: Roman Caesar
Conservation: Ulrich Lang, Kathrin Sündermann (Head), Julia Witter
Registrar: Sabrina Manicke
Depot: Dierk Gessner, Uwe Glaser (Head)
Facility Management, Security, and Coordination of the Supervisory Staff: Hussein Mobark
Housekeeping: Oktay Yildiz

The TOWER MMK was made possible by Tishman Speyer and Commerz Real AG.

Founding Partners
Stefan Quandt, Ernst Max von Grunelius-Stiftung, DekaBank Deutsche Girozentrale, Helaba Landesbank Hessen-Thüringen

The TOWER MMK is supported by New Contemporaries.

MUSEUM MMK FÜR MODERNE KUNST
Domstraße 10
60311 Frankfurt am Main
Germany
T +49 69 212 30447
mmk@stadt-frankfurt.de
www.mmk.art

TOWER MMK
TaunusTurm, Taunustor 1
60310 Frankfurt am Main
Germany
T +49 69 212 73165

MUSEUM MMK FÜR MODERNE KUNST